KW-481-805

ACCOUNTING FOR FIRST EXAMINATIONS

M. CHAHIN, A.C.I.S., A.M.B.I.M., M.I.Ex.

Formerly lecturer in accountancy at Harrow
College of Technology and Ealing Technical College

UNIVERSITY TUTORIAL PRESS

Published by University Tutorial Press Ltd
842 Yeovil Road, Slough, SL1 4JQ

All rights reserved. No portion of this
book may be reproduced by any process
without written permission from the publishers.

Published 1977
Reprinted 1984

© M. Chahin, 1977

ISBN: 0 7231 0747 5

Contents

Preface

This book is intended for students preparing for the examinations in Bookkeeping and Principles of Accounts of the Royal Society of Arts stages I and II, the General Certificate of Education at Ordinary Level and for the Certificate in Secondary Education. It is an expression of many years' teaching experience in bookkeeping and accounts.

The first ten chapters, in which the basic principles are introduced, are written steadily in narrative form, with the intention of involving the reader in situations which arise in the formation and growth of a small business. The exercises at the end of each chapter follow the conventional practice and the student must identify himself with a fictitious businessman whose books he is keeping.

The increasing importance of Management Accounting is reflected in the syllabuses of the examining bodies and the character of the questions set. Those requirements are met by the introduction of elementary aspects of interpretation of accounts, the 'vertical' form of the final accounts and the balance sheet, and a chapter each on Accounting Conventions and Concepts, and Flow of Funds. The chapter on Mechanised Accounting is based on the information kindly supplied by British Olivetti Limited. The specimen bank paying-in slip, cheque and bank statement are reproduced with the permission of National Westminster Bank Limited.

Footnotes are frequently used so that an important point stands out on its own, and yet the main line of thought in the text is undisturbed. The expression 'the firm' is used for convenience throughout the book for all forms of business organisation. Interest rates in the text and in the exercises are based on a relatively stable financial situation.

The following examining bodies are thanked for permission to use their examination questions: The Royal Society of Arts, the Universities of Manchester, Liverpool, Leeds, Sheffield and Birmingham Joint Matriculation Board, the University of London Schools Examination Council, the Institute of Bankers.

I am grateful to my friend Mr A J Tubb, BSc(Econ), FCMA, FCIB, AMBIM, Senior Lecturer, Ealing Technical College, for having read my manuscript and for his valuable suggestions. My thanks are also due to my former colleague, Mr M B Reveres, FCA, FTII, for some very helpful ideas.

Introduction

Why bookkeeping ?

Because I must keep records of everything I possess in my business; I must keep track of everything I buy and sell and of the money my customers owe me, and the money I owe to people who supply goods to be used in my factory or stored in my warehouse. I must write down, in proper form, all payments made to me by my *debtors* (those who owe me money) and all payments I make to my *creditors* (those to whom I owe money). In short, I must write down all the daily *business transactions*—buying and selling goods; paying and receiving money—so that at any time in the future I can easily locate each one whenever it is required.

Commercial and Accounting Terms

Business is carried on for the making of *profit*. Profit is achieved by buying things at a certain price, and selling them at a higher price. The profit can be used to help the business grow. A *manufacturer* buys raw materials, transforms them into finished goods and offers them for sale (at a price above cost), probably to a *wholesaler*. A wholesaler buys from a manufacturer in large quantities and sells to *retailers* (shops for example) in smaller quantities at a profit.

Cash and Credit Transactions

Except in the smallest businesses and certain larger organisations in particular trades, goods are bought and sold on a *credit* basis, that is, there is a time gap between the delivery of the goods and the payment for them. Payment is usually made by cheque, not by cash. Most business in western countries is on a credit basis.

Double-entry System of Bookkeeping

Business transactions must be recorded according to certain clear principles. Over the centuries, the double-entry system of bookkeeping has been developed and today it is generally acknowledged to be the most efficient, and therefore the most satisfactory, method of keeping books of account.

Chapter One

The Meaning of Double-entry Bookkeeping

The Ledger

The system for recording business transactions is called *Double-entry bookkeeping*. The accounts book in which such transactions are recorded is called a *ledger*. The following is a specimen page (or folio) from a ledger. (Each page or folio, (abbreviated to Fol.) is numbered for reference purposes).

EX. 1/1

THE LEDGER

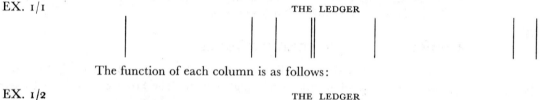

The function of each column is as follows:

EX. 1/2

THE LEDGER

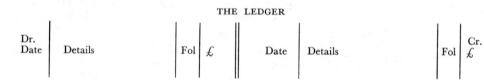

Dr. Date	Details	Fol	£	Date	Details	Fol	Cr. £

Note that the columns to the left and to the right of the centre are identical. The left and the right sides are respectively described as the debit (Dr.) side and the credit (Cr.) side.

Double-entry Bookkeeping

Double-entry briefly expresses the principle that every business transaction can be seen from two aspects; that of the *receiver* (Dr.) on the one hand and that of the *giver* (Cr.) on the other. If on April 15 I buy furniture for my office to the value of £200 from Lockerdesks Ltd., and I promise to pay them at a later date*, Lockerdesks Ltd. would *give* value and Office Furniture would *receive* value. That transaction would appear in my ledger as follows:

EX. 1/3

Dr.	RECEIVED		GIVEN	Cr.

LOCKERDESKS LTD.

April 15 Office Furniture   £ 200

OFFICE FURNITURE

Dr.
April 15 Lockerdesks Ltd.   £ 200

This example illustrates the following points:

---

*I buy now and pay later: that is, I buy on credit.

LOCKERDESKS LTD

1. The right, or credit side of the ledger is the *given* side.

   Lockerdesks Ltd. have *given* value.

   Their account is *credited*.

   They are my creditors.

   I owe them £200.

   Their account has a credit balance.

OFFICE FURNITURE

2. The left, or debit side of the ledger is the *received* side.

   Furniture Account has *received* value*.

   Furniture Account is *debited*.

   It has a debit balance.

Note that the questions asked and the answers given are always *from the point of view of the account*:

> Q Have Lockerdesks Ltd. given or received?
> A They have given.

> Q Has Furniture Account given or received?
> A It has received*.

Exercise 1

1 Which is the Received side of the ledger, the left or the right side?
2 Does the Given side of the ledger represent the debit or the credit side?
3 From which point of view is a transaction looked at before it is entered into the ledger? (a) Proprietor (b) Firm (c) Account.
4 What does 'buying on credit' mean?
5 (a) Define 'My creditor'. Does he owe me or do I owe him value?
  (b) Define 'My debtor'. Does he owe me or do I owe him value?
6 Enter the following transactions in your ledger:

			£
July	5	Bought (Office Furniture) a desk on credit from A Price.	45
	7	Bought (Office Machinery) a typewriter on credit from B Thomas	63
	10	Bought (Office Furniture) a filing cabinet on credit from Slikfiles Ltd.	30
	28	Speedadders Ltd., sold you an adding machine (Office Machinery Account) on credit	100

7 Enter the following transactions in your ledger:

Sept.	2	Bought machinery for the factory (Machinery Account) on credit from Machine Tools Ltd.	600
	4	Bought a motor van (Motor Van Account) on credit from Excel Cars Co.	700
	10	Bought a showcase and had some counters and shelves fitted in the warehouse (Fixtures and Fittings Account) by Contelves Ltd., (on credit)	550

---

*It is at first difficult to accept the abstract idea of Furniture Account 'receiving'. It might be helpful to think in terms of an *addition* to the furniture the business might already possess (not shown in the example). The quantity of furniture would then increase because more has been *received*. Therefore, *debit* Furniture Account.

Chapter Two

Starting a Business

I Inherit £10,000

My name is John Fry, during the month of March, 19·1, I inherited £10,000 and I received a cheque for this amount.

EX. 2/1

I decided to invest this sum of money in a small business as capital, and I took the following steps (Items 1 and 1a): I opened the business account at my bank and paid in the cheque by first completing a bank paying-in slip:

To the left of the perforation is the *counterfoil*. The bank clerk rubber stamps the date on it, initials it and hands it to me. (He retains the right-hand portion.) This is the document from which I make the debit entry in my cash book, as follows:

BANK ACCOUNT*

CASH BOOK

19·1		£
April 1	Capital (1)	10,000

CAPITAL—JOHN FRY

	19·1		£
	April 1	Cash (1a)	10,000

Item 1   Bank *received* £10,000 (Dr.).

Bank is the firm's debtor to the extent of £10,000.

Bank owes the firm £10,000.

Item 1a   Capital Account—John Fry: My personal account in the firm's ledger.

I have *given* the firm £10,000 (Cr.).

The firm owes me £10,000.

I am a creditor of the firm.

My account, Capital, in the firm's ledger is credited.

EX. 2/2   Item 2 and 2a (April 10). I bought freehold premises on Cave Street for the purpose of conducting the business, paying £6,000 by cheque.

BANK ACCOUNT*

(CASH BOOK)

19·1		£	19·1		£
April 1	Capital (1)	10,000	April 10	Freehold Premises (2)	6,000

FREEHOLD PREMISES

19·1		£
April 10	Cash (2a)	6,000

Item 2   Bank has *given* (on behalf of the firm) £6,000 (Cr.).

Bank is the firm's creditor to the extent of £6,000.

Bank claims £6,000 from the firm.

Item 2a   Freehold Premises has *received* value (on the same principle as Office Furniture received value in example 1/3 (Dr.)).

EX. 2/3   Item 3 and 3a (April 15). I bought some furniture for my office from Lockerdesks Ltd. *on credit*, promising to pay them at the end of the month, £200.

OFFICE FURNITURE

		£
April 15	Lockerdesks Ltd. (3)	200

LOCKERDESKS LTD.

		£
April 15	Office Furniture (3a)	200

Item 3   Office Furniture has *received* value (Dr.).

Item 3a   Lockerdesks Ltd. have *given* value (Cr.).

They are the firm's creditors to the extent of £200.

They claim £200 from the firm.

The above transactions and accounts appear together in my ledger as follows:

---

*In practice, entries into the Bank Account (which is a record of money paid into and drawn out of the bank) are so frequent, that a separate book, called the Cash Book, a sort of second volume of the ledger, is justified. The Bank Account is usually abbreviated to *Cash* (short for Cash Book).

EX. 2/4

BANK ACCOUNT
(CASH BOOK)

Dr.		£			£ Cr.
April 1	Capital (1)	10,000	April 10	Freehold Premises (2)	6,000

CAPITAL—JOHN FRY*

		April 1	Cash (1a)	10,000

FREEHOLD PREMISES

April 10	Cash (2a)	6,000

OFFICE FURNITURE

April 15	Lockerdesks Ltd. (3)	200

LOCKERDESKS LTD.

		April 15	Office Furniture (3a)	200

Note that:

1 On the debit side of the Cash Book, the particulars read 'Capital' while
   On the credit side of Capital, the particulars read 'Cash'.
2 On the credit side of the Cash Book, the particulars read 'Freehold Premises' while
   On the debit side of Freehold Premises, the particulars read 'Cash'.
3 On the debit side of Office Furniture, particulars read 'Lockerdesks Ltd.' while
   On the credit side of Lockerdesks Ltd., particulars read 'Office Furniture'.

This style of cross-reference is consistent throughout the system of double-entry bookkeeping with which we are concerned. In Account A, the particulars read 'B', while in Account B, the particulars read 'A'.

Every Transaction Affects Two Accounts

I now accept the principle that each transaction affects two accounts, one of which has a debit entry and the other a credit entry. Therefore, in any given trading period, the two sides of the ledger should add up to the same figure.

Thus, in order to prove the arithmetical accuracy of the entries in the ledger, eg. that I have in fact made identical figure entries on opposite sides of two corresponding accounts, I should draw up a *trial balance* (usually at the end of each month). Supposing that example 2/5 represented all the transactions for the month of April, the trial balance at the end of April would be produced as follows:

EX. 2/5

TRIAL BALANCE
AS ON 30th APRIL, 19·1

	£		£
Cash at bank	4,000	Capital	10,000
Freehold Premises	6,000	Lockerdesks Ltd.	200
Office Furniture	200		
	10,200		10,200

*****Important** In accounting practice, the firm and the owner(s) of the firm are separate from one another; they are said to be *two separate entities*. Therefore, the firm owes me, John Fry, £10,000.

The following is the alternative and more acceptable form of trial balance:

TRIAL BALANCE
AS ON 30TH APRIL, 19·1

	Dr. £	Cr. £
Capital		10,000
Freehold Premises	6,000	
Office Furniture	200	
Lockerdesks Ltd.		200
Cash at Bank*	4,000	
	10,200	10,200

When the trial balance 'balances', that is, when the totals of the two sides are identical the arithmetical accuracy of the ledger accounts is proven. (A more detailed explanation of the trial balance is given in Chapter 16.)

Exercise 2

1 Enter the following transactions in your ledger:

Oct. 1 You go into business with capital £20,000. You open a bank account and pay in your capital.
     3 You move into freehold premises, which you buy outright for £10,000, paying by cheque.
     5 You buy office furniture on credit from Smithers Ltd., £150.
   20 You buy machinery for use in the factory from A Morton on credit, £780 (Machinery Account).

Balance the Cash Book. Produce a trial balance for the month ended 31st October, 19·1.

2 Enter the following transactions in your ledger:

Sept. 1 You went into business with capital £5,000 in cash which you paid into the bank.
     2 Bought office furniture, paying £90 by cheque.
     8 Purchased various fixtures and fittings, paying £60 by cheque.
   10 Bought a typewriter (Office Machinery Account), and paid for it with a cheque for £55.
   12 Bought an adding machine from C Morse on credit, £72.
   17 Bought a showcase (Fixtures and Fittings Account) from M Parks on credit, £23.
   18 Bought a used motor van (Motor Van Account) on credit from Autovans Ltd., £535.
   20 Bought a rug for the office (£28) paying by cheque.
   24 Bought a winch for the warehouse (Machinery Account) on credit from Portman Ltd., £32.
   26 Paid C Morse his account with a cheque for £72.
   30 Paid Portman Ltd., their account by cheque.

Open a Bank Account and the necessary ledger accounts, and take out a trial balance for the month ended 30th September, 19·1.

3 Marsh Mallow goes into business with a capital of £15,000 and employs you to write up his books (keep his books). You are required to enter the following in Marsh Mallow's ledger, balance the Cash Book as on February 28th, and take out a trial balance at that date:

---

*This £4,000 is the *difference between* (or *balance of*) the two sides of the Bank Account; the Bank received £10,000 and gave £6,000. The firm has £4,000 in the bank; the bank owes the firm £4,000. When the account is 'balanced' it appears as follows:

BANK ACCOUNT
(CASH BOOK)

April 1	Capital	10,000	April 10	Freehold Premises		6,000
			30	Balance (or difference)	c/d	4,000
		10,000				10,000

May 1 Balance   b/d   4,000
This balance of £4,000 is described as a *debit balance*. The firm has £4,000 in the bank at the start of the month of May. The balance is *carried down* (c/d) on 30th April and *brought down* (b/d) on 1st May as the starting figure for May.

Feb. 7 Paid capital into bank.

10 Moved into rented premises and paid rent in advance by cheque, £200 (Bank Account and Rent Account).

14 Fitted up some shelves and counters in the warehouse, costing £280. Paid the contractors by cheque. (Bank Account and Fixtures and Fittings Account.)

15 Bought some office furniture worth £140 and paid by cheque (Bank Account and Office Furniture Account).

25 Bought some office machinery on credit from Type-Adder Machine Co., £110 (Office Machinery Account and Type-Adder Machine Co's Account).

4 Enter the following into the Cash Book and the appropriate ledger accounts. Produce a trial balance as on 31st March, 19·1.

		£
Mar.	1 M Edwards (you are keeping his books) starts business with capital in the bank.	8,000
	2 Moved into rented premises and paid rent in advance (Rent Account and Bank Account).	100
	14 Bought some furniture for the office on credit from B Smith.	85
	18 Purchased a trolley and some scales for the warehouse (Machinery Account) on credit from R Dodds.	55
	29 Paid B Smith the amount due to him by cheque.	85

Chapter Three

Purchases and Sales of Goods on Credit

In accounting, the expression 'Purchases', when standing alone, implies purchases of goods for re-sale. In example 1/3, I bought office furniture for the firm's own use. I might have said I purchased it, but it was not a purchase in the technical sense because office furniture bought for the greater efficiency of my own business, is not, in the normal course of trade, for sale. (See Chapter 15 for a fuller explanation of this distinction.)

Credit Transactions

I (John Fry) am now ready to begin business as a wholesaler of china and glass, purchasing goods from manufacturers and re-selling them at a profit to retailers. *Most business is transacted on a credit basis*, that is, there is a time gap of perhaps one month between delivery of goods and payment for them. I shall buy goods from my suppliers on credit, and I shall in turn sell to my customers on credit.

EX. 3/1

PURCHASES OF GOODS ON CREDIT

£

April 17 Purchased goods on credit from C Moss, value   400
April 21 Purchased goods on credit from P Wood, value   100

After the goods have been delivered to me, I receive an invoice (a bill) for them from each of the two suppliers. These I carefully put in a strong file, usually a binder, which is called the Purchases Day Book or more briefly the Purchases Book. I file the invoices in order of date. Using the file as my source of information, I make the following entries in the ledger*:

C MOSS

     £

April 17 Purchases   400

P WOOD

April 21 Purchases   100

PURCHASES

£

April 17 C Moss   400
     21 P Wood   100
_____
     500

*In practice, the purchase invoices are periodically (say, monthly) added up on an adding machine. The total is then entered on the debit side of the Purchases Account. That total is equal to the sum of the purchases shown on the credit side of each supplier's account. The Purchases Account in the above example 3/1 would then show only the total purchases, £500, to balance the two credit entries under the accounts of C Moss and P Wood respectively:

PURCHASES

£

April 30 Goods   500

(See Chapter 6 for a fuller explanation.) It is suggested that the method shown in example 3/1 is used for the present.

CREDIT ENTRIES:

C Moss and P Wood have *given* value.

Their respective accounts are credited.

They are my creditors.

I owe them £400 and £100 respectively.

DEBIT ENTRIES:

Purchases Account has *received* value (or, to aid understanding at this early stage, *the firm* has received value).

Purchases Account is debited with both items.

Purchases Account shows the total value of goods bought for re-sale.

EX. 3/2

SALES OF GOODS ON CREDIT

	£
April 20 Sold goods on credit to S Porter	230
April 23 Sold goods on credit to Providence Ltd.,	470

Following the dispatch of the above orders to my two customers, I send each of them an invoice. I retain a carbon copy which I again carefully *file in a binder*, (called the Sales Day Book or more briefly, the Sales Book), in date order. From the binder (Sales Book) as my source of information, I make the following ledger entries*:

S PORTER

	£
April 20 Sales	230

PROVIDENCE LTD.

	£
April 23 Sales	470

SALES

		£
April 20	S Porter	230
23	Providence Ltd.	470
		―――
		700

DEBIT ENTRIES

S Porter and Providence Ltd. have received value.

Their respective accounts are debited.

They are my debtors.

They owe me £230 and £470 respectively.

CREDIT ENTRIES

Sales Account has given value. (Or, again to aid understanding at this stage, *the firm* has given value.)

Sales Account is credited with both items.

Sales Account shows the total value of goods sold to date.

During the month of April, payments were made and cheques were received as follows:

---

*The comments made on the Purchases Account above, apply also to the Sales Account which appears as follows:

SALES

	£
April 30 Goods	700

EX. 3/3

		£
April 22	Purchased a job lot of goods offered for sale on a cash-and-carry basis (not on credit). Paid (by cheque)	50
28	Paid the printers by cheque the amount due to them for printing invoices (Stationery Account)	15
29	Paid for carriage on the goods sent to Providence Ltd.	5
29	Settled the Electricity Account by cheque	10
29	Paid P Wood's account by cheque	100
30	Received a cheque from Providence Ltd., in part settlement of their outstanding account	200
30	Paid Lockerdesks Ltd., their outstanding account	200

These receipts and payments appearing:

(i) in the Cash Book and

(ii) in their own respective accounts, *together with all the transactions from the start of my business to the present moment*, are included in the accounts shown below, which incorporate all those so far in my ledger:

CASH BOOK

		£				£
April 1	Capital	10,000	April 10	Freehold Premises		6,000
30	Providence Ltd.	200	22	Purchases		50
			28	Stationery		15
			29	Carriage		5
			29	Heating and Lighting		10
			29	P Wood		100
			30	Lockerdesks Ltd.		200
			30	Balance	c/d	3,820
		10,200				10,200
May 1	Balance	b/d	3,820			

CAPITAL—JOHN FRY

					£
			April 1	Cash	10,000

FREEHOLD PREMISES

April 10	Cash	6,000

OFFICE FURNITURE

April 15	Lockerdesks Ltd.	200

LOCKERDESKS LTD.

April 30	Cash	200	April 15	Office Furniture	200

C MOSS

			April 17	Purchases	400

P WOOD

April 29	Cash	100	April 21	Purchases	100

S PORTER

April 20	Sales	230

PROVIDENCE LTD.

April 23	Sales		470	April 30	Cash		200
				30	Balance	c/d	270
			470				470
May 1	Balance	b/d	270				

PURCHASES

April 17	C Moss	400
21	P Wood	100
22	Cash	50
		550

SALES

April 20	S Porter	230
23	Providence Ltd.	470
		700

STATIONERY

April 28 Cash   15

CARRIAGE

April 29 Cash   5

HEATING AND LIGHTING

April 29 Cash   10

Notes on every Account so far opened

A comment on each of the above accounts should be useful:

BANK

All receipts and payments during April have been shown and the Cash Book has been balanced at the end of the month, the balance having been brought down on May 1st (see footnote p.7). It shows:

A *debit balance* of £3,820: it is an *asset*.[1]

The firm has £3,820 in the bank.

The bank owes it £3,820.

The bank is a debtor of the firm to the extent of £3,820.

CAPITAL

This account has a *credit balance*.

It is my personal account in the firm's ledger.

The firm owes me £10,000, being the amount I invested in the business.

I, John Fry, am a creditor of the firm.

Capital Account is one of the firm's *liabilities*.[2]

FREEHOLD PREMISES

This account has a debit balance.

It is an asset.[1]

OFFICE FURNITURE

This account has a debit balance.

It is an asset.[1]

LOCKERDESKS LTD

This account has no balance; for most practical purposes it does not exist any longer. From April 15th to April 29th it had a credit balance and it was a liability.[2] It indicated that the firm owed Lockerdesks Ltd. £200. On April 30th a cheque for £200 in settlement of the account was sent to Lockerdesks Ltd. and *the account was closed*, ie. the totals of the cash columns on each side of the ledger were identical and *they were ruled off* thus ▬▬▬.

C MOSS

This account has a credit balance; it is a liability.[2]

The firm owes C Moss £400.

C Moss is one of the firm's creditors.

---

[1]An item the firm owns; an item in favour of the firm. All assets have debit balances.

[2]An item, the value of which the firm owes; an item unfavourable to the firm. All liabilities have credit balances.

Both the above notes are generalisations. Sometimes a debit balance is not favourable, although it would be classified as an asset; and there are certain accounts with credit balances which are certainly not unfavourable, although they would be classified under liabilities. These refinements will arise later on, at a time when the basic principles of accounting will have been grasped and most of the reasons for the *apparent* anomalies understood.

PURCHASES
This account has a debit balance.
Shows total value of goods purchased during April.

SALES
This account has a credit balance.
Shows total value of goods sold during April.

STATIONERY; CARRIAGE; HEATING AND LIGHTING
These accounts have debit balances.
The concerns represented by these accounts, say, the printers, British Rail, Gas and/ or Electricity Board, have *received* money in return for goods supplied (stationery) or services rendered (transport, heating and lighting).*

THE TRIAL BALANCE
The following trial balance proves the arithmetical accuracy of the above accounts; it proves that each transaction has been entered on the debit side of one account and the credit side of another account. (There is more about the Trial Balance later in the book.)

EX. 3/4

TRIAL BALANCE
AS ON 30TH APRIL, 19·1

	Dr. £	Cr. £
Capital—John Fry		10,000
Freehold Premises	6,000	
Office Furniture	200	
S Porter	230	
Providence Ltd.	270	
C Moss		400
Purchases	550	
Sales		700
Stationery	15	
Carriage	5	
Heating and Lighting	10	
Cash at Bank	3,820	
	11,100	11,100

The Trial Balance shows only the 'Live' Accounts

Note that the trial balance shows only the live accounts, those which have balances, the open accounts. It does not show accounts which have been ruled off, eg., Lockerdesks Ltd., P Wood. The ruled-off accounts are closed, and for most practical purposes, they do not exist. Any one of them might be opened again. If, for example, sometime in the future I buy more goods for re-sale from, say, P Woods, or more furniture from Lockerdesks Ltd., I would reopen and continue to use the accounts of P Wood and Lockerdesks Ltd.

Specimen Documents and their Meaning

ORDER
I must send C Moss, my supplier, an 'Order' for the goods I require showing quantities, description of goods, catalogue number and prices, terms of trade and payment:

---

*Reminder** Remember to consider all entries from the point of view of the account (*not* from the point of view of the firm).

No. A453

ORDER
John Fry,
Wholesaler China and Glass,
Cave Street,
London SE

10th April, 19·1

Mr C Moss
The Pottery
Main Street
Hanley, Staffs.

PLEASE SUPPLY:

  TEA SETS:
    1 set each of the following patterns:
    M/41–60, N/25–34, O/12–21, P/18–27
          Total 50 sets @ £5 per set
  DINNER SETS:
    1 set each of the following patterns:
    AS/1–10, AZ/11–15
          Total 15 sets @ £10 per set
  Delivery: Soonest—From stock
  Carriage: Paid
  Payment: 30 days net

INVOICE

Soon after C Moss has dispatched the goods, he sends me an invoice (a bill). When I receive it, I check it against the order sent to Moss to ensure that one agrees with the other as to quantities and prices; the arithmetical accuracy of the invoice is also checked. Then it is entered on the credit side of the supplier's account and his ledger folio (page number or reference) is shown at the foot of the invoice. It is then filed in the Binder, called the Purchases Book* (example 3/3).

DELIVERY/DISPATCH NOTE

This is a *partial* carbon copy of the invoice; the money values are omitted. C Moss sends it to me either enclosed with the goods, or at the same time as the dispatch of the goods, by separate post, to enable me to check quantities on unpacking them when they arrive.

STATEMENT

When payment is due, C Moss sends me a reminder to pay. This document is called a *Statement*. It is an abbreviated version of my account in his ledger.

INVOICE COPY FOR THE SUPPLIER'S OWN RECORDS

A third carbon copy of the invoice, a complete one, is the document from which C Moss records the sale in his own ledger. He files it in his Sales Invoices Binder called the Sales Book.*

INVOICE

No. EE/3

C Moss,
Manufacturer,
The Pottery,
Main Street,
Hanley, Staffs.

17th April, 19·1

Mr John Fry
Cave Street
London SE

Your Order No. A453   Carriage: Paid   Terms: 30 days net
TEA SETS:
    1 set each of the following patterns:
    M/41–60, N/25–34, O/12–21, P/18–27
          Total 50 sets @ £5   £250

*For more details of this important process, please refer to Chapter 6 on Books of Original Entry.

DINNER SETS:
        1 set each of the following patterns:
        AS/1–10, AZ/11–15
        Total 15 sets @ £10   150

                                        400
                                      Net

DELIVERY/ADVICE NOTE

No. EE/3

C Moss,
Manufacturer,
The Pottery,
Main Street,
Hanley, Staffs.

17th April, 19·1

Mr John Fry
Cave Street
London SE
Your Order No. A453   Carriage: Paid

PLEASE RECEIVE

TEA SETS:
        1 set each of the following patterns:
        M/41–60, N/25–34, O/12–21, P/18–27
        Total 50 sets

DINNER SETS:
        1 set each of the following patterns:
        AS/1–10, AZ/11–15
        Total 15 sets

STATEMENT

C Moss,
Main Street,
Hanley, Staffs.

14th May, 19·1

Mr John Fry
Cave Street
London SE

19·1
April 17   To Goods   £400

                          Net 30 days

Exercise 3

1 What does selling on credit mean?

2 (a) What is an Invoice? (b) What is a Dispatch Note? (c) What is a Statement?

3 Whose account does Capital Account represent?

4 Why is Capital a liability?

5 Define each of the following items either as a liability or an asset:
    (a) Balance at bank (b) Freehold Premises (c) A creditor (d) Capital Account
    (e) Furniture (f) A debtor (g) Machinery.

6 (a) What does Purchases Account show? (b) What does Sales Account show?

7 (a) Is it better to have a debit or a credit balance in your cash book? Give reasons
    for your answer.
    (b) I sell some goods to a customer on credit. Is he my debtor or my creditor?
    Should his account in my ledger have a debit or a credit balance? (Consider all
    accounts from the point of view of the account. Ask yourself: is the *customer* a debtor
    or a creditor; has he received or given?)

8 Do Expense Accounts (eg., Carriage, Rent and Rates, Heat and Light, Telephone
    and Postages) normally have debit or credit entries? Give reasons for your answers.

9 What is the purpose of a Trial Balance?

10 Enter the following transactions in your ledger. Balance the accounts as on May 31st and take out a trial balance:

			£
May	1	Purchased goods on credit from M Robins	60
	5	Sold goods on credit to A Price	90
	16	Price paid his account in full	90
	20	Paid M Robins part of the amount due to him	30
	29	Sold goods and received cheque in payment	20

11 Enter the following transactions in Dick Turpin's ledger, whose accounts you keep. (Or, if you prefer it, your name is Dick Turpin.) Take out a trial balance at 31st December, 19·1.

			£
Dec.	1	Sold goods against a cheque CASH OR OR SALES	105
	3	Purchases of goods on credit from C Green	115
	4	Bought goods for re-sale and paid by cheque	58
	8	Sold goods to B Black on credit	80
	12	Bought more goods on credit from C Green	200
	16	B Black paid the amount due from him	80
	19	Paid C Green	115
	20	Sold more goods to B Black on credit	190
	26	Purchased on credit from R Mumford goods for re-sale	66
	29	Received cheque from Black in settlement of his account	190

12 Enter the following transactions in M Brown's ledger. Balance the accounts at the end of June and take out a trial balance:

			£
June	1	M Brown's capital in cash at bank is	8,000
	4	Bought office furniture on credit from M Parson	100
	7	Bought goods for re-sale and paid by cheque	75
	9	Purchased goods on credit from R Pim	240
	13	Sold goods on credit to E Shylock	135
	19	Bought typewriter (Office Machinery Account) from S Morris	82
	22	Paid M Parson the amount due to him by cheque	
	29	Received cheque from E Shylock in settlement of his account	

13 Enter the following October transactions in the ledger of B Rich. Leave sufficient space between each account for additional entries in November, underneath their respective accounts:

			£
Oct.	1	Paid capital £5,000 into bank	
	4	Purchased goods for re-sale and paid for them by cheque	83
	5	Purchased goods on credit from N Prior	367
	10	Paid rent by cheque (Rent Account)	120
	12	Sold goods on credit to A Morris	682
	25	Paid by cheque the amount due to N Prior	
	28	Received cheque from A Morris for half the amount due from him	

Balance the accounts as on 31st October, take out a trial balance for the month ended 31st October, 19·1, and continue into the month of November, using the same accounts:

			£
Nov.	6	Purchased goods on credit from N Prior	477
	9	Sold goods on credit to A Morris	211
	12	Paid rent by cheque	120
	20	Received cheque from A Morris for the balance of his October account	

Balance the above accounts and take out a trial balance as on 30th November, 19·1.

In doing the following exercises, remember that entries are always looked at *from the point of view of the account.*

14 The following is the account of T Smith, one of your customers:

T SMITH

Nov.	1	Balance	b/d	30		Nov.	10	Cash		30	Payed
	15	Sales	*Bought on credit*	80			28	Cash		80	Payed
	20	Sales	" " "	70			30	Balance	c/d	70	Owes me
				180						180	
Dec.	1	Balance	b/d	70							

Carefully explain the meaning of each of the above entries. In which accounts are the double entries to be found?

15 You are keeping the books of M Bush. *me* You are required to show the ledger account of one of his customers, D Cox, only. No double entries are required for the purpose of this exercise:

			£
Feb.	1	Balance due from D Cox *" customer*	107
	10	Sold to D Cox on credit goods value ⊙R	186
	16	D Cox paid by cheque the amount due from him on Feb. 1 CR	
	20	Sold to D Cox more goods DR	52
	28	D Cox paid half the amount due from him CR	

Balance D Cox's account and bring down the balance. What is the meaning of that balance?

16 R White is one of your customers. Enter the following transactions in his account only. No double entries are required for the purposes of this exercise. Balance his account on 30th April.

			£
April	1	Balance due from R White	160
	4	Received cheque from R White in part payment of his account	100
	6	Sold goods to R White on credit	30
	10	Charged R White for carriage on the goods sold to him in March, as agreed	5
	20	Received cheque from R White in full settlement of his account	
	28	Sold more goods to R White on credit	105

17 S Monk is one of your suppliers. The following transactions took place in October. Enter them in Monk's account and balance it at the end of the month. No double entries are required for the purposes of this exercise:

			£
Oct.	1	Balance due to Monk	90
	5	Purchased goods value	60
	6	Paid the amount due to Monk on Oct. 1	

Chapter Four

The Trading and Profit and Loss Account

Gross Profit

I am in business in order to make a profit, that is to say, *to increase my capital*. Profit is made by buying goods at a certain price and selling at a higher price. Gross profit is the excess of the selling price over the buying price, before any expenses, such as rent and rates, heating and lighting, carriage, stationery, wages and salaries, are deducted. In the foregoing transactions (example 3/3), goods purchased for £550 were sold for £700. This shows a gross profit of £150.

Net Profit

Net profit is the amount that remains after expenses are deducted from the gross profit. This assumes that the total value of expenses does not exceed the gross profit. If it did, the resulting figure would be a *net loss*. These explanations may be illustrated in arithmetical form as follows:

EX. 4/1

THE TRADING ACCOUNT

Sales (from the Sales Account)	700
Deduct cost of the goods—Purchases (from the Purchases Account)	550
Gross Profit	150

THE PROFIT AND LOSS ACCOUNT

Deduct expenditure ('Overheads'):		
Stationery	15	
Carriage	5	
Heating and Lighting	10	30
Net Profit (to be added to Capital and so increase the amount originally invested)		120

The above is a *Trading* and *Profit* and *Loss Account*. The Trading Account shows items which influence the amount of the Gross Profit (or Gross Loss); which arises as a result of trading operations; buying and selling goods. The Profit and Loss Account shows items which are charged against gross profit and thus influence the amount of the Net Profit (or Net Loss). Nowadays, these two accounts are combined, as in the following more formal setting of the above:

EX. 4/2

TRADING AND PROFIT AND LOSS ACCOUNT
FOR MONTH ENDED 30TH APRIL, 19·1

	£
Sales	700
Purchases	550
	——
Gross Profit	150

Deduct expenditure:		
Stationery	15	
Carriage	5	
Heating and Lighting	10	30
		——
Net Profit transferred to Capital Account		120
		══

The conventional method of setting out the above *vertical form* of the Trading and Profit and Loss Account is as follows:

EX. 4/3

TRADING AND PROFIT AND LOSS ACCOUNT
FOR MONTH ENDED 30TH APRIL, 19·1

		£			£
Purchases		550	Sales		700
Gross Profit	c/d	150			
		——			——
		700			700
		══			══
Stationery		15	Gross Profit	b/d	150
Carriage		5			
Heating and Lighting		10			
Net Profit transferred					
to Capital		120			
		——			——
		150			150
		══			══

I am in business to make a profit, ie., to increase my capital. The Net Profit is transferred to Capital Account and added to it, thus increasing it by £120. This extra £120 implies the availability of additional cash for various purposes. The Capital Account now appears as follows:

EX. 4/4

CAPITAL—JOHN FRY

April 1 Bank		10,000
30 Net Profit		120
		————
		10,120

The Capital Account is then closed and the balance brought down:

EX. 4/5

CAPITAL—JOHN FRY

		£			£
April 30 Balance	c/d	10,120	April 1 Cash		10,000
			30 Net Profit		120
		————			————
		10,120			10,120
		════			════
			May 1 Balance	b/d	10,120

Balance is the difference between the two sides of an account. The *credit balance* of the Capital Account is £10,120 since there is nothing on the debit side.

HAVE I MADE A GOOD PROFIT?

According to the above figures, in one month's trading, my capital has increased by £120, from £10,000 to £10,120. Is the return on my investment of £10,000 satisfactory? By what percentage has it increased in one month (or 1/12 of a year)? The formula for working out this information is:

EX. 4/6

$$\frac{\text{Net Profit}}{\text{Capital}} \times 100$$

for the trading period, ie., one month in this example. (Multiply by 12 to arrive at result of one year's trading.)

$$\frac{120}{10,000} \times 100 \times 12 = 14\tfrac{1}{2}\% \text{ (approx.)}$$

This is quite a satisfactory return on capital invested. Would I have done better if I had invested my £10,000 elsewhere? It is unlikely.

Why a Gross Profit as well as a Net Profit?

GROSS PROFIT

(a)   For comparison of one year's percentage of gross profit over sales with that of any other year. This month's percentage over sales is:

$$\frac{\text{Gross Profit}}{\text{Sales}} \times 100 = \frac{150}{700} \times 100 = 21\% \text{ (approx.)}$$

To clarify this important principle, the (fictitious) figures of two years' trading may be taken and compared as follows:

TRADING ACCOUNT

		19·1	19·2		19·1	19·2
Purchases		6,000	5,000	Sales	8,000	7,000
Gross Profit	c/d	2,000	2,000			
		8,000	7,000		8,000	7,000
				Gross Profit b/d	2,000	2,000

Both years show a gross profit of £2,000. But which of the two years is the more profitable one? The percentage of profit over sales of one year against that of another will answer that question:

$$19\cdot1: \frac{2,000}{8,000} \times 100 = 25\%; \quad 19\cdot2: \frac{2,000}{7,000} \times 100 = 28\tfrac{1}{2}\% \text{ (approx.)}$$

Was the second year's business perhaps done more efficiently, thus producing a higher percentage profit on smaller trading figures?

(b)   For comparison of percentage of gross profit and net profit over sales of the current year with those of previous years. Suppose that percentage of gross profit over sales this year is the same as that of last year (on approximately the same proportionate purchases and sales), but that percentage of net profit over sales this year is less than that of last year, then my expenses must have increased this year. I might be able to find the cause of that and possibly correct it.

NET PROFIT

Makes possible an assessment of return on capital invested, as in example 4/6 above.

Transferring and Closing the Accounts

Under the double-entry system, every debit entry in one account must have its corresponding credit entry in another account, and vice-versa. Where then are the double-entries of the items appearing in the Trading and Profit and Loss Account? The following are the accounts concerned:

EX. 4/7

PURCHASES

April 17 C Moss	400	
21 P Wood	100	
22 Bank	50	
	550	

SALES

	April 20 S Porter	230
	23 Providence Ltd.	470
		700

STATIONERY

April 28 Cash	15

CARRIAGE

April 29 Cash	5

HEATING AND LIGHTING

April 29 Cash	10

After the Trial Balance

After the trial balance is satisfactorily produced (*and not before*), the balances of the Purchases and Sales Accounts are transferred to the Trading Account, and the balances of the Stationery, Carriage and Heating and Lighting Accounts are transferred to the Profit and Loss Account. The effect of transferring an account is to close it. A *closed* account is considered non-existent for bookkeeping purposes. The above accounts now appear as follows:

EX. 4/8

PURCHASES

April 17 C Moss	400	April 30 Transferred to Trading	
21 P Wood	100	Account	550
22 Bank	50		
	550		550

SALES

April 30 Transferred to Trading		April 20 S Porter	230
Account	700	23 Providence Ltd.	470
	700		700

STATIONERY

April 28 Cash	15	April 30 Transferred to Profit and	
		Loss Account	15

CARRIAGE

April 29 Cash	5	April 30 Transferred to Profit and	
		Loss Account	5

HEATING AND LIGHTING

April 29 Cash	10	April 30 Transferred to Profit and	
		Loss Account	10

TRADING AND PROFIT AND LOSS ACCOUNT
FOR MONTH ENDED 30TH APRIL, 19·1

Purchases		550	Sales		700
Gross Profit	c/d	150			
		700			700
Stationery		15	Gross Profit	b/d	150
Carriage		5			
Heating and Lighting		10			
Net Profit transferred to Capital		120			
		150			150

CAPITAL—JOHN FRY

April 30 Balance	c/d	10,120	April 1 Cash		10,000
			30 Net Profit transferred from Profit and Loss Account		120
		10,120			10,120
			May 1 Balance	b/d	10,120

The Balance Sheet

This is dealt with in detail in Chapters 13 and 14. For the present, the following essential matters only need be noted:

1 The Balance Sheet is *not* an account. It is a statement showing the financial state of the business at a given time.

2 The Balance Sheet is usually brought out once a year.

3 Its two sides are described respectively as Liabilities (left side) and Assets (right side).

LIABILITIES

Consist of all accounts with credit balances, eg., Capital, Creditors. Credit balances represent amounts due to claimants in various guises, eg., suppliers of goods on credit and Capital which is my (John Fry's) personal account representing my claim of the amount I invested in the firm, plus or minus subsequent entries, e.g, net profit or net loss.

ASSETS

Consist of all accounts with debit balances, eg., Machinery, Debtors, representing items owned by or in favour of the firm. (But see footnote p.12).

Items which appear in the Balance Sheet

Only accounts with outstanding balances, after the completion of the Trading and Profit and Loss Account, appear in the Balance Sheet, eg., Capital, Creditors, Freehold Premises, Furniture, Debtors, Cash. If you now refer to the trial balance on p.13 and ignore the accounts in it which have since been transferred to the Trading and Profit and Loss Account (p.19) (and therefore closed, and for most practical purposes non-existent), you are left with the following accounts:

ACCOUNTS WITH DEBIT BALANCES (ASSETS)
Bank Account (Cash Book)
Freehold Premises
Office Furniture
Debtors:
    S Porter
    Providence Ltd.

ACCOUNTS WITH CREDIT BALANCES (LIABILITIES)
Capital
Creditors (eg., C Moss.)

These accounts have outstanding balances as at 30th April, and they appear in the Balance Sheet as follows:*

EX. 4/9

BALANCE SHEET OF JOHN FRY
AS AT 30TH APRIL, 19·1

LIABILITIES	£	£	ASSETS	£
Capital J Fry	10,000		Freehold Premises	6,000
Add Net Profit	120		Office Furniture	200
		10,120	Debtors (Total)	500
			Cash at bank	3,820
Creditors (Total)		400		
		10,520		10,520

Summary

We have been dealing with:

1 Ledger accounts, including the Bank Account (or Cash Book).

2 At the end of a given trading period, we have brought out a trial balance consisting of all open accounts—accounts with outstanding balances, eg., cash, debtors, other assets such as freehold premises, office furniture; and liabilities such as creditors and capital.

3 After the successful completion of the trial balance:
    (a) Purchases and Sales Accounts have been tranferred to the Trading Account and the gross profit has been computed.
    (b) Expense Accounts such as wages, heating and lighting, carriage, have been transferred to the Profit and Loss Account and the net profit has been computed.

Thus, the accounts transferred have been closed.

4 Any remaining accounts with balances have then been shown in a Balance Sheet.

Producing Final Accounts and Balance Sheet from a given Trial Balance

If the above factors have been grasped, it should be possible to compile a Trading and Profit and Loss Account and Balance Sheet from the items given in a Trial Balance. The following example illustrates this.

---

*These accounts are not *transferred* to the balance sheet; they are merely *shown* in it. Transferring an account means closing it; showing it does not.

EX. 4/10   From the following trial balance you are required to produce the Trading and Profit and Loss Account of M Able, for month ended 30th September, 19·1 and a Balance Sheet as at that date:

TRIAL BALANCE OF M ABLE
AS ON 30TH SEPTEMBER, 19·1

	Dr. £	Cr. £
Capital		40,127
Land and Buildings	30,000	
Machinery and Plant	4,250	
Furniture and Fittings	823	
Motor Van	542	
Purchases and Sales	7,341	9,476
Wages	934	
Salaries	160	
Heating and Lighting	28	
Carriage on Sales	13	
Telephone and Postages	29	
Debtors and Creditors	10,795	8,432
Cash at bank	3,120	
	58,035	58,035

TRADING AND PROFIT AND LOSS ACCOUNT
FOR MONTH ENDED 30TH SEPTEMBER, 19·1

Purchases	7,341	Sales		9,476
Gross Profit	2,135			
	9,476			9,476
Wages	934	Gross Profit	b/d	2,135
Salaries	160			
Heating and Lighting	28			
Carriage on Sales	13			
Telephone and Postages	29			
Net Profit transferred to Capital	971			
	2,135			2,135

EX. 4/11

ALTERNATIVE TO EX. 4/10 VERTICAL METHOD
TRADING AND PROFIT AND LOSS ACCOUNT
FOR MONTH ENDED 30TH SEPTEMBER, 19·1

	£	£
Sales		9,476
Purchases		7,341
Gross Profit		2,135
Less Expenditure:		
Wages	934	
Salaries	160	
Heating and Lighting	28	
Carriage on Sales	13	
Telephone and Postages	29	1,164
Net Profit transferred to Capital		971

BALANCE SHEET OF M ABLE
AS AT 30TH SEPTEMBER, 19·1

LIABILITIES	£	£	ASSETS	£
Capital—M Able	40,127		Land and Buildings	30,000
Add Net Profit	971		Machinery and Plant	4,250
		41,098	Furniture and Fittings	823
Trade Creditors		8,432	Motor Van	542
			Trade Debtors	10,795
			Cash at bank	3,120
		49,530		49,530

Exercise 4

1 From the following items in your ledger take out a Trial Balance; compile a Trading and Profit and Loss Account for the year ended 31st December, 19·2 and Balance Sheet at that date:

Capital	7,000
Purchases	10,000
Sales	16,000
Total Expenses	2,000
Debtors	7,000
Creditors	3,000
Machinery	1,000
Furniture and Fittings	700
Cash at bank	5,300

2 From the following trial balances prepare their respective final accounts for the years ended 31st December 19·1 and 19·2, and balance sheets as at those dates; in each case state the percentage of:

   (i) Gross profit on sales;

   (ii) Net profit on capital.

(a)

TRIAL BALANCE

ON 31ST DECEMBER, 19·1

	Dr. £	Cr. £
Capital		9,952
Freehold Premises	9,000	
Office Furniture	190	
Purchases	17,562	
Sales		21,444
General Expenses	1,544	
Debtors and Creditors	6,572	4,392
Cash at bank	920	
	35,788	35,788

(b)

TRIAL BALANCE

ON 31ST DECEMBER, 19·2

	£	£
Capital		17,320
Freehold Premises	18,500	
Machinery and Plant	1,700	
Furniture and Fittings	400	
Purchases and Sales	15,000	22,500
Debtors:		
H Kent	270	
M Simpson	310	
Creditors:		
R Benson		410
B Carry		60
Cash at Bank	530	
Sundry Expenses	150	
Wages and Salaries	3,430	
	40,290	40,290

3 You are employed as Raine Waters' bookkeeper and you are required:

  (a) to enter the following December transactions in his ledger;

  (b) to produce a trial balance on 31st December, 19·1;

  (c) to produce a Trading and Profit and Loss Account for month ended 31st December, 19·1, and a balance sheet as at that date.

		£
Dec.	1 R Waters started business with capital in the bank	9,000
	6 Purchased goods for re-sale from M Peters*	450
	7 Paid rent by cheque	120
	8 Sold goods to D Mango	710
	20 Settled gas bill (Heating and Lighting Account) by cheque	25
	25 Bought goods and paid for them by cheque	55
	29 Sold goods and received cheque for their value which was paid into bank	40

4 On January 1st A Blow started business with capital of £7,000 which he put into his bank and employed you to keep his books. The following transactions took place:

		£
Jan.	1 Bought office furniture on credit from Matchwood Ltd.	90
	4 Purchased goods fo re-sale from I May Ltd.	676
	7 Purchased goods for re-sale from B Douglas	327
	8 Sold goods to M Cross	982
	12 Sold goods and received payment by cheque. Paid it into bank	23
	12 Bought machinery. Paid for it by cheque	800
	13 Paid cheque, British Rail (Carriage Account)	9
	15 Settled electricity bill by cheque	17
	17 Paid wages and salaries	248
	22 Sold goods to D Hugo	450
	29 Received cheque from M Cross in part payment of his account	500

Required: Ledger Accounts, Cash Book, Trial Balance, Trading and Profit and Loss Account for month ended 31st January, 19·1 and a Balance Sheet as at that date.

---

*It is to be understood that purchases and sales of goods are made on credit, unless 'by cheque' or 'for cash' is specified.

Chapter Five

Returns Inwards and Returns Outwards

Returns Inwards (or Sales Returns)

On May 1st, I received an order from M Silver, value £620, which was dispatched to him on May 5th. A few days later he complained that some of the goods, valued at £10, were defective, and I agreed to have them back. The defective goods arrived on May 16th, and on that day I sent Mr Silver a *credit note* for £10; a document which acknowledged his claim for the value of the returned goods (example 5/1).

EX. 5/1

CREDIT NOTE

John Fry,
Wholesaler China and Glass
Cave Street,
London SE

16th May, 19·1

To Mr M Silver
   Brighton
   Sussex

   Breakages returned and today received:
   2 only Tea Sets Pattern M @ £5 each   £10

From the carbon copy, carefully filed in a binder, called the Returns Inwards *Book* (as distinct from Returns Inwards *Account* in the ledger), an entry was made on the credit side of Silver's Account, thus reducing his debt from £620 to £610*; the double-entry being on the debit side of the Sales Returns (or Returns Inwards) Account. At this stage, the Sales Account is not affected. The relevant accounts, some of them in existence since the beginning of the business in April and being continued into May, appear as follows:

EX. 5/2

M SILVER

	£		£
May 5 Sales	620	May 16 Sales Returns (or Returns Inwards)	10

RETURNS INWARDS
(SALES RETURNS)

May 10 M Silver	10		

SALES

April 30 Trading Account	700	April 20 S Porter	230
		23 Providence Ltd.	470
	700		700
		May 5 M Silver	620

---

*Reminder   An account implies subtraction of one side from the other.

On May 10th, Providence Ltd., one of my customers, wrote to say that £15 worth of the goods sent to them in April were of the wrong pattern. These were returned to me and I sent them a credit note for their value, £15. The ledger entries having been made, the accounts concerned appear as follows:

EX. 5/3

M SILVER

May 5 Sales	620	May 16 Sales Returns (or Returns Inwards)			10

PROVIDENCE LTD.

April 23 Sales	470	April 30 Bank			200
		30 Balance	c/d		270
	470				470
May 1 Balance	b/d	270	May 20 Sales Returns (or Returns Inwards)		15

RETURNS INWARDS
(SALES RETURNS)

May 5 M Silver	10
20 Providence Ltd.	15

SALES

April 30 Trading Account	700	April 20 S Porter	230
		23 Providence Ltd.	470
	700		700
		May 5 M Silver	620

After satisfactory completion of the Trial Balance, at the end of the trading period, May 31st, the Returns Inwards Account is transferred to the debit side of the Sales Account in order to show clearly the true or net sales for the period:

EX. 5/4

RETURNS INWARDS
(SALES RETURNS)

May 5 M Silver	10	May 31 Sales	T*	25
20 Providence Ltd.	15			
	25			25

SALES

May 31 Returns Inwards (or Sales Returns)	T* 25	May 5 M Silver	620

The net sales are then transferred to the Trading Account (where the Sales Account is shown in detail), at the same time closing the Sales Account, thus:

EX. 5/5

SALES

May 31 Returns Inwards	T*	25	May 5 M Silver	620
Trading Account		595		
		620		620

*T = Transfer from one account to another.

TRADING ACCOUNT
ON 31ST MAY, 19·1

Sales		620
Less Returns Inwards		25
		595

Returns Outwards (or Purchases Returns)

Exactly the same sequence of ledger entries applies for goods that I return to my suppliers:

1 I return goods to my supplier as damaged in transit.

2 I receive a credit note from him for the value of the damaged goods, acknowledging my claim.

3 I debit the supplier's account with the value shown on the credit note, which I file away in a special binder called Returns Outwards *Book* (as distinct from the Returns Outwards *Account* in the ledger).

4 The double-entry to 3, is the credit side of the Purchases Returns (or Returns Outwards) Account.

5 At the end of the trading period, usually a year, the Purchases Returns (or Returns Outwards) Account is transferred to the credit side of the Purchases Account in order to show the true or Net Purchases for the period.

6 The balance of the Purchases Account is then transferred to the debit side of the Trading Account and shown there in detail, as in the case of Sales in example 5/5.

EX. 5/6 May 8th, on checking the goods received from C Moss against his invoice of April 17th I found that there were damaged goods worth £30. This was reported to him and I received a credit note from him acknowledging his debt.

C MOSS

		£			£
May 10	Purchases Returns (1) (or Returns Outwards)	30	April 17	Purchases	400

PURCHASES RETURNS
(RETURNS OUTWARDS)

May 31	Purchases (2)	T	30	May 10	C Moss (1a)	30

PURCHASES

			£				£
April 17	C Moss		400	April 30	Trading Account	T	550
21	P Wood		100				
22	Bank		50				
			550				550
May 10	P Wood		350	May 31	Returns Outwards (2a)	T	30
				31	Trading Account	T	320
			350				350

TRADING ACCOUNT
FOR MONTH ENDED 31ST MAY, 19·1

Purchases	350	
Less Returns Outwards	30	
	320	

Exercise 5

Enter the following transactions in appropriate accounts in your ledger. Take out a trial balance for each question 1 and 2:

1

			£
Oct.	1	Purchased goods from S Burton	200
	5	Sold goods to P Searl	300
	15	P Searl returned some of the goods sold to him on October 5th, as defective. Sent him credit note	18
	17	Purchased more goods from S Burton	150
	26	Returned to S Burton goods; wrong design. Received credit note from Burton	20

2

			£
Mar.	3	Received cheque from R Adam as payment in advance for goods he wished to buy	150
	4	Purchased goods on credit from W Rawlins	320
	7	Sold goods to M Tring	490
	20	Returned to W Rawlins damaged goods purchased on March 4th. Received credit note from him	26
	21	M Tring returned over-delivery of goods. Sent him credit note	30
	27	Dispatched goods to R Adams, paid for on March 3rd.	150
	30	Received cheque from M Tring in part payment of his account	200
	31	Paid W Rawlins' account in full	

3

			£
May	1	M Allison started business with Capital at bank	1000
	3	Bought office furniture and paid by cheque	200
	5	Purchased goods from M Bright	492
	7	Paid rent	54
	10	Paid wages, drawing the cash out of bank	60
	11	Sold goods to B Smith	711
	16	Returned goods to M Bright, purchased on May 1st, as damaged. Received credit note from him	15
	24	Purchased goods, paying by cheque	27
	31	Sold goods and received cheque in payment	43

Enter the above in Allison's Cash Book and Ledger. Prepare Trial Balance, Trading and Profit and Loss Account, and a Balance Sheet as at 31st May, 19·1.

(a) What is the percentage of gross profit on Sales?

(b) Net profit on Capital?

4

			£
July	5	D Grant began business with cash at bank	4,000
	6	Purchased a Motor Delivery Van (used)	310
	7	Bought goods for re-sale on credit from C David	320
	11	Paid Rent and Rates, one quarter in advance	340
	12	Purchased goods from P Martin	890
	15	Returned goods to C David, as faulty	45
	18	Sold goods to K Mason	2,000
	22	General Expenses paid by cheque	130
	25	K Mason returned over-delivery of goods	50
	31	Clerk's Salary for month	140

Required T Grant's Ledger Accounts, Trial Balance, Final Accounts and Balance Sheet as at 31st July, 19·1.

5 From the following Trial Balance you are required to produce the Trading and Profit and Loss Account of W Redman and a Balance Sheet as at 30th April, 19·4.

TRIAL BALANCE

FOR MONTH ENDED 30TH APRIL, 19·4

	Dr. £	Cr. £
Capital		6,000
Loan Account—W Lock		2,000
Machinery	3,000	
Furniture	500	
Motor Vans	1,000	
Sundry Expenses	650	
Purchases and Sales	2,300	3,500
Returns Inwards and Outwards	120	100
Debtors and Creditors	3,520	2,300
Cash at bank	2,810	
	13,900	13,900

6 Bell is one of your customers. Enter the following items in M Bell's account. No double-entries are required for the purposes of this exercise:

Sept. 1 M Bell owes you £100;
    2 Sold to M Bell goods value £70;
    6 M Bell paid the amount that he owed on August 31st;
   12 M Bell returned goods as damaged in transit. Sent him credit note for their value £10

Balance Bell's account on 30th September and carry down the balance. Is it a debit or a credit balance? Is Bell your debtor or your creditor?

7 You are keeping Robert Owen's books (or your name is Robert Owen). John Peel is one of Owen's suppliers. You are required· to record the following transactions in Peel's account only, in Owen's ledger. No other accounts are required for the purpose of this exercise:

Nov. 1 Amount due to Peel £500;
    4 Returned to Peel goods value £40 and received his credit note;
   10 Paid the amount due to Peel to date;
   14 Purchased goods from Peel £450;
   20 Paid transport charges on above and entered it against Peel £10.

Balance Peel's account on November 30th. Is Peel Owen's debtor or creditor? How would you describe Owen's balance in Peel's ledger?

8 From the following information write up J Jones account in the books of R Robinson. Balance the account at the end of the month.

1970		£
Sept. 1	Robinson owed Jones	170
3	Jones sold Robinson goods	150
14	Robinson returned goods	20
27	Robinson settled amount due on September 1st	

RSA (adapted 1970)

Chapter Six

The Books of Original Entry

The Cash Book

From the very beginning of this work, the Bank Account has been supplemented by a second title, the Cash Book. The numerous money transactions occurring daily make the use of the Bank Account in the ledger cumbersome and inconvenient. A Cash Book, a kind of second volume to the ledger, is used *instead of* (*not* as well as) the Bank Account; the Cash Book is the Bank Account. Thus, we have a book of original entry; that is, before any cash entries are made in the ledger, they must first appear in the Cash Book, then be posted from the Cash Book to their respective accounts in the ledger. The Cash Book is unique among the firm's books in that it has a double function:

1 It is a book of original entry; entries are made into it from the copies of the paying-in book (debit) and the stubs of the cheque book (credit). These entries are then posted to their respective ledger accounts.
2 It is itself also a ledger account since it represents my banker's account.

OTHER BOOKS OF ORIGINAL ENTRY

The books introduced below do not contain accounts (accounts appear only in the ledger—the Cash Book being part of the ledger—and in no other book); they merely show details and generally help to streamline the double-entry system.

The Purchases (Day) Book—Method 1

In Chapter 3, the entries to record credit purchases of goods for re-sale was explained. The following is the sequence of activities which follow the receipt of suppliers' invoices:

1 After checking the accuracy of the invoices, they are filed into a binder called the Purchases Day Book (Purchases Book).
2 Each invoice value is entered on the credit side of the corresponding supplier's account in the ledger.
3 The supplier's ledger folio is marked on the relevant invoice to show where the entry in the ledger may be found, to indicate that it has been dealt with.
4 At the end of the month, the value of each invoice is tapped out on an adding machine and the grand total of credit purchases for the month thus produced, is entered on the debit side of the Purchases Account.

You will observe that the sum of the individual credit entries in the suppliers' accounts should be equal to the grand total appearing on the debit side of the Purchases Account. Thus, in the trial balance, you would have, perhaps, several suppliers' accounts on the credit side, together corresponding to one total figure against Purchases Account on the debit side[1] (assuming that none of the creditors had been paid). Cash purchases[2] are dealt with as hitherto—Credit Cash Book and Debit Purchases Account. Cash purchases must not be entered in the Purchases Book (or Purchases File).

Purchases (Day) Book—Method 2

There are still many businesses where the suppliers' invoices are first entered in a special book called Purchases Book, from which postings (entries) are made to the ledger. The following example illustrates this method by reproducing example 3/3, with the Purchases Book added:

EX. 6/1

PURCHASES BOOK

		Ledger Folio	£
April 17	C Moss	10	400
21	P Wood	14	100
30	Total credit purchases	143	500

LEDGER

C MOSS[10]

	April 17 Purchases	PB[1]	400

P WOOD[14]

April 29 Cash	CB[2]	100	April 21 Purchases	PB	100

PURCHASES[143]

April 30 Goods (total *credit* purchases)	PB	500
22 Cash	CB[2]	50
		550

---

[1]Purchases Book.
[2]Cash Book. Note that cash transactions, ie., payments made over the counter as opposed to credit transactions, *do not* appear in the Purchases Book at any time. These are called Cash Purchases (even if payment is by cheque). The payment for such purchases appears on the credit side of the Cash Book from which it is posted to the debit side of the Purchases *Account* in the ledger.

The Sales (Day) Book—Method 1

The principles relating to the recording of credit purchases explained above, also apply to credit sales. The binder or file in which the carbon copies of invoices are put, acts as a Sales Day Book (Sales Book). The following is the sequence of activities after the customers' invoices have been typed:

1 The carbon copies of the sales invoices are filed into a binder called the Sales Book.
2 Each invoice is entered on the debit side of the corresponding customer's account in the ledger.
3 The customer's ledger folio is marked on the carbon copy of the invoice to indicate that it has been dealt with and to show where the entry in the ledger may be found.
4 At the end of the month, the value of each invoice is tapped out on an adding machine and the grand total of credit sales for the month thus produced is entered on the credit side of the Sales Account. Cash Sales are dealt with as hitherto— Debit Cash Book, Credit Sales Account.

The Sales (Day) Book—Method 2

There are still many businesses where the customers' invoices are first entered in a special book called the Sales Book. The following example illustrates the sequence in which the entries are made:

EX. 6/2

SALES BOOK

April 20	S Porter	56	230
23	Providence Ltd.	58	470
30	Total credit sale	156	700
May 5	M Silver	65	620
29	A N Other and Others	69	1,000
31	Total credit sales	156	1,620

LEDGER

S PORTER[56]

April 20 Sales		SB	230

PROVIDENCE LTD.[58]

April 23 Sales		SB	470

M SILVER[65]

May 29 Sales		SB	620

A N OTHER AND OTHERS[69]

May 29 Sales		SB	1,000

SALES[156]

	April 30 Goods	SB	700
	May 31 Goods	SB	1,620

Returns Inwards and Returns Outwards Books

Precisely the same principles apply to the Sales Returns and Purchases Returns as to those of Credit Sales and Credit Purchases.

The trial balance is made up usually at the end of each month to prove the arithmetical accuracy of the ledger entries. The Trading and Profit and Loss Account however is normally made up once a year. The Purchases, Sales and the Returns Inwards and Returns Outwards *Accounts* would each have twelve entries to represent totals of twelve months, posted from the respective Day Books, plus any *cash* transactions posted from the Cash Book to Purchases and Sales Accounts. Transfers of accounts, eg., from Returns Outwards Account to Purchases Account; from Returns Inwards Account to Sales Account; from Expenses Accounts to Profit and Loss Accounts, normally take place at the end of the year only, *after* the trial balance at the end of the year has been satisfactorily brought out.

Note that interim accounts and a balance sheet to show the state of the business may be brought out at any time that they are required.

Exercise 6

1 The following accounts appear in your ledger. Explain the meaning of every entry in each column.

(a)

L PHILLIPS

			£					£
July	10	Cash	CB	100	July	1	Balance	b/d	208
	20	Returns	ROB	10		12	Purchases	PB	82
	30	Cash	CB	98					
	31	Balance	c/d	82					
				290					290
					Aug.	1	Balance	b/d	82

(b)

S MOORE

				£					£
Nov.	15	Returns	ROB	6	Nov.	3	Purchases	PB	42
	26	Cash	CB	36		20	Purchases	PB	119
	30	Balance	c/d	119					
				161					161
					Dec.	1	Balance	b/d	119

(c)

W BEE

				£					£
Dec.	1	Balance	b/d	73	Dec.	15	Cash	CB	73
	8	Sales	SB	80		18	Returns	RIB	10
	10	Carriage		2		31	Balance	c/d	165
	18	Sales		93					
				248					248
Jan.	1	Balance	b/d	165					

2 The following Purchases and Returns Outwards Accounts appear in your ledger. Write all you can about each item in them.

PURCHASES

19·2			£		19·2			£
Jan. 31	Goods	PB		980	Dec. 31	Returns Outwards	T	232
Feb. 28	,,	,,		1,120	31	Trading Account	T	11,228
Mar. 15	Cash	CB	110					
31	Goods	PB	930	1,040				
April 30	,,	,,		960				
May 31	,,	,,		810				
June 30	,,	,,		880				
July 31	,,	,,		970				
Aug. 31	,,	,,		1,300				
Sept. 30	,,	,,		1,100				
Oct. 21	Cash	CB	70					
24	,,	,,	130					
31	Goods	PB	1,400	1,600				
Nov. 30	,,	,,		400				
Dec. 31	,,	,,		300				
				11,460				11,460

RETURNS OUTWARDS

19·2			£	19·2			£
Dec. 31	Purchases	T	232	Feb. 28	Goods	RIB	22
				April 30	,,	,,	131
				Oct. 31	,,	,,	79
			232				232

3 Make appropriate entries in the Purchases and Sales Books and relative Returns Books from the following information:

Aug. 2 Sales to M Priest, £33
     5 Purchases from R Cain, £28
   10 Received back from M Priest goods value £5
   12 Bought goods from A Benn, £57
   15 Returned goods to R Cain, £3
   19 Sold more goods to M Priest, £70, plus non-returnable cases, £4
   20 Sales to P Moore, £21
   28 P Moore returned some of the goods sold to him on August 20th, £3

Post the above from the books of original entry to their appropriate ledger accounts and take out Trial Balance on 31st August, 19·1.

4 A B Marks began business on 31st March, 19·1 with capital in the bank, £8,000.

		£
Mar. 3	Bought goods from S Pitt	560
10	Sold goods to M Ord	750
15	Paid by cheque one quarter's rent in advance	300
16	Bought goods from R Morton	410
20	Returned goods as defective to S Pitt	50
25	Sold goods for cash	30
27	M Ord returned goods as over-delivered	10
29	Sold goods to P Victor	940
30	Sundry expenses for the month	100

Enter the above transactions in Marks' books of original entry, post to ledger accounts; take out Trial Balance. Then produce Trading and Profit and Loss Account as on 31st March, 19·1, and a Balance Sheet at that date.

5	Book of Original Entry	Name of Ledger Accounts to be:	
		Debited	Credited

You are required to rule columns similar to those shown above and indicate under the appropriate headings how you would deal with the transactions given below:

(a) Goods valued £125 bought on credit from Metal Supplies Co.

(b) Goods valued £210 sold on credit to S Daniel and Sons.

(c) Paid salaries £250 by means of cheques.

(d) Damaged goods (cost price £20) returned to Metal Supplies Co.

(RSA)

6 The financial year of A Mann ends on 31st December, 19·2. On 30th November his ledger showed the following accounts:

R MORTON

			£
	Dec. 1 Balance	b/d	142

P COLES

		£
Dec. 1 Balance	b/d	221

PURCHASES

		£
Dec. 1 Balance	b/d	8,844

SALES

			£
	Dec. 1 Balance	b/d	15,986

RETURNS INWARDS

		£
Dec. 1 Balance	b/d	133

RETURNS OUTWARDS

			£
	Dec. 1 Balance	b/d	99

Copy the above into your ledger, leaving enough space between each account for the following transactions which took place in December:

Dec. 3 Sold goods to P Coles value £57
    4 Returned to R Morton damaged goods delivered in November, £10
    8 Purchased goods from R Morton, £74
   12 P Coles paid his account to November 30th
   16 Sold more goods to P Coles, £156
   20 Returned from P Coles, goods damaged in transit, £5
   21 Paid R Morton the amount due to him on November 30th
   26 Returned to R Morton goods value £12
   28 Sent Debit Note to P Cole for cases and packing which ought to have been charged to him (added to his invoice) on December 16th, £3

Enter the above in the appropriate books of original entry and post to the ledger. Balance the accounts on 31st December.

7 Give the effect of each of the following errors on the gross profit of a business, stating exactly by how much the gross profit would be increased or decreased. If you think there would be no change, write None.

    (a) The Sales Returns Book was over-added by £20.

    (b) The entries in respect of an invoice for goods bought totalling £60 were omitted from the books. The entries are now made.

    (c) Carriage on sales had been entered in the ledger account as £121 instead of £112.

    (d) An amount of £80 in respect of goods returned to a supplier was entered in the Sales Book instead of the Purchases Returns Book.

RSA (adapted)

Chapter Seven

The Stock Account

Stock at Close of the Trading Period

In the foregoing examples it was assumed that at the end of the month of April all the china I had bought had been sold and there was no stock of unsold goods in my warehouse at the end (or *the close* of the month) of April. The examples had to be kept as simple as possible. But this is an unrealistic situation. In all warehouses, there is always some unsold stock of goods at the end of every trading period. This is called *Stock at Close*.

ASSESSING VALUE OF STOCK AT CLOSE

How do I arrive at the value of Stock at Close? Accounting practice requires that it is estimated either at cost price (its price at the time when purchased), or at its value on the market to-day, whichever is the lower. Formally expressed: *Either at cost or current market value, whichever is the lower*. This is important because the valuation of Stock at Close becomes part of the trading account and like every other entry in the Trading Account, affects the profit; but unlike the other items in the Trading Account, the value of stock is *assessed*. So the profit will be higher than it should be if the value of the Closing Stock is over-estimated and lower than it ought to be if it is under-estimated. There are other methods for assessing the value of stock but they are beyond the scope of this book.

EX. 7/1   Suppose that the stock in my warehouse when purchased had cost £200; but that its market price on April 30th was £180. Then, in the ledger, I would show the value of stock at £180, ie., at the lower figure. Stock (of goods) is something I own, like Cash or amounts due to me from my debtors, and like these Assets, Stock Account has also a *debit balance*.

EX. 7/2   THE STOCK ACCOUNT
A Stock Account is opened and it is debited with £180:

STOCK

April 30 Trading Account*	180

According to the principles of double-entry so far studied, the corresponding double-entry of the above would be on the credit side of the Trading Account:

TRADING ACCOUNT

	£		£
Purchases	550	Sales	700
Gross Profit	330	Stock at close*	180
	880		880

---

*Reminder   In Account A, the details read 'B', while in Account B, the details read 'A' (Chapter 2)

But much better use of the Trading Account would be made (more information would be extracted from it) if the double-entry of Stock were shown as a *deduction* from purchases, on the debit side of the Trading Account[1]:

EX. 7/3
(Extension of
EX. 4/8)

TRADING ACCOUNT

	£		£
Purchases	550	Sales[2]	700
Less Closing Stock	180		
Cost of goods sold	370		
Gross Profit	330		
	700		700

This method brings out the additional information that I purchased goods of value £550, but that only £370 worth was sold for £700. *The cost of the goods I sold for £700, was £370.* The Vertical Form of the above, brings out the information required from a Trading Account even more clearly:

EX. 7/4

TRADING ACCOUNT
FOR MONTH ENDED 30TH APRIL, 19·1

	£	£
Sales		700
Purchases	550	
Less Closing Stock	180	
Cost of goods sold		370
Gross Profit		330

Now, the Stock Account as it stands in example 7/2, is an open account, its double-entry having been made in the Trading Account. As already stated (p.22), all open accounts (or accounts with outstanding balances) at the end of the financial period must appear in the Balance Sheet: debit balances on the Assets (right) side and credit balances on the Liabilities (left) side (example 4/9). The Stock Account has a debit balance, it is also an asset since it represents something I possess. Therefore, it must be shown on the assets side in the balance sheet at the end of the trading period, 30th April, 19·1 in our example:

EX. 7/5

BALANCE SHEET
AS AT 30TH APRIL, 19·1

ASSETS £
Stock 30th April 180

---

[1]**Reminder**   The two sides of an account imply subtraction of one from the other. The closing stock might be added to the credit side of the Trading Account, and then the total of one side of it is subtracted from the other to arrive at gross profit or gross loss (example 7/2). Where expedient, any one item of one side might be deducted from the other side independently; the same gross profit or loss would result. In example 7/3, Closing Stock is deducted from the debit side instead of adding it to the credit side, in order to bring out the cost of the goods that were sold for £700.

[2]**Note**   Total Net Sales at the end of a trading period is sometimes referred to as Turnover.

Opening Stock or Stock at Start (of the Trading Period)

The Closing Stock on April 30th becomes the Opening or Starting Stock for the month of May. On May 1st, I had in hand goods worth £180. On May 31st, the usual trial balance was made up to prove the arithmetical accuracy of the accounts, in which, among all the other open accounts, there were also to be found:

	£
Opening Stock May 1st (Stock Account)	180
Purchases May 1st–May 31st, say	670
Sales May 1st–May 31st, say	1,000
Closing Stock May 31st, say	220

I am required to produce a Trading Account for the month of May from the above figures:

Sequence (or order) of Entries

The following is the order in which the items in the Trading Account are entered:

1 and 1(a)   Transfer the Opening Stock £180 from the Stock Account to the Trading Account, by crediting Stock and debiting Trading Account.

2 and 2(a)   Add the Purchases, £670, to it.

3 and 3(a)   Enter Closing Stock, £220, on the debit side of Stock Account; show it as a *deduction on the debit side* of the Trading Account:

EX. 7/6

STOCK

		£				£
April 30 Trading Account		180	May 31 Trading Account (1)	T		180
May 31 Trading Account (3)		220				

PURCHASES

			£				£
May 31 Goods	PB		670	May 31 Trading Account (2)	T		670

TRADING ACCOUNT
FOR MONTH ENDED 31ST MAY, 19·1

	£		£
Opening Stock 1st May (1a)	180	Sales	1,000
Purchases (2a)	670		
Total value of goods available for sale	850		
Less Unsold stock of goods in hand, ie., Closing Stock 31st May (3a)	220		
Cost of goods sold	630		
Gross Profit	370		
	1,000		1,000

EX. 7/7   OR, in vertical form:

TRADING ACCOUNT
FOR MONTH ENDED 31ST MAY, 19·1

	£	£
Sales		1,000
Opening Stock 1st May	180	
Purchases	670	
	850	
Less Closing Stock 31st May	220	
Cost of goods sold		630
Gross Profit		370

All the accounts in my ledger to 30th April may now be balanced, and a Trial Balance, Final Accounts and a Balance Sheet as at that date may be produced:

EX. 7/8

CASH BOOK

19·1		£	19·1			£
April 1	Capital—John Fry	10,000	April 10	Freehold Premises		6,000
30	Providence Ltd.	200	22	Purchases		50
			28	Stationery		15
			29	Carriage		5
			29	Heating and Lighting		10
			29	P Wood		100
			30	Lockerdesks Ltd.		200
			30	Balance	c/d	3,820
		10,200				10,200
May 1	Balance b/d	3,820				

CAPITAL—JOHN FRY

			£				£
April 30	Balance	c/d	10,300	April 1	Cash		10,000
				30	Net Profit		300
			10,300				10,300
				May 1	Balance	b/d	10,300

FREEHOLD PREMISES

April 10	Cash	6,000

OFFICE FURNITURE

		£
April 15	Lockerdesks Ltd.	200

LOCKERDESKS LTD.

		£			£
April 30	Cash	200	April 15 Office Furniture		200

C MOSS

		£
	April 17 Purchases	400

P WOOD

		£			£
April 29	Cash	100	April 21 Purchases		100

S PORTER

		£
April 20	Sales	230

PROVIDENCE LTD.

		£				£
April 23	Sales	470	April 30	Cash		200
			30	Balance	c/d	270
		470				470
May 1	Balance b/d	270				

PURCHASES

	£	19·1	£
April 17 C Moss	400	April 30 Transfer to Trading Account	550
21 P Wood	100		
22 Cash	50		
	550		550

SALES

	£	April 20 S Porter	£
April 30 Transfer to Trading Account	700	April 20 S Porter	230
		23 Providence Ltd.	470
	700		700

STATIONERY

	£		£
April 28 Cash	15	April 30 Transfer to Profit and Loss Account	15

CARRIAGE

	£		£
April 29 Cash	5	April 30 Transfer to Profit and Loss Account	5

HEATING AND LIGHTING

	£		£
April 29 Cash	10	April 30 Transfer to Profit and Loss Account	10

EX. 7/9

TRIAL BALANCE
AS ON 30TH APRIL, 19·1

	Dr. £	Cr. £
Capital—John Fry		10,000
Freehold Premises	6,000	
Office Furniture	200	
S Porter	230	
Providence Ltd.	270	
C Moss		400
Purchases and Sales	550	700
Stationery	15	
Carriage	5	
Heating and Lighting	10	
Cash at bank	3,820	
	11,100	11,100

The trial balance is made up *before* the transfer of any of the accounts. In our example, the accounts to be transferred are Purchases, Sales, Heating and Lighting, Carriage, Stationery.

STOCK

		£
April 30 Trading Account		180

EX. 7/10

TRADING AND PROFIT AND LOSS ACCOUNT
FOR MONTH ENDED 30TH APRIL, 19·1

		£			£
Purchases		550	Sales		700
Less Closing Stock		180			
Cost of goods sold		370			
Gross Profit	c/d	330			
		700			700
Stationery		15	Gross Profit	b/d	330
Carriage		5			
Heating and Lighting		10			
Net Profit to Capital		300			
		330			330

BALANCE SHEET
AS AT 30TH APRIL, 19·1

LIABILITIES			ASSETS		
Capital	10,000		Freehold Premises		6,000
Add Net Profit	300		Office Furniture		200
		10,300	Stock 30th April		180
Creditors		400	Debtors		500
			Cash at bank		3,820
		10,700			10,700

The Stock Account is shown in this example *after* the trial balance, in order to emphasise that the *closing* stock is entered into its own account just before the Final Accounts are compiled, that is, *after* the trial balance has been taken out. The *closing* stock does not appear in the trial balance (except in tests, exam questions and other special cases). The *opening* stock does.

The trial balance is not normally made up in the ledger. It is a document which is kept in a separate file for reference when required.

Average stock and rate of turnover of stock

The number of times I buy and sell a quantity of stock during the course of a year (or any other given trading period), is useful to know. This is called the Stock-turn, or more precisely, the rate of turnover. A simple arithmetical formula brings out this information:

$$\frac{\text{Cost of Sales}}{\text{Value of Average Stock}} = \text{Rate of Turnover}$$

We are already familiar with the process which produces Cost of Sales (as in the trading account). As to average stock, there are normally only two figures with which we need to be concerned at present: the opening and the closing stocks.

EX. 7/11

	£
On 1st January, 19·1, the value of my stock was	780
On 31st December, 19·1, the value of my stock was	620
On 31st December, 19·1, my trading account showed the cost of sales to be	7,000

$$\text{Average Stock} = \frac{780 + 620}{2} = £700$$

$$\text{Rate of turnover of stock} = \frac{\text{Cost of Sales}}{\text{Average Stock}} = \frac{7,000}{700} = 10 \text{ times}$$

Of course it is possible to add together every purchase made over the year and to divide the total with the number of purchases and thus arrive at an accurate average value of stock.

Ascertaining the Value of Loss of Unknown Quantity of Stock

In the event of any disaster such as fire or theft, how can I estimate the value of stock lost or destroyed? This question is important; the method for its solution involves the fundamental principles that:

1 the two sides of an account imply subtraction of one side from the other;
2 the known items of an account are placed correctly on their respective sides, their difference produces the unknown item.

EX. 7/12   On 20th October, a fire in my premises destroyed all but £100 worth of stock of goods. The account books however were intact and I was able to ascertain that the value of stock on 1st January was £2,000. Purchases to 20th October came to £10,000 and Sales £15,000. My normal gross profit on turnover was 25 per cent. From these figures I was able to produce a trading account for the period ended 20th October:

TRADING ACCOUNT
PERIOD ENDED 20TH OCTOBER, 19·1

	£		£
Stock 1st January	2,000	Sales	15,000
Purchases	10,000	Stock intact after fire at 20th October	100
Gross Profit at 25 per cent on Sales	3,750	Estimated value of stock destroyed (being balance)	650
	15,750		15,750

The difference between all the available figures correctly placed on each side of the trading account produced the value of stock destroyed. This principle is of the utmost importance, particularly at examinations; fortunately, it is not difficult. It is explained in greater detail in the chapter on Incomplete Records (Chapter 23.)
The following rather more interesting example might be instructive:

EX. 7/13   M Brown, a trader, offers the following figures:

19·1		£
Jan 1	Value of Stock brought down from previous trading period	2,100
Dec. 31	Value of Stock at close	1,900
	Sales for year	12,300
	Returns Inwards	300

Brown's ratio of gross profit to turnover is 20 per cent. What do you estimate the value of his purchases for the year to be?
(The numbers against the items in the following trading account, indicate the sequence of the entries.)

TRADING ACCOUNT
AS AT 31ST DECEMBER, 19·1

		£			£	£
Stock 1st Jan.	1	2,100	Sales	2	12,300	
Purchases	11	9,400	*Less* Returns	3	300	
	10	11,500		4		12,000
Less Stock 31st Dec.	9	1,900				
Cost of Sales	8	9,600				
Gross Profit	7	2,400				
	6	12,000		5		12,000

The Stock Book

Another fundamental aspect of the Stock Account is concerned with quantities which are recorded in a *memorandum book* called the Stock Book (not part of the double-entry system). This is not the place for a detailed exposition of that aspect. At this elementary stage, it is sufficient to illustrate a very simple Stock Book.

EX. 7/14

On 1st April, I had in stock 200 articles, costing £3 each. During the month I bought 600 more of those articles at the same price and sold 500 at £4 each:

STOCK BOOK

		Quantities Units IN	Cost £				Quantities Units OUT	Cost £
April	1 Purchases	200	600	April	1/30 Sales		500	1,500
	20 Purchases	600	1,800		30 Balance	c/d	300	900
		800	2,400				800	2,400
May	1 Balances b/d	300	900					

PURCHASES ACCOUNT

April 30 Goods		2,400	April 30 Trading Account	2,400

STOCK ACCOUNT

April 30 Trading Account	900

TRADING ACCOUNT
FOR MONTH ENDED 30TH APRIL, 19·1

	£		£
Purchases (800 @ £3 each)	2,400	Sales (500 @ £4 each)	2,000
Less Closing Stock	900		
	1,500		
Gross Profit	500		
	2,000		2,000

It is possible to show a combination of number of units, price per unit, total cost and selling price and total sales, in the Trading Account:

EX. 7/15

TRADING ACCOUNT
FOR MONTH ENDED 30TH APRIL, 19·1

		Quantities Units IN	Price £	£			Quantities Units OUT	Price £	£
Purchases		800	3	2,400	Sales		500	4	2,000
					Stock at Close	c/d	300	3*	900
Gross Profit	c/d			500					
		800		2,900			800		2,900
Stock 1st May		300							

(as it appears in the Trading Account of the following accounting period.)

*Either at cost or current market value, whichever is the lower.

Exercise 7

1 From the information given below, open Purchases, Sales and Stock Accounts. Transfer as appropriate to the Trading Account and ascertain the Gross Profit and the cost of the goods sold.

		£
Jan. 31	Total purchases for month	2,000
	Total sales for month	2,300
	Stock in hand at close of month	400

2 From the information given below
    (a) Open Purchases, Sales and Stock Accounts and transfer as appropriate to the Trading Account for the month ended 31st August.
    (b) Enter the September items in the same accounts and transfer them to a Trading Account for month ended 30th September, 19·1. In each case indicate the Cost of Sales.

		£
Aug. 31	Total purchases	2,700
	Total sales	3,200
	Stock at close of month	390
Sept. 30	Total purchases	2,690
	Total sales	3,442
	Stock at close of month	311

3 V Baron began business on 1st June with capital £4,000 at bank.

			£
June	4	Purchased goods from A Morris	984
	10	Sold goods to M Ford	1,346
	18	Sold goods and received cheque in settlement	52
	22	Drew money from the bank for wages	207
	30	Paid electricity bill by cheque	18
		Stock in hand 30th June	149

Open the necessary accounts; produce at 30th June a trial balance followed by the Trading and Profit and Loss Account, and a Balance Sheet as at 30th June, 19·1. Then, using the same accounts, enter the following July transactions in Baron's ledger:

			£
July	6	Paid A Morris his outstanding account in full	
	10	Paid British Rail their account	12
	14	Purchased goods from A Morris	724
	20	Drew cheque for wages	202
	21	Received cheque from M Ford in settlement of his account	
	28	Sold goods to M Ford	1,209

Unsold goods in stock at 31st July was valued at £121

Produce a Trial Balance at 31st July, followed by a Trading and Profit and Loss Account, and a Balance Sheet at that date.

4 From the following information calculate the value of R Bott's stock on 30th September, 1970.

	£
1st September, 1970, Stock (at cost)	1,300
Purchases during month	15,000
Sales during month	20,000
Sales returns during month	800
Goods taken by Bott (Selling Price)	400
Gross Profit is 20% on turnover	

(RSA)

5 From the following information, prepare the Trading and Profit and Loss Account of M Twine, for the year ended 31st December, 19·1:

	£
Stock, 1st January, 19·1	3,000
Stock, 31st December, 19·1	2,500
Sales	30,000
Selling Expenses	2,500
Purchases	16,000
Administration Expenses	3,500

From your account, calculate:
(a) the number of times the stock was 'turned over' during the year;
(b) the gross profit/sales percentage;
(c) the net profit/sales percentage.

(*RSA*)

6 During the year 1970, Green bought goods value £8,400 and his sales, on which he made a gross profit of 25 per cent, were £11,600. The value of his stock at the beginning of the year was £1,600. What was the value of his stock at the end of the year? Show details of your calculations.

(*RSA I 1970*)

7 (a) Does the inclusion of Closing Stock in the Trading Account increase or decrease
(i) Gross Profit;
(ii) Net Profit?
Give reasons for your answers.
(b) Re-draw the balance sheet example 4/9 and include in it the Closing Stock of £180 (example 7/5). (Its place among the assets in our example is before Debtors and after Office Furniture.) What corresponding item in the balance sheet would be affected if it were bought (i) on credit; (ii) by cheque?

8 In a burglary at the warehouse of J Cook and Son on the night of 30th September, 1970 part of the stock was stolen.
From the following particulars show in *account form* the estimated value of the loss of stock.

	£
Stock at cost, 1st July, 1970	7,840
Purchases from 1st July to 30th September, 1970	15,600
Sales from 1st July to 30th September, 1970	18,400
Stock remaining after the burglary was valued at	2,420

J Cook & Son's usual gross profit is 25 per cent of selling price

(*RSA*)

9 The premises of T Short were damaged by fire on 15th October, 19·1 and all his stock was destroyed with the exception of goods worth £800 which were salvaged. The value of his stock on 1st January, 19·1 was £10,000.
Purchases to 15th October were £28,400 and sales £39,200. Short was accustomed to making 25 per cent gross profit on sales.
Draw up an account to show the estimated value of stock destroyed by fire.

(*RSA*)

10 A trader dealing in a standard line of goods which he regularly sold at 25 per cent above cost price, discovered on the morning of 18th March, 1974 (a Monday) that during the week-end all his stock had been destroyed by fire. His stock was fully covered by insurance, but no records were immediately available from which he could

calculate how much he should claim from his insurance company. His account books were, however, undamaged, and from them he was able to obtain the following figures:

	£
Stock in hand 1st January, 1974, at cost price	6,000
Purchases from 1st January to 14th March, 1974	14,000
Sales from 1st January to 15th March, 1974	18,000

State the value of the stock destroyed in the fire. Your calculations should be clearly shown.

11 Give the effect of *each* of the following errors on the *gross* profit of a business, stating exactly by how much the gross profit will be increased or decreased. If you think there would be no change write 'None'.
  (a) The Sales Returns Book was over-added by £20.
  (b) The entries in respect of an invoice for goods bought totalling £60 were omitted from the books.
  (c) Carriage on sales had been entered in the ledger account as £121 instead of £112.
  (d) The closing stock was under valued by £649.
  (e) An amount of £80 in respect of goods returned to a supplier was entered in the Sales Book instead of the Purchases Returns Book.

(RSA adapted)

12 On 1st January, 19·1, B Forest, a retailer, had stock valued at £3,750. In planning for the next six months he estimated that his gross sales would amount to £20,500 and that he would have sales returns of £500. He was anxious to have at 30th June, 19·1, stock valued at not more than £3,500. Assuming that this trader's average ratio of gross profit to turnover is 25 per cent, calculate, in account form, the amount to which he should limit his purchases during the period.

13 A firm commenced trading on 1st May, 1971, with a stock of 1,000 articles costing £6 each. During the month it purchased 3,000 more at £5 each, and sold 2,200 at £8 each. Purchasers returned 100 of the articles to the firm in good saleable condition and were allowed for these. At the end of the month 80 of the articles in stock had become damaged and were found to be worthless.
Assuming the stock was sold in the order in which it was purchased, show, in the form of a Trading Account, the gross profit or loss made during the month.

(RSA June 1970)

14 A trader dealing in a single standard article, follows strictly the rule of selling his goods in the order in which he has bought them. On 1st January, 1969, his stock was 1,000 articles, which had cost him 75p each. His subsequent purchases were: on 30th January, 2,000 articles at 80p each; on 27th February, 2,000 articles at 85p each; and on 16th March, 2,000 articles at 90p each. His sales were: for January, 2,400 articles at £1·05 each; for February, 2,000 articles at 95p each; and for March, 1,800 articles at £1 each. The current replacement cost (ie., the price the trader would have had to pay for it in the market on that date) of the stock remaining unsold on 31st March was 85p per article.
Show the Trading Account for the quarter ended 31st March, 1969.

(RSA)

15 For the trading year ended 30th June, 19·2, the figures in a merchant's trading account are: Stocks: 1st July, 19·1, £4,355 and 30th June, 19·2, £1,365; Sales, £80,405; Purchases, £47,330; Returns Inwards, £405; Returns Outwards, £320. In his profit and loss account the summarised net debits for general, administrative, and distributive expenses are £20,000.

  (a) You are required:
    (i)   to draw up the merchant's abridged trading and profit and loss account for the year ended 30th June, 19·2.
    (ii) to state the cost price of the goods sold;
    (iii) to state the amount of the merchant's turnover for the year;
    (iv) to state the percentage rate of gross profit on cost;
    (v) to state the percentage rate of gross profit on turnover;
    (vi) to state the percentage rate of net profit on turnover.

                    (RSA)

16 (a) Explain briefly what you understand by:
    (i)   Last-in, first-out (LIFO), and
    (ii) First-in, first-out (FIFO).

  (b) A firm began the year with a stock of 500 identical items which cost £10 each. On 1st January the firm bought a further 1,500 items at £12 each. During the year, which ended on 31st December, the firm sold 1,600 items for £15 each.

From this information you are required to calculate the gross profit for the year if the firm operated on:

(i) the LIFO basis of stock issue valuation, and
(ii) the FIFO basis of stock issue valuation.

                    (JMB 1971)

17 (a) From the following information you are required to produce a Trading Account for the year ended 31st December 1972:

	£
Opening Stock	10,000
Sales	56,000
Closing stock at cost taken on 4th January, 1973	8,000

Adjustments to the following items are necessary to ascertain the true value of stock at cost on 31st December 1972.

	£
Purchases between 1st and 4th January, 1973	1,800
Sales between 1st and 4th January 1973	2,800
Sales Returns between 1st and 4th January 1973	48

The profit margin is $33\frac{1}{3}\%$ on cost.

  (b) From the details in the above trading account, ascertain the stock turnover for the year.

Chapter Eight

Trade Discount

Purchases of Goods at Trade Discount

As wholesalers are buyers of goods in large quantities, manufacturers usually allow them a substantial discount on their list, or catalogue, prices. This is called a *trade discount*. The trade discount is intended to represent the wholesaler's margin of profit. He is thus able to offer the goods to his retailer customers at manufacturer's list prices.

On 21st May, I purchased from C Moss 15,000 articles listed at £5 per 100, subject to a trade discount of 20%. The goods were delivered and, in due course, I received C Moss' invoice which I entered in the Purchases Book (together with other incoming invoices, eg., one from P Wood, dated 10th May for sundry articles, total value £250 (No trade discount). This is at cost price; I must add a certain percentage to it in order to arrive at my selling price.

EX. 8/1

PURCHASES BOOK

			£	£
May 10	P Wood			
	Sundry goods			250
May 21	C Moss			
	15,000 articles at £5 per 100		750	
	Less 20% trade discount		150	600
				850

The price to my retail customers for the above would be £5 per 100, net; total value £750 for the goods from Moss; gross profit £150. (To arrive at the selling price of the goods from P Wood, I would add an appropriate percentage to the cost, perhaps 25%.) The *net* figures, in the second column of the Purchases Book, are posted to their respective accounts in the ledger:

EX. 8/2

P WOOD

		£
May 10 Purchases		250

C MOSS

May 31 Purchases	600

PURCHASES

May 31 Goods	850

Returns Outwards of Goods Purchased at a Discount

On receiving the above goods from C Moss, I discovered that there were defective articles value £20 *at list price*. I returned these to Moss and, in due course he sent me a credit note, dated 27th May, acknowledging his liability to me for the value of the returned goods. This I entered into the Returns Outwards Book (together with other credit notes, including one from P Wood) and then posted it to Moss' ledger account: (Ignore example 5/6 p.29.)

EX. 8/3

RETURNS OUTWARDS BOOK

	£	£
May 27 C Moss		
400 articles returned as defective @ £5 per 100	20	
Less 20% trade discount	4	
		16
May 31 P Wood		
Sundry articles returned as damaged	30	
		46

Note that when purchasing (or selling) goods at a trade discount, the same percentage must be deducted from the gross value of goods that are returned. The above are posted to the ledger as follows:

EX. 8/4

C MOSS

			£				£
May 27 Returns Outwards	ROB	16		May 21 Purchases	PB	600

P WOOD

May 31 Returns Outwards	ROB	30	May 10 Purchases	PB	250

PURCHASES

May 31 Goods	PB	850	

RETURNS OUTWARDS

	May 31 Goods	ROB	46

Sales of Goods at Trade Discount

On 18th May, I sold to A Salter goods value £860, less 15% trade discount. This was invoiced to Salter. An entry from the copy of the invoice was made in the Sales Book (together with other credit sales, including one to M Silver £620 *net*), which was subsequently posted to Salter's ledger account (example 8/7 below).

Returns Inwards of Goods Sold at a Discount

On 29th May, I agreed to receive back goods worth £20 gross, sold to Salter on 18th May, as they were not of the quality ordered. A credit note was sent to Salter. An entry was made in the Returns Inward Book, together with other returns, including one from M Silver, 16th May £10 *net*, and another from Providence Ltd., 20th May £15 *net*. These were subsequently posted to their respective ledger accounts (example 8/7 below).

EX. 8/5

SALES BOOK

				£	£
May	5	M Silver			620
		Various goods			
	18	A Salter			
		Various goods		860	
		Less 15% trade discount		129	731
					1,351

EX. 8/6

RETURNS INWARDS BOOK

				£
May	16	M Silver		10
	20	Providence Ltd.		15
	29	A Salter		
		Various goods returned, not of quality ordered	20	
		Less 15% trade discount	3	17
				42

EX. 8/7

LEDGER

PROVIDENCE LTD

			£				£
April 23	Sales		470	April 30	Cash		200
				30	Balance	c/d	270
			470				470
May 1	Balance	b/d	270	May 20	Returns		15

M SILVER

May 5	Sales	620	May 16	Returns	10

A SALTER

May 18	Sales	731	May 29	Returns	17

SALES

		May 31	Goods (Total for month)	1,351

RETURNS INWARDS

May 31	Goods (Total for month)	42

All the Ledger Accounts to Date

The Balance Sheet example 7/10, reproduced below, shows all the accounts in my ledger with outstanding balances as at 30th April, 19·1.

EX. 8/8

BALANCE SHEET OF JOHN FRY
AS AT 30TH APRIL, 19·1

LIABILITIES	£	£	ASSETS	£
Capital	10,000		Freehold Premises	6,000
Add Net Profit	300		Office Furniture	200
		10,300	Stock 30th April	180
Creditors		400	Debtors	500
			Cash at bank	3,820
		10,700		10,700

The following transactions took place in May in addition to those in examples 8/4, 5, 6, 7:

		£
May 10	Purchased goods from P Wood	250
11	Received cheque from S Porter in settlement of his account	230
15	Sent cheque to C Moss for the amount due to him 30th April	400
28	Drew cheque for Sundry Expenses	270
31	Received cheque from Providence Ltd. in settlement of their account	255

The above were entered in the ledger in continuation of their respective accounts, as follows:

EX. 8/9

CASH BOOK

			£				£
May 1	Balance	b/d	3,820	May 15	C Moss	10	400
11	S Porter	56	230	28	Sundry Expenses	102	270
31	Providence Ltd.	58	255				

CAPITAL—JOHN FRY[1]

			May 1	Balance	b/d	10,300

FREEHOLD PREMISES[2]

May 1	Balance	b/d	6,000

OFFICE FURNITURE[3]

May 1	Balance	b/d	200

STOCK[138]

April 30	Trading Account	T	180

PURCHASES[143]

May 31	Goods (example 8/4)	PB	850

SALES[156]

		May 31	Goods (example 8/5)	1,351

RETURNS INWARDS[166]

May 31	Goods (example 8/6)	RIB	42

RETURNS OUTWARDS[164]

		May 31	Goods (example 8/4)	ROB	46

S PORTER[56]

May 1	Balance	b/d	230	May 11 Cash	CB	230

PROVIDENCE LTD.[58]

May 1	Balance	b/d	270	May 20 Returns	RIB	15
				31 Cash	CB	255
			270			270

P WOOD[14]

May 31	Returns	ROB	30	May 10 Purchases	PB	250

C MOSS[10]

May	15	Cash	CB	400	May	1	Balance	b/d	400
	27	Returns Outwards	ROB	16		21	Purchases	PB	600

M SILVER[60]

May	5	Sales	SB	620	May	16	Returns	RIB	10

A SALTER[61]

May	18	Sales	SB	731	May	29	Returns	RIB	17

SUNDRY EXPENSES

May	28	Cash	CB	270

The above represents all the accounts in my ledger as they appear to date.

Exercise 8

1 From the following list of transactions, select the appropriate items, and write up the Sales Day Book for 6th September 19·1:

Sold goods to R Jones	£90 less 10% trade discount
to T Williams	£75 less 20% trade discount
for cash	£67 net
to S Smith	£90 net
to T Brown	£80 less 25% trade discount
Returned goods to Barr Supply Co. Ltd., not as ordered £15 net	

(*RSA*)

2 From the following information write up the Sales Day Book of Samson & Co., Ltd. for the day Tuesday, 11th March, 19·1. Samson & Co., Ltd. keep their Sales Day Book in such a manner that it is possible to see both the daily total, and monthly total of sales.

Total brought forward from Monday 10th March, 19.1	£1,700
Robert Home—invoice no. 141D—£120 less 20%	
William Davey—invoice no. 142D—£70 less 10%	
C Gilchrist & Co. Ltd.—invoice no. 143D—£120 less 20%	
J Woodward Ltd.—invoice no. 144D—£50 less 20%	
L McWorthy—invoice no. 145D—£70 net	

(*RSA*)

3 From the following list of transactions select the appropriate items and write up the Sales Book for 6th September, 19·1:

Sold goods to: R Jones	£90 less 10% trade discount
T Williams	£75 less 20% trade discount
S Smith	£90 net
T Brown	£80 less 25% trade discount
Cash-and-carry customer who paid by cheque £67	
Sept. 30 R Jones returned some of the goods sold to him on 6th September, value £20 gross	

4 Enter the following list of transactions into their appropriate books of original entry; post to their ledger accounts; take out trial balance:

Mar. 1 Purchased from S White goods value £160 less 20% trade discount
    4 Sold to M Penn goods value £210, less 15% trade discount
    5 Purchased goods by cheque £10
   15 M Penn returned some of the goods sold to him on 4th March, value £30 gross
   20 Returned to S White some of the goods purchased from him on 1st March, £20 gross
   25 Sold goods and received cheque in payment £15
   28 Purchased goods from P Roberts £70, net
   31 Sold goods to N Crosby £95, net

Transfer the Returns Accounts to Purchase and Sales Accounts respectively, and show the Trading Account extract.

5 M Miller is in business as a wholesaler, and the following are his transactions with B Russell for the month of December, 19·1:

Dec. 1 Balance owed by Miller £350
3 Miller purchased goods valued at £200 less 15% trade discount
3 Russell charged carriage £6 on these goods
8 Miller returned goods valued at £12 (catalogue price), and a further allowance of £1 was made by Russell
14 Miller sent a cheque for the balance owing at 1st December
17 Miller purchased goods valued at £85 net
20 Russell sold Miller goods valued at £45

You are asked:

(a) To prepare from the above information Russell's account as it would appear in Miller's ledger, balancing it and bringing down the balance on 1st January.

(b) To state where the balance of Russell's account would appear in the balance sheet of Miller dated 31st December, 19·1.

(c) To state the amount Miller would have to realise on the goods purchased on the 3rd December in order to obtain 25 per cent gross profit on his outlay.

(*RSA*)

6 It is normal for a business, which receives a large number of purchase invoices, to use a purchase invoice checking procedure before any entries are made in the books. You are required to list the points you would check on each invoice.

(*RSA*)

7 Enter the following credit transactions in the appropriate day book, open ledger accounts, post to ledger and extract a trial balance:

1973		£
June	5 Received invoice from M Smith for goods supplied	95
	6 Sold goods to R Jones	120
	Bought goods from T Brown	130
	Bought goods from M Smith	97
	8 Returned goods to T Brown	25
	Sold goods to R Jones	150
	Allowed R Jones for faulty goods	10

(*RSA 1973*)

Chapter Nine

Cash Discount

Meaning of Cash Discount

My terms of payment to my customers (in some cases) are that if they pay their accounts within 30 days of the invoice date they may deduct $2\frac{1}{2}\%$ from the amount due. This is to induce them to pay within a reasonable time.

Of the four customers in my ledger, the accounts of S Porter and Providence Ltd. are cleared (see pp.54–55). M Silver and A Salter are entitled to $2\frac{1}{2}\%$ cash discount provided they pay within 30 days of their respective invoice dates: they do so.

The following are details of the payments made by the two customers in settlement of their accounts (all calculations are to the nearest £):

EX. 9/1

Customers' name	Date of payment	Amount due £	Cash discount allowed $2\frac{1}{2}\%$ (nearest £)	Amount paid £
M Silver	May 29	610	15	595
A Salter	May 31	714	18	696
			33	

The amounts received, £595 and £696 are debited to the Cash Book and credited to the customers' respective accounts. The discounts allowed, £15 and £18 are also credited to the customers' respective accounts and debited, in total, to a Discounts Allowed Account:

EX. 9/2

M SILVER

		£				£
May	5 Sales	620	May	16	Returns Inwards	10
				29	Cash	595
					Discount	15
		620				620

A SALTER

May	18 Sales	731	May	29	Returns Inwards	17
				31	Cash	696
					Discount	18
		731				731

DISCOUNTS ALLOWED

May	31 Cash	33

Discount Columns in the Cash Book and Discount Accounts

In practice, a business has many more than just two customers. What convenient method is there, then:

1 For recording the discounts allowed, immediately on receipt of payment, so that it is not forgotten?

2 For quickly arriving at the total discounts, for entry into the Discounts Allowed Account at the end of each month?

These problems are solved by drawing an additional column on each side of the Cash Book; on the debit side for Discounts Allowed to debtors (my customers); on the credit side for Discounts Received from creditors (my suppliers). Thus, the above payments *and discounts* first appear in the Cash Book:

EX. 9/3

CASH BOOK

		Discount Allowed £	Bank £				Discount Received £	Bank £
May 29	M Silver	15	595	May 31	P Wood		6	214
31	A Salter	18	696	31	C Moss		15	569
		33					21	

It is from the Cash Book that payments as well as discounts are posted to the ledger, as in examples 9/2, 3, 4. It is evident that creditors P Wood and C Moss have been paid and that I have taken $2\frac{1}{2}\%$ cash discount. Their accounts and the Discounts Received Account now appear as follows:

EX. 9/4

P WOOD

		£			£
April 29	Cash	100	April 21	Purchases	100
May 31	Cash	214	May 10	Purchases	250
	Discount	6			
	Returns	30			
		250			250

C MOSS

May 27	Returns Outwards	16	April 17	Purchases	400
15	Cash	400	May 21	Purchases	600
31	Cash	569			
31	Discount	15			
		1,000			1,000

DISCOUNTS RECEIVED

			Cash	21

Note that:

1 The discount columns in the Cash Book are there only for convenience. They are called *memorandum* columns (Reminder Columns); they are not intended to be part of the double-entry process.

2 The *totals* of the Discounts Allowed and Discounts Received columns in the Cash Book appear on the same side in their own ledger accounts, as they are in the Cash Book, ie., the Discounts Allowed on the debit side, and the Discounts Received on the credit side.

3 At the end of the trading period, the discounts accounts are transferred to the Profit and Loss Account, as follows:

EX. 9/5

DISCOUNTS ALLOWED

			£				£
May 31 Cash	T		33	May 31 Profit and Loss Account	T		33

DISCOUNTS RECEIVED

						£
May 31 Profit and Loss Account T	21	May 31 Cash	T		21

PROFIT AND LOSS ACCOUNT

Discounts Allowed	33	Discounts Received	21

All my customers' and suppliers' accounts are now (31st May) settled—they have no outstanding balances. The Cash Book appears as follows:

EX. 9/6

CASH BOOK

			Discount Allowed £	Bank £				Discount Received £	Bank £
May	1 Balance	b/d		3,820	May 15	C Moss			400
	1 S Porter			230	28	Sundry Expenses			270
	29 M Silver		15	595	31	P Wood		6	214
	31 Providence Ltd.			255	31	C Moss		15	569
	31 A Salter		18	696	31	Balance	c/d		4,143
			33	5,596				21	5,596
June	1 Balance	b/d		4,143					

The following is a trial balance as on 31st May, followed by the Final Accounts and a Balance Sheet as at that date:

EX. 9/7

TRIAL BALANCE
AS ON 31ST MAY, 19·1

	£	£
Capital		10,300
Freehold Premises	6,000	
Office Furniture	200	
Stock 1st May	180	
Purchases and Sales	850	1,351
Returns Inwards and Outwards	42	46
Sundry Expenses	270	
Discounts Allowed and Received	33	21
Cash at bank	4,143	
	11,718	11,718

The value of the Stock at close was £110

TRADING AND PROFIT AND LOSS ACCOUNT
FOR MONTH ENDED 31ST MAY, 19·1

	£	£			£	£
Stock 1st May		180	Sales		1,351	
Purchases	850		*Less* Returns Inwards		42	1,309
Less Returns Outwards	46	804				
		984				
Less Stock 31st May		110				
		874				
Gross Profit	c/d	435				
		1,309				1,309
Sundry Expenses		270	Gross Profit	b/d		435
Discounts Allowed		33	Discounts Received			21
Net Profit transferred to Capital		153				
		456				456

BALANCE SHEET
AS AT 31ST MAY, 19·1

LIABILITIES		ASSETS			
Capital—John Fry	10,300		Freehold Premises		6,000
Add Net Profit	153		Office Furniture		200
		10,453	Stock 31st May		110
			Cash at bank		4,143
		10,453			10,453

EX. 9/8

ALTERNATIVE VERTICAL VERSION
TRADING AND PROFIT AND LOSS ACCOUNT
FOR MONTH ENDED 31ST MAY, 19·1

	£	£	£
Sales	1,351		
Less Returns	42		1,309
Stock 1st May		180	
Purchases	850		
Less Returns	46	804	
		984	
Less Stock 31st May		110	874
Gross Profit			435
Add Discounts Received			21
			456
Less Expenditure:			
Sundry Expenses		270	
Discounts Allowed		33	303
Net Profit transferred to Capital			153

BALANCE SHEET
AS AT 31ST MAY, 19·1

ASSETS		
Freehold Premises		6,000
Office Furniture		200
Stock 31st May		110
Cash at bank		4,143
		10,453
REPRESENTED BY		
Capital—John Fry	10,300	
Add Net Profit	153	
		10,453

Exercise 9

1 On 1st April, the following balances were outstanding in B Adam's ledger:

CAPITAL—B ADAMS

£			£
	April 1 Balance		4,000

MOTOR VANS

April 1 Balance	1,200

STOCK

April 1 Balance	680

C MORTIMER

April 1 Balance	160

A MARTIN

	April 1 Balance	80

CASH BOOK

April 1 Balance	2,040

During the month of April, the following transactions took place:

April 2 Purchased goods from A Martin, £110, less 20% trade discount
8 Paid cheque in settlement of Heating and Lighting Account, £15
10 C Mortimer paid his outstanding account, taking 2½% cash discount
12 Paid printer's bill (Stationery Account), £9
13 Sold to C Mortimer goods worth £220, less 20% trade discount
20 Sold goods and received cheque in payment, £75
28 Wages and Salaries, £300
29 Returned to A Martin goods purchased from him on 2nd April, £15 gross
30 Paid A Martin's account in full, less 2½% cash discount
Value of Stock in hand on 30th April, £750

Enter the above in the appropriate books of original entry; post to ledger. Take out a Trial Balance. Produce a Trading and Profit and Loss Account for the month ended 30th April, 19·1, and a Balance Sheet at that date.

2 On 1st January, 19·1, L Bright had the following assets and liabilities (see footnotes on page 12):

ASSETS	£	LIABILITIES	£
Machinery	2,000	Capital	8,000
Furniture	300	Creditors:	
Stock	700	M Vane	200
Debtors:		L Payne	120
S Rice	400		
T Bride	520		
Cash at bank	4,400		
	8,320		8,320

Open each of the above accounts in L Bright's ledger*. Enter the following transactions in appropriate books of original entry and post to ledger:

Jan. 1 Purchased goods and paid by cheque, £50
    3 Purchased goods from L Payne, £200, less 25% trade discount
    6 Sold to S Rice goods value £300, less 25% trade discount
    8 Purchased from M Vane, goods value £180, less 25% trade discount
  10 Received cheque from T Bride in settlement of his outstanding account on 1st January, less 2½% cash discount
  18 Returned to L Payne goods value £25 gross, purchased from him on 3rd January
  20 Paid L Payne the amount outstanding on 1st January, less 2½% cash discount
  22 Returned to M Vane goods purchased from him on 8th January, £12 gross
  24 Sold to T Bride goods value £260, less 25% trade discount
  26 Received back from S Rice goods worth £16 gross, sold to him on 6th April
  28 Received cheque from S Rice in full settlement of his account, less 2½% cash discount
  31 General Expenses for month £490

    Stock in hand 31st January, £410

Balance the above ledger accounts, take out a Trial Balance, Trading and Profit and Loss Account as on 31st January, 19·1, and a Balance Sheet as at that date.

3 A Chandler buys goods from R Shipper. From the following information write up R Shipper's account in A Chandler's books.

1971
Oct. 1 Balance due to R Shipper, £800
    7 Bought goods from R Shipper, £500, less 20% trade discount
  13 Returned some of the goods purchased on 7th October. List price £100
  14 Paid R Shipper by cheque the amount due on 1st October, less 2½% cash discount
  23 Bought goods from R Shipper, £250 net
  31 Balance the account

                                       (RSA 1971)

4 From the information given below prepare the account of T Rose as it would appear in the Sales Ledger of A Thorn and balance the account at the close of business on 30th, November, 1972.

1972
Nov. 1 Balance due to A Thorn £200
    6 Sold goods on credit to T Rose for £150 (catalogue price), less 20% trade discount
    7 Received cheque from T Rose for the balance due on 1st November, less 2½% cash discount
    9 Sent a credit note to T Rose in respect of damaged goods returned by him valued at £10 (catalogue price)
  27 Sold further goods on credit to T Rose for £240 (catalogue price), less 25% trade discount

                                       (RSA 1973)

5 From the information given below prepare the account of A Bird as it would appear in the ledger of A Fowler.

1970
Jan. 1 Amount owing by A Bird £171
Feb. 6 Credit purchases by A Bird £85 less 20% trade discount
    Carriage charged by A Fowler £5
    Returnable boxes charged by A Fowler £6
    9 A Bird sent A Fowler a cheque for £95 and was allowed £5 cash discount
  10 A Fowler received back the boxes undamaged
  11 A Bird returned part of the goods bought on 6th February, the catalogue price of which was £15
June 9 A Fowler received a cheque for £44 as a first and final dividend, A Bird having been declared bankrupt

                                       (RSA 1970)

---

*Set them out as in question 1, eg.,

CAPITAL—L BRIGHT

		£
19·1		
Jan. 1 Balance		8,000

MACHINERY

19·1	£
Jan. 1 Balance	2,000

6 On 1st February, 1971, G Root owed J Code £120 in respect of goods supplied by Code during January.

During February the following transactions took place:

GOODS SOLD BY J CODE TO G ROOT

Feb. 3 £40 list price, less 10% trade discount
11 £60 list price, less 15% trade discount
23 £140 list price, less 25% trade discount

GOODS RETURNED BY G ROOT

Feb. 17 £10 list price of the goods bought on 3rd February

PAYMENT OF JANUARY ACCOUNT

Feb. 8 2½% cash discount allowed

ALLOWANCE BY J CODE TO G ROOT FOR ARRANGING A SPECIAL DISPLAY OF J CODE'S PRODUCTS
Feb. 27 £12

Write up Root's account in Code's ledger, balancing at 28th February, 1971.

(RSA 1971)

7 From the information given below prepare the account of L Kent as it would appear in the Sales Ledger of F Surrey (a wholesaler), balancing the account and bringing down the balance on 1st March, 19·1.

19·1
Feb. 1 Balance due to F Surrey £82
3 Sales to L Kent (catalogue price) £75, less 20% trade discount
3 F Surrey charged L Kent £1 for containers
7 F Surrey received goods returned by L Kent valued at £150 (catalogue price) and the containers, allowing credit in full for the latter
13 Purchases by L Kent valued at £120 net
23 L Kent sent a cheque for the amount due on 1st February, less 5% cash discount

8 From the following information prepare the account of L Trent as it would appear in the purchases ledger of H Peters for the month of September 1974. The account should be balanced on the last day of the month.

Sept. 1 Amount due to L Trent £240
6 H Peters purchased goods from L Trent catalogued at £180 subject to trade discount of 10%
13 H Peters sent L Trent a cheque for the amount due on 1st September less 5% discount
17 H Peters received from L Trent a debit note for carriage £15
20 H Peters received from L Trent a credit note in respect of goods purchased on the 6th catalogued at £30. Returned as unsuitable
30 H Peters sent L Trent a cheque for £100

9 From the information given below prepare the account of A Thorn as it would appear in the Purchases Ledger of T Rose and balance the account at the close of business on 31st March, 1970.

1970
Mar. 2 Balance due to A Thorn £200
5 Purchased goods on credit from A Thorn for £150 (catalogue price), less 20% trade discount
6 Paid A Thorn by cheque the balance due on 2nd March, less 2½% cash discount
10 Received a credit note from A Thorn in respect of damaged goods returned to him valued at £10 (catalogue price)
28 Bought further goods on credit from A Thorn for £240 (catalogue price), less 25% trade discount

(RSA 1970)

10 Driver, Porter and Guard are three customers of Chair & Sleeper, Wholesale Hardware Merchants.

From the information given below, write up the accounts of Driver, Porter and Guard as they would appear in the Sales Ledger kept by Chair & Sleeper.

1969			£
Feb.	1 Debit balances	Driver	100
		Porter	70
		Guard	10

SALES DURING THE MONTH

1969		
Feb.	3 Driver	70
	5 Guard	45
	7 Driver	20
	14 Porter	80
	21 Porter	70
	28 Guard	40

RETURNS DURING THE MONTH

1969		
Feb.	15 Driver	20
	21 Porter	10

On 12th February, 1969, a letter was received from Guard, pointing out that the total of the invoice dated 5th February should have been £40. He was sent a credit note on the following day.

The balances due on 1st February, 1969, were settled by all three customers on the following dates:

Driver	7th February, 1969
Porter	11th February, 1969
Guard	12th February, 1969

The three customers were entitled to deduct 2½ per cent cash discount.

11 F Brixton, a trader, keeps a Sales Ledger and a Purchases Ledger.*

Show how the following would be recorded in these ledgers:

19·1
May
2 Sold goods on credit to J B Lawson & Sons £184
3 Received invoice for goods purchased from F L Jack Ltd. £607
4 Invoiced goods to R J James at list price £350 less 20% trade discount
9 Received goods returned by R J James valued £70 (list price)
10 Sold goods on credit to J B Lawson & Sons £297
15 Received cheque from J B Lawson & Sons for goods invoiced on 2nd May and paid it into bank
17 Paid F L Jack Ltd. by cheque for goods purchased on 3rd May, less 5% cash discount
20 Purchased goods on credit from F L Jack Ltd. £210
31 Balanced the accounts for the month, bringing down the balances

---

*As F Brixton has so many customers and suppliers, he has divided their accounts into two separate volumes of his ledger, one for customers, the Sales Ledger, and one for suppliers, the Purchases Ledger. (See Chapter 22 for additional information on this subject.) This makes no difference to the manner in which entries are made in the accounts.

12 John Marchmont's trading year runs from 1st July to the following 30th June. With the exception of his sales to his only credit customer, James Crombie, all his sales are made on a cash basis. On 1st July, 19·1, Crombie owed Marchmont £1,210. During the trading year ended 30th June, 19·2, Crombie paid over to Marchmont cheques and cash totalling £9,850, and was allowed £189 cash discount; he was also charged £15 for transport charges on a consignment of goods specially dispatched by air. During the year Crombie returned to Marchmont damaged or unsatisfactory goods, for which Marchmont allowed him £47; and on 30th June, 19·2, Crombie owed Marchmont £176.

Marchmont's cash sales for the year were £19,807. Calculate his total sales for the year, showing clearly your method of calculation.

13 The following Trial Balance of a sole trader, although it adds up to the same total on both sides, is incorrect:

TRIAL BALANCE
AS AT 30TH JUNE, 19·2

	Dr. £	Cr. £
Capital, 1st July, 19·1	9,300	
Drawings		1,050
Stock, 1st July, 19·1	3,725	
Purchases	23,100	
Sales		39,425
Wages and Salaries	6,205	
Lighting and Heating	310	
Equipment	3,600	
Carriage Outwards		230
Returns Inwards	105	
Returns Outwards		290
Discount Allowed	285	
Discount Received		315
Rent, Rates and Insurance	1,115	
Motor Vehicles	1,475	
Cash in hand	110	
Sundry Creditors	4,925	
Sundry Debtors		13,920
Bank Overdraft	975	
	55,230	55,230

Stock in hand 30th June, 19·2, £4,100

Draw up a corrected Trial Balance.
Take out a Trading and Profit and Loss Account for year ended 30th June, 19·2 and a Balance Sheet at that date.

RSA (adapted)

Chapter Ten

The Cash Book

Bank Cash Book

This is the Cash Book with which you are familiar, except that it has an additional column on each side of it for details. If the Cash Book in example 9/6 were shown as a Bank Cash Book, it would appear as in example 10/1 below:

EX. 10/1

CASH BOOK

			Fol	Discount Allowed	Details	Bank				Fol	Discount Received	Details	Bank
May	1	Balance	b/d			3,820	May	25	C Moss				400
	11	S Porter				230		31	General Expenses:				
	29	M Silver		15		595			Wages			210	
	31	Providence Ltd.			255				British Rail			5	
		A Salter		18	696				Rates			55	
						951							270
								31	P Wood		6		214
								31	C Moss		15		569
								31	Balance	c/d			4,143
				33		5,596					21		5,596
June	1	Balance	b/d			4,143							

The Debit Side: 31st May two cheques were paid into the bank on one paying-in slip. The *Details* column is the column from which postings to the ledger accounts are made; the total, £951 is the amount with which the Bank is concerned; the amount that appears in the Bank's own ledger (and in the Bank Statement (Chapter 11)). It is therefore necessary to record not only the individual cheques, but also the *total amount* deposited on any particular date.

The Credit Side: 31st May General Expenses. The sum of £270 was drawn from the bank and used for paying wages as well as amounts due to British Rail and to Rates. Postings to the relevant ledger accounts are made from the Details column, while the Bank is only aware of, and concerned with the total value of the cheque drawn, £270.

Two-Column Cash Book

So far, all transactions have been settled by cheque. There are, however, occasions when goods might be bought or sold for cash, and certain small payments might also be made in cash. Some firms are concerned with regular receipts and payments in cash. It is, therefore necessary to keep, in addition to a Bank Account, a Cash Account, when there are frequent cash payments.

EX. 10/2   On 1st June, my Cash Book showed a balance at bank of £4,143. As I had some cash payments to make on 5th June:

(a) I drew from bank £300 which
(b) I put into the safe in my office

The two accounts **concerned are**:
(a) the Bank Account;
(b) the Cash Account

The necessary entries are made as follows:

BANK

			£						£
June	1	Balance	4,413	June	5	Cash		C*	300

CASH

				£
June	5	Bank	C*	300

EX. 10/3   The following are the receipts and payments in June:

			£
June	6	Bought stationery for cash	2
	10	Paid wages in cash	160
	12	Paid Sundry Expenses by cash	10
	14	Paid gas bill by cheque	49
	20	Sold goods for cash (payment over the counter)	55
	26	Received cheque from W Marks	38
	30	Banked £70 of the total amount left over in the office safe	

BANK

				£						£
June	1	Balance	b/d	4,143	June	5	Cash		C	300
	26	W Marks		38		14	Gas Board			49
	30	Cash	C	70		30	Balance		c/d	3,902
				4,251						4,251
July	1	Balance	b/d	3,902						

CASH

									£
June	5	Bank	C	300	June	6	Stationery		2
	20	Sales		55		10	Wages		160
						12	Sundry Expenses		10
						30	Bank	C	70
						30	Balance	c/d	113
				355					355
July	1	Balance	b/d	113					

These two accounts are combined in a double-column Cash Book, rather than shown separately: the double-column Cash Book is *instead of* the two separate accounts.

---

*C = Contra. An entry in one account against an identical entry on the opposite side in another account.

EX. 10/4

CASH BOOK

			Cash £	Bank £					Cash £	Bank £
June	1	Balance	b/d		4,143	June	5	Cash	C		300
	5	Bank	C	300			6	Stationery		2	
	20	Sales		55			10	Wages		160	
	26	W Marks			38		12	Sundry Expenses		10	
	30	Cash	C		70		14	Gas Board			49
							30	Bank	C	70	
							30	Balance	c/d	113	3,902
				355	4,251					355	4,251
July	1	Balances	b/d	113	3,902						

The Three-Column Cash Book

A third column is added to each side of a double-column Cash Book for cash discounts allowed and received respectively:

EX. 10/5

Sept. 2 Received cheque from Y Andrews £110 in settlement of his account £113
4 B Ryan paid his outstanding account of £100, taking 2% cash discount £98
8 Sold goods for cash £40
10 Paid M Bryant his account £80, less 2½% cash discount
15 Drew from bank £20 and placed it into cash
20 Paid wages in cash £30
28 Paid for stationery £5

CASH BOOK

				Discounts Allowed	Cash	Bank					Discounts Received	Cash	Bank
Sept.	2	Y Andrews		3		110	Sept.	10	M Bryant		2		78
	4	B Ryan		2		98		15	Cash	C			20
	8	Sales			40			20	Wages			30	
	15	Bank	C		20			28	Stationery			5	
								30	Balances	c/d		25	110
				5	60	208					2	60	208
Oct.	1	Balances	b/d		25	110							

A Comprehensive Cash Book

A cash book is even more comprehensive than the three-column version in example 10/5 when the Bank Cash Book has cash columns as well as discount columns. The basis of the Cash Book, however, comprises the Bank and the Details column, together with the Discounts column. The Cash column is optional and is used by a relatively small number of firms. In many businesses the Petty Cash Book serves adequately for all cash transactions; such businesses purchase their goods on credit and pay for them by cheque. Where credit is not allowed, payment is made by cheque before or on delivery of the goods.

Exercise 10

1 On 1st January your Cash Book balances were:

	£
Cash in hand	55
Cash at bank	370

During January the following cash and bank transactions took place:

Jan. 3 Received cheque from P Jones, £78. He had deducted £2 cash discount
    5 S Redman paid his debt in cash £15
    6 Paid Expenses in cash, £5
    8 Transferred from Bank to Cash, £50
  10 Paid D Whiteley by cheque, his outstanding account £40, less 2½% cash discount
  15 Received cheque in payment of M Brown's account £60, less 5% for prompt payment
  18 Sold goods to M York for cash £25
  22 Purchased goods for cash £12
  28 Paid S London his outstanding account by cheque £120, less 2½% cash discount

Enter the above in your Cash Book. At the end of the month, add up the two discount columns and balance the Cash and Bank columns. Then post to the ledger.

2 Write up a trader's Bank Cash Book from the following information:

(a) His balance at the bank at the close of business on 26th May, 19·1, according to his cash book was £983·75.

(b) The counterfoils of his paying-in book give the following details:

May 29 Total paid in £197·13, consisting of cash from sales £49·63, a cheque from L Waterlow for £97·50. Waterlow's cheque was accepted in full settlement of £100 owed by him, a cheque from J Izzard for £50.
  30 Total paid in £48·45, consisting entirely of cash from sales.
  31 Total paid in £75·45, consisting of cash from sales £39·50 and a cheque from H Benskin for £35·95.

(c) The counterfoils of his cheque book show:

May 29 J Omerod & Co. Ltd., £327·70
  30 Ivens & Co., £195
  31 Petty Cash £29·90
    Self £100
    Ashton's Garage £18·10

The cheque to Ivens and Co. was accepted in full settlement of £200 owing to them. The cheque to Ashton's Garage was for petrol, oil, repairs, etc., for the previous month, and no previous record of this transaction had gone through the books.
The Details column of the Cash Book should indicate clearly which ledger account should be debited or credited in respect of each Cash Book entry. Rule off and balance the Cash Book at the close of business on 31st May, 19·1.

RSA (adapted)

3 James Galbraith is a wholesale merchant, but has also a small retail department. On the morning of 27th May, 19·1, a fresh working-page of his Cash Book appears as follows:

Debit side

Date	Particulars	Discount	Cash	Bank
19·1		£	£	£
May 27	To totals brought forward	90	910	4,800

Credit side

Date	Particulars	Discount	Cash	Bank
19·1		£	£	£
May 27	By totals brought forward	60	900	3,100

During the last working-days of May the following transactions affecting the Cash Book take place:

May 27 A cheque for £110 is received from J Harper, and paid into the bank. A cheque for £390 is drawn in favour of Zealand Trading Co., in full settlement of an amount of £400 due to them. Cash amounting to £80 is received into the cash till in respect of the day's retail sales.

28 A cheque for £190, payable to the Milltown Borough Council, is drawn for rates due. Goods are purchased for cash, £50. Cash sales by the retail department are £375.

29 John Carraway settles by cheque, £195, his account for £200, the balance being allowed as discount. His cheque is paid into the bank.

30 A second-hand motor-lorry is purchased by cheque, £675. Cash sales are £80.

31 An open cheque is drawn for £1,000, and the cash received across the bank counter is placed in the cash till. Wages and Salaries, £925, are paid in cash. All cash remaining in the till, in excess of the customary 'over the weekend' balance of £10, is paid into the bank.

You are required:

(a) To copy down the opening Cash Book totals on the morning of 27th May, as given above.

(b) To make the necessary entries in the Cash Book in respect of the transactions from 27th to 31st May.

(c) To rule off and balance the Cash Book at the close of business on 31st May.

(RSA)

4 Write up a trader's Bank Cash Book from the following particulars:

(a) His balance at the bank at the close of business on 27th May, 1970, according to his Cash Book, was £893.

(b) The counterfoils of his paying-in book give the following details:

May 28 Total paid in £196; consisting of cash from sales £49, a cheque from A Plum for £50 and a cheque from B Berry for £97. Berry's cheque was accepted in full settlement of £100 owed by him.

29 Total paid in £48; consisting entirely of cash from sales.

30 Total paid in £75; consisting of cash from sales £40 and a cheque from C Flower for £35.

(c) The counterfoils of his cheque book show:

May 28 Orchard and Co. Ltd., £327
29 Hedges and Co., £195
30 Petty Cash £29 and Self £50, one cheque for £79, Wood's Garage £18.

The cheque to Hedges and Co. was accepted in full settlement of £200 owing to them. The cheque to Wood's Garage was for petrol, oil and servicing for the previous month and no previous record of this had gone through the books.

The particulars columns of the Cash Book should show clearly the name of the ledger account which is to be debited or credited in respect of each entry.

Rule off and balance the Cash Book at the close of business on 30th May.

(RSA)

Henceforth the examples and figures used will not be connected with the foregoing business of John Fry except where useful.

Chapter Eleven

The Bank Reconciliation Statement

The Bank Statement and my Cash Book

Periodically, my Bank sends me a statement representing their version of my account in their books.* I check each item in the Statement against those in the Cash Book to ensure that the two versions of payments in and out of the Bank agree. Almost invariably, however, they do not agree.

How Differences Arise

The differences that arise are due to two factors:

1 (a) Cheques drawn by me and entered in my Cash Book might not have reached the Bank (might not have been 'cleared') at the time when the Statement was being prepared. Therefore, the balance shown on the Statement would be greater than that in my Cash Book by the total value of the cheques not yet cleared; I would appear to have more money in the Bank, according to the Statement, than shown in my Cash Book.

(b) Cheques and cash paid (or 'lodged') into the Bank and entered in the Cash Book, might not yet have been entered in the Statement. Therefore, the balance of the Statement would be less than that of the Cash Book by the total value of cheques paid in but not shown on the Statement; I would appear to have less money in the Bank, according to the Statement, than shown in my Cash Book.

2 (a) Bank Charges might appear in the Statement (for banker's various services to me), and this would be the Bank's first intimation to me of such charges. Therefore, the Statement balance would be lower by that amount than that of my Cash Book.

(b) Amounts debited to my account by the Bank for direct payments made by them on my behalf (eg. standing orders); or amounts credited to my account by the Bank such as the interest on a Deposit Account.

EX. 11/1 The following is an example of a Bank Statement and the corresponding period in my Cash Book:

CASH BOOK

			£	£					£
Dec.	1	Balance	b/d	1,000	Dec.	10	M White		60
	25	M Brown	35			12	B Black		40
		R Benson	98			16	C Green		130
				133		26	Wages		200
						31	Balance	c/d	703

---

*The Bank, being my debtor, has a debit balance in my Cash Book. But since from the Bank's point of view, I am its creditor, my account in the Bank's books has a credit balance.

BANK STATEMENT

		Dr. £	Cr. £	Balance £
Dec.	1 Balance			1,000
	13 M White	60		940
	18 Bank Charges	5		935
	19 C Green	130		805
	26 Cash	200		605
	29 Interest on Deposit		20	625

On checking the items in the Bank Statement against those in the Cash Book, I found that:

1 The Statement contained:

	£
Bank Charges	5
Interest on Deposit Account	20

I entered these items in my Cash Book:

CASH BOOK
(AFTER ADJUSTMENTS)

			£	£					£
Dec.	1 Balance			1,000	Dec.	10 M White			60
	25 M Brown		35			12 B Black			40
	R Benson		98			16 C Green			130
			—	133		26 Wages			200
	31 *Interest on Deposit*			20		31 *Bank Charges*			5
						31 Balance	c/d		718
				1,153					1,153
Jan.	1 Balance	b/d		718					

2 There were:

(a) Cheques paid in but not yet shown on the Statement: M Brown £35, R Benson £98.

(b) Cheques drawn but not yet presented at the Bank for payment: B Black £40.

The following Bank Reconciliation Statement was then produced:

BANK RECONCILIATION STATEMENT
31ST DECEMBER, 19·1

	£	£
Balance as per Bank Statement		625
Add cheques paid in but not yet shown:		
M Brown	35	
R Benson	98	
	—	133
		758
Deduct cheque not yet presented:		
B Black		40
Balance as per Cash Book		718

The two cheques paid in and not shown as well as Black's cheque, will appear in the bank's next statement of my account among other payments-out and lodgements into my account, which had taken place in the meantime:

BANK STATEMENT (CONT.)

19·1		Dr.	Cr.	Balance
Dec. 29	Balance			625
19·2				
Jan. 2	M Brown		35	660
4	R Benson		98	758
7	B Black	40		718

It would be instructive to study in detail the bank statement of Richard Webster reproduced below.* The Detail column shows the cheque numbers, instead of the names of the payees. The abbreviations at the foot of the statement should be of interest.

RICHARD WEBSTER, ESQ.

In account with

National Westminster Bank Limited
Anytown Branch
41 High Street, Anytown, Berks

Date	Detail		Debits	Credits	Balance
4FEB	**Balance forward**				538
11FEB		205	5		533
12FEB		213	4		529
14FEB		003 SO	45		484
24FEB				50	534
25FEB		006 SO	21		
	BANK GIRO CREDIT			122	635
26FEB		214	8		627
6MAR		004 SO	3		624
12MAR		215	3		
		216	2		619
13MAR		217	4		615
14MAR		003 SO	45		570
19MAR		218	1		569
25MAR		006 SO	21		
	BANK GIRO CREDIT			121	669
28MAR		219	30		639
3APR				10	649
12APR		220	57		592
14APR		003 SO	45		547
15APR		632	8		539
17APR		631	2		537
18APR	ADVICE ENCLOSED		2		535
24APR		633	8		527
25APR		006 SO	21		
	BANK GIRO CREDIT			121	627
29APR				5	632
1MAY		634	25		
		637	1		
		635	9		597
2MAY		636	5		592

Abbreviations:	CD Cash Dispenser DV Dividend TR Transfer	O/D indicates an
	DD Direct Debit SO Standing Order	Overdrawn Balance

Ledgers with Adjacent Debit and Credit Cash Columns (as in bank statements)

An increasing number of accountants use ledger ruling with adjacent cash columns This simple method conforms with mechanised accounting and it should therefore be remembered. If it is preferred to the conventional method, it may be used exclusively. The following example illustrates its use:

*Both the name and the account number on the statement are fictitious, as are the figures.

$£$

March 1 J Bradley buys goods from me 100
13 J Bradley buys goods from me 70
31 J Bradley pays amount due 170

CONVENTIONAL METHOD
J BRADLEY

March 1	Sales	100	March 31	Cash	170
13		70			
		170			170

ADJACENT CASH COLUMNS
J BRADLEY

		Dr.	Cr.	Balance
		$£$	$£$	$£$
March 1	Sales	100		100
13	,,	70		70
31	Cash		170	

Exercise 11

1 On the 31st March, 19·1, J Cooper's Cash Book showed a balance of £450 and his Statement of Account from the Bank showed a balance in his favour of £800. On comparing the Statement with his Cash Book, he found that the following entries in the Cash Book had not yet been entered on the Statement:

Cheques paid in on 31st March, £160.
Cheques drawn up to 31st March, £350.

and the following entries on the Statement had not yet been entered in his Cash Book:

Bank Charges, £20.
Payment direct to the Bank by one of his debtors, £180.

Complete the writing up of the Cash Book and draw up a Reconciliation Statement as on the 31st March, 19·1.

(*RSA*)

2 On 30th June, 19·1, W Evans' Cash Book showed a bank balance of £406·40, but the monthly statement from his bank showed at the same date a credit balance of £420. The difference between the two balances was found to be due to the following:

(a) On 10th June a charge of £2 for banker's services had been made by the bank.

(b) An annual subscription of £5·25 had been paid by a bankers standing order on 25th June.

(c) Cheques for £25·40 and £37·95 issued by Evans had not been presented for payment.

(d) A cheque for £41·10 from A Jones paid into the bank on 15th June had been returned marked 'No account'.

Prepare a statement reconciling the above balances.

(*RSA*)

3 On 31st May, 19·1, P Ray's Cash Book showed a debit balance of £740·80 while his Bank Statement at that date had a credit balance of £819.

The following differences were discovered between the Cash Book and the Bank Statement:

Interest due to Ray on investments £73·50 had been collected by the bank and entered in Ray's account, but not shown in the Cash Book.

£25·70 had been paid for fire insurance premium by standing order, but not entered in the Cash Book.

Two cheques drawn on 30th May and entered in Cash Book, one for £32·70 and one £168·44 had not yet been presented for payment.

On 31st May a cheque for £170·74 had been entered in the Cash Book and paid into Bank but not shown in the Bank's Statement.

Show the necessary adjustments in the Cash Book and the balance that should be brought down at 31st May, and then prepare a Bank Reconciliation Statement.

4 On 28th February, 19·1, F Underwood's Bank Cash Book showed the following:

			£
Discount allowed	B/F	Total	94·70
Discount received	B/F	Total	78·67
Main Bank Columns B/F Debit	Total		1,170·73
B/F Credit	Total		1,317·10

A comparison with his bank statement showed the following items which had not been entered in the Cash Book:

	£
A standing order for insurance	5
Bank charges	2·50
A credit transfer from A Brown (This payment was in settlement of an account for £80)	78

You are required to re-open F Underwood's Bank Cash Book, and bring it up to date. What should be the balance shown on the Bank Statement?

(*RSA*)

5 At close of business on 28th February, 1970, a trader's Cash Book showed a balance of £1,017·12, which did not agree with his bank statement, the following being sources of disagreement:

(i)   cheques issued but not presented:
Green £115·10; Riley £237·50; Stokes £38;

(ii) lodgement 28th February not credited by bank:
£185·15;

(iii) traders' credits not entered in Cash Book:
Boxer £5·75; Striker £16·6;

(iv) a standing order for £10·50, being subscription to a trade association, had been paid by the bank but not entered in the Cash Book;

(v)   a charge of £4·22 had been made by the bank for operating the account, but had not been entered in the Cash Book.

You are required to:

(a) make such entries in the cash book as will result in the correct balance being shown;

(b) prepare a statement accounting for the difference between your corrected cash book and the bank statement balance;

(c) show on the statement required in (b) the balance per the bank statement.

(*RSA*)

6 From the following figures prepare a statement—as at 28th February—reconciling the position shown by A Trader's cash book and the statement of his Bank account:

CASH BOOK (BANK COLUMNS)

19·1		£	19·1		£
Feb.	1 Balance	210·00	Feb.	2 Baker	18·35
	10 Smith	60·10		12 Cheque	2·60
	28 Edge	73·50		15 Dodge	12·15

BANK STATEMENT
A Trader, in account with the Blank Bank Ltd.

Date	Particulars	Dr.	Cr.	Balance
19·1		£	£	£
Feb.	1 Balance forward			220·00
	2 Fox	10·00		210·00
	10 Smith		60·10	270·10
	16 Dodge	12·15		257·95

(*RSA*)

Note Both the cash book and the bank statement have been written up to 28th February.
Begin by putting a tick against items which appear in the Cash Book as well as the Bank Statement.
Then deal with the unticked items in the Bank Reconciliation Statement.

7 Mr B Spender has an account at the Bank of Education. He also keeps a private record in a 'Bank Book'. Compare his Bank Statement with his 'Bank Book' for the month of October. Bring the 'Bank Book' up to date, and prepare a reconciliation statement.

BANK BOOK

1971		£	1971	Cheque No.	£
Oct.	1 Balance	250	Oct.	2 11118	50
	7 Cash	170		8 11119	140
	16 T Spencer	120		16 11120	120
				29 11121	40
				11122	160
				Balance	30
		540			540

BANK STATEMENT

1971			Dr.	Cr.	Balance
			£	£	£
Oct.	1				300
	5	11116	20		280
		11118	50		230
	7	Cash		170	400
	11	11120	120		280
	15	11117	30		250
	18	Cheque		120	370
	22	11119	140		230
	28	S.O. Insurance	10		220
	29	Giro Credit		70	290

(*RSA*)

8 The following Statement was received from the Bank, indicating the position during the month of December:

			Payments £	Receipts £	Balance £
Dec.	1	Balance			402
	4	Cheques and Cash		74	476
	5	R F Brown	168		308
	9	Cash		312	620
	10	S E Gas	22		598
	11	Cash		62	660
	12	P M G	74		
		Wages	311		275
	16	Cash		477	752
	18	Cash		241	993
	19	Cash		299	1,292
		Wages	376		916
	23	Charges	3		913
	24	Wages	516		397
	30	Cash		76	473

On Checking this with the Cash Book, the following discrepancies were found:

(i)   The item of £299 on 19th December had been accidentally omitted from the Cash Book.

(ii) The amount of bank charges (23rd December) had not been entered in the Cash Book.

(iii) An item of cash, paid into the Bank on 31st December, £85 did not appear in the Bank Statement.

(iv) Cheques drawn on 28th December in favour of:

	£
Spicers Ltd.	78
F Richardson Ltd.	146
S E Electricity Board	116

are not shown in the Bank Statement.

(a)   State which items require to be entered in the Cash Book before closing the books at the end of December.

(b)   Prepare a statement, reconciling the Bank Statement with the Cash Book, indicating the Balance according to the Cash Book.

(*RSA*)

9 On the 31st March, 19·2, the debit balance in Ring Bros. Bank Account, as shown in the cash book, was £1,568. The Bank Statement at that date showed a credit balance of £1,472. On checking the Bank Statement against the Cash Book the following differences were found:

(i)   Two cheques drawn on the 29th March, 19·2 and entered in the Cash Book, one drawn in favour of C Bloom for £28 and the second drawn in favour of Mears Ltd. for £50 had not yet been presented for payment.

(ii) A standing order £25 payable on the 30th March each year to the Economic Research Institute had been paid by the bank but not yet entered in the Cash Book.

(iii) The following cheques were received on 31st March, 19·2 and entered in the Cash Book but were not paid into the bank until 1st April, 19·2.

	£
M Roe	125
B Kay	49
R Dove	3·50

(iv) Dividends receivable on Corporation Stock £36 had been collected by the bank on behalf of Ring Bros. on 25th March, 19·2 but had not been entered in the Cash Book.

(v) Bank charges of £7·50 debited in the Bank Statement on 31st March, 19·2, had not been entered in the Cash Book.

You are required to prepare the calculation of:

(a) the adjusted cash book balance 31st March, 19·2, and then

(b) a bank reconciliation statement as at 31st March 19·2.

Chapter Twelve

Petty Cash Book

The Imprest System

There are always numerous small items of day-to-day expenses which must be recorded. It is time-consuming (consider the high salary of the cashier) and cumbersome to load the cash book with such items. The responsibility of recording these is therefore delegated to a junior clerk (with a low salary) who enters them in a Petty Cash Book, usually kept on the 'Imprest' system (explained below). Like the Cash Book, the Petty Cash Book has a debit and credit side and is balanced periodically. Suppose it is decided to balance the Petty Cash Book weekly, and that the *imprest* or *float* is £30. On the first Monday at the inception of the Petty Cash Book, the cashier hands the Petty Cashier £30. If by the end of the week £26 had been spent, there would be a balance of £4 to carry forward to the following Monday. The Petty Cashier would then receive £26 *to make up the imprest or float* of £30. Thus, there is a sum of £30 in the Petty Cash Box at the start of each week. The following example illustrates the Petty Cash Book at its inception:

EX. 12/1

Dr. £	Date 19·1		Details		Voucher No.	Cr. £
30	Jan.	1	Cash	CB		
		1	Postage Stamps		1	6
		2	Telegrams		2	2
		3	Stationery		3	1
		3	Fares		4	1
		4	Purchases (of goods for re-sale)		5	10
		4	Postage Stamps		6	5
		5	Writing materials		7	1
		5	Balance	c/d		4
30						30
4	Jan.	8	Balance	b/d		
26		8	Cash	CB		

Petty Cash Vouchers

Every payment made by the Petty Cashier is signed for by the recipient on a numbered voucher showing the reason for payment. The vouchers then become the source-documents from which entries are made in the Petty Cash Book.

Analysis Columns

The Petty Cash Book is usually analysed in order that the total of each recurring kind of expense may be readily ascertained. The analysed version of the above example appears as follows:

EX. 12/2

PETTY CASH BOOK

£	Date	Details	Voucher No.	Totals	Stationery	Postage & Telegrams	Sundry Expenses	Ledger	Ledger Folio
	19·2								
30	Jan. 1	Cash	CB						
	1	Postage Stamps	1	6		6			
	2	Stationery	2	1	1				
	3	Telegram	3	2		2			
	3	Fares	4	1			1		
	4	Postage Stamps	6	5		5			
	4	Purchases Account	5	10				10	L.82
	5	Stationery	7	1	1				
				26	2	13	1	10	
	5	Balance	c/d	4	L.20	L.27	L.31		
30				30					
4	Jan. 8	Balance	b/d						
26	8	Cash	CB						
	8	Fares	8	1			1		

CASH BOOK

	19·2		Fol.	£
	Jan. 1	Petty Cash		30
	8	Petty Cash		26

The respective double-entries corresponding to £30 (1st January) and £26 (8th January) are to be found on the credit side of the Cash Book. (example 12/3).

THE LEDGER COLUMN is intended for items of infrequent occurrence for which there is already a ledger account, such as a cash purchase of goods for re-sale, or a refund to a customer for an overpayment.

THE TOTAL COLUMN Every expense item is entered in this column and at the end of the week it not only shows the total expenditure but also acts as a check for the accuracy of the addition of every other column. The sum of the totals of all the columns should be equal to the figure at the end of the totals column.

Corresponding Ledger Accounts

Each Petty Cash column has a corresponding account in the ledger. Thus, there are ledger accounts for Stationery, Postages and Telegrams, and Sundry Expenses. At the end of regular periods (a week or a month) the total of each column is posted to the debit side of its own account in the ledger (examples 12/2 and 12/3). These ledger accounts might also contain entries posted from the Cash Book. Thus, if a payment by cheque had been made to the printers (say, for letterheads), this would first appear on the credit side of the Cash Book and then posted to the debit side of the Stationery Account. The total weekly expenditure on Stationery shown in the Petty Cash Book, would also be posted to the debit side of the Stationery Account in the ledger. Thus, at the end of the financial year, the Stationery Account shows a grand total of expenditure on stationery consisting of all forms of payment (example 12/3). In due course, this is transferred to the debit side of the Profit and Loss Account. The balance of the Petty Cash Book at the end of the financial year, appears in the Balance Sheet under Current Assets.

EX. 12/3

CASH BOOK

	19·2			£
	Jan.	1 Petty Cash		30
		2 Sundry Expenses	31	6
		8 Petty Cash		26
		10 Stationery Account	20	15
		14 Sundry Expenses	31	10
		15 Purchases	82	125
		15 Petty Cash		x

STATIONERY²⁰

			£				£
Jan.	5 Petty Cash	PC	2	Jan. 31 Balance		c/d	x
	10 Cash (Printers)	CB	15				
	12 Petty Cash	PC	x				
	19 ,, ,,	,,	x				
	26 ,, ,,	,,	x				
			x				x
Feb.	1 Balance	b/d	x				
	2 Petty Cash	PC	x				

PURCHASES⁸²

			£				
Jan.	5 Petty Cash	PC	10	Jan. 31 Returns Outwards		ROB	x
	5 Cash	CB	125	31 Balance		c/d	x
	31 Goods	PB	1,900				
			x				x
Feb.	1 Balance	b/d	x				

SUNDRY EXPENSES³¹

Jan.	2 Cash	CB	6	Jan. 31 Balance		c/d	x
	5 Petty Cash	PC	1				
	12 ,, ,,	,,	x				
	14 Cash	CB	10				
	19 Petty Cash	PC	x				
	6 ,, ,,	,,	x				
			x				x
Feb.	1 Balance	b/d	x				

POSTAGES AND TELEGRAMS

Jan.	5 Petty Cash	PC	13	Jan. 31 Balance		c/d	x
	12 ,, ,,	,,	x				
	19 ,, ,,	,,	x				
	26 ,, ,,	,,	x				
			x				x
Feb.	1 Balance	b/d	x				

. . . and so on for 12 months, at the end of which each account is transferred to the appropriate section of the Trading and Profit and Loss Account.

Exercise 12

1 A Petty Cash Book is kept on the imprest system, the amount of the imprest being £50·00.

Give the ruling for the book, providing suitable columns and enter the following transactions:

> 1972
> Nov. 1 Balance in hands of petty cashier £16·40
>   1 Cash received from chief cashier restoring the imprest
>   2 Cash Purchases £7·45
>   3 Paid sundry travelling expenses £2·50
>   6 Purchased stationery £6·10
>   7 Cleaners wages £7·00
>   8 Repairs to typewriter £5·50
>   8 Bought postage stamps £3·00
>   9 Office tea and sugar £2·50
>   10 Typewriter ribbons £4·20

Balance the book on 10th November and total the analysis columns.

2 A petty cash book is kept on the imprest system, the amount of the imprest being £20, and has four analysis columns for Postage and Stationery, Travelling Expenses, Carriage, and Office Expenses. Give the ruling for the book and enter up the following transactions:

> 19·1
> Jan. 4 Petty Cash in hand £2
>   Received Cash to make up the Imprest
>   Bought stamps £2
>   7 Paid bus fares £1; telegrams £1
>   8 Paid carriage on small parcels £1; paid railway fares £2; bought envelopes £2
>   10 Paid for repairs to typewriters £2; paid carrier's account for December £3
>   11 Paid office tea lady £4

Balance the Petty Cash Book as on 11th January, 19·1, and bring down the balance.

RSA (adapted)

3 A firm manufactures radio and television sets and components. It is a standing rule of the firm that all payments below £5 are made through the Petty Cash, and that payments of £5 and over are made by cheque.

Name the following:

(a) the Subsidiary Book through which the original record in respect of each of the following transactions would be put; and

(b) the document from which this record would be written up:

    (i)   a payment of £5 for a cash purchase of brass screws.

    (ii) a purchase on credit of 1,000 yards of copper wire.

    (iii) an allowance granted by the firm in respect of goods returned by a credit customer.

    (iv) a payment of £4 to British Road Services in respect of inward carriage.

    (v) payment into the firm's bank of the day's total of cheques and cash received from various customers.

    (vi) a sale on credit of 50 television sets.

(RSA)

4 Prepare the ruling of F Gee's Petty Cash Book with analysis columns for postage, carriage, office cleaning and stationery.

The book is kept on the Imprest System, the imprest amount being £35, and you are required to:

(a)   Enter the following transactions:

1975			£
May	1	Balance in hand	25·00
		Paid for office cleaning	1·85
		Paid carriage on parcels	1·45
	2	Bought stamps	1·00
	3	Paid window cleaner	1·40
		Bought envelopes	2·25
		Paid for carriage by rail	1·60
	4	Bought stamps	3·75
		Paid for cleaning materials	1·40
	5	Bought postcards	1·05
	8	Received cheque to make up the imprest amount	

(b)   Balance the Petty Cash Book as on 8th May, 1975, and bring down the balance.

(c)   Post the analysis totals to the ledger.

5 Rule a petty cash book that will record the total expenditure under the headings of:

(a) Postage (b) Stationery (c) Travelling (d) General Expenses (e) Bought Ledger Accounts paid.

Enter the following transactions and balance at the end of the week showing the amounts to be posted to the ledger:

19·1			
June	21	Cash in hand £20	
	22	Paid office tea bill £2	
	23	Paid for typewriter ribbons £1	
	23	Paid railway fares £1·50	
	24	Paid for envelopes £1·50	
	24	Paid Marlow & Co. £1 (Bought Ledger Account)	
	25	Paid for postage stamps £2	
	25	Paid for bus fares £0·50	
	26	Paid for cleaning office windows £2	
	26	Paid for postage on registered letters £1	
	26	Cashed a cheque for the total spent in the week	

(*RSA*)

Chapter Thirteen

The Balance Sheet and the Meaning of Capital (I)

Changes in the Character or Constitution of Capital

An important question at this stage is concerned with the character of Capital which at the moment when I started business on 1st April, consisted entirely of cash at the bank, £10,000. If at that moment a statement of the affairs of the business, or a Balance Sheet were produced, it would appear as follows:

EX. 13/1

BALANCE SHEET

AS AT 1ST APRIL, 19·1

LIABILITIES		ASSETS	
(Items the firm owes)	£	(Items the firm owns)	£
Capital	10,000	Cash at bank	10,000
(Due to me, John Fry, the proprietor)			

Part of the £10,000 was spent in purchasing Freehold Premises; I acquired an asset in the form of Freehold Premises worth £6,000. Thus, at that stage, (a) Capital, a liability, consisted of (b) Freehold Premises £6,000 and Cash at Bank £4,000, two forms of assets. (a) and (b) are shown respectively on the left and right side of the Balance Sheet:

EX. 13/2

BALANCE SHEET

LIABILITIES	£	ASSETS	£
Capital—John Fry	10,000	Freehold Premises	6,000
		Cash at Bank	4,000
	10,000		10,000

Later on, I bought some furniture from Lockerdesks Ltd. *on credit*, that is, I acquired £200 worth of furniture, but at the same time I contracted a corresponding liability in Lockerdesks Ltd. as creditors. The Balance Sheet now shows three items of assets, *less* one of liability, resulting in Capital £10,000:

EX. 13/3

BALANCE SHEET

LIABILITIES	£	ASSETS	£
Capital—John Fry	10,000	Freehold Premises	6,000
Creditors (Lockerdesks Ltd.)	200	Office Furniture	200
		Cash at bank	4,000
	10,200		10,200

This Balance Sheet and the significance of Capital is seen more clearly in arithmetical form as follows:

EX. 13/4

BALANCE SHEET

Assets	£
Freehold Premises	6,000
Office Furniture	200
Cash at bank	4,000
	10,200
Less	
Liabilities	
Creditors	200
Capital, the remainder	10,000
(the amount the firm owes me, the proprietor)	

Definition of Capital

It should now be clearly understood that Capital was entirely in cash only at the moment of my entry into business. I could not begin until part of that cash capital had been transformed into other assets. The definition of Capital thus emerges as follows:

Assets minus Liabilities equals Capital

$$£10,200 - £200 = £10,000$$

Or, more formally expressed: *Capital is the excess of assets over liabilities.*

The Balance Sheet

The Balance Sheet is a statement which shows concisely the financial position of a business. It is always produced at the end of the firm's trading period, usually a year, after all the relevant accounts have been transferred to the Trading and Profit and Loss Account, and after the profit has been added to, or the loss deducted from Capital. The transactions listed and illustrated in example 3/3 produced some accounts which were ultimately *closed* by transfer to the final accounts. The remaining *open* accounts would have appeared in a Balance Sheet.

The Balance Sheet, example 7/8, is reproduced below for reference purposes:

(a) in the conventional layout

(b) in the vertical form

EX. 13/5

BALANCE SHEET OF JOHN FRY
AS AT 30TH APRIL, 19·1

LIABILITIES	£	£	ASSETS	£
Capital	10,000		Freehold Premises	6,000
Add Net Profit	300		Office Furniture	200
		10,300	Stock, 30th April	180
Creditors		400	Debtors	500
			Cash at bank	3,820
		10,700		10,700

BALANCE SHEET OF JOHN FRY

AS AT 30TH APRIL, 19·1

Assets	£	£
Freehold Premises		6,000
Office Furniture		200
Stock, 30th April		180
Debtors		500
Cash at bank		3,820
		10,700
Liabilities		
Creditors		400
		10,300
Represented by:		
Capital (or the Proprietor's Interest)	10,000	
Add Net Profit	300	
		10,300

The following are some important characteristics of the Balance Sheet:

1 The Balance Sheet is not itself an account. It is a statement which can be made up at any time to show the financial position of the business. It is usually brought out once a year.

2 Its two sides are never described as debit and credit, because it is not an account and it cannot, therefore, owe or claim value.

3 No account is ever *transferred* to it; accounts are merely *shown* in it. *Showing* does not involve a double-entry, *transferring* does.

4 The Balance Sheet contains those of the ledger accounts which have balances at the time when it is being prepared.

5 All liabilities have credit balances in their respective ledger accounts. In other words, accounts with credit balances, eg. the personal accounts of creditors, appear on the left, or liabilities, side of the balance sheet.

6 All assets have debit balances in their respective ledger accounts. In other words, accounts with debit balances, eg. the personal accounts of debtors, Machinery, Furniture, Stock, Cash, appear on the right, or assets, side of the Balance Sheet.

7 There is no particular reason why liabilities should appear on the left and the assets on the right side of the Balance Sheet; it is a British accounting convention. In some parts of the world the sides are reversed.

Note: The Capital Account in the Balance Sheet is always shown in detail, as illustrated in the above example.

The Classification of the Items in the Balance Sheet

As stated above, the Balance Sheet shows the financial situation of the business at the end of a trading period, usually a year. So, the more detail in it, the better. Then, whoever is studying it can get a good idea as to how the business stands; or how it is progressing, if comparison is made between one or two successive balance sheets.

LIABILITIES SIDE

CAPITAL ACCOUNT Normally, the value of capital changes only once a year, when profits are added to it or losses deducted. It is therefore relatively 'fixed' in value.

CURRENT LIABILITIES In contrast to Capital Account, which is relatively static, the values of items under this heading are in a state of continuous change. Creditors, for example, are paid off and new ones are created in the normal course of business, as goods are purchased on credit for re-sale.

ASSETS SIDE

FIXED ASSETS are so called because changes in their values are shown only once a year as they *depreciate* (or fall in value) due to wear and tear. Thus, the changes in value are relatively slow, which justifies the expression *fixed* to describe such assets. Examples of fixed assets are: Freehold Premises; Machinery and Plant; Furniture; Fixtures and Fittings; Motor Vans.

CURRENT ASSETS are so called because such accounts fluctuate in value perhaps daily in the normal course of business. The balances of these accounts are always fluid. For example, the value of Stock rises and falls as goods are bought and sold; Debtors pay, and yet new ones are created as goods are sold to customers on credit; the balance at Bank rises and falls, as money is paid in and cheques are drawn.

The above classifications are illustrated in the following version of the balance sheet of example 13/4:

EX. 13/6

BALANCE SHEET OF JOHN FRY
AS AT 30TH APRIL, 19·1

	£	£		£	£
Capital	10,000		FIXED ASSETS		
Add Net Profit	300		Freehold Premises	6,000	
		10,300	Office Furniture	200	
					6,200
CURRENT LIABILITIES			CURRENT ASSETS		
Creditors		400	Stock, 30th April	180	
			Debtors	500	
			Cash at bank	3,820	
					4,500
		10,700			10,700

Drawings Account

I am in business in order to earn a living. From time to time, then, I must draw some money from the business bank for my own personal use, for expenses which have nothing to do with my business. This is called 'drawings'. On 30th April I write out a cheque to 'self' for £160 and I collect that amount in cash from the bank. I credit the Cash Book and debit a Drawings Account:

CASH BOOK

	£
April 30 Drawings	160

DRAWINGS—JOHN FRY

	£
April 30 Bank	160

Consider what, in fact, I have done. When I began trading, I put £10,000 into the business bank. The Capital Account (my personal account in the firm's ledger) was credited with that amount; showing that the firm owed me £10,000. Obviously, then, on taking £160 out of the firm's bank for my own use, I reduced my claim as a creditor of the firm by £160; I reduced the Capital Account by £160. To show this reduction, Drawings Account is transferred (after the trial balance has successfully been completed, and not before) to the Capital Account. The accounts affected now appear as follows:

EX. 13/7

CASH BOOK

			£				£
April	1	Capital—John Fry	10,000	April 10	Freehold Premises		6,000
	30	Providence Ltd.	200	22	Purchases		50
				28	Stationery		15
				29	Carriage		5
				29	Heating and Lighting		10
				29	P Wood		100
				30	Lockerdesks Ltd.		200
				30	*Drawings*		160
				30	Balance	c/d	3,660
			10,200				10,200
May	1	Balance	b/d 3,660				

DRAWINGS—JOHN FRY*

			£			£
April 30	Cash		160	April 30	Transfer to Capital	160
					(*After the trial balance*)	

CAPITAL—JOHN FRY

			£			£
April 30	Drawings	T	160	April 3	Bank	10,000
30	Balance	c/d	10,140	30	Net Profit	300
			10,300			10,300
				May 1	Balance	10,140

In the Balance Sheet, the Capital Account appears in detail, as follows:

EX. 13/8

BALANCE SHEET
(LIABILITIES SIDE ONLY)

	£	£
Capital—John Fry	10,000	
Add Net Profit	300	
	10,300	
Less Drawings	160	
		10,140

The assets side will be affected to the same extent by a reduction of the bank balance by £160.

*See example 13/9 for alternative Current Account.

DRAWINGS IN THE FORM OF GOODS

When the owner of the firm helps himself to goods from stock for his own use, their value, at cost, is debited to Drawings Account. The corresponding entry is on the credit side of Purchases Account, because for all practical purposes total value of Purchases has been reduced by the value taken out of stock. Alternatively, Sales Accounts, instead of Purchases, might be credited; it can be argued that the goods could have been sold to a customer, in some special circumstance, at cost. All sales are not necessarily at a profit, eg. Drawings, samples, disposal of unwanted stocks because, perhaps, of changing fashions and designs.

The Proprietor's Current Account

An alternative account to Drawings Account (and possibly preferable to it) in which cash taken for his own use by the proprietor of the business might be shown, is a Current Account. Unlike the Drawings Account, a Current Account is not transferred to Capital Account, except in special circumstances. My Capital Account is then described as 'fixed', ie. it does not change either by the subtraction of drawings from it or the addition of profit to it. Both these items, as well as any other transactions I might have with my firm, are shown in my Current Account. Thus, if I preferred to keep a Current Account and to let my Capital Account remain 'fixed', example 13/7 would appear as follows:

EX. 13/9

CAPITAL—JOHN FRY

		£
	April 3 Cash	10,000

CURRENT ACCOUNT—JOHN FRY

		£			£
April 30 Cash—Drawings		160	April 30 Net Profit		300
30 Balance	c/d	140			
		300			300
			May 1 Balance	b/d	140

The balance sheet shows Capital and Current Accounts separately:

EX. 13/10

BALANCE SHEET OF JOHN FRY
AS AT 30TH APRIL, 19·1
(EXTRACT FROM LIABILITIES SIDE)

	£	£
Capital Account		10,000
Current Account		
Net Profit	300	
Less Drawings	160	
		140

From a purely technical point of view, a current account in a sole trader's ledger has the advantage, over the more conventional drawings account, of uniformity with this practice in Partnership accounts (Chapter 26).

Exercise 13

1 From the following items, prepare M Trustee's Balance Sheet as at 31st December, 19·1. Show the items properly classified (example 13/6) in their order of liquidity[1], starting with the least liquid (see examples 13/5):

	£
Freehold Premises	25,000
Stock in hand, 31st December	1,110
Creditors	890
Cash at bank	350
Debtors	1,930
Drawings	5,000
Machinery	2,500
Furniture and Fittings	1,000
Profit and Loss Account—Cr. (i.e., Net Profit)[2]	6,000
Capital	30,000

2 From the following Trial Balance prepare final accounts for year ended 31st March, 19·2, and a correctly classified Balance Sheet at that date:

TRIAL BALANCE
AS AT 31ST MARCH, 19·2

	£		£
Purchases	6,221	Sales	12,434
Opening Stock 1st April 19·1	340	B White	844
Freehold Premises	13,109	Capital	13,490
Wages	2,776		
Salaries	1,454		
Heating and Lighting	233		
Machinery at cost	1,200		
R Smith	622		
M Brown	700		
Cash at bank	113		
	26,768		26,768

Stock in hand 31st March 19·2 £100

3 (a) From the following items, prepare the Balance Sheet of M Cox as at 31st December, 19·1. Classify the items in their correct order of liquidity (example 13/6):

	£
Cash at bank	350
Machinery	2,500
Stock	270
Drawings	5,000
Creditors	890
Debtors	930
Motor Vans	1,840
Net Profit	6,000
Furniture and Fittings	1,000
Freehold Premises	25,000
Capital	30,000

(b) In example 13/1, Drawings were added to the credit side of the Cash Book. Explain why the balance sheet would still balance.

---

[1] Liquidity   The most liquid of the items on the assets side of a balance sheet is Cash. Less liquid (or less easily available in terms of cash) than Cash are the Debtors. Then comes Stock, which has yet to be sold and still later paid for, and so on to the least liquid item, Freehold Premises.

[2] In the Profit and Loss Account, a profit is represented by a credit balance. If the Profit and Loss Account had been an ordinary ledger account, its favourable balance (the net profit) would have been carried down to its credit side. Instead, it is transferred to the credit side of Capital Account. Thus, a Profit and Loss Account is described as having a credit balance when it shows a profit.

4 Re-draft the following Balance Sheet of N Seaton after correcting the errors contained therein and correctly group the figures to show the totals of Fixed Assets, Current Assets, Current Liabilities and Capital.

BALANCE SHEET

FOR THE YEAR ENDED 31ST DECEMBER, 1970

	£		£
Liabilities		*Assets*	
Capital	10,000	Cash	124
Debtors	3,210	Bank Overdraft	750
Expenses paid in advance[1]	230	Creditors	2,570
Net Profit for the year	2,432	Stock	2,328
		Drawings	1,500
		Freehold Premises	6,000
		Motor Vehicles	2,480
		Expenses accrued[2]	120
	15,872		15,872

[1]Current Asset
[2]Current Liability

(*RSA 1971*)

5 State what you consider would be the effect of each of the following transactions on the capital of a trader's business. State, in each case, whether the capital would be increased or decreased and by what amount. If you think there would be no change simply write 'None'.

(i) The receipt of £50 from one of the trader's debtors.

(ii) The payment of an insurance premium of £20.

(iii) The sale of goods on credit for £100 which had cost the trader £75.

(iv) The cash purchase of a filing cabinet for the office for £27.

(*RSA adapted*)

6 Each of the following transactions of a sole trader affects either the Balance Sheet, or the Trading and Profit and Loss Account, or in some cases both.

(i) The trader settles an account for £100, due to a creditor, by sending the creditor a cheque for £97·50, the balance being allowed as discount.

(ii) The trader withdraws £60 from his Business Account at the bank for his personal expenses.

(iii) A Debtor's Account for £25, being irrecoverable, is written off as a bad debt.

(iv) A second-hand motor van, costing £425 and standing in the books at that figure, is sold on credit for exactly that sum.

(v) A debtor who owes £50, settles his indebtedness in full.

(vi) At the close of the trading year an entry is passed for bank charges £9·50.

(vii) The trader moves into new premises, which he rents. In consequence, his old premises, which he owned freehold and which stand in the books at £6,500 were sold for £7,000.

You are required to write down the words Balance Sheet or Profit and Loss Account, as may be appropriate against each of the items (i) to (vii). If in your judgement the correct answer should be both, write down the word 'both'.

(RSA)

7 (a) Distinguish between a 'Trial balance' and a 'Balance sheet'.

(b) Explain why, if it is correctly prepared, a Balance Sheet always 'balances'.

(JMB)

Chapter Fourteen

The Balance Sheet and the Meaning of Capital (II)

Working Capital

Of frequent interest to businessmen, is the question: 'How much of my capital, in terms of cash, is quickly available to me?' In other words, 'What part of my assets can I quickly transform into cash, for use in my business?' Or, more formally expressed, what is the *Working Capital* of the business? The answer to this vital question may be found among the cash and near-cash items of the Current Assets and Current Liabilities. Near-cash items are stocks of goods which are ready for sale and so ready for conversion into cash in the near future; and debtors, who normally pay within one month of invoice date. When the total of the Current Liabilities is deducted from the total of the Current Assets, the resulting figure is the Working Capital of the business. In defining Working Capital more formally, it is said to be *the excess of current assets over current liabilities*. I can now re-cast my balance sheet (example 13/6) so that the Working Capital is thrown up:

EX. 14/1

BALANCE SHEET OF JOHN FRY
AS AT 30TH APRIL, 19·1

	£	£		£	£
Capital	10,000		FIXED ASSETS		
Add Net Profit	300		Freehold Premises	6,000	
	———		Office Furniture	200	
	10,300			———	6,200
Less Drawings	160		CURRENT ASSETS		
	———	10,140	Stock	180	
			Debtors	500	
			Cash at bank	3,660	
				———	
				4,340	
			Deduct		
			CURRENT LIABILITIES		
			Creditors	400	
			Working Capital	———	3,940
Capital employed		10,140	Net value of assets		10,140

The working capital shows that after all the creditors have been paid there would still be £3,940 available for purchasing more goods for re-sale, or, perhaps, for buying machinery, or adding a new wing to the premises; that is, in one way or another expanding the business by making it more efficient and more productive.

THE EFFECT OF PROFIT (OR LOSS) ON WORKING CAPITAL
Thus, ultimately, all the items affecting working capital as well as the working capital itself, are thought of in terms of cash. The amount of available cash depends upon profits made or losses sustained. Profit implies an increase in capital.

The Net Value of Assets and Capital Employed

The net value of assets, that is the assets (fixed as well as current) remaining after allowances have been made for current liabilities, represents the Capital, in various forms, that is employed by the firm.

EX. 14/2

VERTICAL LAY-OUT OF THE BALANCE SHEET

AN ALTERNATIVE TO THE CONVENTIONAL SETTING IN EX. 14/1:

BALANCE SHEET OF JOHN FRY
AS AT 30TH APRIL, 19·1

	£	£	£
FIXED ASSETS			
Freehold Premises		6,000	
Office Furniture		200	
			6,200
CURRENT ASSETS			
Stock	180		
Debtors	500		
Cash at bank	3,660		
		4,340	
CURRENT LIABILITIES			
Creditors		400	
WORKING CAPITAL			3,940
NET VALUE OF ASSETS			10,140
Represented by proprietor's			
Capital		10,000	
Add Net Profit		300	
		10,300	
Less Drawings		160	
CAPITAL EMPLOYED			10,140

Long Term Liabilities

Suppose that the firm borrowed £5,000 from R Corry, repayable in five years. That would affect:

(a) the Cash Book (Dr.) by increasing the balance at bank;

(b) R Corry's Loan Account (Cr.) by showing him as a creditor.

The Loan Account appears in the Balance Sheet under a heading called Long Term Liabilities. The firm's balance sheet example 14/1 now appears as follows:

BALANCE SHEET OF JOHN FRY
AS AT 30TH APRIL, 19·1

	£	£		£	£
Capital	10,000		FIXED ASSETS		
Add Net Profit	300		Freehold Premises	6,000	
			Office Furniture	200	
	10,300				6,200
Less Drawings	160		CURRENT ASSETS		
		10,140	Stock	180	
Long Term Liabilities			Debtors	500	
Loan Account		5,000	Cash at bank	8,660	
				9,340	
			Deduct		
			CURRENT LIABILITIES		
			Creditors	400	
			Working Capital		8,940
CAPITAL EMPLOYED		15,140	Net Value of Assets		15,140

Overtrading*

If the Current Liabilities exceed the Current Assets, or, if the Working Capital is small, then the business is said to be *overtrading*. It means that the available cash and near-cash (stock and debtors) items would together fall short of the amount due to the creditors; a dangerous situation. The following extract from a balance sheet illustrates such a situation:

EX. 14/3

BALANCE SHEET (EXTRACT)

CURRENT ASSETS	£
Stock	1,000
Debtors	4,000
Cash at bank	500
	5,500
CURRENT LIABILITIES	
Creditors	8,000

Working Capital—Deficiency (2,500)

The firm would also be described as overtrading in a situation where there is a tendency for business to be increasing at a high rate and the cash at bank is low. Such a situation implies the purchase of relatively large stocks of raw materials on credit, and the creation of an abnormally high amount due from debtors; both stock and debtors constitute *tied-up capital*, that is, money which is not immediately available; it will be available only when the stocks of goods are sold, and when they are finally paid for by the customers. Should creditors hear of these circumstances, they might in a panic insist upon immediate payment of the moneys due to them and thus perhaps force the firm into bankruptcy; for the money to pay them would not be available, since the sum of the Current Assets would be less than the total Current Liabilities. My own financial position, as presented in example 14/1, 2, is very sound.

'Quick Assets' Ratio, or the 'Acid Test' of Liquidity*

An even safer assessment of the stability of the business is to ignore all but the Cash and the Debtors and to see how the sum of these two 'quick assets' (assets quickly available in terms of cash) compare with the Current Liabilities. Stocks are ignored under this method because they have to be sold before their value in terms of cash is available; there is never any guarantee that sales will in fact take place. The Balance Sheet, example 14/1–2 shows favourable figures, even under this more stringent 'acid test' of liquidity.

---

*The subjects of Overtrading and Quick Assets Ratio are not usually introduced at this stage. But it is felt that a few words on them might help to bring reality into the principles, and to make the student aware of the significance of Balance Sheet figures. Expansion on the brief statements made above is beyond the scope of this book.

The following figures are offered for comparison purposes:

WORKING CAPITAL	£		QUICK ASSETS RATIO	£
CURRENT ASSETS			Debtors	4,000
Stock	2,000		Cash	500
Debtors	4,000			4,500
Cash	500			
	6,500		*Less:*	
CURRENT LIABILITIES			Creditors	5,000
Creditors	5,000		Deficiency	500
Working Capital	1,500			

An apparently adequate figure

Exercise 14

1 What do you understand by the following account concepts?
Why are they important?

(a) Overtrading.

(b) Rate of turnover (or stock-turn).

(c) 'Acid-Test' ratio.

(d) Percentage of Gross Profit on turnover.

2 From the following balances prepare the balance sheet of B Hopeful as at 31st
December, 19·1:

		£
Trade Debtors		1,200
Insurance paid in advance		40
Stock at 31st December, 19·1		4,625
Wages outstanding		85
Trade Creditors		3,720
Profit and Loss Account to 31st December, 19·1	Dr.	240
Bank Overdraft		1,250
Motor Van at cost less depreciation		800
Premises at cost		2,500
B Hopeful's Capital	Cr.	5,000
Drawings Account		650

Show the working capital and comment on the financial position disclosed by the
balance sheet.

(*RSA*)

3 What is working capital and how is it calculated?
The working capital of John Brown was £5,000 before the following transactions
occurred and you are required to say what effect, if any, each of these would have on
the figure of working capital.

(i) Purchase of fixed assets by cheque £4,650.

(ii) Sale of goods (costing £100) to R Jones for £125.

(iii) Loan from a bank, £5,000 repayable in 5 years.*

(iv) Payment of £60 to H Walters in full settlement of his account of £62.

(v) Bought goods on credit from J Saunders, £30.

(vi) Receipt of balance, due from a debtor £200 less 5% cash discount.

(*RSA 1973*)

---

*Long Term Liability; not a Current Liability (Author)

(a) From the following details find D Jones' capital and show his Balance Sheet at 31st March, 19·1:

Debtors £4,374; Stock £3,586; Loan from K Hind £3,000
Creditors £2,546; Motor vans £1,464; Furniture and Fittings £1,584
Premises £8,000; Bank Overdraft £2,000.

(b) In relation to your completed Balance Sheet, answer the following questions:

    (i)   What is the total of fixed assets?

    (ii) How would you find the working capital, and what is its amount?

    (iii) Was Jones solvent or insolvent? Give your reasons.

(RSA)

5 Given below in abridged form is the balance sheet of C Cantone:

BALANCE SHEET
AS AT 1ST MARCH, 19·1

	£		£
C Cantone—Capital Account	2,355	Machinery	1,500
Creditors	1,890	Stock	2,100
		Debtors	625
		Cash at bank	20
	4,245		4,245

The following transactions took place on 2nd March, 19·1:

(i)   Cantone receives a loan of £500, which he used to pay £200 to a creditor and £300 for the purchase of new machinery.

(ii) A debtor pays £120 on account.

(iii) Cantone purchases on credit goods for re-sale (stock) costing £75.

(iv) Old machinery is sold for £100 in cash; the book value was £250.

(v)   It is decided to correct the valuation of stock on 1st March, 19·1, reducing it by £320.

(vi) Goods were sold on credit for £190 (cost price £145).

Show Cantone's Balance Sheet as it would appear on 2nd March, 19·1, after the transactions, as noted, had been recorded.

(RSA)

6 M Roberts began to trade on 1st September, with a capital of £900 at bank.

			£
Sept.	1	Purchased goods by cheque	360
	3	Purchases goods from M Proctor	180
	7	Bought and paid by cheque Furniture and Fittings	450
	8	Paid by cheque for packing materials	10
	10	Sold to S Brown goods	480
	18	Sold to D Monk goods	360
	25	S Brown paid his account, less 2½% cash discount	
	29	Total expenses for the month paid for by cheque	50

Stock in hand at 30th September was valued at £200.

From the above information you are required to produce appropriate Ledger Accounts, Trial Balance on 30th September and Trading and Profit and Loss Account, as well as a Balance Sheet as at 30th September. Also:

(a) Classify the items in the Balance Sheet.

(b) Set out the Balance Sheet so that the Working Capital is shown.

7 On 31st December, 19·1, the Balance Sheet of James Galbraith, a manufacturer, showed his Capital Account to be £13,750. Taking into consideration the successive effects of the transactions mentioned below, state the amount of Galbraith's Capital at the close of business on each of the dates given:

(i) 2nd January, 19·2. Raw Materials, costing £115, were purchased on credit.

(ii) 3rd January, 19·2. The account of a creditor, to whom £120 was owing, was settled in cash, discount at $2\frac{1}{2}\%$ being deducted by Galbraith.

(iii) 6th January, 19·2. Galbraith's Bank Statement up to 31st December, 19·1, was received. It contained an item of £5·25 in respect of Bank Charges for the half-year, for which Galbraith had not made an entry in his books.

(iv) 7th January, 19·2. A debtor, who owed £85, settled by cheque his indebtedness in full.

(v) 8th January, 19·2. Galbraith withdrew from his business bank account £50 as personal drawings.

(RSA)

8 (a) From the following information, draw up a clear statement to show the result of A Finch's trading during 19·1. He started his business on 1st January by investing £1,000 in it. During the year he had borrowed, for use in the business, £500 free of interest from his aunt, Miss Wren, which had not been repaid, and had withdrawn £730 from the business bank account for his own use. At the end of the year it was found that customers owed £90 and that £110 was owing to suppliers. The stock was £410, valued at cost, and the business had furniture and equipment of £630, valued at cost less depreciation. There was a balance of £306 in the bank account and £4 in petty cash.

(b) What difference would it have made to the result of your calculation if you had been told that the market value of the stock at the end of the year was £530?

9 (a) Explain why, throughout the entire life of a business, its assets always equal its liabilities.

(b) 'A profit is simply an increase in assets.' Explain why you believe that this statement is correct or incorrect.

(c) The assets held by a business are in general classified either as fixed or current. Explain (a) the reason for this distinction and (b) how you would decide in which category a particular asset should be placed.

10 At 1st September, 19·1, the Balance Sheet of R Keen was as follows:

BALANCE SHEET
AS AT 1ST SEPTEMBER, 19·1

	£		£
Sundry creditors	2,190	Cash in hand	20
Outstanding expenses	60	Sundry debtors	2,340
Bank overdraft	750	Stock	1,930
Capital	4,600	Fixtures and Fittings	280
		Machinery	3,030
	7,600		7,600

Having made the necessary arrangements, Keen decided, as from that date, to make the following changes:

(i) to borrow £8,000 from his wife at 6% per annum interest;

(ii) to pay off the bank overdraft, the outstanding expenses, and £290 of the creditors;

(iii) to purchase his premises for £4,000, the payment to be made by cheque on 1st September, 19·1;

(iv) to purchase new stock on credit for £300;

(v) to reduce the value of the machinery by £330 and his old stock by £230.

You are asked to prepare Keen's Balance Sheet immediately after the above changes have been made.

(RSA)

11 L G Silvertree started business with £25,000 on 1st January, 1971. Below is set out information relating to his first year of trading, and a Balance Sheet on 31st December, 1971. Study this information, and then answer the questions below.

Sales during year £45,000
Gross profit for year £9,000

BALANCE SHEET
AS AT DECEMBER 31st, 1971

	£	£		£	£
Capital 1st Jan., 1971	25,000		Premises (At cost 1st Jan., 1971		20,000
Add net profit	4,500		Motor Vans (At cost		
			1st Jan., 1971	3,750	
	29,500		*Less* depreciation	750	
Less drawings	3,000				3,000
		26,500	Stock		4,000
Loan on Mortgage (7%)			Debtors		3,000
1st Jan., 1971		4,000	Bank		2,500
Creditors		2,300	Cash		500
Rates unpaid		200			
		33,000			33,000

(a) What is the percentage of net profit to capital?

(b) What is the percentage of net profit to turnover?

(c) By what percentage have the vans been depreciated?

(d) If the vans are depreciated by the straight line method, at the end of which year will they be completely written off?

(e) What was the 'capital employed' on January 1st, 1971?

(f) Calculate the 'capital employed' on 31st December, 1971.

(g) What was the working capital at the commencement of trading on 1st January, 1971?

(h) What was the working capital on December 31st, 1971?

(i) Calculate the purchases made during the year.

(j) What is the average mark up on cost price?

(k) All transactions were strictly net. How much money had been paid by customers during the year?

(l) Write down the total value of the fixed assets on December 31st, 1971.

(m) Write down the total value of the current assets on December 31st, 1971.

(n) Write down the total value of the current liabilities on December 31st, 1971.

(o) What sum should be debited to profit and loss account for mortgage interest for the year ended December 31st, 1971?

(RSA 1972)

Chapter Fifteen

Capital Expenditure and Revenue Expenditure

On starting business, I might have bought the following items:

(a) certain essential items, such as:
Freehold Premises, Machinery and Plant, Furniture and Fittings, Motor Delivery Vans.
that is to say, the Fixed Assets of my business (example 13/6).

(b) goods for re-sale (normally at a profit).
Payments might also have been made for:

(c) day-to-day expenses, for example:
Heating and Lighting, Wages and Salaries, Packing materials, Telephone charges, Carriage, Stationery.

The difference in character between these categories (a), (b), (c), will be evident after a brief consideration of each one in turn.

Capital Expenditure

(a) Classified under Capital Expenditure, these items are intended to make the business more efficient and more productive. They are items of a relatively permanent nature and are the Fixed Assets of the firm. *They appear as such on the debit side of their own respective accounts in the ledger* and on the right hand side of the Balance Sheet.

Revenue Expenditure

(b) describes stocks of goods purchased for re-sale, which appear as Purchases and Stocks in the Trading Account.

(c) other items of Revenue Expenditure consist of day-to-day expenses, which appear on the debit side of the Profit and Loss Account as losses. Items of revenue expenditure are ephemeral or transitory; many of them are for services (Heat and Light, Carriage); other items are being used up continually (Stationery); others again are financial losses (Discounts Allowed, Bad Debts).

Aspects of Capital Expenditure

Sometimes, the category under which certain items of expenditure should be placed, is problematical. Consider the carriage payable on some furniture I buy for my own use at home for £200. On receipt of the invoice for it, I find that I have been charged £5 for delivery. How much has the furniture, in fact, cost me? Not £200 but £205. By a similar and perfectly valid argument, carriage paid on furniture or machinery bought for use in my business, adds to the total cost of those items.

EX. 15/1   On 10th July, I bought a piece of machinery value £300 on credit from Nutbolt Ltd. Later on, British Rail sent me a delivery charge for £10 which I paid by cheque on 15th July. The accounts concerned appear as follows:

CASH BOOK
(BANK ACCOUNT)

		£
	July 15 Machinery Account	
	(Carriage on Machinery)	10

MACHINERY

		£
July 10	Nutbolt Ltd.	300
15	Cash (Carriage on above)	10

NUTBOLT LTD.

		£
	July 10 Machinery	300

Now, suppose that this machine had to be firmly fixed to the floor of my premises, involving additional costs for materials (say, concrete and timber) £18 and labour (wages to the men doing the job) £20, and that these amounts were paid by cheque. These charges, too, add to the original cost of the machinery purchased. The machinery would not have been delivered if I had not agreed to pay for the additional cost of delivery; I could not have used it before securely installing it. The extra charges for delivery and installation, increased the cost from £300 to £348. They first appear in the Cash Book on the credit side, as payments; they are then posted to Machinery Account which now appears as follows:

MACHINERY

		£
July 10	Nutbolt Ltd.	300
17	Cash—Carriage	10
25	Cash	
	Materials (Installation)	18
	Wages (Installation)	20
		348

How much has the machine cost me? Not £300 but £348. In a situation, then, where expenses are additions to the cost of items classified under Capital Expenditure, they are themselves categorised as Capital Expenditure.

EX. 15/2   Variations on the above principle (example 15/1) are the unavoidable expenses involved in buying freehold property, such as legal charges and estate agent's commission. In fact, I did receive two bills (*debit notes*) dated respectively 26th July, concerned with the purchase of my freehold premises:

	£
Legal charges and solicitors fees	180
Estate agent's commission	150

These were paid by cheque on 26th July and subsequently posted from the Cash Book to Freehold Premises Account. Freehold Premises Account now appears as follows:

FREEHOLD PREMISES

		£
April 1	Cash	6,000
July 26	Cash	
	Legal charges	180
	Agent's commission	150
		6,330

Soon after taking possession of my business premises, I realised that they were too small. But there was some space for the erection of a new wing which Builders Ltd. estimated would cost £1,500. At the same time, I gave them instructions to erect a partition to divide the office into two parts, which they estimated would cost £100. These, too, are examples of capital expenditure.

Revenue Expenditure Contrasted with Capital Expenditure

EX. 15/3

I felt also that some parts of the walls of the premises (which was an old building) could do with repairs, and other parts would look better if a coat or two of paint were applied. The cost of these jobs was estimated at £200. There are, then, three additional items of expenditure to consider:

	£
(a) A new wing to the premises—Capital expenditure	1,500
(b) A partition—Capital expenditure	100
(c) Repairs and decorations—Revenue expenditure	200

(a) A NEW WING adds to the capital of £6,000 already expended on Premises. To all intents and purposes a new building is being proposed, attached to the old one; it is *Capital Expenditure* of £1,500.

(b) A PARTITION is also an addition to the building. It is *Capital Expenditure* of £100.

(c) REPAIRS and DECORATIONS are *not* additions to the building; they simply renovate it; they put it as near as possible back to its state when it was first built. Repairs and Decorations are items of *Revenue Expenditure*, in this instance costing £200.

INSTRUCTIONS TO THE BUILDERS TO PROCEED

I accepted the builders' estimates and instructed them to proceed with the work. The partition and the repairs and decorations were completed by the end of July and a cheque was sent to them, value £300 in settlement of their account. This was entered on the credit side of the cash book, taking care to show how it was divided between Premises Account (Partition £100) capital expenditure, and Repairs and Decorations Account £200, revenue expenditure (the latter to be transferred eventually to the debit, or losses, side of the Profit and Loss Account). The accounts and the items concerned appear as follows:

EX. 15/4

FREEHOLD PREMISES

		£
April 10	Cash	6,000
July 31	Cash	
	Partition	100

REPAIRS AND DECORATIONS

		£
July 31	Cash	200

Builders Ltd. sent me their invoice for the new wing long before it was completed. They asked for a deposit of 10% on the total cost, and a cheque for £150 was sent to them on July 31st. The new wing was completed on 14th October. These items, too, were entered in their appropriate accounts:

EX. 15/5

FREEHOLD PREMISES

	£
April 10 Cash	6,000
July 31 Cash	100
Oct. 14 Builders Ltd. (New wing)	1,500

BUILDERS LTD.

	£		£
July 31 Cash (Deposit on new wing to Premises)	150	Oct. 14 Freehold Premises	1,500

Note that the total value of Freehold Premises is now £7,600 (plus legal and agents charges), although I still owe Builders Ltd. £1,500 less £150 deposit.

SUMMARY

(i) Premises have *received* additional value of £1,500 (Dr.)
Builders Ltd. have *given* (or will *give*) services and materials, value £1,500 (Cr.)
Builders Ltd. have *received* money, £150 (Dr.)
Bank has *given* money, £150 (Cr.).

(ii) In account A, the particulars read B, while in account B, the particulars read A (Chapter 2 p.6).

(iii) Remember to consider all ledger entries from the point of view of the account with which you are at any given time concerned.

(iv) Remember that a ledger account implies the subtraction of one side from the other.

EX. 15/6   The following are the accounts we have been concerned with in this chapter:

CASH BOOK

			£				Details £	Bank £
July 1 Balance		b/d	3,902	July	17	British Rail (Carriage on Machinery)		10
					25	Machinery installation		
						Materials	18	
						Wages	20	38
					26	Freehold Premises		
						Legal charges		180
						Agent's commission		150
					31	Builders Ltd.		
						Partition (Premises Account)	100	
						Repairs and Decorations Account	200	
								300
					31	Builders Ltd.		
						New wing to Premises (Deposit)		150

FREEHOLD PREMISES

		£
April 10	Cash	6,000
July 26	Cash	
	Legal charges	180
	Agent's commission	150
31	Cash	
	Builders Ltd. (Partition)	100
Oct. 14	Builders Ltd.	
	New wing	1,500

MACHINERY

		£
July 10	Nutbolt Ltd.	300
17	Cash—Carriage on above	10
25	Materials and labour to install above	38

BUILDERS LTD.

	£		£
July 31 Cash—Deposit on cost of new wing	150	Oct. 14 Freehold Premises New wing	1,500

NUTBOLT LTD.

	£
July 10 Machinery	300

REPAIRS AND DECORATIONS

	£
July 31 Cash	200

A Useful Exercise

A useful exercise would be to enter items of Capital Expenditure, such as those mentioned under Fixed Assets, in the Profit and Loss Account to see:

1 what would happen to the profits—if there are any left!
2 how bare the assets side of the Balance Sheet would look;
3 how little if at all, the capital would increase, or, more likely, how seriously it would be reduced, since the Profit and Loss Account would almost certainly show a heavy loss, deductable from Capital;
4 how there would be no balance in the Fixed Asset Accounts in the ledger, since they would have been transferred to the Profit and Loss Account! It would look as if the firm did not possess any freehold premises, machinery, furniture or motor vans, since all these accounts would have been closed on being transferred to the Profit and Loss Account!

Fixed Assets or items of Capital Expenditure, as long as they exist, have debit balances, are not transferred to any account, except at the end of their productive lives, and are *shown* in (not transferred to) the Balance Sheet.

Exercise 15

1 State whether the following transactions of a sports club should be classified as capital expenditure or revenue expenditure:

(a) The re-decoration of the club premises.

(b) The installation of a new wine bar.

(c) The building of an extension to the club dressing rooms.

(d) The purchase of wines and spirits.

(e) The purchase of a record player for use in the club lounge.

2 Explain the distinction between capital expenditure and revenue expenditure. State under which heading you would classify each of the following items incurred by a manufacturing business and give reasons for your decision in each case:

(a) Cost of a freehold building.

(b) Legal charges on the purchase of a freehold building.

(c) Replacement of furniture which has been destroyed by fire.

(d) Relaying floors destroyed by dry rot.

(RSA II)

3 Arthur Makin has an engineering business. His business, which is expanding, owns its factory and distributes its products by its own motor lorries.

(a) Give one example each of capital expenditure, revenue income, and revenue expenditure that you might expect to find in the above firm.

(b) How would you deal with the examples chosen in the final accounts of the firm?

(RSA)

4 (a) What do you understand by Capital Expenditure and Revenue Expenditure? Why is this distinction important in bookkeeping?

(b) Steven and James, retailers, have spent £250 for complete re-decoration of their premises. Steven says this is Capital Expenditure but James says it is Revenue Expenditure. State with your reasons which of them you consider to be right.

(c) What difference will it make to the profits for the year if Steven's rather than James's view is adopted, but one fifth of the cost is written off?

(RSA)

5 (a) Some of the following items of expenditure should be debited to asset accounts and others to expense accounts. Answer 'Asset A/c' or 'Expense A/c' as the case may be:

(i) repairs to an office typewriter; (ii) the fitting of a new engine to the firm's delivery van; (iii) the cost of installing a new plant in the factory; (iv) re-decorating the works canteen; (v) erecting a partition in the general office; (vi) repairing a wall in the boiler house; (vii) raising the height of the factory chimney by another 4 ft.

(b) What type of expenditure is involved in the items debited to the asset accounts?

(c) State—very briefly and clearly—the guiding principle which you followed in deciding to debit certain items to Expense Accounts.

(RSA)

6 Classify the following as either capital or revenue expenditure. Give reasons for your decisions.

   (a) Legal expenses incurred in connection with the purchase of a new warehouse.

   (b) Cost of rebuilding the wall of a boiler-house.

   (c) Cost of replacing a rotten wooden floor in the factory office.

   (d) Cost of replacing the damp course in the factory wall with a new improved damp course.

(RSA II)

7 On the 1st January, 19·1, the Land and Buildings Account of James Grant showed a balance of £5,000, and on the same day Grant sold on credit to Arthur White part of his land for £350 which had originally cost £250. At the 30th June, Grant completed the purchase of additional buildings at a cost of £500. Alterations carried out in June by his own workpeople cost Grant £280 in wages and £120 for materials, and the architect's fee was £30.

You are required to prepare the Land and Buildings Account, bringing down the balance that should appear in his Balance Sheet dated 31st December, 19·1

(RSA)

8 (a) The following statement, which is incomplete, sets out information regarding the position, at a particular date, of five different businesses identified in the statement A, B, C, D and E. Copy it and insert the missing amount in each case.

	Liabilities £	Capital £	Assets £	Deficiency £
A	231		420	
B		7,310	12,830	
C	1,942	5,617		
D	9,715			1,234
E			8,162	418

   (b) What bookkeeping terms are used to indicate the following:

     (i) assets held not for re-sale but merely to increase the profit earning capacity of the business;

     (ii) loans to the business of a semi-permanent nature;

     (iii) debts falling due to be settled by the business in the immediate future;

     (iv) assets which fluctuate in the ordinary course of trading.

Which of the above items would you use in determining the amount of the working-capital?

   (c) Are the following statements (i) and (ii) true or false?

     (i) The amount of capital is increased when fixed assets are bought.

     (ii) Capital expenditure increases net profit.

(RSA)

9 (a) How would you distinguish between capital expenditure and revenue expenditure?

   (b) State, with reasons, in which of the two categories you would place each of the following items:

     (i) cost of repairs to plant, £792;

     (ii) cost of an addition to an existing machine which will improve its performance, £600;

(iii) cost of repairing and replacing woodwork, which had been destroyed by woodworm, in a building which had been in the same ownership since it was built, £2,000.

Would it make any difference to your answer if you were told that the building had been purchased recently. and its state was known when the contract to buy it was signed?

Chapter Sixteen

The Journal

The Journal is a Book of Original Entry. It consists of items for which the other books of original entry are unsuitable. The following are some of its functions:

To record purchases of capital goods, such as machinery;

To record credit (and debit) notes before they are entered in their respective accounts;

To record correction of errors;

To record transfers of items from one account to another.

The Journal as a Book of Original Entry for Recording the Purchase of Capital Goods

In Chapter 3, the function of the books of original entry was explained:

1 The Cash Book, to record moneys received and paid;

2 The Sales Book to record credit sales;

3 The Purchases Book to record credit purchases of goods *intended for re-sale in the ordinary course of trade.*

The thoughtful student might now ask: 'Where is the original entry for purchases of *capital* goods, such as machinery, furniture, to be found?' *Purchases of capital goods (Capital Expenditure) must not appear in the Purchases Book.* That kind of purchase is first shown in detail in the Journal. The two adjacent cash columns in the Journal indicate the corresponding debit and credit entries that are to be made in the ledger, while the first two lines in the Details column, represent the debit (first line) and credit (second line) accounts. The remainder of the Journal entry describes the nature of the entry and it is called the *Narration.*

EX. 16/1   THE USE OF THE JOURNAL AS A BOOK OF ORIGINAL ENTRY FOR RECORDING THE PURCHASE OF CAPITAL GOODS

Let us take for example:

(a) the furniture bought on credit from Lockerdesks Ltd.

(b) the machinery bought on credit from Nutbolt Ltd.

Entries first appear in the Journal, from which they are posted to the ledger as follows:

JOURNAL

		Fol.	Dr. £	Cr. £
April 15	Office Furniture	5	100	
	Lockerdesks Ltd.	13		100
		£		
	Desk	40		
	Chairs	10		
	Typewriter	50		

May 10 Machinery		6	300	
Nutbolt Ltd.		14		300
Trolley	30			
Weighing Machine	200			
Winch	70			

LEDGER
OFFICE FURNITURE[5]

			£
April 15 Lockerdesks Ltd.	J		100

LOCKERDESKS LTD.[13]

			£
April 15 Office Furniture	J		100

MACHINERY[6]

			£
May 10 Nutbolt Ltd.	J		300

NUTBOLT LTD.[14]

			£
May 10 Machinery	J		300

An alternative place for recording purchases of capital goods is in a Purchases Book; in which a separate column might be used specially for recording purchases of capital goods, and postings to the ledger may then be made from that column.

The use of the Journal for Recording Credit and Debit Notes

The only Credit Notes that have so far been introduced, record the value of goods returned against sales or purchases, which have been entered into the Returns Inwards and Returns Outwards Books respectively. But Credit Notes might be sent for other reasons as well.

EX. 16/2

Suppose that Builders Ltd., who erected a partition in my office (example 15/4) had overcharged me by £10. On discovery of the error, they sent me a credit note which I entered in the Journal as follows:

JOURNAL

		Dr.	Cr.
19·1		£	£
Dec. 2 Builders Ltd.		10	
Freehold Premises			10
Overcharge on cost of			
erection of partition			

LEDGER
FREEHOLD PREMISES

	£				£
April 10 Cash	6,000	Dec. 2 Builders Ltd.	J		10
July 26 Cash					
Legal charges	180				
Agent's commission	150				
31 Cash					
Builders Ltd.	100				
(Partition)					
Oct. 14 Builders Ltd.	1,500				
(New wing)					

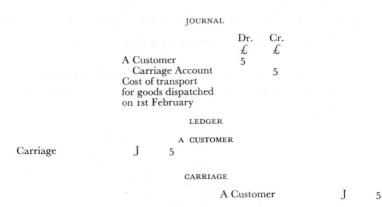

BUILDERS LTD.

	£		£
July 31 Cash—Deposit on cost of new wing	150	Oct. 14 Freehold Premises New wing	1,500
Dec. 2 Freehold Premises J	10		

EX. 16/3   Having rendered an invoice for goods I supplied to A Customer, it was discovered that a charge for transport had been omitted. I sent him a debit note and from the carbon copy, I made an entry in the Journal:

JOURNAL

	Dr. £	Cr. £
A Customer	5	
Carriage Account		5
Cost of transport for goods dispatched on 1st February		

LEDGER

A CUSTOMER

Carriage	J	5

CARRIAGE

	A Customer	J	5

The use of the Journal for the Correction of Errors

As we now know, a trial balance is normally brought out to prove the arithmetical accuracy of the ledger accounts. But the trial balance does not always balance at the first attempt. Then it is necessary to check every ledger account, to add up the entries in the Day Books and check the postings from them to the ledger, until all the errors have been found and corrected. In practice, when there are numerous accounts to check, this is a tedious and time-consuming process. However, it must be done, and it is done systematically. As each error is located, it is recorded in a temporary account called the Suspense Account. The first entry in it is the trial balance error, *on the same side as the lesser of the two sides of the trial balance.* When the last of the errors comes to light and it is entered in the Suspense Account, that account should balance. The trial balance will then also balance.

EX. 16/4

TRIAL BALANCE

	£		£
Various items	9,600	Various items	9,800
Suspense Account*	200		
	9,800		9,800

SUSPENSE ACCOUNT

	£
**Trial balance error	200

---

*This balance of £200 represents *the difference of all the errors* in the trial balance.

**The Suspense Account is a temporary account; opened as an expedient. There is therefore, no double entry to this £200.

Suppose now, for the sake of simplicity, there were only two errors:

(a) The *Sales Book* had been overcast by £250 (consequently the credit entry in the *Sales Account* was too much by £250).

(b) £50 paid by M Smith had not been credited to his account, although an entry had been made on the debit side of the Cash Book (included in the £9,600 shown in the trial balance above).

What is needed is:

(a) to decrease the credit side of Sales Account by £250; and

(b) to credit Smith's account with £50;

The corresponding double-entries are in the Suspense Account. The following are the journal and ledger entries for the correction of those errors:

EX. 16/5

JOURNAL

	Dr.	Cr.
Sales	250	
Suspense Account		250
Sales Book overcast		
Suspense Account	50	
R Smith		50
Item not posted from Cash Book		

LEDGER

SALES

		£			£
Suspense Account	J	250	Goods	SB	x

R SMITH

		Suspense Account	J	50

SUSPENSE ACCOUNT

		£			£
Trial balance error		200	Sales	J	250
R Smith	J	50			
		250			250

The Suspense Account balances. This indicates that all the errors have been found and the trial balance might now be completed and ruled off.

Other errors which might be corrected by journal entry:

ERROR OF COMMISSION

Suppose that a cheque for £60 received from S Norton, a customer, was in error posted to the credit of S Morton and Co., another customer; this would not prevent the trial balance from balancing. On discovery of the error, a journal entry is made to effect a correction of this *Error of Commission*.

EX. 16/6

JOURNAL

	Dr.	Cr.
S Morton & Co.	60	
S Norton		60
Cheque from S Norton posted to credit side of Morton & Co. in error		

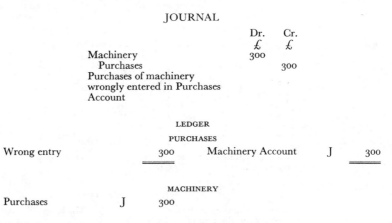

LEDGER

S NORTON

	£			£
		S Morton & Co.	J	60

S MORTON AND CO.

S Norton	J	60	Cash	CB	60

The debit entry in S Morton and Co.'s account cancels the wrong entry; the credit entry in S Norton's account is the one that should have been made in the first place.

ERROR OF PRINCIPLE

It was emphasised above that Capital Expenditure must not be confused with Revenue Expenditure. But supposing that in a moment of forgetfulness the machinery purchased from Nutbolt Ltd. was entered into the Purchases Account on the debit side (together with the purchases of goods intended for re-sale), instead of to the debit side of Machinery Account. The trial balance would still balance. A journal entry is needed to correct this *Error of Principle*:

EX. 16/7

JOURNAL

	Dr.	Cr.
	£	£
Machinery	300	
Purchases		300
Purchases of machinery wrongly entered in Purchases Account		

LEDGER

PURCHASES

Wrong entry		300	Machinery Account	J	300

MACHINERY

Purchases	J	300			

More examples of the error of principle:

(i)   Carriage, say, £10, paid on capital goods, wrongly included in Carriage Account.

(ii)   Materials, say, £15, for installing machinery, wrongly included in Purchases Account.

(iii)   Wages paid, say, £18, for installing machinery, wrongly included in Wages Account.

The corrections:

(i)   Carriage on capital goods, eg. Office Furniture, is Capital Expenditure and should be added to the item on which carriage was paid.

(ii)   Materials used for installing, say, machinery, should be added to the cost of machinery.

(iii)   Wages paid for installing, say, machinery, should be added to the cost of machinery.

The following journal entries and their corresponding ledger accounts deal with the correction of the above errors:

EX. 16/8   JOURNAL

		Dr.	Cr.
Machinery		10	
Carriage			10
Transfer of item entered in			
wrong account			
Machinery		15	
Purchases			15
Transfer of item entered in			
wrong account			
Machinery		18	
Wages			18
Transfer of item entered in			
wrong account			

Note   The following 'composite' form presents concisely the above necessarily repetitive entries.

Machinery	43	
Carriage		10
Purchases		15
Wages		18
Transfer of items entered in		
wrong account	43	43

LEDGER

MACHINERY

	Fol.	£
Cash	CB	300
Carriage	J	10
Purchases	J	15
Wages	J	18

CARRIAGE

Cash (Including carriage on machinery)	CB	x	Machinery	J	10

PURCHASES

Goods (Including materials used for installations of machinery)	PB	x	Machinery	J	15

WAGES

Cash (Including wages paid for installations of machinery)	CB	x	Machinery	J	18

Carriage on Purchases (Carriage Inwards)

Carriage paid on purchases (Carriage Inwards) of goods for re-sale, in the ordinary course of business, say £5.

As in the case of carriage paid on capital goods, so carriage paid on Purchases must be added to the cost of the goods in order to show their true cost. It might be necessary to transfer the amount from Carriage Account to Purchases Account. This would be done by a journal entry, as in the previous examples. However, it is better to have a Carriage on Purchases Account, which is transferred to the Trading Account and shown as an addition to Purchases as follows:

EX. 16/9

TRADING AND PROFIT AND LOSS ACCOUNT (EXTRACT)

Opening Stock		x	Sales		x
Purchases	x				
Add Carriage Inwards	x				
	—				
	x				
Less Returns Outwards	x				
(Purchases Returns)	—				
Net value of Purchases		x			
		x			
Less Closing Stock		x			
		—			
Cost of Sales		x			
Gross Profit	c/d	x			
		—			
		x			x
		=			=
Carriage on Sales		x	Gross Profit	b/d	x

Carriage on Sales (Carriage Outwards)

While, obviously, carriage on goods bought increases their cost, it would not be true to say that carriage paid on goods sold increases the total value of goods sold. Carriage on Sales is an overhead expense and it is transferred to the debit side of the Profit and Loss Account, as shown above.

Journal Opening Entries

At the commencement of a business, its assets and liabilities are brought together in the journal, under *Opening Entries*, before they are posted to their new ledger accounts.

EX. 16/10

W Carr started business with a small capital. He could not afford to employ a book-keeper, nor did he know anything about accounts himself. He managed to keep up a rough and ready method for reminding himself to what extent he owed money to his creditors, and the amounts due to him from his debtors. The Bank Statement kept him informed as to the state of his bank account.

However, at the end of the year, 31st December, 19·2, he was obliged to employ an accountant in order to ascertain his profit or loss, but especially to satisfy the requirements of H.M. Inspector of Taxes. The accountant elicits the following information from Carr as to the state of his business at 31st December:

Carr possessed: Office Furniture and Machinery worth £300; Stock of goods at cost £200; Debtors: M Day £190, C Mann £230; Creditors: L Parson £210. His bank statement showed a credit balance of £520.

This information is entered in the journal as follows:

JOURNAL OPENING ENTRIES

			Fol.	Cr. £	Dr. £
19·2					
Dec.	31	Office Furniture and Machinery	2	300	
		Stock	3	200	
		Debtors:			
		M Day	4	190	
		C Mann	5	230	
		Cash at bank	CB	520	
		Creditors:			
		L Parson	6		440
		Capital—being excess of assets over liabilities			1,000
				—	—
		Assets, liabilities and capital at 31st December, 19·2		1,440	1,440

Separate ledger accounts are then opened and each item is posted to its respective account. (In the above example, the ledger folios have already been inserted):

CAPITAL—W CARR[1]

				19·2				£
				Dec. 31 Balance			J	1,000

OFFICE FURNITURE AND MACHINERY[2]

19·2				£
Dec. 31 Balance		J		300

STOCK[3]

19·2				£
Dec. 31 Balance		J		200

M DAY[4]

19·2				£
Dec. 31 Balance		J		190

C MANN[5]

19·2				£
Dec. 31 Balance		J		230

L PARSON[6]

			19·2			£
			Dec. 31 Balance		J	440

BANK
(CASH BOOK)

19·2				£
Dec. 31 Balance		J		520

Once the accounts are properly set out in the ledger, Carr can continue to make entries in them on the same pattern, (with an occasional check-up by his accountant). The following transactions illustrate how the above accounts are continued:

19·3			£
Jan. 10	Paid to Parson the amount due to him by cheque		440
	14	Received cheque from M Day in settlement of his account	190
	19	C Mann settled his account by cheque	230
	22	Sold goods to M Day on credit	150

BANK
(CASH BOOK)

19·2				£	19·3				£
Dec. 31 Balance		J	520		Jan. 10 L Parson		6	440
19·3								
Jan. 14 M Day		4	190					
19 C Mann		5	230					

M DAY[4]

19·2				£	19·3				£
Dec. 31 Balance		J	190		Jan. 14 Cash		CB	190
19·3								
Jan. 22 Sales		SB	150					

C MANN[5]

19·2				£	19·3				£
Dec. 31 Balance		J	230		Jan. 19 Cash		CB	230

L PARSON[6]

19·3				£	19·2				£
Jan. 10 Cash		CB	440		Dec. 31 Balance		J	440

SALES[58]

				19·3				£
				Jan. 31 Goods		SB		150

Exercise 16

1 Journalise the following:

(a)
Jan. 1 Purchased machinery on credit from Makeshift Ltd. £700
4 Purchased on credit Office Furniture from Penner & Co. £60
6 A cheque payment of £67 to A Smith & Sons was debited to A Smithson's account in error
10 £18 received from D Jones had been posted to the account M Jay
14 £10 received from A Cain was wrongly posted to C Able's account

(b)
Mar. 3 £10 received in payment of the sale of an old desk from the office had been posted to the Sales Account
11 The purchase of a calculating machine for the office, value £230, had been posted to Purchases' Account

(c)
May 15 The proprietor of the business, K Hod, took goods from the firm for his own use (Drawings Account and Purchases Account), £30
20 £245 has been included in the Wages Account which sum represents expenditure on an extension to K Hod's private house

(d)
June 11 Sold our own used motor van to Autovans Ltd. £200 (Motor Vehicles Account and Autovans Account)
25 £40 expended by the trader on his own expenses had been posted to the Office Expenses Account

2 Show by means of journal entries how the following errors should be corrected in the books of C Careless:

(a) Fixtures and Fittings purchased for £300 had been debited to the Purchases Account.

(b) Goods sold to G Watson for £50 had been debited to G Weston.

(c) Goods value £174 bought on 8th December from L Johnston & Co. was credited in error to the account of L Johnson & Sons.

(d) Careless's final stock had been undervalued by £200.

3 Make the necessary entries in A Peak's books of original entry and his ledger to record the following:

Invoices received

Mar. 2 Bird & Sons—goods for re-sale £85
3 Office Supplies Ltd.—new filing cabinet £40
6 Mallard Bros.—goods for re-sale £190

Invoices sent out for goods dispatched

Mar. 3 A Gunn £93
4 G Stock £80

Credit note received

Mar. 7 Bird & Sons, overcharge £7

Credit note sent out

Mar. 6 A Gunn—Return of crate £4

Cheque book counterfoils

Mar. 2 Properties Ltd.—Rent £40
3 A Trader—goods for re-sale £33
6 Mallard Bros., on account £50

Bank paying-in slip

Mar.   7 Cash and cheques £268 (Cash sales £192;
          G Stock £76—in settlement for goods supplied
          on 4th March)

No trial balance is required, nor should the accounts be balanced.

(RSA)

4 Prepare journal entries to show the effect of the following transactions in the books of W Smith:

  (a) A motor van was valued in the books at £140. It was taken by H P Carr at an agreed price of £100 in part exchange for a new van value £500.

  (b) The correction of the posting of a credit of £5 to the account of A Wright instead of A Wrightson.

  (c) A new machine was installed by the firm's own labour and £150 wages and £100 purchases are to be charged as part of the capital cost.

5 Show, by journal entries, how the following transactions of A White, a dealer in electrical goods, would be dealt with in his ledger:

  Mar.   2 White received a credit note from P Green for £2 which he had omitted to deduct when settling Green's account
         5 White received a credit note from B Brown for goods returned to the value of £7
        10 White bought on credit from Pink & Co. five electric fires at £10 each and took one home to keep for his own use
        12 White sold on credit to C Gray a refrigerator for £92 taking in part exchange a filing cabinet valued at £32 for use in the office

(RSA)

6 Prepare the journal entries which would be necessary to deal with the following transactions:

  (a) Interest at 5% per annum charged to the account of V Tardy whose debit balance of £70 was due for payment at the end of 19·1.

  (b) Purchased on credit from L Dove & Co. Ltd. a new motor van at a price of £750 subject to trade discount of 10% and an allowance of £100 for an old vehicle taken by Dove & Co. in part exchange.

  (c) When paying S Jones, a creditor, we had deducted £7 as cash discount. Jones has disallowed this discount.

  (d) Machinery valued at £1,000 purchased on credit from Steel Engineering Company had been debited to the Purchases Account.

  (e) A sale to Derby & Co. amounting to £275 had been entered in the Sales Day Book as £257 and this latter figure had been posted to the respective ledger accounts.

7 Draft the journal entries with appropriate narrative to record the following in the books of B Robinson, on 4th November, 1971.

  (a) Waterways Ltd. disallowed a £5 discount that Robinson deducted when paying an account to Waterways Ltd.

  (b) An account for £500 for repairs to premises was received from Builders Ltd. The account was payable at 31st December, 1971.

(RSA 1971)

8 Prepare the journal entries and brief narration in the books of Jones & Son to record the following:

    (a) Included in the Purchase Account was £450 for Materials used in building an extension to the firm's premises.

    (b) £50 received from K Hunt had been wrongly credited to the account of K Hunter.

    (c) The loss arising on the sale for £40 of an office machine, the book value of which is £60. (Debit Profit and Loss Account.)

(RSA 1973)

9 Prepare the journal entries which would be necessary to deal with the following transactions:

    (a) The loss arising on the sale for £56 of a machine, the book value of which is £75. (Debit Profit and Loss Account.)

    (b) £163 has been included in the Wages Account which sum represents expenditure on an extension of a freehold premises.

    (c) A cheque for £10 paid to A Turney was debited to a personal account in his name. It should have been charged to Legal Expenses Account.

    (d) During the year the proprietor had taken goods for his own use at a total cost value of £80. No previous entry had been made in the books in this respect.

10 Write down, against each of (i) to (vii) below, the name of the Book of Original Entry which would be used for the first record from each of the documents described:

    (i) A letter from the bank, returning dishonoured a customer's cheque paid in three days previously.

    (ii) An inward invoice for fixtures and fittings purchased on credit.

    (iii) A receipted petty cash slip signed by the firm's cleaners.

    (iv) An invoice received from one of the firm's suppliers of goods.

    (v) The office copy of a credit note sent out to one of the firm's customers.

    (vi) A credit note received from one of the firm's suppliers.

    (vii) The office copy of an invoice sent out to one of the firm's customers.

11 From the following information write up, as it would appear in the Sales Ledger of John Lorimer, a timber merchant, the account for June, 19·1, of Charles Barron, a builder, one of his customers. Particular care should be taken to place the various entries in their correct order of date.

    (i) The debit balance of Barron's account on 1st June, 19·1, was £387.

    (ii) The Sales Day Book contains three entries under Barron's name: 3rd June £200, 7th June £360, and 26th June £285.

    (iii) The Cash Book contains the following entries concerning Barron: on 3rd June a debit of £350 in the Bank column, on 10th June a debit of £195 in the Bank column and an entry of £5 in the corresponding Discount column, and on 25th

June a debit of £351 in the Bank column and an entry of £9 in the corresponding Discount column.

(iv) The Returns Inwards Book has an entry of £5 under Barron's name on 28th June.

(v) There are two entries concerning Barron in the Journal. On 19th June he was credited, to the debit of Fixtures and Fittings Account, with £118, being the cost of a new counter and shelves erected in Lorimer's offices. On 26th June the cash discount, taken by Barron when settling—too late, incidentally—for the goods purchased on 7th June, was disallowed.

Rule off and balance Barron's account as at 28th June, 19·1, the last working day of the month.

12 (a) T Briggs, a wholesaler, extracted a Trial Balance from his ledgers at the end of his financial year on 31st January, 19·1. In which column, debit or credit, would you expect the balances in the following accounts to appear?

(i) Carriage Outwards.

(ii) Returns Inwards.

(iii) Rent Received.

(iv) Stock in Trade.

(v) Freehold Buildings.

(b) Certain types of bookkeeping errors do not affect the agreement of a trial balance; one such error is called an error of principle. What is an error of principle?

13 C Piggott, at the end of his financial year on 31st January, 19·2, extracted and agreed a trial balance of his books. He then prepared a first draft of his Trading and Profit and Loss Account for the year and the Balance Sheet, and at that stage asked you to check his work. In doing so the following matters were found, calling for amendment:

(i) A new machine costing £480 had been included in Trade Purchases; this is to be corrected.

(ii) The Sales Day Book had been over-added by £100 and this error was compensated by posting twice a cheque for £100 drawn by C Piggott, to his Drawings Account.

(iii) A Credit for £10 in respect of Goods returned by C Brownson had been posted to C Browne in error.

(iv) On 31st July, 19·1, A Reynolds had lent C Piggott £1,000, which was paid in to the business bank account and credited to C Piggott as capital; this should have been credited to a loan account in Reynolds' name.

You are asked:

(a) To state how these amendments should be made in the books, framing your answer, where appropriate, in the form of Journal entries.

(b) To state, giving your calculations, by how much the Net Profit, shown by C Piggott's draft Profit and Loss Account for the year, would be increased or decreased by the corrections.

(RSA adapted)

14 The following undiscovered errors were made during 1970 in a set of books:

(i) A debit balance on a customer's account was carried forward £6 short.

(ii) The total of the discounts allowed in August (£12) was posted to the credit of the Discounts Account.

(iii) The Sales Day Book was undercast by £100 in July.

(iv) A customer's personal account had no entry for his discount of £2 which appeared in the discount column of the Cash Book.

(v) A credit balance of £3 standing on a customer's account had been omitted when drawing up the Trial Balance.

(a) State in each case, which side of the Trial Balance as at 31st December, 1970, would be the greater as a result of that particular error and the amount of the difference caused by it; and

(b) State the amount of the difference in the totals of the Trial Balance, indicating whether debit or credit.

(c) Show a Suspense Account.

(RSA 1971)

15 At the end of the financial year on 31st December, 19·1, the trial balance of A Bee, a wholesaler, did not agree, and the amount of the difference was carried to a Suspense Account.
During the audit of his books the following errors were found:

(i) The total of the Sales Book was under-added by £90.

(ii) The total of the Discount Allowed by A Bee in December, amounting to £60 was not posted to the Discount Allowed Account.

(iii) Goods purchased on credit for £80 from K Jay had been posted to the credit of J Kay.

(iv) £20 received for the sale of furniture from his office had been posted to the credit of the Sales Account.

(a) Show the journal entries necessary to correct the above errors.

(b) Show the Suspense Account after the necessary corrections have been made.

16 On 31st December, 19·1, the Trial Balance of A Wendy & Co., shows the debit side to be £60 greater than the credit. After checking, the following errors were discovered:

(a) The Bought Ledger had been overcast by £120.

(b) A cash payment of £135 for a lathe was posted to the cash book only.

(c) A cheque for £70 received from A Swindel had not been posted to his account.

(d) A returnable crate (£5) had been received from a debtor, R Tee. The posting to his personal account was omitted.

Show the Suspense Account and Journal entries to correct the errors.

17 (a) Write a brief explanation of the purpose of a trial balance and how it is used by the accountant.

(b) A firm's bookkeeper was unable to agree the Trial Balance and he entered the amount by which it was out of balance in a Suspense Account.
The following errors were subsequently discovered:

(i) The debit side of the General Expenses Account had been over-cast by £100.

(ii) £600 paid for office furniture had been debited to Office Expenses Account.

(iii) The discounts received and allowed in the month of November amounted to £30 and £50 respectively and had been posted to the wrong sides of the Discount Account.

(iv) Returns outwards amounting to £148 had been posted to the personal accounts only.

(v) A total in the Sales Day Book of £540 had been carried forward as £450.

Show the journal entries which are necessary to correct the above errors. You should assume that Control Accounts are not kept by this firm.

18 L Smith carries on business as a radio dealer. On 1st January, 19·1, his assets were: Cash in Hand, £67; Cash at Bank, £396; Trade Debtors: L Roberts, £47; K Thompson, £80; Stock, £396; Fixtures and Fittings, £376; Premises, £4,000. His liabilities were: Trade Creditor: H Tims, £84; Loan from J Walters, £500.
Ascertain Smith's capital and open the accounts necessary to record the above position.
His order book shows that during January 19·1, he ordered and received delivery on credit of the following goods for re-sale:

Jan.   2 From H Keeping Ltd., four radios at £64 each, less 5% trade discount
      16 From H Tims, batteries value £36
      18 From Fix Co. Ltd., twelve radios at £22 each

His other transactions during January were:

Jan. 15 Sold for cash, three of the radios for £30 each
      21 Returned one of the radios to Fix Co. Ltd., being faulty
      23 K Thompson paid by cheque the amount owing by him, less 2½% cash discount, which was allowed
      24 Purchased new fixtures for the shop and paid for them by cheque, £40
      25 Paid by cheque the amount owing to H Tims at 1st January
      27 Sold on credit one record player for £85 to S Pope
      28 Paid by cash: Wages, £40; Shop cleaning, £2; Office teas, £1; Postage stamps, £2

Record the above transactions in the books of L Smith, using proper subsidiary books to enter the transactions and posting these to the ledger. Balance the accounts and draw up a trial balance on 31st January. The stock on 31st January, was £300. Produce a Trading Account, Profit and Loss Account, and Balance Sheet as at 31st January, 19·1.

Chapter Seventeen

Adjustments at the end of the Financial Year

The Amount That Ought to Have Been Paid

When preparing the Final Accounts at the end of the firm's financial year, care must be taken to show the amount that *ought* to have been paid against each item, not merely what has actually been paid, thus ensuring that a true profit or loss figure is produced.

Payments Due but Unpaid ; or Payments Accrued

Suppose that on 1st January, 19·2, I, John Fry, rented some extra storage space in a warehouse at £160 per year, and assume that my financial year ends on 31st December (as in all the examples in this Chapter). If by the end of the year only three-quarters (£120) of the total rent had been paid, the full amount (£160) should nevertheless be shown in the Profit and Loss Account, since that is the amount that *ought* to have been paid. The following entries in the Rent Account show how that difficulty is overcome:

EX. 17/1

RENT

19·2		£	19·2		£
Jan./Dec. Cash		120	Dec. 31 Transferred to Profit and		
Dec. 31 Balance	c/d	40	Loss Account		160
		160			160
			19·3		
			Jan. 1 Balance, being rent due	b/d	40

SUGGESTED ORDER OF ENTRIES IN THE RENT ACCOUNT

1 Cash

2 Ask the question: 'How much rent should I have paid for the whole year?' The answer, £160 (*not* £120) is the amount that must appear on the debit side of the Profit and Loss Account; credit Rent Account with £160 (because this is the amount that the landlord *ought* to have been paid)* and debit Profit and Loss Account.

3 Rule off the account and carry the balance down to the credit side to show that I owe the landlord, my creditor, £40.

The above adjustment achieves two purposes:

(a) The debt to my landlord, £40, is clearly shown as a credit balance in the Rent Account—a liability.

---

*More precisely stated: This is the value of the service *given* to me by my landlord; hence the credit entry.

(b) The true amount of the annual rent which *ought* to have been paid is shown in the Rent Account and transferred to the Profit and Loss Account; an adjustment which will help to bring out a true profit or loss for the year.

Payments in Advance; or Prepayments

Suppose that on 1st January, I pay £1,000 in advance for two years' advertising, and it is agreed that this amount is divided equally between years 19·2 and 19·3. The £1,000 is posted from the credit side of the Cash Book to the debit side of the Advertising Account. On 31st December, 19·2, I ask myself: 'How much of this £1,000 relates to this year?' The answer is £500. Therefore, £500 *not* £1,000, is transferred to the Profit and Loss Account. The Advertising Account then appears as follows:

EX. 17/2

ADVERTISING

19·2			£	19·2			£
Jan.	1	Cash (1)	1,000	Dec.	31	Profit and Loss Account (2)	500
					31	Balance, being payment in advance (3) c/d	500
			1,000				1,000
19·3							
Jan.	1	Balance (4) b/d	500				

The figures 1–4 in brackets indicate the sequence of entries.

This account shows:

(a) That the advertising agency owe me £500, they are my debtors to the extent of £500—an asset—until the payment in advance is used up in advertising in 19·3.

(b) The correct charge for advertising for one year, £500, is transferred to the Profit and Loss Account.

A rather more difficult example to illustrate Prepayments, might be Insurance. Assume on 1st April, 19·2, I take out a fire policy for my premises and its contents. Assume also that the Insurance Company's financial year runs from 1st April, 19·2 to 31st March, 19·3, although my own financial year is between 1st January and 31st December. On 1st April, I pay the Insurance Company £24, being one year's premium in advance, ie. from 1st April, 19·2 to 31st March, 19·3. When on 31st December, 19·2, the end of *my* financial year, I close the Insurance Account, I find an entry for £24 on the debit side. I ask myself: 'How much of this £24 really belongs (is actually attributable) to the year 19·2?' The answer is £18. This covers the nine months from 1st April, when the premium was paid, to 31st December, the end of my financial year. The remaining £6 is for the first three months, 1st January to 31st March of the year 19·3, paid in advance. These matters are expressed in the Insurance Account as follows:

EX. 17/3

INSURANCE

19·2			£	19·2			£
April	1	Cash (1)	24	Dec.	31	Profit and Loss Account (2)	18
					31	Balance (3) c/d	6
			24				24
19·3							
Jan.	1	Balance, being amount prepaid to 31st March (4) b/d	6				

The Insurance Account clearly shows:

(a) A prepayment to the Insurance Company, the Company owe me £6; they are my debtors to the extent of £6—an asset.

(b) The true amount of Premium, £18, representing insurance payable for nine months of my trading year, which *ought* to be transferred to the Profit and Loss Account.

How does the Insurance Account appear in the following year, 19·3?
On 1st April, 19·3, I pay my annual premium, £24, in advance as before.
On 31st December, 19·3, the end of my financial year, the Insurance Account appears as follows:

EX. 17/4

INSURANCE

19·2		£	19·2		£
April 1 Cash (1)		24	Dec. 31 Profit and Loss Account (2)		18
			31 Balance (3) c/d		6
		24			24
19·3			19·3		
Jan. 1 Balance b/d, being amount prepaid (4)		6	Dec. 31 Profit and Loss Account (6)		24
April 1 Cash (5)		24	31 Balance (9) c/d		6
	(7)	30		(8)	30
19·4					
Jan. 1 Balance b/d, being amount prepaid (10)		6			

On 31st December, 19·3, I ask myself the usual question: 'How much of the £30 appearing on the debit side of Insurance Account is actually attributable to this year?' This time the answer is £24, being premium for a full year which I transfer to the Profit and Loss Account.

Method of Presentation in the Profit and Loss Account

The above three examples, Rent, Advertising and Insurance, appear in the Profit and Loss Account as follows:

EX. 17/5

PROFIT AND LOSS ACCOUNT (EXTRACT)
YEAR ENDED 31ST DECEMBER, 19·2
DEBIT SIDE ONLY

	£	£
Rent (amount actually paid)	120	
Add amount due	40	
		160
Advertising (amount actually paid)	1,000	
Less Prepayment	500	
		500
Insurance (amount actually paid)	24	
Less Prepayment	6	
		18

In each case the amount properly attributable to year 19·2 has been shown in the second column, made up from (a) the amount actually paid, (b) plus the amount due or minus the amount prepaid.

Method of Presentation in the Balance Sheet

In the balance sheet,* the above ledger accounts with outstanding balances appear as follows:

EX. 17/6

BALANCE SHEET (EXTRACT)

AS AT 31ST DECEMBER, 19·2

Current Liabilities	£	Current Assets	£	£
Rent due (or Rent accrued)	40	Prepayments:		
		Advertising	500	
		Insurance	6	
				506

Effect of Adjustments on Profit or Loss

Adjustments, of course, affect the Profit (or Loss). If payments due and payments in advance at the end of the year were not somehow taken into consideration and corresponding adjustments made, an untrue profit (or loss) figure would be thrown up in the Profit and Loss Account. Take the above accounts again as examples and suppose that the gross profit is £5,000:

EX. 17/7

PROFIT AND LOSS ACCOUNT

(WITHOUT ADJUSTMENTS)

		£	£		£
Amounts actually paid:				Gross Profit	5,000
Rent			120		
Advertising			1,000		
Insurance			24		
Net Profit	c/d		3,856		
			5,000		5,000
				Net Profit b/d**	3,856

PROFIT AND LOSS ACCOUNT

(WITH ADJUSTMENTS)

		£	£		£
Amounts that ought to have been paid:				Gross Profit	5,000
Rent		120			
Add amount due		40			
			160		
Advertising		1,000			
Less Prepayment		500			
			500		
Insurance		24			
Less Prepayment		6			
			18		
Net Profit	c/d		4,322		
			5,000		5,000
				Net Profit b/d**	4,322

*__Reminder__   The balance sheet is made up of all the accounts in the ledger which have outstanding balances.

**__Reminder__   Net Profit is represented by a *credit* balance in the Profit and Loss Account. It is normally transferred to the credit side of Capital Account, because the profit made by the firm is due to me, John Fry, the proprietor.

Exercise 17

1 P Carter, a retailer, occupies his shop at an annual rent of £468, payable quarterly in arrear. During 19·1 he paid the rent due from him on 23rd March, 25th June and 30th September, but at 31st December had not paid the quarter's rent due. Show the rent account in P Carter's ledger, after the preparation of his Profit and Loss Account for the year.

2 The Trial Balance extracted from the books of J Cakebread at 31st December, 19·1, includes the following debit balances:

	£
Rent	750
Rates	500
Wages	36,000
Interest on Loan	100
Insurance	120

The following adjustments have to be made before the preparation of the final accounts:

	£
Rent outstanding	250
Rates paid in advance	125
Wages accrued due	500
Interest on loan unpaid	100
Insurance paid in advance	30

Show the Ledger Accounts from which the Trial Balance was prepared, give the closing entries and bring down all balances.

(RSA)

3 From the following information prepare the Electricity Account in the Ledger of L Welsh, a manufacturer:

	£
Amount due at 31st December, 19·1	64
Payments during the year 19·2:	
15th January	64
20th April	54
17th July	42
15th October	47

The bill for electricity supplied during the three months ended 31st December, 19·2, was £82 and was not paid until 19th January, 19·3.

4 At 1st January, 19·1, T Tennant owed a quarter's rent, £200, in respect of business premises that he occupied. During the next twelve months he paid £200 by cheque on each of the following dates: 14th January, 26th March, 25th June and 27th December.

(a) Prepare Tennant's Rent Account as it would appear after his Profit and Loss Account for the year ended 31st December, 19·1, had been drawn up.

(b) What entry relating to rent should appear in his Balance Sheet dated 31st December, 19·1?

5 In January, 19·1, a transport undertaking, which will be preparing its first accounts to 30th June, 19·1, started to acquire a fleet of fifteen vehicles. Each vehicle was licensed on the day it was bought and all licences expired on 31st December. From the following information prepare the Motor Licences Account and transfer the appropriate amount to the firm's Profit and Loss Account for the year ending 30th June, 19·1.

19·1
Jan.   2 Paid by cheque licences for vehicles 1 to 10 at the full annual rate of £24 each
Mar. 26 Paid by cheque licences on vehicles 11 to 14 at the part annual rate of £18 each
Sept.   1 Paid by cash licence on vehicles 15, £8

6 A retailer sub-lets the flat over his shop at an annual rental of £312, payable quarterly in arrear. During 19·1 the tenant paid the rent due from him on 25th March, 30th June and 29th September, but at 31st December he had not yet paid the quarter's rent due. Show the rent account in the retailer's ledger, as it would appear after the preparation of his Profit and Loss Account for the year.

(RSA)

7 Goodsell commenced trading on 1st January, 1970, on which date he took over a showroom suite at an annual rental of £1,700.
On 1st August, 1970, a section of the premises was sub-let at an annual rental of £300. During the year ended 31st December, 1970, at which date Goodsell ends his financial year, the following payments had been made in respect of rent:
25th March, £425; 24th June, £425; 29th September, £425
and the following amounts had been received from the sub-tenant:
2nd August, £75; 1st November, £75.
Write up separate accounts for Rent Payable and Rent Receivable and balance them at the financial year end, showing the appropriate transfers to Profit and Loss Account.

(RSA 1971)

8 A trader sub-lets part of his premises to two tenants, Hill and Dale. At December 31st, 1971, Hill owed £80 rent for the month of December and Dale had paid a month's rent, £120 for the month of January 1972 in advance.
During the following year the trader received £1,120 from Hill, representing rent for the fourteen months to January 31st, 1973, and £1,200 from Dale, representing rent for the ten months to November 30th, 1972.
The trader makes up his accounts annually at December 31st.
Show the Rent Receivable Account in the trader's ledger for the year 1972.

(RSA 1973)

9 A firm has in its ledger a combined Rent and Rates Account, which on 1st July, 19·1, read as follows:

RENT AND RATES

19·1		£	19·1		£
July	1 To Balance b/d, being rates prepaid to 30th September	40	July	1 By Balance b/d, being rent due 24th June	100

The following transactions affecting this account took place during the financial year ended 30th June, 19·2.

(a) Rent due on 24th June, 19·1, was paid by cheque on 4th July.

(b) Rent due on 29th September, 19·1, £100, was paid by cheque on the due date.

(c) Rates for the half-year 1st October, 19·1, to 31st March, 19·2, £85, were paid by cheque on 31st October, 19·1.

(d) Rent due on 25th December, 19·1, £100, was paid by cheque on 22nd December, 19·1.

(e) Rent due on 25th March, 19·2, £100, was paid by cheque on 5th April, 19·2.

(f) Rates for the half-year 1st April, 19·2, to 30th September, 19·2, £85, were paid on 1st May, 19·2.

(g) On 18th June, 19·2, the usual reminder that a quarter's rent, £100, was due and payable on 24th June was received from the landlords. This payment had not been made when the financial year ended on 30th June.

You are required to copy the heading and opening balances in the firm's Rent and Rates Account, as given above; to complete the account for the financial year ended 30th June, 19·2, to rule it off and balance it at the close of business on 30th June, 19·2.

10   TRIAL BALANCES
                                   YEAR ENDED 30TH JUNE, 1976

	Dr.	Cr.
Freehold Premises	20,000	
Machinery	2,000	
Furniture and Fixtures	500	
Motor Van	800	
Purchases and Sales	16,000	33,500
Stock 1st July, 1975	1,700	
Carriage on Sales	150	
Carriage on Purchases	130	
Discounts Allowed and Received	145	162
Returns Inwards and Outwards	220	138
Cash at Bank	1,400	
Cash in hand	150	
Rates	1,300	
Insurance	172	
Wages	10,500	
Debtors and Creditors	2,600	1,400
Drawings	6,200	
Capital		28,767
	63,967	63,967

Notes
1 Stock at close of the year was valued at £1,850
2 Rates £325 had been paid in advance
3 Wages due but unpaid amounted to £700
4 There was £15 due to British Railways
5 Insurance premium £43 prepaid

From the above information you are required to produce a Trading and Profit and Loss Account for year ended 30th June, 1976, and a Balance Sheet at that date.

11 Curran pays all his car expenses by cheques drawn on his business bank account. In the books of his business all these payments are debited to the account for motor expenses.
To cover private use of the car he treats half the expenses as private and transfers this proportion of them to his personal drawings account.

On 1st January, 19·1, he owed £16 for repairs and had paid insurance in advance £12. During 19·1 he drew cheques to the value of £193, and on 31st December, 19·1, he owed £13 for repairs and had paid insurance in advance £14.

Show the account for motor expenses in Curran's ledger for 19·1 after the accounts for the year had been closed.

(RSA II)

Chapter Eighteen

Bad Debts and Provision for Bad Debts

Bad Debts

A debtor might fail to pay the amount due from him, perhaps because he goes bankrupt, that is to say, for over a fairly long period his current liabilities exceed his current assets, or the working capital might be inadequate. Failing to pull his business through the difficult times, he has to admit to his creditors that he cannot pay them. On bankruptcy, his assets are sold up at the best price they can fetch and possibly some part of his debts might be paid from the proceeds:

EX. 18/1 On 1st June, I received an order for goods worth £80 from an old-established retailer, R Acton. The goods and the invoice for them were dispatched on 3rd June. Only three weeks later, I heard that he was unable to pay his debts and that he had been forced to close down his business. Acton's debt must now be written off as bad*:

R ACTON

19·4		£	19·4		£
June	1 Sales	80	June 28	Bad Debts	80

SALES

June	1 R Acton	80

BAD DEBTS

June 28	R Acton	80

At the end of the trading period, the Bad Debts Account is transferred to the Profit and Loss Account:

BAD DEBTS

June 28	R Acton	80	Dec. 31	Profit and Loss Account	80

PROFIT AND LOSS ACCOUNT
YEAR ENDED 31ST DECEMBER, 19·1

Bad Debts	80

The Bad Debt thus transferred to the Profit and Loss Account, reduces the profit for the year by £80. If the proceeds from the sale of Acton's assets had made it possible for him to pay his creditors, say, one quarter of their claim (in our example £20), then £60 would have been transferred to the Bad Debts Account (and subsequently to the Profit and Loss Account).

---

*The book of original entry for each of the following examples is the journal. The journal entries are all shown at the end of this chapter.

R ACTON

June	1 Sales	80	June	20 Cash	20
				28 Bad Debts	60
		80			80

Provision for Bad Debts

Chapter 17 explained that the Profit and Loss Account must show amounts that *ought* to have been paid in a particular trading period, not what had actually been paid. Thus, a true figure for profit or loss is calculated. In accordance with the same principle, at the end of a trading year, say, 31st December, 19·4, outstanding debtors who are likely to default, are shown on the debit side of the Profit and Loss Account in the guise of a *reserve* or *provision*. Thus, if I think that a total of £100 due to me now, 31st December, 19·4, will not be paid when it falls due for payment in January, 19·5, for any reason, I anticipate that loss by making a 'loss' entry in the Profit and Loss Account now; because that loss is properly attributable to this year, and it ought to reduce this year's profits, not next year's. Such anticipated bad debts are *provided for* in a Provision for Bad Debts Account, as follows:

EX. 18/2

PROVISION FOR BAD DEBTS

			£
	19·4		
	Dec. 31 Profit and Loss Account		100

PROFIT AND LOSS ACCOUNT

	£
Provisions for Bad Debts	100

Thus, to keep the matter as simple as possible, we have two accounts which are concerned with respectively 1. Debtors who have defaulted and 2. Debtors who might default, that is:

1 Bad Debts: Moneys due to me that I know for certain will not be paid;

2 Provision for Bad Debts: Moneys due to me that are *unlikely* to be paid (but they *might* be paid).

Both these items appear on the debit side of the Profit and Loss Account and they reduce the profit by corresponding amounts. But while in the case of 1. the entry represents a true loss, the entry in the case of 2. merely serves to earmark £100 of the the profits against the *possibility* of a loss; £100 from profits is put aside, or 'reserved', so that if and when default of debtors actually occur,

(a) It will already have affected the Profit in the correct trading period;

(b) The business will have provided itself with the finance to meet the anticipated loss by appropriating part of the profit of the *relevant* trading period, for that particular purpose.

Thus, a provision, as illustrated here, is also a safeguard; it helps to strengthen the financial position of the business.

Increasing the Provision for Bad Debts

The Provision for Bad Debts Account remains open in the ledger for the whole of the trading period following that on which it was made, ie. the year 1st January, 19·5 to 31st December, 19·5:

EX. 18/3

PROVISION FOR BAD DEBTS

		£
	19·4	
	Dec. 31 Profit and Loss Account	100

On 31st December, 19·5, I consider the list of my outstanding debtors and decide that the total value of likely defaulters might come to £150. Now, last year's profit was reduced by £100 and it was earmarked for just this purpose. But it has not been used; it is only a reserve; the bad debts that actually occurred in the year 19·5 were shown in the Bad Debts Account. So the £100 in the Provision for Bad Debts Account is still intact. All that needs to be done is to increase it by £50 to bring it up to the requirements of financial stability. This means taking £50 out of the profits of year 19·5, by debiting the Profit and Loss Account with that amount. The double entry is of course on the credit side of the Provision for Bad Debts Account:

PROVISION FOR BAD DEBTS

19·5			£	19·4		£
Dec. 31 Balance		c/d	150	Dec. 31 Profit and Loss Account		100
				19·5		
				Dec. 31 Profit and Loss Account		50
			150			150
				19·5		
				Dec. 31 Balance	b/d	150

This shows that a total of £150 has been set aside from profits specifically as a buffer (a 'hedge') against losses through bad debts.

Decreasing the Provision for Bad Debts

The Provision for Bad Debts Account remains open in the ledger for the whole of the trading period 1st January, 19·6 to 31st December, 19·6, showing an outstanding credit balance of £150. On 31st December, 19·6, I consider the list of my debtors and decide that the total value of likely defaulters might come to £120. Now, the account shows a provision for £150, ie., £30 in excess of my requirements for the year 19·6. The Provision for Bad Debts Account must therefore be reduced by that amount. This means paying back to profits the amount (or excess) not needed to cover the current year's anticipated bad debts. To achieve this:

EX. 18/4

1 Debit Provision for Bad Debts with £30 to reduce it to £120;

2 Credit Profit and Loss Account with £30 to adjust it to the reserve actually required for the current year.

PROVISION FOR BAD DEBTS

19·6			£	19·6		£
Dec. 31 Profit and Loss Account			30	Jan. 1 Balance	b/d	150
31 Balance		c/d	120			
			150			150
				19·6		
				Dec. 31 Balance	b/d	120

Effect on Balance Sheet

The Balance Sheet shows all the accounts in the ledger which have outstanding balances. The Provision for Bad Debts has an outstanding credit balance, but, unlike other reserves, it is *not* shown on the liabilities side, it is shown as a deduction from debtors on the assets side. The purpose is to show at a glance the *true amount* that I can expect to receive from my debtors:

BALANCE SHEET (EXTRACT)
AS AT 31ST DECEMBER, 19·6

CURRENT ASSETS	£	£
Debtors (say)	5,000	
Less Provision for Bad Debts	120	
		4,880

How is the Provision for Bad Debts Assessed?

There are various methods for arriving at a figure for the Provision for Bad Debts. Two of the most straightforward methods are:

1 Consider the outstanding debtors carefully, select the ones of long standing, who are unlikely to pay; add them up, and make a provision for the total.

2 Basing my conclusions on experience, I know that an average of 2% per year of outstanding debts are, for one reason or another, unlikely to be paid. If total debtors at the end of the trading period come to £5,000, 2% Provision on that figure would be £100.

Bad Debts Recovered

When a debtor whose account has been written off, eventually and unexpectedly pays, the Cash Book is debited and then it is the Bad Debts Account (or a Bad Debts Recovered Account) which is credited, not his personal account; the debtor's personal account was closed when it was transferred to the Bad Debts Account and there is no debit balance against which to enter the payment.

EX. 18/5   On 17th May, 19·6, I received a cheque from M Benn whose account had been written off as irrecoverable. The following entries were made to record this:

CASH BOOK

	£			£
May 17 Bad Debts (recovered) M Benn	35			

BAD DEBTS

		£			£
Dec.	R Acton	80	May 17 Cash—M Benn		35
			Dec. 31 Profit and Loss Account		45
		80			80

Combined Provision for Bad Debts and Bad Debts Account

It is possible to show in the same account, the bad debts actually suffered during the year and the bad debts recovered, as well as the Provision for Bad Debts that is to be made at the end of the year.

EX. 18/6   On 1st January, 19·6, the Provision for Bad Debts Account had a credit balance of £332. During the year January/December 19·6, £210 was written off on the bankruptcy of a customer, and £60 was unexpectedly received on 10th September in settlement of an account which had been written off as bad. It is considered advisable to provide £500 for bad debts on 31st December, 19·6.

The most important item here is the £500 provision which must be shown as a credit balance in the Provision for Bad Debts Account, brought down at the end of the financial year. In the Provision for Bad Debts Account below, the sequence of entries to record these matters has been numbered:

PROVISION FOR BAD DEBTS

19·6		£	19·6			£
Jan./Dec. Bad Debts (2)		210	Jan. 1	Balance (1)	b/d	332
Dec. 31 Balance (4)	c/d	500	Sept. 10	Cash (3)		60
			Dec. 31	Profit and Loss Account (8)		318
				(The difference between the		
		(6)710		two sides)		(7)710
			19·7			
			Jan. 1	Balance (5)	b/d	500

Journal Entries of the Examples given in this Chapter

				£	£
EX. 18/1	June 28	Bad Debts		80	
		R Acton			80
		Debt written off on Acton's bankruptcy			
EX. 18/2	19·4				
	Dec. 31	Profit and Loss Account		100 ·	
		Provision for Bad Debts			100
		Provision against doubtful debts			
EX. 18/3	19·5				
	Dec. 31	Profit and Loss Account		50	
		Provision for Bad Debts			50
		Increase in Provision for Bad Debts			
EX. 18/4	19·6				
	Dec. 31	Provision for Bad Debts		30	
		Profit and Loss Account			30
		Decrease in Provision for Bad Debts			
EX. 18/5	19·6				
	May 17	Cash*		35	
		Bad Debts			35
		Bad debt recovered (M Benn)			
EX. 18/6	19·6				
	Dec. 31	Provision for Bad Debts		210	
		A Customer			210
		Bad debt written off on bankruptcy			
		Profit and Loss Account		318	
		Provision for Bad Debts			318
		Amount to increase Provision to £500			

*The original entry for this is normally the Cash Book and it does not appear in the Journal. But examiners sometimes require *all* original entries to be shown in journalised form.

Exercise 18

1 (a) Two of your customers went into bankruptcy. They were:

G Scott who owed you £340; M Prince who owed you £500.

Scott's assets were insufficient to allow for any dividend to his creditors. His account was therefore written off in full. M Prince's assets yielded enough to provide for a first and final dividend of 35% per creditor. In due course you received a cheque for £175 and you closed M Prince's account

(b) Three years (or three weeks) later you received a cheque from Scott in full payment of his old debt. You are required to make suitable entries in your books to record the above.

2 On 1st January, 1971, the provision for doubtful debts stood at £350. During the year £130 was written off as bad debts. On 31st December, 1971, the total debtors stood at £8,000. Adjust the provision for bad debts to 5% of the total debtors. Prepare the relevant accounts showing the amount which should be debited to profit and loss account.

(RSA 1972)

In answering questions 3–5 below, show in each case the Provision for Bad Debts Account, the Profit and Loss Account and the Balance Sheet entries:

3 (a) 31st December, 19·1. Total debtors £10,000.

You are required to create a Provision for Bad and Doubtful Debts of 5% on sundry debtors.

(b) 31st December, 19·2. Total debtors £13,000.

Continue the Provision Account 3(a) above and increase it so that 5% on sundry debtors is maintained.

4 (a) 31st December, 19·1. Total debtors £8,000.

You are required to create a Provision for Bad and Doubtful Debts of 5% on sundry debtors.

(b) 31st December, 19·2. Total debtors £10,000.

Continue the Provision Account 4(a) above and increase it so that 5% on sundry debtors is maintained.

(c) 31st December, 19·3. Total debtors £7,000.

Continue the Provision Account 4(a) and 4(b) above and decrease it so that 5% provision on sundry debtors is maintained.

5 On 1st January, 1975, a firm's Provision for Bad Debts Account showed a balance of £300. During the year the firm's bad debts amounted to £400. At the end of the year it was decided to carry forward a provision of 5% on the firm's debtors, which amounted to £10,000.

6 On 1st July, 1972, a firm's Provision for Bad Debts Account showed a balance of £175. During the year ended 30th June, 1973, the firm's bad debts amounted to £185 and £30 had been received for a debt previously written off. At the end of the year it was decided to carry forward a provision of 5% on the firm's debtors, which amounted to £4,000.

(RSA)

7 At 31st December, 19·1, a firm's Provision for Bad Debts was £240. During the next twelve months Bad Debts amounting to £137 were incurred, and it was decided to carry forward a sum equal to 5% of the debtors, £4,000. In 19·3, there was recovered £26 which had previously been written off, and the Bad Debts written off amounted to £129. By 31st December, 19·3, the debtors had risen to £5,000 but the provision was maintained at 5% of that amount.

(a) Prepare the account for the Provision for Bad Debts for the years 19·2 and 19·3.

(b) State the total amount charged against the firm's profits for the same period.

(c) Show the entry which should be made in the firm's balance sheet for 31st December, 19·3, in respect of debtors.

(RSA)

8 Joan Peters is in business as a wholesale draper. It is her practice to maintain a bad and doubtful debts reserve equal in amount to 5% of the debts outstanding at the end of each financial year.

From the following information prepare the Bad Debts Account for the year 19·2 (including the reserve for bad and doubtful debts):

	£
Total Debtors on 31st December, 19·1	3,220
„ „ „ „ „ 19·2	4,340
Debts written off as irrecoverable:	
On 30th June A Luke	15
N Abel	120
30th Nov. B John	97
K Simon	49

On 1st November, 19·2, a first and final dividend of 10p in the £ was received in respect of the debt due from Abel (previously written off on 30th June, 19·2) and on 18th December, £20 in respect of a debt due from O Adam (written off in a previous year).

Balance the account as on 31st December 19.2, and show the amount chargeable against the Profit and Loss Account for the year.

(RSA)

9 N Thorn maintains a bad and doubtful debts provision equal in amount to 5% of the debts outstanding at the end of each financial year.

From the following information prepare the Provision for Bad and Doubtful Debts Account for the year 19·2.

	£
Total debtors on 31st December, 19·1	4,500
„ „ „ „ „ 19·2	5,360

Debts written off as irrecoverable:

	£
On 31st May, 19·2 T Tomkins	26
On 31st May, 19·2 S Carter	145
On 31st July, 19·2 P Lane	40
On 30th November, 19·2 N Lucas	57

On 1st October a first and final dividend of 15p in the £ was received in respect of the debt from P Lane written off on 31st July, 19·2. On the 17th November, 19·2, £30 was received in respect of a debt due from K Jones which had been written off in a previous year.

Balance the account as on 31st December, 19·2 and show the amount charged to the Profit and Loss Account for the year.

(RSA)

10 On 31st December, 19·1, the sales ledger of T & Co. showed the following debtors:

	£
Smith	250
Brown	128
Jones	22
Robinson	230
Williams	140

A bad debt reserve had been provided equal to 10% of the total debts outstanding. Trading continued during the year 19·2 with these and other customers except that there were no sales to Jones and Robinson; the former made no payment in respect of the amount due from him, while Robinson paid only £200 during the year.
On 31st December, 19·2:

(i)   it was found that the sales ledger debit balances, including those due from Jones and Robinson, totalled £952;

(ii) it was decided to write off as Bad Debts the amounts then due from Jones and Robinson; and

(iii) it was decided to adjust the Bad Debt Reserve to 8% of the remaining debts.

You are asked to show the entries recording the above in the appropriate ledger accounts for the financial year ended 31st December, 19·2, including the entries in the firm's Profit and Loss Account for the year.

(*RSA*)

11 Alexander Skeen, a merchant, has the following arrangements in respect of bad debts. The balance in his Sales Ledger of all debtors who fail during any trading year to discharge their indebtedness are charged to Bad Debts Account as soon as Skeen is sure that recovery is unlikely; in addition, he has as a result of experience, maintained a Provision for Bad Debts Account at 3% of the total of Sundry Debtors at the date of his Final Accounts. This Provision is varied upwards or downwards at the end of each trading year in accordance with changes in the Sundry Debtors' total.
In his Balance Sheet as at 31st December, 19·1, the gross total of his Sundry Debtors was £3,700 and the balance on his Provision for Bad Debts Account corresponded with this. During 19·2 the following events occurred on the dates named:

10th February   Skeen received from the trustee in bankruptcy of J Willcox, who owed him £54 (still standing as a debit in the Sales Ledger), a first and final dividend of 50p in the £.

8th April   On 1st January, 19·2, H Watkins owed Skeen £87. Skeen is now advised by his own solicitor that Watkins has emigrated and that there is no hope of recovering anything from him.

22nd July   During 19·1 the account of T Norie had been written off as a bad debt. Norie's solicitor now sends in a cheque for £78, being payment in full of the debt itself, £75, plus £3 as interest by way of compensation.

15th December   Preparatory to drawing up his Final Accounts for the year, Skeen writes off the following small debts: A Chivers £6, W Hartley £8, and F Bickersdyke £12.

19th December   Skeen receives from his own solicitor an account for £8·40 for Legal Charges in connexion with debt recovery during the year.

On 31st December, 19·2, the total of Sundry Debtors' balance still open in the Sales Ledger was £2,900.

You are required to write up the Bad Debts, Provision for Bad Debts, Interest and Legal Charges accounts in Skeen's ledger for the year 19·2, and to show how the relevant items would appear in his Profit and Loss Account for the year.

(*RSA*)

12 The Balance Sheet of George Smith at 31st December, 1972, was as follows:

BALANCE SHEET
AS AT 31ST DECEMBER, 1972

	£		£	£
Capital at 1st January, 1972	4,000	Fixtures and Fittings at cost	2,000	
Net Profit for the year	2,000	*Less* Depreciation	400	
Provision for doubtful debts	200			1,600
Trade creditors	1,200	Motor Vehicles at cost	3,000	
		Less Depreciation	1,000	
				2,000
		Stock		1,500
		Debtors		1,400
		Bank		900
	7,400			7,400

You are informed that no account has been taken of the following items:

(i) Rates prepaid at 31st December, 1972, £36.

(ii) Electricity due for the October–December 1972 quarter, £22.

(iii) Wages include £20 per week for the owner.

(iv) Debtors include a debt of £120 which is considered to be irrecoverable and should be written off and the provision for doubtful debts is to be 5% of the debtors at 31st December, 1972.

You are required to:

(a) prepare a statement showing the adjustment to the net profit;

(b) rewrite the balance sheet showing clearly the following totals: fixed assets; current assets; current liabilities; revised owners capital.

(*RSA 1973*)

13

TRIAL BALANCE
YEAR ENDED 31ST DECEMBER, 19·1

	£	£
Capital Account, C Green		12,874
Purchases and Sales	68,485	73,998
Wages	2,837	
Returns Inwards and Outwards	58	392
Provision for Bad Debts		100
Sundry Debtors and Creditors	4,880	8,405
Bad Debts	26	
Machinery	1,900	
Sundry Expenses	1,310	
Cash in hand	352	
Cash at Bank	3,896	
Stock at 1st January	12,025	
	95,769	95,769

From the Trial Balance (p.139) prepare a Trading and Profit and Loss Account for year ended 31st December, 19·1, and a Balance Sheet at that date. The following should be taken into consideration:

(a) Stock at 31st December was valued at £10,800.

(b) Make a provision of 5% on Sundry Debtors for Bad Debts.

(c) Carriage on Purchases due and unpaid £120.

(d) Reserve £150 as a bonus to staff.

14 The following trial balance was extracted from the books of Essex, a trader, as at 31st December, 1972:

	£	£
Capital Account		22,000
Freehold Land and Building	11,000	
Furniture and Fittings	1,200	
Purchases	63,420	
Sales		78,880
Stock in trade 1st January 1972	8,300	
Trade Debtors	8,125	
Trade Creditors		5,426
Rates and Insurance	850	
General Expenses	2,165	
Wages and Salaries	7,155	
Balance at Bank	1,966	
Drawings	2,570	
Bad Debts	465	
Provision for Doubtful Debts		175
Rents received		735
	107,216	107,216

The following matters are to be taken into account:

(a) Stock in trade 31st December, 1972, £9,420.

(b) Wages and salaries outstanding at 31st December, 1972, £247.

(c) Rates and Insurance paid in advance at 31st December, 1972, £105.

(d) Part of the building was let to a tenant who owed £85 for rent at 31st December, 1972.

(e) The provision for doubtful debts is to be increased by £70.

(f) Essex took for his own use goods costing £52.

You are required to prepare a trading and profit and loss account for the year 1972 and a balance sheet at 31st December, 1972.

(RSA adapted)

Chapter Nineteen

Depreciation of Fixed Assets

What is Depreciation?

The Oxford Dictionary defines 'To depreciate' as 'To diminish in value; to lower market price of'. The best and most universally accepted example of an asset with a 'lowering market price', is a motor car.

Wear and Tear

I buy a motor car today for, say, £1,000. How much can I sell it for in a year's time? If I have used it with care, and the mileage is not excessive, I might get £800 for it, or a little more, if I am lucky. The difference between the price I paid for it, the cost, £1,000, and its selling price, £800, represents a loss in the efficiency and appearance of the car over a period of a year due to *wear and tear*. That difference of £200 is called *depreciation*. The inescapable fact of wear and tear, and consequent diminution, or depreciation, in value, applies to most fixed assets, including machinery, furniture, fixtures and fittings, motor vans as well as motor cars.

Obsolescence

Another reason for the depreciation in the value of assets, is obsolescence. A machine might be efficient enough as far as its intended capacity is concerned; but if another and more efficient machine comes on the market, it is often good economics to dispose of the old machine and install the new one in its place. Here the rate of depreciation really depends on the market value of the old machine, which falls steeply when a more efficient machine suddenly becomes available. The greater producitivity of the new machine (producing more in a given time than the old machine) might more than make up for the loss sustained on selling the old machine before its anticipated span of life. But consider the interesting situation during a period of rapid inflation, such as that in the years 1973–1975: I buy a machine for, say, £1,000 whose life is estimated to be five years, which implies a depreciation rate of 20% per annum. After only two years, when its value had fallen by £400, a more efficient machine appears on the market; its price is £1,500; I think it would be good policy to install it in my factory if only the loss on disposal of the old machine was not too great. Its book value stands at £1,000 − £400 = £600, but due to the inflationary economic situation, I think I can probably get more than £600 for it. You might well ask who is likely to buy an old machine at such an apparently high price when there is a new one on the market? There are small firms whose productive capacity is relative to their size, these firms may possess machinery which is even older than my current one. They cannot finance (and do not see any need for financing) the purchase of the expensive, latest article at £1,500 (which two years ago would have been offered probably at around £1,200). Such a firm might be pleased to purchase my old, but still efficient machine for £800 or even perhaps more. However optimistic this might sound, it is certainly not an impossible proposition since the purchasing power of the cash received for the old machine today, has fallen considerably and is not in the least comparable with its purchasing power two years ago (always assuming a steeply inflationary period). These matters can be very complex and any further discussion on them is beyond the scope of this work; as are the accounting processes which deal with the *appreciation* of assets, such as the value of freehold land and buildings.

The above attempts to illustrate the complexities of the nature of depreciation. The most common methods for calculating depreciation are:

(a) The Straight Line or Equal Instalment method.

(b) The Diminishing (or Reducing) Balance method.

(c) The Revaluation method.

EX. 19/1

Straight Line or Equal Instalment Method

HOW IT WORKS

1 Assess the number of years of the asset's satisfactory operation.

2 Estimate its scrap value at the end of that period.

3 Deduct the scrap value from the cost.

4 Divide the remainder by the estimated number of years of its life, to arrive at the equal annual instalments that are to be deducted from the asset.

Take, for example, a piece of machinery I buy for £5,000.

1 I think it will have a useful life of five years.

2 At the end of five years, I estimate it will fetch £500.

3 I deduct this from its cost: £5,000 − £500 = £4,500.

4 I divide £4,500 by five years: $\dfrac{£4,500}{5} = £900$ per year.

Thus, I have now a formula for arriving at depreciation on the Straight Line, or Equal Instalment method:

$$\frac{\text{Cost—Scrap value}}{\text{Number years asset's life}} = \text{Depreciation per year}$$

$$\text{or} \qquad \frac{5,000 - 500}{5} = £900 \text{ per year depreciation}$$

Over a period of five years, the Ledger Accounts and the Balance Sheet appear as follows:

STRAIGHT LINE OR EQUAL INSTALMENTS METHOD

MACHINERY

19·1			£				£
Jan. 1	Cash		5,000				

DEPRECIATION

19·2					19·1				
Dec. 31	Balance	c/d	1,800		Dec. 31	Profit and Loss Account			900
					19·2				
					Dec. 31	Profit and Loss Account			900
			1,800						1,800
19·3					19·3				
Dec. 31	Balance	c/d	2,700		Jan. 1	Balance	b/d		1,800
					Dec. 31	Profit and Loss Account			900
			2,700						2,700
19·4					19·4				
Dec. 31	Balance	c/d	3,600		Jan. 1	Balance	b/d		2,700
					Dec. 31	Profit and Loss Account			900
			3,600						3,600
19·5					19·5				
Dec. 31	Balance	c/d	4,500		Jan. 1	Balance	b/d		3,600
					Dec. 31	Profit and Loss Account			900
			4,500						4,500
					19·6				
					Jan. 1	Balance	b/d		4,500

PROFIT AND LOSS ACCOUNT
FOR YEAR ENDED 31ST DECEMBER

19·1	Depreciation	900
19·2	Depreciation	900
19·3	Depreciation	900
19·4	Depreciation	900
19·5	Depreciation	900

BALANCE SHEET
AS AT 31ST DECEMBER

		£	£
19·1	Machinery	5,000	
	Less Depreciation	900	
			4,100
19·2	Machinery	5,000	
	Less Depreciation	1,800	
			3,200
19·3	Machinery	5,000	
	Less Depreciation	2,700	
			2,300
19·4	Machinery	5,000	
	Less Depreciation	3,600	
			1,400
19·5	Machinery	5,000	
	Less Depreciation	4,500	
			500

At the end of five years:

1 The Machinery Account is transferred to a Machinery Disposals Account (Dr.).

2 The Depreciation Account is transferred to Machinery Disposals Account (Cr.).

3 The proceeds from the sale of the machinery, say, £560, is posted from the Cash Book (Dr.) to Machinery Disposals Account (Cr.).

4 The difference, £60, between the estimated disposal price, £500, and the actual amount for which the machinery is sold, £560, is transferred to the Profit and Loss Account.

MACHINERY

19·1		£	19·6		£
Jan. 1 Cash		5,000	Jan. 31 Machinery Disposals		5,000

DEPRECIATION

19·6			19·6			
Jan. 31 Machinery Disposals		4,500	Jan. 1 Balance	b/d	4,500

MACHINERY DISPOSALS

19·6			19·6		
Jan. 31 Machinery		5,000	Jan. 31 Depreciation		4,500
Dec. 31 Profit and Loss Account		60	Cash		560
		5,060			5,060

PROFIT AND LOSS ACCOUNT
FOR YEAR ENDED 31ST DECEMBER, 19·6

	Machinery Disposals	60

Diminishing (or Reducing) Balance Method

On 1st January, 19·1, I bought machinery worth £10,000, paying for it by cheque. I estimated that its market value would fall by 20% per year, calculated each year on the diminishing balance of its account (not on its original cost). There are two methods for the manner in which the necessary accounts are set out, the Old Method and the More Recent method used increasingly since the Companies Act of 1948 *by most business organisations*. Both are shown in the following examples over a period of three years:

EX. 19/2

DIMINISHING BALANCE METHOD
(A) CONVENTIONAL METHOD (B) NEW METHOD

(A) CONVENTIONAL METHOD

MACHINERY

19·1			£	19·1				£
Jan.	1	Cash	10,000	Dec.	31	Depreciation		2,000
					31	Balance	c/d	8,000
			10,000					10,000
19·2				19·2				
Jan.	1	Balance b/d	8,000	Dec.	31	Depreciation		1,600
						Balance	c/d	6,400
			8,000					8,000
19·3				19·3				
Jan.	1	Balance b/d	6,400	Dec.	31	Depreciation		1,280
						Balance	c/d	5,120
			6,400					6,400
19·4								
Jan.	1	Balance b/d	5,120					

DEPRECIATION

19·1				19·1			
Dec.	31	Machinery	2,000	Dec.	31	Profit and Loss Account	2,000
19·2				19·2			
Dec.	31	Machinery	1,600	Dec.	31	Profit and Loss Account	1,600
19·3				19·3			
Dec.	31	Machinery	1,280	Dec.	31	Profit and Loss Account	1,280

PROFIT AND LOSS ACCOUNT
FOR YEAR ENDED 31ST DECEMBER

19·1	Depreciation	2,000
19·2	Depreciation	1,600
19·3	Depreciation	1,280

BALANCE SHEET
AS AT 31ST DECEMBER

		£	£
19·1	Machinery	10,000	
	Less Depreciation	2,000	
			8,000
19·2	Machinery	8,000	
	Less Depreciation	1,600	
			6,400
19·3	Machinery	6,400	
	Less Depreciation	1,280	
			5,120

(B) MORE RECENT METHOD

MACHINERY

19·1			£		£
Jan.	1	Cash	10,000		

DEPRECIATION

19·1				19·1			
Dec. 31	Balance	c/d	2,000	Dec. 31	Profit and Loss Account		2,000
19·2				19·2			
Dec. 31	Balance	c/d	3,600	Jan. 1	Balance	b/d	2,000
				Dec. 31	Profit and Loss Account		1,600
			3,600				3,600
19·3				19·3			
Dec. 31	Balance	c/d	4,880	Jan. 1	Balance	b/d	3,600
				19·3			
				Dec. 31	Profit and Loss Account		1,280
			4,880				4,880
				19·4			
				Jan. 1	Balance	b/d	4,880

PROFIT AND LOSS ACCOUNT
FOR YEAR ENDED 31ST DECEMBER

19·1	Depreciation	2,000
19·2	Depreciation	1,600
19·3	Depreciation	1,280

BALANCE SHEET
AS AT 31ST DECEMBER

		£	£
19·1	Machinery	10,000	
	Less Depreciation	2,000	
			8,000
19·2	Machinery	10,000	
	Less Depreciation	3,600	
			6,400
19·3	Machinery	10,000	
	Less Depreciation	4,880	
			5,120

The differences between the conventional and the new methods are:

Conventional

1 Depreciation is deducted direct in the asset account.

2 Depreciation Account is transferred to the Profit and Loss Account, and closed each year. No balance.

3 Balance Sheet: The *balance* of the asset at the end of each year is shown, from which the *current year's* depreciation only is deducted.

More Recent

1 Machinery Account shows cost only, until the asset is disposed of.

2 Depreciation Account shows the accumulation of past annual reserves. The balance represents the sum of the values deducted from profits each year.

3 The Balance Sheet: The *cost* of the asset is shown every year, from which the *total*, or *accumulated* depreciation is deducted.

Of these two methods the conventional method is little used nowadays, certainly never by Limited Companies, since the Companies Act 1948 disallows it. The Companies Act requires that the balance sheet should show the cost of the asset and the accumulated depreciation, in other words, the more recent method for the depreciation of the assets as illustrated above (or the Straight Line method) is required.

The Revaluation Method

This method is best suited for assets which are not used regularly. An example of such an asset is a motor vehicle which might be used for travelling longer distances in one year than in another. Again, certain specialised machinery might be used for more hours in one year than in another. Consequently, higher (or lower) rates of depreciation might be charged against profits in one year than in another. In such cases, the value of the asset in question is assessed afresh each year. Suppose that a motor vehicle bought for £1,000 in year 19·2 is depreciated by £200 at the end of that year, and that it is depreciated by £300 at the end of the year 19·3: The balance sheets for the two successive years, showing the motor vehicle account as well as the Machinery Account (example 19/2) appear as follows:

EX. 19/3

BALANCE SHEET

AS AT 31ST DECEMBER, 19·2

	Cost	Depreciation	Book value 19·2	Book value 19·1
	£	£	£	£
Fixed Assets				
Machinery	10,000	3,600	6,400	8,000
Motor Vehicle	1,000	200	800	—

BALANCE SHEET

AS AT 31ST DECEMBER, 19·3

	Cost	Depreciation	Book value 19·3	Book value 19·2
	£	£	£	£
Fixed Assets				
Machinery	10,000	4,880	5,130	6,400
Motor Vehicle	1,000	500	500	800

The Choice Between Straight Line and Diminishing Balance Method

While cases where the Revaluation Method might be used are usually obvious, there can be frequent differences of opinion as to the choice between the Straight Line and the Diminishing Balance Method. A constant rate of depreciation (Straight Line) does not take into account the considerable increase, with age of the asset, in expenses for repairs and replacement of parts. But under the Diminishing Balance Method the Provision for Depreciation becomes lighter with the passage of years, as the cost of repairs rises.

What Happens to the Amount Provided for Depreciation?

As illustrated in examples 19/1–3, Depreciation appears in the balance sheet as a deduction from its corresponding asset. As an account with a credit balance, it might have been shown on the liabilities side of the balance sheet, but it serves a much better purpose if it is set out as a deduction from assets on the right-hand side of the balance sheet where its entry can be described as multi-purpose because it then shows:

1 The amount of depreciation.

2 Its corresponding asset.

3 The book value of the asset, after deduction of depreciation.

The Provision for Depreciation decreases the profit (or increases the loss) in the Profit and Loss Account; which means that there is extra cash at bank equal to the provision. Whether or not that extra cash is earmarked for the replacement of assets depends entirely upon the policy of the firm. There is no law to compel the firm to use the accumulated provision specifically for purchasing assets.

Exercise 19

1 (a)

J ENGINEER'S LEDGER
MACHINERY ACCOUNT

19·1			£	19·1		£
Jan.	1	Balance	7,000	Dec. 31	Scrapper Co.	150
Dec.	31	Machinery Ltd.	3,000		Loss on sale	350
		Installation	150		Depreciation	650
					Balance	9,000
			10,150			10,150
19·2						
Jan.	1	Balance	9,000			

Write a short explanation of the information given by the entries in the above account.

(b) Journalise the following:

Depreciation of $12\frac{1}{2}\%$ is to be written off Machinery £1,500 and $7\frac{1}{2}\%$ off Fixtures and Fittings £500.

2 On 1st January, 19·1, a manufacturing concern purchased from AB Ltd., a machine valued at £2,000. It was decided to depreciate the machine at the rate of 10% per annum on the diminishing balance.

(a) Show the Machinery Account for the next three years, bringing down the balance on 1st January, 19·4.

(b) If the firm had depreciated the machine by 10% per annum on the *original value* (Straight Line method), what difference would this have made to the firm's profits during the three years?

3 Arthur Briggs, a sole trader, prepares his accounts annually to 31st December. He provides for depreciation at 25% per annum by the reducing balance method taking a full year's depreciation in the year of purchase.
He started on 1st January, 1970, when he purchased a motor van for £600, a further van was purchased on 1st April, 1971, for £800. The motor vehicle account is kept at cost and a provision for depreciation account is used.
You are required to show the provision for depreciation account for the years 1970, 1971 and 1972.
Calculations should be made to the nearest pound.

(*RSA I*)

4 A firm purchased a machine by cheque for £1,500 on 1st January, 19·1. Its probable working life was estimated at ten years and its probable scrap value at the end of that time as £200. It was decided to write off depreciation by equal annual instalments over the ten years. Show the Machinery Account for the two years ended 31st December, 19·2.

(*RSA I*)

5 T Brown started business on 1st January, 19·1, and on that date purchased machinery by cheque for £3,000. He decided to close his books each year at 31st December and to depreciate machinery at the rate of 10% per annum, on the fixed instalment method, assuming a scrap value of nil at the end of the life of the machines.
On 1st May, 19·2, he purchased by cheque another machine for £600.
You are required to show:

(a) The Machinery Account as it would appear in the ledger from 1st January, 19·1, to 31st December, 19·3, inclusive, and

(b) How this asset would appear in the Balance Sheet at 31st December, 19·3.

(RSA I)

6 On 1st February, 1970, a manufacturer bought a new packing machine (No. 1) at a cost of £720. Owing to the expansion of the business, this machine was found to be no longer suitable and it was sold for £500 on 31st October, 1970, and on the same day replaced by a larger machine (No. 2) which cost £1,920.
Depreciation is charged at the rate of 25% per annum on the fixed instalment method. Write up the Packing Machine Account for the year ended 31st December, 1970, making your calculations in months.

(RSA I)

7 William Williams Ltd., has Machinery and Plant written down to £250 in their books. On 1st March, 19·1, the company decided to re-equip the factory with modern plant. The following transactions took place:

19·1			£
Mar.	3	Sold old machinery for scrap. Cash	300
	3	Purchased new machinery on credit from Machinery & Plant Ltd.	7,000
	7	Of the wages paid on this date, £300 was estimated as the amount due to the company's own staff for fixing and wiring new machines	
	10	Paid Machinery & Plant Ltd., on account	3,000

Show by means of journal entries how the above would be recorded in the books of William Williams Ltd.

(RSA I)

8 A Builder had a motor van, the written down value of which, on 31st January, 19·1, was £200. On 1st February, 19·1, he bought (for cash) a further motor van for £800 and a car for £600. He decided to write off depreciation at 20% per annum on the reducing balance system. On 31st January, 19·3, he sold the car for £450 (cash).
You are asked to prepare the Motor Vehicle account as it would appear in A Builder's books for each financial year ended 31st January, 19·2, and 19·3, showing the amount written off as depreciation each year.

(RSA)

9 On 1st January, 19·1, S Savage, a motor dealer, had in stock two cars which he valued respectively at £600 and £500. On 31st March he sold the first car, which he had been depreciating at the rate of 20% per annum, for £520 cash. On 30th June he obtained for the other car a re-conditioned engine for £80, which was installed. At 30th September he purchased from BCM Garage Ltd., on credit a van for £900. At the end of the year he decided to depreciate both vehicles at the rate of 10% per annum. You are asked:

(a) To prepare Savage's Motor Vehicle Account, balancing it and bringing down the balance on 1st January, 19·2.

(b) To state in which group of assets you would place the balance obtained.

(RSA)

10 (a) A firm provides for depreciation of its machinery, at 10% per annum on the diminishing balance system. This depreciation is calculated by reference to the number of months during which the machines are in use.

On 31st December, 19·3, the machinery consisted of three items, purchased as under:

		£
On 1st January, 19·1	Cost	3,000
On 1st July, 19·2	Cost	2,400
On 1st October, 19·3	Cost	1,400

Show the entry in the firm's journal for depreciation for the year to 31st December, 19·3, and show your calculations in the narration.

(b) How does the provision for bad debts affect the net assets of a business when the provision is increased?

(c) Explain why you would make a charge for depreciation when preparing the profit and loss account of a business using machinery. How would you decide the appropriate amount to charge for a particular year?

(RSA II)

11 (a) On 1st January, 19·1 a haulage contractor purchased four motor lorries for £2,400 each. At the end of each year depreciation is provided for at the rate of 20% per annum on the Straight Line Method, this depreciation being recorded in a separate Provision Account.

One of these vehicles was sold on 1st January, 19·3 for £1,500 and on the same date a new lorry was purchased for £2,700.

Show the appropriate ledger accounts for the years 19·1, 19·2 and 19·3.

(RSA I)

(b) On 1st January, 19·1, a company purchased four machines for £2,000 each. The balance on Machine Account has been carried down at cost and the annual charge for depreciation, calculated at the rate of 10% per annum on cost, has been credited to a Provision for Depreciation Account.

On 1st January, 19·2, one of the machines was sold for £1,722 and on the same day two additional machines were purchased at a cost of £2,400 each.

On 1st January, 19·3, another of the original machines was sold for £1,625 but was not replaced.

You are required to show:

(i) The Machinery Account and the Provision for Depreciation Account as well as Assets Disposal Account for the years 19·1, 19·2 and 19·3.

(ii) How the machinery would appear in the Balance Sheet as on 31st December, 19·3.

(RSA II)

12 Immediately after the completion of his Trading Account for the financial year ended 31st December, 19·1, T Bacon's books showed the following balances:

	Dr. £	Cr. £
T Bacon's Capital Account		1,500
T Bacon's Drawing Accounts	1,310	
Plant and Machinery	906	
Fixtures and fittings	269	
Stock	558	
Trade debtors	2,138	
Trade creditors		1,644
Discount allowed	398	
Rent and rates	602	
Office salaries	2,246	
Office expenses	68	
Motor vehicles	1,858	
Heat and light	176	
Accrued expenses		130
Discounts received		706
Cash in hand	84	
Motor expenses	510	
Payments in advance	88	
Lloyds Bank Ltd.—Current Account		1,477
Trading Account		5,754
	11,211	11,211

You are required to prepare T Bacon's Profit and Loss Account for the year ended 31st December, 19·1 and his Balance Sheet as at that date.

You are to take into account:

(a) It is considered that one of the book debts amounting to £114 is bad and should be written off.

(b) Plant and machinery to be depreciated by £203 and motor vehicles by £200.

(c) Bacon wishes his Balance Sheet to show separate groupings and total figures of Fixed Assets, Current Assets and Current Liabilities and his Working Capital.

(RSA I)

13 S Skinner is in business as a sole trader and on 31st December, 19·2, the balances on his books were as shown below:

	£	£
Capital (as on 31st December, 19·1)		11,000
Drawings	1,300	
Debtors and Creditors	2,500	1,650
Cash in hand	120	
Bank Overdraft		700
Provision for Bad Debts		100
Discount Allowed and Received	290	295
Rent Received		150
Stock at 31st December, 19·1	3,400	
Purchase and Sales	25,434	35,242
Returns Inwards	202	
Wages	4,120	
Carriage Inwards	246	
Salaries	2,430	
Rates	195	
Insurance	70	
Heating	416	
Bank Charges	59	
Carriage Outwards	355	
Machinery (as on 31st December, 19·1)	5,000	
Leasehold Premises	3,000	
	49,137	49,137

Notes:

1 On 31st December, 19·2, unsold stock was valued at £3,960.
2 Machinery is to be depreciated 10%.
3 The provision for Bad Debts is to be increased by £25.
4 Skinner's tenant owed a quarter's rent, £50.

From the foregoing information you are asked to prepare S Skinner's Trading and Profit and Loss Account for the year ended 31st December, 19·2, and Balance Sheet as on that date.

From the information given in Question 13 you are asked:

(a) To state and total Skinner's current assets at 31st December, 19·2.

(b) To calculate his working capital at 31st December, 19·2.

(c) To calculate the correct net profit if it were found that the final stock, originally taken as £3,960, had been overvalued by £155.

(d) To advise Skinner as to the financial action he could take if his creditors pressed for payment early in 19·3.

(RSA)

14 The following balances were extracted from the books of A Trader, a wholesale merchant, on 31st March, 1970. You are required to draw up a Trial Balance—ascertaining his capital as you do so and from it prepare the Trading and Profit and Loss Account for the year:

	£
Drawings	950
Returns Outwards	90
Carriage Outwards	105
Debtors	2,175
Creditors	645
Motor Car	600
Cash in hand	55
Sales	23,900
Furniture, Fixtures and Fittings	1,600
Bank Overdraft	900
Wages and Salaries	4,300
Returns Inwards	104
Commission Paid	910
Commission Received	103
Motor Car Expenses	120
Stock at 1st April, 1969	2,250
Purchases	17,050
Bank Interest and Charges	57
Rent, Rates and Insurance	570
General Expenses	714
Bad Debts	91
Discount Allowed	70
Discount Received	330

In preparing the Trading and Profit and Loss Account take note of the following:

(i) The stock was valued at £3,535 on 31st March, 1970.

(ii) Wages and salaries should be apportioned as to one-quarter to Trading Account and three-quarters to Profit and Loss Account.

(iii) Rent, rates and insurance should be apportioned as to two-thirds to the Trading Account and one-third to the Profit and Loss Account.

(iv) The Furniture, Fixtures and Fittings are to be depreciated by 20%.

You are not required to produce a Balance Sheet.

15 A Bull is in business as a commodity market broker. At 31st December, 19·1, the following Trial Balance was extracted from his books:

	£	£
Capital: 1st January, 19·1		16,450
Drawings	3,600	
Commission earned		14,384
Staff Salaries	4,430	
Rent and Rates	1,800	
Postages and Cables	931	
Telephone	342	
Lighting and Heating	182	
Insurance	120	
Travelling and Entertaining	523	
Furniture and Fittings	840	
Office machinery	1,650	
Debtors	3,472	
Creditors		2,583
Interest received		450
General expenses	126	
Cash in hand	23	
Balances at bank:		
Deposit account	10,000	
Current account	5,828	
	33,867	33,867

You are required to prepare a Profit and Loss Account for the year ended 31st December, 19·1, and a Balance Sheet as at that date, taking the following into consideration:

(a) Furniture and Fittings and Office Machinery are to be depreciated by 10%.

(b) Insurance paid in advance, £40.

(c) Provision is to be made for a staff bonus of £500.

(d) Rates prepaid, £75.

Note A Trading Account is NOT required.

16 (a) The following trial balance was extracted from the books of John Norwich, a trader, at 31st December, 19·3:

	£	£
Capital account		20,461
Freehold land and building	13,000	
Furniture and fittings	840	
Motor Van (cost 1st January, 19·1: £950)	650	
Purchases	47,619	
Sales		69,778
Bad debts	430	
Rent and rates	1,201	
Wages and salaries	10,042	
Van expenses	942	
General expenses	1,041	
Rent received		540
Drawings	3,618	
Stock in trade 1st January, 19·3	5,089	
Trade debtors	8,462	
Trade creditors		7,012
Provision for doubtful debts 1st January, 19·3		280
Balance at bank	5,137	
	98,071	98,071

The following matters are to be taken into account:

(i) Stock in trade 31st December, 19·3, £5,871.

(ii) Wages and salaries accrued 31st December, 19·3, £208.

(iii) The provision for doubtful debts is to be increased by £59.

(iv) Rates paid in advance 31st December, 19·3, £52.

(v) Provide for depreciation on the motor van on the basis that it will be in service for four years from the date of purchase and will then be traded in for £350.

(vi) Part of the building was let to a tenant who owed £160 for rent due at 31st December, 19·3.

(vii) Van expenses include the cost of unused spare parts amounting to £89.

Required:

Norwich's trading and profit and loss account for 19·3 and a balance sheet at 31st December, 19·3.

(b) 'If you charge depreciation when trade is bad it only makes profits look even worse than they are, so it is better to postpone the charge until things improve.' Explain why you agree or disagree with this statement.

(RSA II)

Chapter Twenty

Departmental Accounts

So far it has been assumed that a firm deals only in one uniform article, or that it has one department; but if, for example, my factory produced two (or more) articles (or if I had two departments in my shop) A and B, how could I be sure that each one of them was profitable, if they were not classified in the books of account?

The Purchases and Sales Books

As many columns as there are articles or departments are introduced in the Purchases and Sales Books, with an extra column in which every item is shown. The following illustrates such an analysis:

EX. 20/1

PURCHASES BOOK

		Fol.	Totals £	A £	B £
Sept. 10	Orm Supplies Ltd.		800	800	
16	Mark Bros. Ltd.		750		750
20	Athos and Aramis		750	450	300
			2,300	1,250	1,050

SALES BOOK

		Fol.	Totals £	A £	B £
Sept. 4	Peters		350		350
9	Mathers		490		490
12	Amos		570	570	
21	Bright		1,300	900	400
28	Crease		500		500
			3,210	1,470	1,740

The Purchases and Sales Accounts

These entries are posted in the usual way to the ledger, crediting suppliers and debiting customers' accounts (which are not affected by the analysis). The totals of the Purchases and Sales Books are posted to similarly ruled Purchases and Sales Accounts in the ledger.

EX. 20/2

PURCHASES ACCOUNT

	Totals £	A £	B £				Totals £	A £	B £
Sept. 30 Goods	2,300	1,250	1,050	Sept. 30 Trading Account	T		2,300	1,250	1,050

SALES ACCOUNT

		Totals £	A £	B £			Totals £	A £	B £
Sept. 30 Trading Account	T	3,210	1,470	1,740	Sept. 30 Goods		3,210	1,470	1,740

The Trading Account

At the end of the trading period, the Purchases and Sales Accounts (and a similarly ruled Stock Account) are transferred to a three-column Trading Account.

EX. 20/3

TRADING ACCOUNT

FOR MONTH ENDED 30TH SEPTEMBER, 19·1

	Totals	A	B			Totals	A	B
	£	£	£			£	£	£
Purchases	2,300	1,250	1,050	Sales		3,210	1,470	1,740
Gross Profit	910	220	690					
	3,210	1,470	1,740			3,210	1,470	1,740

Thus, the Gross Profit for A and B separately (as well as in total) can be seen at a glance, and their respective merits may be assessed without difficulty. What, for example, is the percentage of profit on turnover (i) for A; (ii) for B?

$$\text{A:} \quad \frac{220 \times 100}{1,470} = 15\% \text{ (approx.)}$$

$$\text{B:} \quad \frac{690 \times 100}{1,740} = 40\% \text{ (approx.)}$$

The Profit and Loss Account

The second section of the Trading and Profit and Loss Account is not usually analysed. If it is not, then the above first section continues as follows:

EX. 20/4

PROFIT AND LOSS ACCOUNT

	£			£	£
General Expenses	750	Gross Profit A: b/d		220	
Net Profit	160	B:		690	
					910
	910				910

When required to analyse the Profit and Loss Account, then the columns in the Trading Account are continued into the Profit and Loss Account and suitable apportionment of the expense items are allotted to A and B respectively. If A and B represent departments in a shop, the proportions of expense allotted to each department might be based upon the extent of the floor area occupied by each. Suppose that it was decided to allot expenses in the following proportions: A 1/3; B 2/3. Then the Profit and Loss Account, analysed precisely as the Trading Account, continues as follows and the profits (or losses) are transferred to Capital Account:

EX. 20/5

PROFIT AND LOSS ACCOUNT

	Totals	A	B			Totals	A	B
	£	£	£			£	£	£
General Expenses	750	250	500	Gross Profit	b/d	910	220	690
Net Profit transferred				Net Loss transferred				
to Capital	190		190	to Capital		30	30	
	940	250	690			940	250	690

CAPITAL ACCOUNT

Balance	b/d		x
Net Profit	B:	190	
Less Net Loss	A:	30	
			160

If, however, the business is not departmental and it is concerned with the manufacture of, say, two mutually exclusive articles, A and B, then the indirect expenses (the expenses other than raw materials and production-wages), such as Rent and Rates, Heating and Lighting, can only be arbitrarily apportioned to the two articles; perhaps according to the proportion of turnover per article relative to total turnover.

EX. 20/6   The following are the balances as on 30th June, 19·2, appearing in the ledger of A Wholesaler who has two departments, A and B:

	£	A £	B £
Stocks 1st July, 19·1		6,000	8,000
Sales		11,360	12,630
Purchases		10,080	1,450
Stocks 30th June, 19·2		6,100	6,650
Wages	1,500		
Advertising	150		
Carriage on Sales	30		
Packing Materials	60		
General Expenses	30		

Required, in vertical form, the Trading and Profit and Loss Account of A Wholesaler. The expenditure is to be apportioned as to A 1/3; B 2/3.

DEPARTMENTAL ACCOUNT, VERTICAL FORM
TRADING AND PROFIT AND LOSS ACCOUNT
FOR YEAR ENDED 30TH JUNE, 19·2

	Totals £	Dept. A £	Dept. B £
Sales	23,990	11,360	12,630
Stocks 1st July, 19·1	14,000	6,000	8,000
Purchases	11,530	10,080	1,450
	25,530	16,080	9,450
Less Stocks 30th June, 19·2	12,750	6,100	6,650
Cost of Sales	12,780	9,980	2,800
Gross Profit (being excess of Sales over Cost of Sales)	11,210	1,380	9,830
Wages	1,500	500	1,000
Advertising	150	50	100
Carriage	30	10	20
Packing Materials	60	20	40
Stationery	30	10	20
	1,770	590	1,180
Net Profit transferred to Capital	9,440	790	8,650

If One of the Articles is Being Produced at a Loss (or at too Small a Profit), Should its Production be Stopped?

The advisability of keeping a non profit making article in production or a low-profit department open, might be in question.

Suppose the same raw materials are used in the manufacture of A and B. This enables the manufacturer to buy the raw materials in larger quantities than if he confined production only to one article. Such a policy achieves economies of large scale production by:

1 Enabling the manufacturer to purchase raw materials in maximum quantities at lowest prices.

2 Keeping machinery in operation during all the working hours, none remaining idle.

3 Making maximum use of the space available in the factory.

If B is being produced at a profit and A at a small loss, I, the manufacturer, have to ask myself: 'Should I stop manufacturing A? What would be the consequence if I did?' If I confined production to B, I would have to buy raw materials in smaller quantities, at higher cost; I would have to dispose of some of my machinery and probably make a loss on the original capital expended upon them. The effect on B would be a rise in its price, followed, of course, by a fall in demand, resulting in lower sales and smaller profits. I would have to ask myself: 'Which is the greater loss; the loss from A, which must be deducted from B's profit, to arrive at net gain, or the fall in profit of B, on stopping production of A?'

If a Department's Profits are Unsatisfactory, Should it be Closed?

Suppose there are two departments in my shop: Cotton Goods and Woollen Goods. Although Cottons are very profitable, local demand is limited and sales are unlikely to increase. Demand for Woollens, on the other hand, has fallen and profits are low and unsatisfactory. The basic situation is that the whole of the space available in the premises ought to be used because irrespective of the sort of arrangements made within them, expenses such as Rent and Rates, Heating and Lighting, must be paid for the whole of the premises. The space occupied by Woollens must sustain a part of such expenses, proportional to the area occupied. If, then, Woollens are discontinued:

(a) even the small profit it yields is forfeited;

(b) customers who come into the shop to purchase Woollens, and incidentally are attracted to and purchase Cottons as well, would no longer visit the shop;

(c) the general prestige of the shop diminishes.

In the circumstances, the best course is not to close down Woollens but either:

(a) to continue as before or

(b) to diversify,

eg., introduce Nylons in a part of the Woollens Department or, much more drastic, change the character of the department completely and offer, perhaps, stationery (if there is not already a stationery shop in the area). Thus the capital equipment (Premises, Furniture and Fixtures) are fully employed; and the expense items described above, fully justified.

This departmental accounting, this breaking down of total figures, is one of the simplest, yet among the most important devices for planning the organisation of a business so that its various aspects are made to help each other, and yet to help themselves in the process. A careful breaking down of accounts is intended to quickly suggest possible areas of the business which might be hindering its overall efficiency. At the same time it brings out the relative profitability of one aspect of the business to that of other aspects.

Many of the expenses in the Profit and Loss Account cannot be controlled to fit the volume of production because they are fixed by outside agencies: Rent is fixed by the landlord and the firm has agreed to pay it; local authorities fix the Rates and they are payable irrespective of profit or loss; Heat and Light are services which are essential throughout the firm. These and other items in the second section of the Trading and Profit and Loss Account, such as salaries, which are fixed and are payable irrespective of production and profit, are beyond the control of production managers or managers of departments. On the other hand, the volume of goods to be produced, the quantity and value of stocks to be kept in hand, are to a large extent within the powers of managers.

Exercise 20

1 S Menswear & Co., are outfitters. They take stock and close their books on 31st December. The business is divided into two departments; Department A which sells suits, and Department B which sells overcoats. At stocktaking on 31st December, 19·1, there are 250 suits which cost £15 each and 160 overcoats which cost £10 each. When these articles are valued it is found that the market value of the suits has declined to 10% below cost and the market value of the overcoats has risen to $7\frac{1}{2}\%$ above cost.

Taking these facts into account and using the following balances, prepare S Menswear & Co's. Trading Account for 31st December, 19·1:

	Dept. A £	Dept. B £
Stocks (1st January, 19·1)	750	600
Net purchases for the year	3,000	3,500
Net sales for the year	5,550	6,000

2 NF Metal Merchants Ltd's business is divided into four departments: copper, tin, lead and zinc. On 31st March, 19·1, the following balances were extracted from the books.

	Copper £	*Tin* £	*Lead* £	*Zinc* £
Stock 1st January, 19·1	11,500	9,000	7,000	4,000
Purchases	230,000	18,000	35,000	48,000
Sales	221,350	22,750	39,050	45,100
Warehousing charges	475	25	250	300
Stock 31st March, 19·1	23,000	4,500	3,500	8,000

Prepare, on the columnar system, the Trading Account for the quarter ended 31st March, 19·1.

3 You are employed by John Briggs, a wholesaler in electrical appliances. The principle sales lines are televisions, radios and refrigerators.

Trade discount is allowed on televisions and refrigerators of 20%; radios 15%; and on other electrical goods 10%.

Credit sales, at catalogue prices for the 2nd and 3rd of October, 19·1, were as follows:

Oct. 2 J Rolfe   6 radios at £30 each
           R Forber 2 televisions at £240 each
                      4 refrigerators at £72·50 each
                      6 radios at £36 each
Oct. 3 D Miller 12 refrigerators at £80 each
                     6 electric fans at £15 each
           K Shaw   4 televisions at £95 each
                     2 electric fires at £20 each

You are required to:

(a) Write up a suitably analysed sales day book for 2nd and 3rd October.

(b) State which nominal ledger posting should be made from the sales day book.

(*RSA 1973*)

4 K Smith is a wholesaler and on 31st December, 19·1, his sales ledger showed the following amounts due to him:

A Wills, £40; H Bottomley, £180; R Law, £70; V Benn, £256.

(a) The entries in his sales day book for the month of January, 19·2, are as follows:

SALES DAY BOOK

			Total	Sweets	Tobacco	Cigarettes	Other items
19·2			£	£	£	£	£
Jan.	10	A Wills	60	18	15	27	
	14	R Law	93			93	
		V Benn	435	276		150	Carriage 9
	21	H Bottomley	48			48	
	28	L Lister	306	39	117	150	
	31	A Wills	105	99			Carriage 6
			1,047	432	132	468	15

(b) During the month of January, 19·2, the following further transactions occurred:

Jan. 6 V Benn returned goods valued £15
      8 Cheques were received from A Wills and R Law in settlement of the amounts due from them less 5% cash discount
    18 H Bottomley paid the amount due from him less 2½% discount
    28 L Lister sent a cheque for £85

You are asked to make the necessary postings from the sales day book to the ledger, and to carry down the balances in the personal accounts on 31st January, 19·2.

5 T Ironmonger services and repairs cars. He also sells used cars. On 31st December, 1975, he extracted the following Trial Balance from his books:

	Dr. £	Cr. £
Capital		10,500
Drawings	4,000	
Purchases parts and materials for repairs	720	
Cars	7,000	
Sales		14,925
Receipts from repairs and servicing		6,500
Stocks (1st January, 1975) parts and materials for repairs	300	
Cars	6,000	
Wages		
Car mechanics	2,300	
Shop assistant	800	
Tools (1st January, 1975)	1,310	
Power, Light and Heat	400	
Rent, Rates and Insurance	2,200	
Debtors and Creditors	5,000	2,413
Furniture and Fixtures	1,280	
Cash in hand and balance at bank	3,028	
	34,338	34,338

Prepare Ironmonger's Trading Account (in column form) and his Profit and Loss Account for the year ended 31st December, 1975, and a Balance Sheet as at that date. The following matters are to be brought into account:

On 31st December

(i) Stocks of parts and materials for repairs valued at £200, and stocks of cars at cost £8,000.

(ii) Tools at cost £300.

(iii) Furniture and Fixtures to be depreciated by £75.

(iv) Accrued: Rates £110; Power, Light and Heat £70.

(v) Prepaid insurance £60.

Notes:

1 Power, Light and Heat, Rent and Rates and Insurance are to be allocated equally to workshop, and to the showroom-and-offices respectively.

2 Prepare the Trading Account in column form to show the gross profit or loss on repairs and car sales and the total gross profit or loss.

Chapter Twenty One

Accounting Conventions, Concepts and Assumptions

The Business as a Going Concern

When the accounts of a firm are being prepared, it must be assumed that it will continue as a going concern indefinitely. Given this assumption, then the assets are shown at cost, less estimated depreciation. As we have already stated (Chapter 19), the cost of an asset, less estimated depreciation, is not necessarily also its current market price. If, when preparing the accounts, the accountant knows that the business is about to close down, then he would attempt to assess the saleable value of the assets, which would most probably be quite different from that of cost-less-depreciation book value.

Conventions and Conservatism

When an accountant is setting out his figures in a particular manner, he is attempting to convey to others how a particular account, or the business as a whole, stands at a given moment in time. To achieve this, he must adhere to the conventions of accounting. It is no use expressing the debt of a customer or the final accounts of the firm in any other way but that in which all other accountants understand them at a glance. The methods we have been studying have developed to their present-day state of efficiency over the centuries, during which the earlier attempts have been modified, sharpened and altered again and again; and the process is still going on. It is essential that the conventional (and apparently conservative or unchanging) principles and processes should be strictly adhered to, otherwise the information I, as an accountant, am trying to convey, will not be readily understood by every other accountant.

Objectivity

Not only must I adhere to the principles (or *concepts*) and conventions of accounting, but the accounting information must be truthfully recorded; it must not be biased. In other words, the information must be expressed *objectively* and this is best achieved by keeping to the accepted rules of accounting. For example, accountants accept that the best way to show the value of an asset is at cost price, and this is the value that they normally show. It would be confusing and open to much wasteful discussion, if some accountants showed cost price and others showed what they thought might be the current market value and others again, recorded what they thought the asset was worth to their particular business during a given period. Thus, concepts or principles can be based on objective (outward-looking) not subjective (prejudiced) argument. Objectivity in Accounting is of the utmost importance; it is achieved by the rules, or concepts, governing the manner in which business activities or transactions are recorded.

Money Measurement Concept

The very objectivity of conventional accounting described above, has, however, a limitation which is inherent within itself; the inescapable fact that values must be shown in money terms. Accounting cannot show whether the business is being conducted at maximum efficiency, nor can it show the friction that might exist between management and labour (causing serious loss in production). Nor, again, can it show the state of competition as between the products of the firm and similar goods on the market manufactured by others. It cannot show impending rises in wages and salaries which could seriously affect cost and profit.

The Instability of the Purchasing Power of Money

One of the most serious disadvantages of the Money Measurement Concept is that the purchasing power of money fluctuates, sometimes very seriously. Sometimes its purchasing power rises; but this happens for relatively short periods. The long-term tendency is for it to fall, and this has been demonstrated to us all very forcibly in recent years. If we assume that twenty-five years ago the purchasing power of the £ was 100p, its value now is less than 30p. Since that time, prices have risen (purchasing power of money has been falling), sometimes very steeply as in the years 1973–75. If a piece of machinery I purchased five years ago cost £1,000, today the same sort of machine would cost considerably more. Indeed, as an extreme example, if my machine is in a fair condition, I might manage to sell it today for £1,000 (at original cost) because a new, identical machine might cost £1,800.

Again, the price of property has risen at an unprecedented rate. Suppose my freehold premises, purchased six years ago, stand in my books at £10,000. If I bought an adjoining building of identical size and age for £20,000, the Buildings Account would show a balance of £30,000, when in fact it ought to show £40,000, since the market price of my original building seems to be £20,000, not £10,000. The figure of £30,000 is only historically true.

Materiality

This describes the relative value placed upon various goods used or services received by the firm. As a simple illustration of this concept, take the Petty Cash Book which is analysed by columns, each representing a specific expense, such as Postage and Telegrams, Travelling and Fares, Stationery, Cleaners. You will notice that each one of these is a regular expense and therefore recording it in its own right is justified. There is also a column for 'Sundry Expenses' which is intended for the odd items not worth recording in their own right, as their individual values are too insignificant (or their incidence too infrequent); that is, their individual values are not *material* (meaning 'not substantial or important'). But the idea of materiality—what is worth recording and what is not, varies according to the financial standard of the firm or the individual.

Some machinery worth £1,000 would represent a valuable asset to a small firm and would certainly have its own particular account in the ledger. In big business, however, it would be an insignificant value and the value of such a machine would probably be lumped together with other machinery of similar value. In such a business the value of an item which would justify an account of its own, might be £10,000 and in a yet bigger concern it might rise to £100,000. There is no law which lays down rules as to what is or is not 'material'; it is a matter for individual decision.

Consistency

Much of the fore-going in this Chapter points to one common rule: that of consistency. In all aspects of accounting the same methods should be followed year after year so that:

1 useful and valid comparisons might be made between the results of one period of trading with another;

2 any accountant is able to understand the meaning of the figures presented to him. Changes and modifications are of course introduced from time to time and this is desirable if they indicate greater efficiency in the presentation of accounts. But when such alterations in processes of accounting are made, then notes should be provided clearly indicating the nature of the changes so that the necessary allowances and adjustments may be made by interested persons.

Chapter Twenty Two

Divisions of the Ledger and Control Accounts

So far, our dealings have been with very small businesses where all the accounts might be kept in a single ledger by an experienced clerk. When, however, the firm expands and the number of accounts increase, it becomes necessary to split the ledger into a number of sections, each represented by a separate *volume* and the work might then be divided between as many clerks as there are volumes or ledgers. There are three main classes of accounts:

Real Accounts

describe the accounts of the firm's fixed assets, such as Freehold Premises and Machinery.

Nominal Accounts

describe the Revenue Accounts of the business, that is, the accounts appearing in the Trading and Profit and Loss Account.
Real and Nominal Accounts are called *Impersonal Accounts.*

Personal Accounts

describe the accounts of the customers and suppliers of the firm, as well as the personal account of the proprietor, that is the Capital Account.

This classification implies a separation of the accounts into a number of ledgers, consisting of:

General Ledger (or Impersonal Ledger)

contains the Real Accounts and Nominal Accounts.

Personal Ledgers

consist of the Sales Ledger, with all the customers' accounts (Debtors); Purchases (or Bought) Ledger, containing all the suppliers' accounts (Creditors).

Private Ledger

containing such accounts as Capital, the Trading and Profit and Loss Account, Investment Accounts.

Divisions of the Sales and Purchases Ledgers

It should not be difficult to see that the increasing numbers of customers (and suppliers) accounts in a thriving business would soon necessitate an additional ledger for the personal accounts. In practice, therefore, two separate ledgers are kept, the Purchases (or Bought) Ledger and the Sales Ledger; and when the business justifies it, two clerks might be employed for the jobs, called the Sales Ledger Clerk and Bought Ledger Clerk respectively. Yet additional divisions of the personal ledgers might be necessary as customers (and suppliers) increase. For example, one Sales Ledger might contain Town Customers and another Country Customers. Alternatively, the customers might be divided between alphabetically classified Sales Ledgers: A–D, E–K, L–R, S–Z.

Analysis of the Books of Original Entry to Correspond with the Classification of the Ledgers

The Sales Book (as well as the Purchases Book) and the Cash Book, must have as many columns as there are ledgers. For example:

EX. 22/1

SALES BOOK

Date	Details	Fol.	£ A—D	£ E—K	£ L—R	£ S—Z	£ Total

Postings from each column are made to a corresponding Sales Ledger, eg., a Sales Ledger for customers A–D, another one for customers E–K, and so on.

Control Accounts

The problem now arises as to the best method of checking the figures of each clerk responsible for a ledger. To keep the matter as simple as possible, suppose I have only one Sales and one Purchase Ledger, kept respectively by a Sales Ledger Clerk and Bought Ledger Clerk. The Chief Clerk or the Secretary would keep two *Control Accounts* called respectively Sales Ledger Control Account (or Total Debtors Account), and Purchases (or Bought) Ledger Control Account (or Total Creditors Account).

Sales Ledger Control Account (or Total Debtors Account)

The items in this account consist of monthly totals taken from the books of original entry, that is:

1 The Sales Book provides the total credit sales for the month.

2 Returns Inwards Book provides total value of returned goods.

3 The Cash Book provides total money received from, and cash discount allowed to customers.

When these figures are set out in a Sales Ledger Control Account, *on the same sides as they would appear in customers' accounts*, the difference, or balance brought down (to the debit side of the Control Account) represents the total outstanding debtors. That figure should be equal to the sum of the outstanding balances of all the customers' accounts in the Sales Ledger.

EX. 22/2   Suppose I have three customers in my Sales Ledger, Arthur, Bernard and Charles. Their Accounts appear as follows:

SALES LEDGER

ARTHUR

			£					£
Feb.	1 Balance	b/d	100	Feb.	12 Cash			100
	16 Sales		90		28 Balance	c/d		220
	21 ,,		130					
			320					320
Mar.	1	b/d	220					

BERNARD

			£					£
Feb.	1 Balance	b/d	400	Feb.	14 Returns Inwards			30
	3 Sales		280		18 Cash			390
					Discount			10
					28 Balance	b/d		250
			680					680
Mar.	1 Balance	b/d	250					

CHARLES

			£					£
Feb.	1 Balance	b/d	320	Feb.	15 Cash			312
	20 Sales		610		Discount			8
					28 Returns Inwards			25
					28 Balance	c/d		585
			930					930
Mar.	1 Balance	b/d	585					

The problem is how to check these figures entered by the Sales Ledger Clerk without actually going over every single entry. It is solved by opening a Sales Ledger Control Account, consisting of *totals taken from the books of original entry*. A Control Account corresponding to the above accounts appears as follows:

EX. 22/3

SALES LEDGER CONTROL ACCOUNT

			£					£
Feb.	1 Balance	b/d	820	Feb.	28 Cash	CB		802
	28 Sales	SB	1,110		Discount	CB		18
					Returns Inwards	RIB		55
					Balance			1,055
			1,930					1,930
Mar.	1 Balance	b/d	1,055					

The sum of the balances in the Sales Ledger agrees with this £1,055. It consists of:

	£
Arthur	220
Bernard	250
Charles	585
	1,055

Purchases (or Bought) Ledger Control Account (or Total Creditors Account)

Precisely the same method is used for checking the entries in the Purchases Ledger, that is, by opening a Purchases Ledger Control Account.

How Control Accounts Help Managers

Apart from acting as a means for checking the entries made by ledger clerks, and thus, incidentally, making fraudulent entries difficult to go unnoticed, Control Accounts also serve to show members of the management how the relationship between total debtors and creditors stands, very quickly. There is no need for them to have to wait for individual accounts to be balanced and extracted from the ledger before a total can be produced. This helps management to exercise a more efficient control generally. (In this context, see Chapter 14, on Quick Assets Ratio to remind you why it helps management to know the ratio between total debtors and total creditors.)

EX. 22/4

Contra Entries

Sometimes a customer is also a supplier (or vice-versa). Suppose that Charles in Example 22/3 above, is also a supplier and that his account in the Purchases Ledger stands as follows:

PURCHASES LEDGER

CHARLES

			£
	Feb. 1 Balance	b/d	130

My debt of £130 to Charles can easily be cleared by transferring his balance in the Purchases Ledger to the credit side of his account in the Sales Ledger, as follows:

PURCHASES LEDGER

CHARLES

		£			£
Feb. 28 Sales Ledger	T	130	Feb. 1 Balance	b/d	130

SALES LEDGER

CHARLES

		£			£
Feb. 1 Balance	b/d	320	Feb. 15 Cash		312
26 Sales		610	Discount		8
			28 Returns Inward		25
			28 Purchases Ledger	T	130

Corresponding entries of course appear in the Sales and Purchases Ledger (or Bought Ledger) Control Accounts. Note that transfers of this sort are like payments and, accordingly, entries appear on the side in Control Accounts where payments normally appear in personal accounts. If I had paid Charles' outstanding balance in the Purchases Ledger, his account would have been debited; if Charles had paid me £130, his account in the Sales Ledger would have been credited; hence Bought Ledger Control Account is debited and Sales Ledger Control Account credited, just as if payments had been made.

Customers' Accounts with Credit Balances

In what circumstances would a customer's account have a *credit* balance? Suppose that I sold some goods to Martin and that he settled his account promptly in order to take advantage of cash discount. He has now a clear account; no outstanding balance. Subsequently, he returns some of the goods because of defects in them, and I send him a credit note for their value. Thus, customer Martin's account in my ledger shows a credit balance.

There might be other customers with credit balances, those who were given an allowance on carriage, or returned containers after they had settled their accounts. The *total* of such credit balances appears on the credit side of the Sales Ledger Control Account.

Suppliers' Accounts with Debit Balances

There might be suppliers' accounts with debit balances for similar reasons.

EX. 22/5

On 31st May, the following *totals* were taken from the respective books of original entry, and shown in the Sales and Purchases Ledger Control Accounts:

			£
May	1	Debit balances in Sales Ledger	2,000
May	1	Credit balances in Purchases Ledger	1,500
May	31	Sales	9,400
		Purchases	7,300
May	1	Credit balances in the Sales Ledger	200
May	1	Debit balances in the Purchases Ledger	100
		Cash paid by customers	8,000
		Cash paid to suppliers	6,000
		Discounts received on credit accounts	150
		Discounts allowed to debtors	200
		Sales Returns	90
		Purchases Returns	180
		Contra Accounts	320
		Bad Debts	130
May	31	Credit balances in Sales Ledger	150
May	31	Debit balances in Purchases Ledger	90

SALES LEDGER CONTROL ACCOUNT
MONTH ENDED 31ST MAY, 19·4

		£			£
Balance	b/d	2,000	Balance	b/d	200
Sales		9,400	Cash		8,000
Balance	c/d	150*	Discounts		200
			Returns Inwards		90
			Purchases Ledger	c	320
			Bad Debts		130
			Balance	c/d	2,610
		11,550			11,550
Balance	b/d	2,610	Balance	b/d	150

---

*This figure is entered *before* the account is balanced; the debit balance £2,610 is influenced by this(*) figure.

PURCHASES LEDGER CONTROL ACCOUNT
MONTH ENDED 31ST MAY, 19·4

		£			£
Balance	b/d	100	Balance	b/d	1,500
Cash		6,000	Purchases		7,300
Discounts		150	Balances	c/d	90*
Returns Outwards		180			
Sales Ledger	c	320			
Balance	c/d	1,940			
		8,890			8,890
Balance	b/d	90	Balance	b/d	1,940

Exercise 22

1 (a) Explain what is meant by each of the following:

(i)   a real account;

(ii) a nominal account;

(iii) a current account;

(iv) a personal account.

(RSA I)

(b) Divide the following into real accounts, nominal accounts and personal accounts:

(i)   Capital;

(ii)   Wages;

(iii) R Brown, a customer;

(iv)   Sales Account;

(v)   Bank;

(vi)   Drawings;

(vii) Rates;

(viii) Smith & Co. Ltd., Suppliers.

2 After the preparation of the Trading and Profit and Loss Account for the year ended 30th June, 19·3, which showed a net profit of £3,103, the following balances appear in the books of a sole trader:

IMPERSONAL LEDGER

	£
Debit balances	
Rates	60
Stock	3,555
Land and Buildings	8,500
Fixtures and Fittings	1,125
Motor Vehicles	1,895
Credit balances:	
Rent	165
Provision for Bad Debts	105

---

*This figure is entered *before* the account is balanced; the credit balance £1,940 is influenced by this (*) figure.

PRIVATE LEDGER

Credit balance:
Capital (1st July, 19·2)   15,135
Debit balance:
Drawings   1,440

CASH BOOK

Debit balances:
Bank   924
Cash   68

SALES LEDGER

Total of Debit balances   1,978
There are no Credit balances

BOUGHT LEDGER

Total of Credit balances   1,037
There are no Debit balances

You are required:

To draw up from the above information the trader's Balance Sheet as at 30th June, 19·3, in such a way as to show, grouped together, the trader's fixed assets, current assets, and current liabilities, with the total of each group and the details of his Capital Account and showing the trader's working capital.

(RSA I)

3 A firm keeps a Sales Ledger which is checked by means of a Control Account. The following figures are available for the Control Account for the month of January, 1976:

	£
Debit balance, 1st January, 1976	9,100
Sales	11,213
Returns Inwards	298
Payments received from customers	10,180
Discounts allowed	269
Transfers of Credit balances in the Bought Ledger to the Sales Ledger	120

Required:

(a) The Control Account for January 1976.

(b) Indicate by a suitable entry in the folio column, the source from which each of the above figures is obtained.

(c) What does the balance of the Control Account represent?

4 J Corbridge keeps his sales ledger on the self-balancing principle and the following details, relating to the month of October, 19·1, are taken from his records:

	£
Balances on Sales Ledger at 1st October, 19·1 (Debit)	8,949
Balances on Sales Ledger at 1st October, 19·1 (Credit)	29
Sales during the month	5,297
Allowances to customers	152
Transfers from Sales Ledger to Debit of Purchases Ledger	78
Bad Debts written off	132
Legal charges debited to customers	45
Cash received from customers	6,107
Balance on the Proprietor's Account transferred to his Drawings Account	41
Discounts allowed to customers	229
Credit balances in ledger at 31st October, 19·1	131

Draft the Sales Ledger Total (or Control) Account as it would appear in the General Ledger.

5 C Lincoln keeps his books so that a Purchases Ledger Control Account and a Sales Ledger Control Account are shown in his General Ledger and balanced at the end of each month.

From the following details show how these accounts would appear in the General Ledger for the month of October 19·1.

19·1		£
Oct. 1	Debit balances in Sales Ledger	13,693
1	Credit balances in Sales Ledger	295
1	Debit balances in Purchases Ledger	116
1	Credit balances in Purchases Ledger	11,966
31	Sales	19,945
31	Purchases	17,046
31	Sales returns and allowances	367
31	Purchases returns and allowances	200
31	Cash received from customers	20,461
31	Cash paid to suppliers	15,318
31	Discount received	112
31	Discount allowed	359
31	Bad Debt written off	41
31	Sales Ledger Debit balance transferred to Purchases Ledger	78
31	Debit balances in Purchases Ledger	102
31	Credit balances in Sales Ledger	121

(RSA II)

6 The following information relating to the year 1971 appears in the books of Beeston Ltd.

	£
Sales Ledger balances 1st January, 1971	5,169
Purchases Ledger balances 1st January, 1971	4,121
Cash received from customers	63,248
Payment to suppliers	42,488
Sales	65,741
Purchases	44,419
Returns Inwards	1,142
Returns Outwards	586
Bad debts written off in 1971	1,322
Increase in provision for doubtful debts at 31st December, 1971	181
Received from supplier in respect of an overpayment	62
Credit balance on Sales Ledger at 31st December, 1971	124

Required: The sales ledger control account and the purchases ledger control account for 1971. Carry down the balances on the accounts at the end of 1971.

(RSA II 1972)

7 There is a difference in the balances on the books of Clover Ltd. In an attempt to locate the difference, Total Accounts for the Purchases and Sales Ledgers are prepared from the following figures:

1970		£
Jan. 1	Balances on Purchases Ledger	40,921
1	Balances on Sales Ledger	50,420
Dec. 31	Purchases during year	498,216
31	Sales during year	628,421
31	Discounts received	8,289
31	Discounts allowed	10,498
31	Purchases returns during year	825
31	Sales returns during year	1,422
31	Cash paid to suppliers	456,227
31	Cash received from customers	582,989
31	Purchases Ledger balances	73,976
31	Sales Ledger balances	83,309

Prepare the Total Accounts and state what they reveal.

(RSA II 1972)

Chapter Twenty Three

Incomplete Records and Single Entry

Single Entry Accounts

One of the important reasons for keeping accounts is to ascertain through a Trading and Profit and Loss Account the profit or loss made at the end of a year's trading. What other method besides the Double-entry system is there for the calculation of profit or loss? Consider the relationship of capital to profit or loss. A profit increases capital, a loss decreases it. If then, capital at the beginning of the trading period is less than capital at the end of it, the difference represents a profit.

EX. 23/1

	£	
If on 1st January, 19·1 Capital is	7,000	and
if on 31st December, 19·1 Capital is	7,500	
Then the profit or increase in Capital is	500	

The question now arises: if the figure for capital at the start of the year is given, how is the capital at the end of the year calculated? The answer is to be found in the definition of capital, ie., the excess of assets over liabilities. To arrive at the unknown figure of capital, list all the assets and liabilities in the form of a Statement of Affairs (to all intents and purposes, a balance sheet)*, and the excess of the assets over the liabilities is the capital.

EX. 23/2

Given on 1st January Capital £7,000. On 31st December my assets and liabilities consisted of items which I set out in a Statement of Affairs, as follows:

STATEMENT OF AFFAIRS
AS AT 31ST DECEMBER, 19·1

LIABILITIES	£	ASSETS	£
Capital (Excess of assets over liabilities)	7,500	Machinery	5,000
Creditors	500	Furniture	300
		Motor Vans	1,000
		Stock	700
		Debtors	600
		Cash at bank	400
	8,000		8,000

Thus, capital on 31st December, emerges as £7,500, and the difference between capital at the start and the close of the year is £500 as illustrated above, example 23/1.

---

*Statement of Affairs figures are *not* obtained from a proper set of accounts; Balance Sheet figures are so obtained.

Now, suppose that during the year I have drawn out for personal use £1,100. Does this increase or decrease the profit? Where did that £1,100 come from? It must have come out of profits. The true profit is therefore £500+£1,100=£1,600. This is set out formally as follows:

EX. 23/3

STATEMENT OF PROFIT

	£
Capital 31st December, 19·1	7,500
Capital 1st January, 19·1	7,000
Increase in Capital	500
Add Drawings	1,100
Profit for year	1,600

Consider the interesting result if the above figures for capital at the start and the close of the year were reversed:

EX. 23/4

STATEMENT OF PROFIT

	£
Capital 1st January, 19·1	7,500
Capital 31st December, 19·1	7,000
Decrease in Capital	500
Add Drawings	1,100
Profit for year	600

Note that when drawings are taken into consideration, the apparent loss for the year (£500) is turned into a profit (£600).

On the other hand, if additional capital had been introduced into the firm during the year, either in the form of cash or in any other form, eg., fixed assets, that must be deducted so that the figure for the profit or loss at the end of the year is not distorted. There are many small firms which do not keep a complete set of books. They usually keep a Cash Book and, perhaps, a ledger, which does not by any means contain a complete set of accounts. The proprietor of such a business can carry much of the necessary information in his head. But he cannot produce accounting details easily. However, H.M. Inspector of Taxes requires that a proper set of accounts showing profit or loss and a balance sheet must be produced at the end of each trading year. For that reason, if for no other, the trader with incomplete records employs an accountant to calculate the necessary figures.

Incomplete Records

In Chapter 7 (Stock Account) we have seen how it is possible to arrive at the value of a missing item in an account, if all the other relevant items which normally appear in it are available (example 7/12). This simple arithmetical principle can be applied in other instances besides the Trading Account.

EX. 23/5 R Crow does not keep a proper set of accounts. At the end of the financial year he calls upon me to produce a Trading and Profit and Loss Account. He says that he does not know the total value either of his purchases or sales. But I am able to ascertain the value of his total debtors and total creditors at the start of the year (end of last year), and at the end of the year, as well as the total cash received from debtors and total cash paid to creditors through the year, all of which I list as follows:

SALES		£	PURCHASES		£
Debtors 1st January	b/d	1,000	Creditors 1st January	b/d	600
Cash received from Debtors			Cash paid to Creditors		
1st January/31st December		5,000	1st January/31st December		3,500
Debtors 31st December		1,300	Creditors 31st December		900

It is now possible to calculate the sales for the year arithmetically as follows:

EX. 23/6 Calculating Credit Sales

	£
Total cash received from debtors, January/December, 19·2	5,000
Deduct the amount due from debtors at 31st December, 19·1 brought down on 1st January, 19·2. (This amount must have been paid sometime during the year 19·2. It is therefore included in the total payment of £5,000. Since we are calculating the sales for year 19·2, any figures concerned with 19·1 must be eliminated.)	1,000
Total cash received against credit sales January/December, 19·2	4,000
Add outstanding debtors at 31st December, 19·2 (representing unpaid credit sales in 19·2)	1,300
Credit sales for year 19·2	5,300

The above can be shown more neatly in the form of a Total Debtors' Account. Entries into it are made as in a single debtor's (say a customer's) account as follows. (Remember that the two sides of an account imply the subtraction of one side from the other.)

EX. 23/7

				£				£
19·1					19·1			
Jan.	1	Balance	b/d	1,000	Jan./Dec. Cash			5,000
Dec.	31	*Total Credit Sales*		5,300	Dec. 31 Balance		c/d	1,300
				6,300				6,300

TOTAL DEBTORS

Calculating Credit Purchases

An arithmetical calculation similar to example 23/6 produces the missing figure for Purchases as follows:

EX. 23/8

	£
Total cash paid to creditors January/December, 19·2	3,500
Deduct the amount due to creditors at 31st December, 19·1	600
Total cash paid against credit purchases January/December, 19·2	2,900
Add outstanding creditors at 31st December, 19·2	900
Credit purchases for year 19·2	3,800

More formally:

EX. 23/9

TOTAL CREDITORS

19·2			£	19·2			£
Jan./Dec. Cash			3,500	Jan. 1 Balance		b/d	600
Dec. 31 Balance	c/d		900	Dec. 31 *Total Credit*			3,800
			4,400				4,400

The above calculation accounts are sometimes called *Control Accounts* which have already been discussed in the previous Chapter. The above represents a very important principle.

Since an account implies subtraction of one side of it from the other, if *any* three of the four items in the above calculations are given, then the calculation of the missing fourth item is a simple matter. If, for example, we are given:

EX. 23/10

	£
Balance due to Creditors on 1st January, 19·1	600
Balance due to Creditors on 31st December, 19·1	900
Credit purchases for the year 19·1	3,800

the missing item, Total Cash Paid to Creditors, during the year, will emerge if the available figures are set out in a Total Creditors Account:

EX. 23/11

TOTAL CREDITORS

19·1			£				£
Dec. 31 Balance	c/d		900	Jan. 1 Balance		b/d	600
Jan./Dec. *Total cash paid*			3,500	Dec. 31 Purchases			3,800
			4,400				4,400

By using the same arithmetical method, it is possible to calculate *Total Cash Received* from debtors during a given period.

EX. 23/12

The following is a summary of the bank account of Copeman, a retail trader, for the year 19·3.

BANK SUMMARY

	£	19·1	£
Balance 1st January, 19·3	1,448	Payments to trade creditors	28,364
Shop takings banked	34,722	Rent and Rates	1,488
		Drawings	5,816
		Balance 31st December, 19·3	502
	36,170		36,170

You are given the following additional information:

	31st Dec., 19·2	31st Dec., 19·3
	£	£
Furniture	1,000	1,000
Stock in trade	5,260	4,380
Trade debtors	2,900	3,270
Trade creditors	3,750	3,946

During 19·3 wages amounting to £1,300 and some general expenses were paid in cash out of shop takings. All the remaining shop takings were paid into the bank and all other payments were made by cheque.

You are required to prepare a trading and profit and loss account for 19·3 and a balance sheet at 31st December, 19·3.

TRADING AND PROFIT AND LOSS ACCOUNT
YEAR ENDED 31ST DECEMBER, 19·3

	£	£			£	£
Stock 1st January		5,260	Sales			
Purchases		28,560	Credit		370	
		———	Cash		34,722	
		33,820	Cash (Wages and Expenses			
Less Stock 31st December		4,380	paid out of shop takings)		1,300	
					———	36,392
Cost of Sales		29,440				
Gross Profit		6,952				
		———				———
		36,392				36,392
		———				———
Rent and Rates		1,488	Gross Profit	b/d		6,952
Wages and Expenses		1,300				
Net Profit		4,164				
		———				———
		6,952				6,952
		———				———

BALANCE SHEET OF COPEMAN
AS AT 31ST DECEMBER, 19·3

Capital 1st January	6,858		Furniture	1,000
Add Net Profit	4,164		Stock 31st December	4,380
	———		Debtors	3,270
	11,022		Cash at bank	502
Less Drawings	5,816			
	———	5,206		
Creditors		3,946		
		———		———
		9,152		9,152
		———		———

CALCULATIONS

TOTAL CREDITORS

19·3		£	19·3			£
Jan./Dec. Cash		28,364	Jan. 1 Balance	b/d		3,750
Dec. 31 Balance	c/d	3,946	Dec. 31 Purchases			28,560
		———				———
		32,310				32,310
		———				———

TOTAL DEBTORS

Jan. 1 Balance		2,900	Dec. 31 Balance	c/d	3,270
Sales		370			
		———			———
		3,270			3,270
		———			———

STATEMENT OF AFFAIRS
AS AT 1ST JANUARY, 19·3

LIABILITIES			ASSETS	
Capital (Excess of Assets over			Furniture	1,000
Liabilities)		6,858	Stock	5,260
Creditors		3,750	Debtors	2,900
			Cash at bank	1,448
		———		———
		10,608		10,608
		———		———

Exercise 23

1 Smith's Balance Sheet at 31st December, 1970, showed the value of his assets as
£21,000, and amounts owing to creditors £9,000.

At 31st December, 1969, his assets were £15,000 and amounts owing to creditors
£8,000.

During the year 1970, Smith had introduced £2,000 as additional capital.

Calculate the amount of Smith's profit for the year 1970.

(RSA I 1971)

2 W Davis is the proprietor of a small café. His sales are strictly cash, and he banks all
takings every night. All purchases are paid for by cheque on delivery. He lives on the
premises with his family.

A statement of affairs on 1st January, 1968, showed his position to be as follows:

	£		£
Capital	4,670	Premises	3,000
		Furniture	1,000
		Stock	150
		Bank	500
		Cash	20
	4,670		4,670

A study of his Cash Book provides the following information:

	£
Takings during year ended 31st December, 1968	10,000
Purchases during year ended 31st December, 1968	7,400
Personal expenses during year ended 31st December, 1968	1,500
Light and Heat during year ended 31st December, 1968	200
Cleaning during year ended 31st December, 1968	30
Wages during year ended 31st December, 1968	500
New furniture bought during year	200
Cash in hand, 31st December, 1968	30
Bank balance, 31st December, 1968	660

You are asked to prepare a statement showing W Davis' profit or loss for the year
ended 31st December, 1968, and a Balance Sheet on that date.

The following are to be taken into consideration:

(i)   Valuation of stock on 31st December, 1968 is £150.

(ii) £100 of the Light and Heat was allocated to his private accommodation.

(RSA I)

3 On 1st January, 19·1, A Singleton decided to go into business. His only asset was a
bank balance of £1,000. For the next six months he kept no books except a cash book.
At 30th June, 19·1, his cash balance was £45 and his bank balance £215. Singleton
estimated his debtors at £640 and stock in hand at £700, and he had a van worth
£400. His creditors amounted to £950. During the half-year he had drawn £530 for
his personal expenses.

(a)   Draw up a statement showing the profit or loss Singleton had made by 30th
June, 19·1.

(b)   State two items of information, which you consider important, that Singleton
cannot ascertain from the statement you have prepared.

(RSA I)

4 H Cook maintains a store. His records are incomplete and you have been called in to prepare his accounts.

You ascertain the following:

AT 1ST JANUARY, 19·1

	£		£
Stock	2,100	Debtors	1,300
Creditors	960	Rates in advance	80
Motor vehicles	1,200	Cash at bank	900

AT 31ST DECEMBER, 19·1

	£		£
Stock	2,240	Debtors	1,040
Creditors	1,000	Rates in advance	96
Motor vehicles	1,000	Cash at bank	2,344

Drawings during the year were £1,200 and a legacy of £400 received on 1st March, 19·1, had been paid into the bank.

You are required:

(a) To draw up two statements showing:

 (i) Capital at 1st January, 19·1.

 (ii) Capital at 31st December, 19·1.

(b) To compile a statement showing the profit for the year ended 31st December, 19·1.

(*RSA I*)

5 T Newman started business on 1st January, 1968, with a balance at the bank of £4,000, of which he had borrowed £1,000 from V Trusting. Newman did not keep a complete set of records but at 31st December, 1968, a valuation showed the following assets and liabilities:

	£
Furniture and Fittings	1,200
Motor Van	900
Stock in hand	1,700
Trade debtors	540
Cash at bank	1,300
Trade creditors	1,240

The loan from Trusting was still outstanding and interest at 5% per annum was to be charged on this loan. During the year, Newman had drawn £16 per week in anticipation of profits.

From the above information draw up a statement showing the profit or loss for the year ended 31st December, 1968, and a Balance Sheet at that date.

(*RSA I*)

6 On 1st July, 1969, G Smith started business as a Building Decorator and Repairer with £3,000 in the bank. He kept no books but banked all receipts and paid all accounts by cheque. His bank statement disclosed the following information for the year ended 30th June, 1970.

	£
Receipts for work done	4,000
Cost of new motor van	1,000
Cost of materials purchased	1,750
Motor van expenses	270
Insurance	20
Cost of new equipment	1,300
Drawings for private expenses	1,000
Payments to Building Society for private house	400
Rent of yard	100

On 30th June, 1970, stock was valued at £350 and debtors amounted to £150. G Smith decided to write 20% depreciation off his motor van, and 10% off his equipment.

Prepare G Smith's profit and loss account for the year ended 30th June, 1970, and a Balance Sheet on that date.

You will find it useful to calculate his Balance in Bank on 30th June, 1970 before attempting the Balance Sheet.

(*RSA I 1970*)

7 The following are summaries of the assets and liabilities of John Smith, a retail trader, at the dates stated:

	1st Jan., 19·1 £	31st Dec., 19·1 £
Debtors	4,186	5,319
Creditors	2,918	2,184
Stock	3,750	4,100
Loan from J Green (repayable 19·7)	3,000	3,000
Cash in hand	175	125
Bank balance	1,273	
Bank overdraft		628
Plant and Machinery	4,500	5,000
Land and Buildings	15,000	15,000
Fixtures and Fittings	800	700

During the year, Smith had drawn £200 per month on account of profits.
You are required to give:

(a) A statement showing Smith's Capital at 1st January, 19·1.

(b) A statement showing the profit/loss for the year.

(c) A Balance Sheet at 31st December, 19·1, showing Capital Account in detail.

8 Brown has never kept a proper set of books. He asks you to introduce a double-entry system, and gives you the following valuations at 30th June, 1973:

	£
Motor vans	1,750
Stock	700
Debtors	300
Premises	15,000
Bank	1,350
Creditors	410
Mortgage	9,000
Insurance in advance	95
Rates unpaid	120
Loan interest unpaid	400

You are required to:

(a) set out an opening journal entry and calculate Brown's capital on 1st July, 1973;

(b) make a list of the books you would purchase to introduce a simple system.

(*RSA 1973*)

9 (a) Define Single Entry, and state briefly the disadvantages of this system.

(b) A manufacturer, Philip Morgan, kept his books on what is known as the Single Entry system. The position of the business at the 31st December, 19·1 revealed the following:

	£
Plant and machinery	1,600
Stock in trade	1,300
Sundry debtors	1,750
Cash at bank	300
Sundry creditors	1,875

At the 1st January, 19·1, his capital was £5,500.

During the year his drawings amounted to £500, and the sale of his private motor car realised £200, which he paid into the business bank account.

You are required to prepare the Statement of Affairs showing the financial position of Philip Morgan as at the 31st December, 19·1, compile his Capital Account at that date, and ascertain his profit or loss for the year.

(*RSA*)

10 C Monger, a wholesaler, does not keep proper books of account. The following information was obtained from his records on 31st December, 1970.

1st January, 1970	£
Stock	7,400
Trade debtors	6,000
Trade creditors	2,100
1st January to 31st December, 1970	
Receipts from Trade Debtors	55,530
Payments to Trade Creditors	46,320
Warehouse wages	2,000
Carriage on purchases	1,570
31st December, 1970	
Stock	8,200
Trade Debtors	5,750
Trade Creditors	2,740

From the above information you are required to:

(a) Calculate Monger's Purchases and Sales, showing your workings.

(b) Draw up his Trading Account for the year ended 31st December, 1970.

(*RSA I 1971*)

11

BALANCE SHEET

	£		£
Creditors	721	Freehold premises	1,560
Capital	3,150	Machinery and plant	420
		Stock	876
		Debtors	982
		Cash	33
	3,871		3,871

The above is a copy of Samuel Wood's Balance Sheet as on the 31st December, a year ago. The only books kept are a Cash Book and a Ledger. The following is a summary of his receipts and payments for the year ended 31st December, 19·1:

RECEIPTS	£	PAYMENTS	£
Cash on account of credit sales	4,276	Creditors for goods purchased	3,954
Cash sales	1,863	Wages	743
Capital paid in	200	General expenses	627
		Additions to machinery	160
		Drawings	536
	6,339		6,020

On 31st December, 19·1, the amount due to creditors was £816, and the debtors and stock amounted to £918 and £854 respectively. You are required to prepare Trading and Profit and Loss Accounts for the year ended 31st December, 19·1, and a Balance Sheet as on that date, after making adjustments in respect of the following:

(a) Depreciation of 10% is to be written off the machinery and plant, including additions during the year.

(b) £150 is to be provided for doubtful debts.

(c) The sum of £38 for goods supplied to the proprietor was included in the debtor's balances at 31st December, 19·1

(RSA)

12 A list of the assets and liabilities of S Small, a trader, on 31st December, 1969, is given below:

	£
Capital	7,041
Trade creditors	3,984
Trade debtors	2,048
Furniture and Fittings	2,890
Stock in trade	3,491
Creditors for general expenses	86
Cash at bank	2,682

The following figures relating to the year 1970, have been taken from his books:

	£
Receipts from customers	70,928
Payments to suppliers	59,292
Drawn from the bank for private purposes	3,000
General expenses paid	2,923
Salaries and wages paid	5,627

On 31st December, 1970, Small's books showed that trade debtors amounted to £2,242 and trade creditors amounted to £4,928. General expenses paid in advance were £40 and stock in trade was valued at £4,291.

On 31st December, 1970, goods costing £2,000 were received from suppliers. The invoice was not received until 4th January, 1971, and no entries were made in the books to record the receipt of these goods until 5th January, 1971.

Depreciation on furniture and fittings is to be charged at the rate of 10% per annum on the value at 1st January in each year.

You are required to prepare:

(a) A summary of Small's Bank Account for 1970.

(b) A Trading and Profit and Loss Account for 1970.

(c) A Balance Sheet as at 31st December, 1970.

(RSA II 1971)

13 The balance sheet of Sally, a trader, as at 31st December, 1970, was as follows:

BALANCE SHEET

	£		£
Capital	12,290	Furniture and Fittings	820
Trade creditors	6,792	Stock in trade	8,920
		Trade debtors	8,410
		Balance at bank	932
	19,082		19,082

During 1971, Sally introduced £2,710 additional capital into the business, purchased a motor van for the business for £800 paying for it with a cheque drawn on her private bank account, and withdrew goods valued at £40 (cost price) for her own use. Sally also drew £3,290 from the business bank account in 1971 for her own private use.

On 31st December, 1971, trade debtors amounted to £9,420, trade creditors amounted to £7,104, stock in trade amounted to £9,220 and the balance at the bank was £2,410.

The total expenses debited to the profit and loss account for 1971 amounted to £11,040 of which £228 was unpaid at 31st December, 1971. The figure for expenses included £160 for depreciation of the motor van and £82 for depreciation of furniture and fittings.

Sally calculated her selling prices by adding 25% to the cost price of all goods.

You are required:

(a) To calculate the net profit for 1971.

(b) To construct the trading and profit and loss account for 1971.

(*RSA II 1972*)

14 The following figures relating to the year 1969 are extracted from the books of Longford:

	£
Balance at bank 1st January, 1969	100
Cash sales	10,460
Cash paid for purchases	7,410
Creditors for purchases	
31st December, 1968	470
31st December, 1969	550
Wages paid	1,240
General expenses paid	1,120
Stock	
31st December, 1968	730
31st December, 1969	840
Capital, Longford, 1st January, 1969	980
Personal drawings, Longford	640
Plant and Furniture at cost, 1st January, 1969	620

All sales are for cash and there are no creditors at the beginning or at the end of the year, other than those for which details given above. No discounts were received. Longford lodges all his receipts at his bank and all payments are made by cheque.

You are asked to prepare:

(a) A summary of Longford's bank account for 1969.

(b) A Trial Balance as at 31st December, 1969.

(c) A Trading and Profit and Loss Account for 1969 and a Balance Sheet at 31st December, 1969.

(*RSA II*)

15 The balance sheet of Fletcher, a trader, at 31st December, 1970, was as follows:

	£		£
Capital	201	Fixed assets	200
Trade creditors	649	Stock	482
		Payment in advance	50
		Bank balance	118
	850		850

You are given the following additional details from Fletcher's books:

(i)   Sales for 1971 were £10,270; the whole amount was received in cash and paid into the bank.

(ii) Purchases Ledger Control Account for 1971:

	£		£
Cash	6,265	Balance 1st January, 1971	649
Balance 31st December, 1971	709	Purchases	6,325
	6,974		6,974

(iii) Payments made in 1971 for expenses were £583, of which £20 was paid in advance for 1972.

(iv) Stock in trade at 31st December, 1971, was £415.

(v) Fletcher drew £3,000 during 1971 for his personal expenses.

Note: All payments were made by cheque.

You are required to give:

(a) A summary of Fletcher's bank account for 1971.

(b) His trading and profit and loss account for 1971 and balance sheet at 31st December, 1971.

Ignore depreciation of fixed assets.

(Institute of Bankers 1972)

16 A Jones opened a small retail shop on 1st April, 1969. Sales were made only for cash and after certain outgoings had been paid for out of the till and a cash float of £5 retained, the remaining cash was paid into the bank weekly. Suppliers' accounts were settled by cheque. An analysis of his bank statement for the year ended 31st March, 1970 is as follows:

BANKINGS

	£
Paid in to commence business	1,000
Total of weekly lodgements	4,020
	5,020

The outgoings paid out of the till totalled £250 for the year, made up of wages £200, stationery £12, Sundry trade expenses £38. Since he kept no record of takings, Jones agreed that the preparation of the accounts can be based on the assumption that the rate of gross profit is 25% of the Selling Price of goods sold. Jones further agreed that the remainder of the estimated takings not otherwise accounted for can be taken as being personal drawings. On 31st March, 1970, the value of goods on hand on a cost basis was £300, and the stock of paper bags, etc, was valued at £5. The outstanding liabilities were:

	£
Suppliers	239
Electricity	10
Incidentals	5
Paper Bags	2
Rent and insurance	10

Depreciation at the rate of 10% per annum is to be written off fixtures and fittings.

CHEQUES DRAWN, ETC.

	£
Fixtures and Fittings	500
Purchases	3,736
Rent, Rates, Postages and Insurance	235
Electricity and Gas	23
Paper bags, etc.	18
Bank charges	5
Balance at 31st March, 1970	503
	5,020

Prepare the Trading and Profit and Loss Account for the year ended 31st March, 1970, and a Balance Sheet at that date.

Chapter Twenty Four

The Accounts of Non-Trading Organisations

The Accounts of Local Sports or Social Clubs

In the strictest sense, non-trading organisations, such as local sports or social clubs, exist entirely for the benefit of their members. That being the case, the question of profit does not arise. What is called 'profit' in the trader's Profit and Loss Account, is called 'surplus' (to be used for the benefit of members) in the club's corresponding 'Income and Expenditure' Account.

Cash Book with Analysis Columns

What in Club Accounting is slightly different from most business accounting is that a Club's Cash Book has several columns on the credit side, each one for a specific, regular payment, such as Rent and Rates, Heating and Lighting, Wages and Salaries, Sundry Expenses, Postages and Telephone, etc.

These columns are used throughout the accounting year, carrying the page totals forward to the end of the year, when the total amount spent on each item may be seen at a glance. A similar treatment is given to the debit side of the Cash Book which might, perhaps, have three columns, for example, Subscription received from members, Donations given by well-wishers and Locker Rents paid by members. These columns, too, are written up regularly and a total for each is produced at the end of the year.

The Receipts and Payments Account

These totals are then shown in a Receipts and Payments Account; a summarised version of the Cash Book. The Receipts and Payments Account gives the basic information from which the Income and Expenditure Account is computed. The following is a simple example:

EX. 24/1

RECEIPTS AND PAYMENTS ACCOUNT

OF THE MERCIA CLUB

YEAR ENDED 31ST DECEMBER, 19·1

		£			£
Balance 1st January, 19·1	b/f	100	Rates		60
Subscriptions		486	Heating and Lighting		80
Locker rents		248	Wages and Salaries		400
			Postages and Telephone		50
			Sundry Expenses		20
			Balance	c/d	224
		834			834
Balance	b/d	224			

From the above I am required to prepare an Income and Expenditure Account, taking into consideration the following information:

(a) Subscriptions due and unpaid £20 (The club has 250 members and the annual subscription is £2 per member).

(b) Subscriptions paid in advance £6.

(c) Locker rents due £2.

(d) Rates paid in advance £10.

Note: The club owned freehold premises value £5,000 and Furniture and Equipment worth £300.

INCOME AND EXPENDITURE ACCOUNT
YEAR ENDED 31ST DECEMBER, 19·1

	£	£		£	£
Rates	60		Subscriptions	486	
Less Rates prepaid	10		*Add* subscriptions due	20	
				506	
		50			
Heating and Lighting		80	*Less* subscriptions prepaid	6	500
Wages and Salaries		400			
Postages and Telephones		50	Locker Rents	248	
Sundry Expenses		20	*Add* Rents due	2	
Surplus		150			250
		750			750

Income and Expenditure Account

There is no difference in the way in which adjustments are made as between a Profit and Loss Account and an Income and Expenditure Account. In the above example, subscriptions paid by members include £6 paid in advance by enthusiastic supporters of the club; yet there are others who have not paid their current year's subscriptions. In writing up the Income and Expenditure Account, I have to remind myself that whatever happens, the amount to be shown is that which *ought* to have been paid. In our example, the club has 250 members and the subscription is £2 per year. Then, the amount that must appear on the credit side of the Income and Expenditure Account *must be* £500, after subscriptions due have been added to the total received by 31st December, and subscriptions paid in advance have been deducted. In the balance sheet, the subscriptions due appear under Current Assets and subscriptions prepaid appear under Current Liabilities. Club Secretaries usually write off subscriptions if they are not paid within a reasonable time after the due date because if members do not pay on or about that time, they are unlikely ever to do so. Examiners sometimes instruct candidates to ignore unpaid subscriptions.

The Accumulated Fund

The Capital of a non-trading organisation is called the Accumulated Fund. On instructing candidates to show the Balance Sheet of a club, examiners sometimes omit the figure for the Accumulated Fund *at the beginning of the year* (to which the Surplus at the end of the year must be added), and they expect the candidate to calculate it. This is a simple matter of deducting total liabilities from total assets *at the beginning of the year*.

EX. 24/2   The following is the Balance Sheet of the above Mercia Club:

BALANCE SHEET
AS AT 31ST DECEMBER, 19·1

LIABILITIES	£	£	ASSETS	£	£
Accumulated fund, 1st January, 19·1			Freehold Premises	5,000	
			Furniture and Equipment	300	
Assets					5,300
Premises	5,000		Debtors		
Furniture and Equipment	300		Subscriptions due	20	
Cash at bank	100		Locker Rents unpaid	2	
		5,400		22	
Add Surplus 31st December	150	5,550			
			Rates Prepaid	10	
Subscriptions prepaid		6	Cash at bank	224	256
		5,556			5,556

Treatment of Profit or Loss of Special Club Events

When a small club throws a party, holds a Social or a Dance, the amounts involved for refreshments are so small that they are most conveniently shown *on the one side* of the Income and Expenditure Account. The Secretary first assesses, by inspection of the figures, whether a profit or loss has been made. If it is a profit, he shows all the figures concerned on the credit side of the Income and Expenditure Account; if it is a loss, the figures are shown on the debit side.

EX. 24/3   The Mercia Club held a Social. Refreshments value £260 were purchased. Sales to the members came to £375. At the end of the festivities there remained £20 worth of stock in hand.

INCOME AND EXPENDITURE ACCOUNT (EXTRACT)
CREDIT SIDE

	£	£
Sales of Refreshments		375
Purchases of Refreshments	260	
Less Stock in hand	20	
		240
Profit on Refreshments		135

Where, however, a large club is concerned, in which substantial quantities of drinks and refreshments are regularly provided for members (some clubs have even a restaurant on the premises), then an ordinary Trading (Bar Trading Account) and Profit and Loss Account would be made up. For, such a club is not entirely for the benefit of its members; it is very much like an ordinary business; it is a profit-making establishment.

Exercise 24

1 (a) Distinguish between:

    (i) A Receipts and Payments Account.

    (ii) An Income and Expenditure Account.

    (iii) A Profit and Loss Account.

(b) Prepare the Income and Expenditure Account for the Western Vale Hockey Club for 19·1 from the following information:

	£
Subscriptions for the year	500
Receipts for hire of pitch	50
Club dances (Net income)	36
Rent paid	120
Secretarial expenses	60
Wages (Groundsman)	208
Paid for repairs to Club-house	80
Lighting and other Club-house expenses	112

On 31st December, 19·1, £15 was due to the Club for the hire of the pitch and £26 was unpaid for repairs to the Club-house.

2 The following is a summary of the receipts and payments of the Westend Cricket Club for the period from the date of formation on 1st April, 19·1, to 31st March, 19·2.

	£		£
Subscriptions	234	Purchase of land	1,700
Gate Money	124	Purchase of Refreshments	123
Sale of Refreshments	162	Equipment	62
Loan secured on land and Club-house	2,600	Printing, Stationery, etc.	21
		Travelling Expenses	18
		Sundry Expenses	21
		Club-house—paid on account	1,150
		Balance c/d	25
	3,120		3,120
Balance b/d	25		

Prepare the Income and Expenditure Account of the Club for the year ended 31st March, 19·2, taking into consideration the following:

(a) There is an unpaid account for provisions amounting to £12.

(b) Subscriptions received included £10 paid in advance.

(c) The stock of provisions on hand at 31st March, 19·2, was valued at £8.

(RSA adapted)

3 The following is the Receipts and Payments Account of a Social club for the year ended 31st December, 19·2.

RECEIPTS AND PAYMENTS ACCOUNT

RECEIPTS	£	PAYMENTS	£
Balance (1st January, 19·2)	31	Games equipment	24
Subscriptions:		Printing, postage and stationery	13
19·2	272	Periodicals	18
19·1	12	Competition prizes	12
Profit on refreshments	35	Sundry expenses	20
Competition fees	18	Wages	78
		Rent	120
		Rates	37
		Balance	46
	368		368

(a) Prepare the club's Income and Expenditure Account, having regard to the following:

    (i)   Subscriptions due but unpaid for 19·2 amounted to £18.

    (ii) The club had furniture and games equipment at the beginning of the year valued at £80 and this is to be depreciated by 20%. (No depreciation is to be written off additions made during 19·2.)

    (iii) Of the rates payment, £13 was in respect of 19·3.

(b) State the amount of the Society's Accumulated Fund as at 31st December, 19·2.

4 From the following information prepare the Income and Expenditure Account for the year ended 31st August, 1972, and a Balance Sheet on that date:

	£
The Downhill Social Club	
Cash in hand and bank on 1st September, 1971	250
(This includes £20 subscriptions for 1971/2)	
Subs received for year ended 31st August, 1972	750
Subs due and unpaid for year to 31st August, 1972	40
Subs received in advance for year 1972/3	10
Rent of hall paid	150
Rent of hall due and unpaid	50
Secretarial expenses paid	70
Paid for annual outing for old age pensioners	100
Heating and Lighting paid	120
Caretakers wages paid	500
Cash in hand and at bank on 31st August, 1972	70

(RSA I 1972)

5 From the following particulars prepare the Income and Expenditure Account of the Barnhill Drama and Music Club for the year ended 31st December, 1970, and its Balance Sheet at that date:

	£
Accumulated Fund at 1st January, 1970	368
Cash in hand	5
Cash at bank	92
Musical equipment	150
Drama equipment	190
Postages and Stationery	12
Receipts from sale of tickets for performances	323
Hire of costumes for plays	33
Subscriptions received from members	
For 1970	99
For 1971	4
Donations from supporters	15
Royalties paid on plays performed	21
Rent of hall for weekly meetings	76
Hire of theatre for special performances	230

Provision is to be made for the following matters which have not yet been passed through the books of the Club:

1 Rent paid in advance amounts to £4.

2 Subscriptions still due for 1970 amounts to £6.

3 Depreciation at 10% is to be written off the Musical and Drama equipment.

(RSA I 1971)

6 From the following Receipts and Payments Account of the Midlawn Tennis Club, prepare an Income and Expenditure Account for the season ended 30th September,

19·1, and a Balance Sheet as on that date, taking into account the information and instructions detailed at the foot:

RECEIPTS AND PAYMENTS ACCOUNT
FOR SEASON ENDED 30TH SEPTEMBER, 19·1

RECEIPTS	£	PAYMENTS	£
Balance 1st April, 19·1	45	Wages	110
Entrance fees	5	Stationery	11
Subscriptions	190	Rent	28
Visitors fees	20	Repairs	12
Profit on catering	30	Balance 30th September, 19·1	129
	290		290

(a) £10 subscriptions are owing for the season ended 30th September, 19·1, and £3 had been paid in advance for the 19·2 season.

(b) £15 is owing for wages.

(c) The Pavilion was valued at £600 and the equipment at £140 at 1st April, 19·1.

(d) Depreciate the pavilion by 2% and the equipment by 5%.

(e) The balance on accumulated fund at 1st April, 19·1, was £785.

(*RSA*)

7 The following figures were supplied to you by the treasurer of the Forsyth Tennis Club. They refer to the year ended 31st December, 1968:

1968
Jan. 1 Balance in bank and in hand   £300
         Rates due and unpaid   10
         Subscriptions owing to the Club 5

Receipts and Payments for the year ended 31st December, 1968, were as follows:

	£
Subscriptions (including £5 arrears)	350
Tournament (Entrance fees received)	70
Tournament (Cost of prizes)	40
Postages and Stationery	10
Light and Heat (Club-house)	30
Rates (including arrears for 1968, £10)	60
Cost of new roller, bought for cash	40
Repairs to netting	10
Club-house Decorations (expected to last 5 years)	50
Wages of part-time groundsman	250

On 31st December, 1968, subscriptions £15 due for the year 1968 had not been paid, but were certain to be received.

The rates paid included £10 for the first quarter of 1969. The Club's furniture and fittings is depreciated by £20 every year.

You are asked to prepare the Forsyth Tennis Club's Receipts and Payments Account and Income and Expenditure Account for the year ended 31st December, 1968. A Balance Sheet is *not* required.

(*RSA I*)

8 The treasurer of the Mergerland Social Club gives you the following Receipts and Payments Account. You are asked to prepare an Income and Expenditure Account for the year ended 30th September, 1971.

THE MERGERLAND SOCIAL CLUB
RECEIPTS AND PAYMENTS ACCOUNT
FOR THE YEAR ENDED 30TH SEPTEMBER, 1971

RECEIPTS	£	PAYMENTS	£
Balance 1st October, 1970	200	Rent of hall	150
Subscriptions	375	Cost of Refreshments	140
Sales of Refreshments	255	Secretarial expenses	90
		Games equipment	160
		Balance	290
	830		830

The following changes in the valuation of stocks and equipment should be taken into consideration:

	1st Oct., 1970 £	30th Sept., 1971 £
Stationery and Stamps	10	7
Catering supplies	15	9
Games equipment	750	800

(RSA I 1971)

9 The treasurer of the C D Club supplies the following information:

(a) Total Club Membership is 240. All have paid their annual subscription of £2·50 except 20 members who are in arrears of one year's subscription.

(b) During the year, the following payments had been made:

	£
Rent	400
Light and Heat	110
Cleaning	52
Sundry Expenses	48
At the end of the year there was an unpaid electricity bill	16

(c) Dances held during the year produced gross proceeds, £100. Expenses in connection with the dances came to £40.

(d) A total of £120 was spent on purchases of refreshments and the sales of refreshments amounted to £160. The stock of refreshments in hand at the end of the year was valued at £20 compared with £30 at the beginning of the year of account.

(e) Cash in hand and at bank at the end of the year was £146 and the value of furniture was estimated at £380.

(f) The capital of the Club at the beginning of the year of account was £516.

From the above information, prepare an Income and Expenditure Account for the year ended 30th September, 1975, and a Statement of the Club's financial position at that date.

10 On 1st January, 1970, the financial position of the Mid-Sussex Gundog Society was:

LIABILITIES	£	ASSETS	£
Accumulated Fund	220	Equipment	125
Trainer's fees accrued	10	Subscriptions due 1969	35
		Cash at bank	70
	230		230

During the year ended 31st December, 1970, receipts and payments were as follows:

RECEIPTS	£	PAYMENTS	£
1st January, 1970 Balance at bank	70	Printing	80
Subscriptions for 1969	20	Stationery and Postage	23
Subscriptions for 1970	140	New Equipment	18
Subscriptions in advance for 1971	25	Hire of Training Ground	50
Field Trials entrance fees	144	Trainer's fees (including £10 for 1969)	40
Receipts from Advertisements in		General expenses	15
Society Year book	55	Field Trials:	
		Judges fees	100
		Expenses	21
		31st December, 1970 Balance at bank	107
	454		454

The following items must also be taken into account:

(a) £18 is owing for subscriptions 1970.

(b) The balance of subscriptions for 1969 still outstanding is to be written off as a bad debt.

(c) The balance of equipment at 1st January, 1970, was to be depreciated by 20%.

(d) There is an amount of £12 owing for printing expenses.

You are required to prepare the Income and Expenditure Account for the year ended 31st December, 1970, and a Balance Sheet as at that date. All calculations to be shown in detail.

(RSA I 1971)

11 (a) The accounts of a social club are made up annually as at 31st December. At 31st December, 19·1, subscriptions in arrears amounted to £69 and subscriptions received in advance for the year 19·2 amounted to £43. During 19·2, £837 was received in respect of subscriptions; this included the £69 arrears for 19·1 and £29 in advance for 19·3. At 31st December, 19·2, subscriptions in arrears amounted to £76.

The annual income and expenditure account is credited with all subscriptions in respect of the year to which the account relates, on the basis that all arrears will afterwards be collected.
Show subscriptions account for the year 19·2.

Note: There are no separate accounts for subscriptions in arrear or for subscriptions in advance.

(RSA I)

(b) During the year ended 31st December, 19·1, the treasurer of an archery club received £325 on account of subscriptions, of which £40 represented subscriptions in advance for the year 19·2. During the year ended 31st December, 19·2, £340 was received on account of subscriptions. Of this sum £25 represented subscriptions for the year 19·1, which, on 1st January, 19·2, were in arrear, and £20 represented subscriptions in advance for the year 19·3. Subscriptions in arrear for the year 19·2 at 31st December, 19·2, were £15 and it may be assumed that none of the subscribers in arrear will fail to pay up in due course.

Give a statement showing the amount that should be credited in the club's Income and Expenditure Account for the year ended 31st December, 19·2, on account of subscriptions income, and how this amount is arrived at.

12 After the passing of certain entries for the calculation of the profits or losses on the restaurant and bar, the trial balance of the Bluewater Sailing Club on 31st December, 19·1, is as follows:

	Dr. £	Cr. £
Club motor launch	850	
Members' subscriptions received		3,140
Capital Fund, 1st January, 19·1		7,230
Club sailing boats	1,200	
Hiring fees received for Club boats		620
Leasehold Premises	5,000	
Maintenance expenses of launch and Club boats	240	
Furniture and Equipment	800	
Cash in hand	25	
Balance at bank	600	
Stock of wines and spirits	105	
Racing entrance fees received		335
Cost of racing prizes distributed	105	
Salaries of secretary and office assistant	1,650	
Sundry creditors		295
Printing and Stationery	90	
Wages of Club boatman	520	
General expenses	225	
Rates	325	
Loss on restaurant catering	185	
Profit on bar		380
Office expenses, postages and telephone	80	
	12,000	12,000

You are required to draw up the Club's Income and Expenditure Account for the year, and a Balance Sheet as at 31st December, 19·1, taking the following into account:

(a) The motor launch, the fleet of Club boats, and the Furniture and Equipment should all be depreciated by 10%.

(b) On 1st January, 19·1, the Club's lease had 20 years to run, and a proportionate amount for the current year should be written off Leasehold Premises.

(c) Members' subscriptions for the current year, amounting to £60, were in arrear and unpaid on 31st December, 19·1.

(RSA I)

13 The Assets and Liabilities of the Emperor social club on 31st December, 1969, were as follows:

	£
Freehold premises at cost	5,000
Furniture and fittings at cost	3,000
Stock of restaurant and bar supplies	1,293
Members' subscriptions in advance	25
Members' subscriptions in arrears	42
Amount owing for newspapers and periodicals	26
Creditors for restaurant and bar supplies	427

A summary of the Club's Bank Account for the year to 31st December, 1970, is given below:

BANK ACCOUNT

	£		£
Balance 1st January, 1970	672	Restaurant and bar supplies	9,420
Members' subscriptions:		Wages	5,405
for 1969	31	Stationery and postages	210
for 1970	6,671	General Expenses	1,921
for 1971	89	Newspapers and periodicals	74
Restaurant and bar takings	10,840	Materials for extension to freehold	
Income from sale of old periodicals to		premises	620
members	8	Balance 31st December, 1970	661
	18,311		18,311

The amount spent on wages as shown in the summary Bank Account given above includes £492 spent on wages incurred in connection with the extension to the freehold premises.

Depreciation on furniture and fittings is to be provided for at the rate of 10% per annum on cost.

On 31st December, 1970, the stock of restaurant and bar supplies was valued at £1,429; £28 was owing for newspapers and periodicals; £528 was owing for restaurant and bar supplies, and members' subscriptions in arrears amounted to £56.

You are required to prepare:

(a) A Trading Account for the Restaurant and Bar for 1970.

(b) An Income and Expenditure Account for 1970.

(c) A Balance Sheet as at 31st December, 1970.

(RSA II 1971)

Chapter Twenty Five

Manufacturing Accounts

Manufacturers

So far we have been concerned only with the accounts of merchants; businesses which buy goods and re-sell them without changing their nature in any way. There are of course, also many manufacturers who transform raw materials into finished goods. Their final accounts must necessarily show more information than those of merchants, for in their case it is important to ascertain not only the cost of the goods sold but also a breakdown of such costs under two main classifications:

1 Prime cost or Variable cost.

2 Factory overhead expenses or Fixed costs.

Prime Costs

Prime Costs describe the total cost of: Direct materials, Direct labour and Direct expenses.

These quantities and costs vary according to the number of articles manufactured. These are also referred to as *variable costs*, and are concerned most intimately with the manufacture of a given article.

DIRECT MATERIALS

In an engineering factory the steel sections used for producing the final article are the raw materials. In the textiles business, cotton or wool is the raw material for the piece goods which are the end product.

DIRECT LABOUR

describes the men and women actually working at the machines; the lathe or the drill operators; the spinning and weaving machine operators. Their wages are described as direct wages or manufacturing wages.

DIRECT EXPENSES

occur in special cases:

(i)   If a builder hired a crane, the cost of hiring would be a direct expense.

(ii) If a manufacturer is allowed to produce a patented article and he pays royalties on the profits made from it, such royalties would be classified under Direct Expenses.

Factory Overhead Expenses or Fixed Costs

These describe the total cost of:

INDIRECT EXPENSES

Any expenses which only indirectly add to the cost of production, such as depreciation of Machinery and Plant or a proportion of the bill for Heating and Lighting representing the fuel consumed by the factory (the remainder being for fuel consumed in the administrative offices).

INDIRECT WAGES

are paid to labour in the factory, other than the actual machine operators, such as foremen, winch operators, truck drivers, stackers, cleaners, porters.

The examples below show the main sections, and the items classified under them, of a Manufacturing, Trading and Profit and Loss Account:*

EX. 25/1   The following balances were extracted from my ledger on 31st December, 19·4, and classified in a Manufacturing, Trading and Profit and Loss Account: (the depreciation on factory machinery and office machinery respectively was calculated at a given percentage).

MANUFACTURING ACCOUNT
FOR YEAR ENDED 31ST DECEMBER, 19·4

PRIME COST	£	£		£
Stock of raw materials 1st January		400	Cost of Production c/d to Trading Account	26,095
Purchases of Raw Materials	4,145			
Add Carriage Inwards	100			
	4,245			
Less Returns Outwards	150	4,095		
		4,495		
Less Stock of Raw Materials 31st December		550		
Cost of Materials consumed		3,945		
Manufacturing wages		20,000		
Prime Cost		23,945		
FACTORY EXPENSES				
Heating and Lighting (¾)	300			
Rent and Rates (¾)	750			
Depreciation of machinery and plant	1,000			
Factory Expenses		2,050		
		25,995		
Add Work in progress 1st January		300		
		26,295		
Less Work in progress 31st December		200		
Cost of production		26,095		26,095

Stocks of Work in Progress

In a manufacturing business there is almost invariably a quantity (or stock) of unfinished (or partly finished) goods, or *work in progress*, at the beginning and at the end of the trading period, the value of which must be brought into account if an accurate cost of production is to be obtained. Such stocks are respectively added and subtracted from the cost of production so far calculated and the total true cost of production thus obtained is entered on the credit side of the manufacturing account and carried down to the debit side of the trading account.

The Trading Account

EX. 25/2   Besides the Factory Cost of Production, the only other items to be found in the Trading Account are stocks of *Finished Goods* at the start and the close of the trading period; and sales of Finished Goods. Sometimes manufacturers buy goods which they re-sell without changing their nature. Such Purchases of Finished Goods also appear in the Trading Account.

*You may refer to the fully worked out Example 25/4 at the same time as its sections, Examples 25/1–3.

Thus, the Trading Account contains only items of Finished Goods. Continuing the above example, the Trading Account appears as follows:

TRADING ACCOUNT
FOR YEAR ENDED 31ST DECEMBER, 19·4

	£		£
Stock of Finished Goods		Sales of Finished Goods	56,000
1st January	2,000		
Cost of Production b/d	26,095		
Purchases of Finished Goods	1,000		
	29,095		
Less Stock of Finished Goods			
31st December	2,300		
	26,795		
Gross Profit c/d	29,205		
	56,000		56,000

The Classified Profit and Loss Account

The items in the Profit and Loss Account are classified under three headings: Administration; Selling and Distribution; Financial charges. Continuing the above example, the Profit and Loss Account appears as follows:

EX. 25/3

PROFIT AND LOSS ACCOUNT
FOR YEAR ENDED 31ST DECEMBER, 19·4

	£	£		£
ADMINISTRATION EXPENSES				
Salaries	5,600		Gross Profit b/d	29,205
Rent and Rates (¼)	250			
Heating and Lighting (¼)	100			
Depreciation Office				
Machinery	50			
General Expenses	1,250			
		7,250		
SELLING AND DISTRIBUTION				
EXPENSES				
Salesman's Salary	2,200			
Salesman's Commission	4,600			
Advertising	800			
Carriage on sales	180			
		7,780		
FINANCIAL CHARGES				
Discounts allowed	1,100			
Less Discounts received	150			
		950		
Bank Interest		120		
Net Profit		13,105		
		29,205		29,205

The Manufacturing Account Classified (Cost Analysis of a Manufacturing Account)

The various components which combine to bring out the essential aspects of the total cost of manufacture can now be shown together:

Total Cost of Production is made up of
{ Prime Cost
  Factory Overhead expenses } Factory cost of goods produced
  Administration expenses
  Selling and Distribution expenses
  Financial Charges

The above examples 25/1–3 of Manufacturing, Trading and Profit and Loss Accounts, are of course combined, and they appear set out in the vertical form as follows:

EX. 25/4

MANUFACTURING, TRADING AND PROFIT AND LOSS ACCOUNT
FOR YEAR ENDED 31ST DECEMBER, 19·4

	£	£	£
Sales of Finished Goods			56,000
PRIME COST			
Stock of Raw Materials			
1st January		400	
Purchases of Raw Materials	4,145		
Add Carriage Inwards	100		
	4,245		
Less Returns Outwards	150	4,095	
		4,495	
Less Stock of Raw Materials		550	
31st December			
Cost of raw materials used		3,945	
Manufacturing wages		20,000	
Prime Cost		23,945	
FACTORY EXPENSES			
Heating and Lighting (¾)	300		
Rent and Rates (¾)	750		
Depreciation of machinery			
and plant	1,000	2,050	
Factory Expenses		25,995	
Add Work in progress			
1st January		300	
		26,295	
Less Work in progress			
31st December		200	
Cost of Production		26,095	
Stock of Finished Goods			
1st January		2,000	
Purchases of Finished Goods		1,000	
		29,095	
Less Stock of Finished Goods			
31st December		2,300	
			26,795
Gross Profit			29,205
ADMINISTRATION EXPENSES			
Salaries	5,600		
Rent and Rates (¼)	250		
Heating and Lighting (¼)	100		
Depreciation Office Machinery	50		
General Expenses	1,250	7,250	
SELLING AND DISTRIBUTION			
EXPENSES			
Salesman's Salary	2,200		
Salesman's Commission	4,600		
Advertising	800		
Carriage on Sales	180		
		7,780	
FINANCIAL CHARGES			
Discounts allowed	1,100		
Less Discounts received	150	950	
Bank Interest	120	1,070	16,100
Net Profit			13,105

Note: When you are not required to draw up a manufacturing account, and yet you are instructed that the business whose final accounts you are required to make up is a manufacturing business, it is advisable to show wages (and perhaps one or two other manufacturing items, eg. depreciation of factory machines, as well) in the trading account. The trading account in such instances would be set out (Vertical form) as follows:

EX. 25/5

TRADING ACCOUNT

	£	£
Sales		x
Opening Stock	x	
Purchases	x	
	x	
Less Closing Stock	x	
	x	
Manufacturing Wages	x	
Cost of Sales		x
Gross Profit		x

The above may, of course, be set out in the conventional form if preferred.

Exercise 25

1 (a) Give a clear definition of the meaning of gross profit.

(b) From the following list select those items you think should be used in the Trading Account of a tailor, and prepare this account for the half-year ended 31st March, 19·2:

	£
Sales for the half-year	4,000
Purchases of cloth, etc.	1,277
Purchases of sewing machines	90
Carriage on sales	52
Returns and allowances outwards	54
Purchases of packing materials	12
Office heating and lighting	55
Heating and lighting of workrooms	106
Office salaries and expenses	672
Advertising	92
Wages of workpeople	852
Rent and rates (¾ workrooms; ¼ office)	240
Electricity for machines	150
Carriage on purchases	32
Discount allowed	36
Discount received	61
Stocks of cloth, etc.:	
1st October, 19·1	307
31st March, 19·2	388

(*RSA I*)

2 The following balances were extracted from the books of Moped Ltd., on 31st December, 19·1:

	£
Stock of raw materials 1st January, 19·1	1,800
Stock of manufactured goods 1st January, 19·1	2,200
Purchases:	
Raw Materials	14,000
Goods for re-sale	2,000
Manufacturing wages	12,000
Sales	40,000
Rent and Rates:	
Factory	600
Office	300
Lighting, heating and power for factory	400
Lighting and heating for office	200
Administration Expenses	1,400
Office Salaries	1,100
Stocks on 31st December, 19·1 were:	
Raw Materials	2,100
Manufactured Goods	2,600

You are asked to prepare a Manufacturing, Trading and Profit and Loss Account for 19·1, classifying the items under their relevant headings. No Balance Sheet is required.

(RSA II adapted)

3 The following figures relating to the year 19·2, have been taken from the books of KTG Ltd.

	£
Sales	72,800
Stock of materials (1st January) at cost	1,608
Materials purchased	19,471
Stock of materials (31st December) at cost	1,482
Manufacturing wages	26,430
Work in progress (1st January) at factory cost	874
Work in progress (31st December) at factory cost	947
Factory expenses	7,828
Office and administration expenses	3,725
Depreciation of plant and machinery	3,250
Depreciation of delivery vans	625
Stock of finished goods (1st January) at factory cost	2,532
Stock of finished goods (31st December) at factory cost	3,569
Factory power	1,835
Advertising	517
Delivery vans' running expenses	713
Salesman's salary and commission	2,315

You are requested to prepare a Manufacturing Account, a Trading Account and a Profit and Loss Account for the year 19·2.

(RSA II)

4 You are required to prepare a Manufacturing Account, Trading Account and a Profit and Loss Account for the year 1971, for Painter Ltd., from the figures given below. Indicate in the accounts the significance of the various sub-totals and balances carried down:

	£
Stocks on 1st January, 1971:	
Raw materials at cost	6,000
Work in progress at factory cost	3,290
Finished goods at factory cost	7,280
Purchases of raw materials	42,940
Purchases of finished goods for re-sale—all sold in 1971	1,240
Manufacturing wages	60,984
Factory expenses	17,891
Office and administration expenses	8,922
Depreciation of plant and machinery	7,000
Factory power	4,982
Travellers' salaries and commissions	6,921
Delivery expenses	4,228
Advertising	2,989
Rates and insurance	800
Light and heat	400
Sales	172,498
Stocks at 31st December, 1971:	
Raw materials at cost	8,921
Work in progress at factory cost	4,557
Finished goods at factory cost	9,480

Three-quarters of:

(i)   Rates and Insurance, and

(ii) Light and Heat

are to be allocated to factory and one-quarter to office.

(RSA II 1972)

5 (a) The following items are extracted from the Final Accounts of M Bunson, year ended 31st December, 1972:

	£
Purchases of raw materials	19,752
Sales of finished goods	49,400
Stock of raw materials:	
1st January, 1972	5,568
31st December, 1972	4,642
Stock of finished goods, 1st January, 1972 at selling price	6,574
Stock of finished goods, 31st December, 1972 at selling price	5,890
Factory wages	15,700
Factory overheads:	
Power	212
Heat and Light	68
Rent and Rates	1,680
Gross Profit for year	10,206
Net Profit for year	3,740
Capital	17,000

From the above information calculate:

(i)   Cost of raw materials used during the year.

(ii) Cost of production of goods manufactured during the year.

(iii) The percentage of Net Profit on Capital.

(iv) Value at selling price of goods manufactured during the year.

(b) Under what main headings would the following items appear in cost analysis:

(i)   Raw materials for the manufactured goods.

(ii)   Rent of factory.

(iii) Commission to Salesman.

(iv) Wages to machine operators.

(v)   Depreciation of duplicating machines in the office.

(vi) Factory Manager's salary.

(vii) Royalty paid for manufactured items.

(viii) Discounts allowed.

6 Tavana and Quick, who are old friends, run separate businesses, manufacturing a similar product.

Tavana runs his business on the sound but rather conservative lines followed by his father; he serves a long-established group of customers and does not actively seek new business. Quick on the other hand, wants to expand and is prepared to pay for advertising and other promotion expenses.

Tavana complains that, although he works harder than Quick, and operates a factory of comparable size, yet he is much less well off.

Tavana and Quick agree that the financial results of their two businesses should be compared, and they invite your help.

You obtain the following information from the two sets of books:

	Tavana £	Quick £
Factory:		
Current value 31st December, 1971	40,000	41,000
Plant:		
(in both cases the acquisitions are spread evenly over the years)		
Balance at 1st January, 1971, at cost	35,000	33,000
Depreciation to 31st December, 1970 (10% per annum on cost)	11,000	10,800
Sales for 1971	128,000	172,000
Variable cost of sales	96,000	129,000
Selling expenses	10,000	18,000
Administration expenses	15,000	13,000
Working capital 31st December, 1971	26,500	31,500

You are required to give:

(a) Separate Trading and Profit and Loss Accounts for 1971 and Balance Sheets at 31st December, 1971, for the two businesses in column form.

(b) A report on the accounts you prepare which will explain the less favourable results of Tavana's business.

(Institute of Bankers 1972)

Chapter Twenty Six

Bills of Exchange

I, the Creditor, Draw a Bill (of Exchange) and my Debtor Accepts it

When I sell goods worth, say, £1,000, on one month's credit, I, in effect, deprive myself of the cash value of the goods for one month, and, in these days of high interest rates, that is a serious matter. A bill of exchange is a financial instrument which may smooth over this difficulty because:

1 My customer gets his goods on a credit of one month, or more; yet at the same time,

2 I can cash the bill he accepts by either:

   (a) Discounting it at my bank or at another financial house, or

   (b) Transferring it by endorsement to one of my creditors.

The examples below should make clear the meanings of these terms, and the accounting processes they involve:

EX. 26/1   I, John Fry, sell goods worth £1,000 on credit to A Smith:

		A SMITH
		£
Sept. 2	Sales	1,000

I, *the creditor*, immediately draw a bill at thirty days on Smith:

No. 1032 *Exchange for* £1,000   London 2 Sep. 19.1

At Thirty days *pay to my order the sum of*

Value received   **One Thousand Pounds**

To Mr. A. Smith
41, Moon Street
London EC1

Smith accepts the above bill; that is, he agrees to the terms stated on the face of the bill:

1 That he has received value of £1,000.

2 That he agrees to a credit of thirty days, plus three days grace (allowed on all bills, making the period not thirty days but thirty-three days) when payment for £1,000 will fall due.

3 That he will have £1,000 cash available to meet the bill on 5th October.

Smith expresses his liability to meet the bill by writing across its face 'Accepted' and signing it thus:

No. 1032 *Exchange for* £1,000   London 2 Sep. 19.1

At Thirty days *pay to my order the sum of*

One Thousand Pounds

Value received

To Mr. A. Smith
41, Moon Street
London EC1

EX. 26/2   Immediately on drawing the bill, I credit Smith's account (just as if he had paid his account) thus closing it; debiting Bills Receivable Account at the same time:

A SMITH

	£		£
Sept. 2 Sales	1,000	Sept. 2 Bills Receivable	1,000

BILLS RECEIVABLE

	£		£
Sept. 2 A Smith	1,000		

When, at the end of thirty days (plus three days grace), Smith honours the bill, then the money is transferred from his bank to mine; I debit my cash book and credit Bills Receivable Account:

BILLS RECEIVABLE

	£		£
Sept. 2 A Smith	1,000	Oct. 5 Cash	1,000

and the bill is then settled.

Discounting a Bill

It was stated above that 'I can cash the bill by discounting it'. If the £1,000 is required for immediate purposes, the bill may be cashed, ie., 'discounted', for a relatively small charge, comparable to a cash discount:

EX. 26/3   On 10th September, I ask my bankers to discount Smith's bill and to credit my account with its face value, less their discounting charge of, say £50:

A SMITH

	£		£
Sept. 2 Sales	1,000	Sept. 2 Bills Receivable	1,000

BILLS RECEIVABLE

Sept. 2 A Smith	1,000	Sept. 10 Cash—Smith's bill discounted	1,000

DISCOUNT ON BILLS

Sept. 2 Cash	50		

CASH BOOK

Sept. 10 Bills Receivable	1,000	Sept. 10 Discount on bills	50

Here, it is presumed that all will go smoothly, and that on 5th October, Smith will honour the bill and I shall hear no more about it.

A Dishonoured Bill

If, however, Smith defaults, the bill is said to be dishonoured and I (not Smith) am liable to my bankers for the £1,000 due to them.

EX. 26/4

If then, the bill is dishonoured, Smith's debt to me must be reinstated, that is, Smith's account must once again be debited with the £1,000 he still owes me; the double-entry being on the credit side of Bills Receivable Account, which is thus closed:

A SMITH

		£			£
Sept.	2 Sales	1,000	Sept.	2 Bills Receivable	1,000
Oct.	5 Bills Receivable (Bill dishonoured)	1,000			

BILLS RECEIVABLE

					£
Sept.	2 A Smith	1,000	Oct.	5 A Smith (Bill dishonoured)	1,000

If Smith is to be charged interest on the now overdue account (say, £10), then his account is debited with £10, thus increasing his debt to £1,010. He might then accept a fresh bill maturing (payable) at a mutually agreed date. The double-entry for the interest is on the credit side of the Interest Account, transferred at the end of the financial year to the Profit and Loss Account (Cr.), as is the Discount on Bills Account (Dr.).

Noting Charges

Another charge with which Smith might be debited on dishonouring his bill, is a legal charge by the bank to me. It might be described as a solicitors (or the archaic 'notary public', hence 'Noting') charge.

The bank sends me a debit note for that fee: it also appears on the Bank Statement as a debit. The double-entries in my books are: Cash Book (Cr.); A Smith (Dr.).

Transferring a Bill by Endorsement

At the beginning of this Chapter, it was stated that the bill might be transferred by endorsement to a third party:

EX. 26/5

April 20 (a) I draw a bill at three months for £500, which R Day accepts
April 28 (b) I endorse the bill over to M Kerry.

R DAY

	£			£
		April 20	Bills receivable (a)	500

BILLS RECEIVABLE

April 20 R Day (a)	500	April 28	M Kerry (b)	500

M KERRY

April 28 Bills Receivable (b)	500

Retired Bills

If a bill is paid before its date of maturity, it is said to be retired. In such a case a discount or a rebate might be allowed, since payment was made before due date. On the other hand, under new arrangements the credit to the acceptor, or the drawee, of the bill might be extended. Thus, the old bill is cancelled before maturity (debit customer, credit Bills Receivable), and a new one drawn to replace it (credit customer, debit Bills Receivable) maturing at a later date.

Bills Payable

The bill of exchange in example 26/1, drawn by me, the creditor, and accepted by Smith, my debtor, is from my point of view a bill receivable since it represents payment I expect to receive. But it represents a bill payable to Smith, since it is payment he expects to make sometime in the future. On the other hand, if I agree to accept a bill drawn on me by R Brown, one of my creditors, then that is, from my point of view, a bill payable. It is entered in my ledger as follows:

EX. 26/6

	R BROWN			
	£			£
Bills payable	x	Balance		x
	BILLS PAYABLE			
		R Brown		x

Bills of Exchange in the Balance Sheet

Bills Receivable and Bills Payable appear in the balance sheet under Current Assets and Current Liabilities respectively. If a bill has been discounted, it would not appear on the balance sheet since there would be no balance in the Bills Receivable Account. Instead, the bank balance would be greater by the value of the discounted bill. And yet, the bill might be dishonoured and the bank balance would then fall by the value of the dishonoured bill. In order to represent this situation accurately, a note is appended at the foot of the balance sheet reading:

'There is a contingent liability of £x on bills discounted as at ·1/·1/19·1 (the date of the balance sheet).'

The Journal

All the entries above, except those involving the Cash Book are first entered in the Journal, eg. example 26/2:

	£	£
Bills Receivable	1,000	
A Smith		1,000
Bill for £1,000 at 30 days accepted by A Smith		

The Register of Bills

This is a memorandum book (not part of the double-entry system) in which a bill is recorded at the time when it is drawn. The bill drawn on A Smith (example 26/1) might be registered as follows:

EX. 26/7

REGISTER OF BILLS RECEIVABLE

No.	Date	Drawee	Amount £	When Due	Remarks
1029					
1030					
1031					
1032	2.9.01	A Smith	1,000	5.10.0.	Dishonoured

Exercise 26

(i) Show J Crow's account and the Bills Receivable Account in your ledger:

Jan. 1 You sell J Crow goods value £100
       1 J Crow accepts a bill at 30 days against your invoice
Feb. 2 J Crow honours his bill, and the transaction is closed

(ii) Make the necessary ledger entries in W Harris's ledger to record the following transactions:

(a) 1st March. Sold goods value £800 to P Cole who accepted a bill at thirty days. The bill was duly honoured.

(b) 10th March. Sold goods value £300 to M Roe who accepted a bill at thirty days. On 15th March Harris discounted the bill at his bankers. Discounting charge £7.

(c) 18th March. Sold goods value £700 to R Tyne, who gives Harris his acceptance (ie., accepts a bill) at sixty days for that amount. On due date, Tyne says he cannot meet the bill. It is dishonoured. He asks for a fresh bill at thirty days and agrees that an interest charge of £10 should be added.

2 On 1st July, 19·1, Amos received from Bates his acceptance for two months for £800 for goods supplied on that date. He discounted the bill on the same day with his bankers for £785. On the due date his bankers notified him that Bates had dishonoured the bill on presentation. Show the necessary entries in Amos's ledger.

3 A owes B the sum of £1,000 and gives him his acceptance at six months for this amount plus £25 for interest, payable 31st December, 19·1. A retires the bill on 1st October, 19·1, by a cash payment of £650 and a bill at three months for the balance for £375 which bill B discounts with his bankers at 5%. Make the necessary entries to record these transactions in B's ledger.

4 X owed Y £1,555 for goods supplied. The account was settled on 1st October, 19·1 by X giving Y a cheque for £305, a three months' bill of exchange for £600 and a five months' bill for the balance.
The first bill was met when due and at the same time the second was withdrawn in consideration of two further bills, equal in amount, due on 1st June, 19·1 and 1st September 19·1 respectively. Interest on the first renewal was payable forthwith in cash, calculated at the rate of 4% per annum.
Show the above transactions as they would appear in Y's ledger and cash book up to March 19·1. Ignore days of grace and calculate the interest on the basis of months.

(RSA)

5 On 1st January, 19·1, the following balances appeared in the books of Oxford Ltd:

DEBTORS	£	CREDITORS	£
Hull Ltd.	250	Bristol & Sons Ltd.	300
Exeter & Co.	400	Cardiff Bros.	100

Open the accounts to record the above in the books of Oxford Ltd., and record the following transactions in the Journal and Ledger and Cash Book:

19·1
Jan.   2 Accepted a bill drawn by Bristol & Sons Ltd., for the balance due at one month
Jan.   9 Received bill for two months from Exeter & Co., for £400 duly accepted
Jan. 16 Hull Ltd., forwarded draft duly accepted at two months for balance due
Jan. 23 Accepted Cardiff & Co.'s bill for three months for £100
Feb.   5 Bill due to Bristol & Sons Ltd., duly honoured
Feb.   9 Discounted Exeter & Co.'s draft at 6% per annum
Mar. 19 Proceeds of Hull Ltd.'s bill collected by bankers and credited in account

(RSA)

6 On 1st March, A purchased from B goods to the value of £1,200 and settled the account by means of three Bills of Exchange for £400 each, due respectively in two, three and four months. A week later B discounted the first of the three with his bank, receiving £398, the others he held. The first two bills were paid at maturity. The third A was unable to meet and it was retired by arrangement, A paying £100 in cash and giving B a fresh bill for three months to cover the balance with interest at the rate of 5% per annum. B discounted this bill on 7th July for £300. Set out the entries recording the above in B's ledger.
(The Cash Book is not required.)

(Institute of Bankers)

7 Record the following matters in ledger accounts (including Bank) to be kept by B:
On 1st January, 19·1, A owes B £300 and B owes C £500.
On that day A accepts a bill at three months in favour of B for £300. On 4th January B endorses the bill over to C in part settlement of his indebtedness. On 31st January B hands C a cheque for the balance of his account less 5% discount on that balance. On presentation of the bill on the date due by C against A, it is dishonoured, whereupon B pays C a cheque for £300. On 31st May, A (who has been declared bankrupt) pays a first and final dividend of £0·50 in the pound.

(RSA)

8 On 1st January, 19·1 A sells goods to B for £800. On the same day, B sells goods to C for £500. Subsequent transactions are:

19·1
Jan.   2 A draws a bill (No. 1) at 3 months on B for £300, which B accepts
Jan.   3 B draws a bill (No. 2) at 3 months on C for £400, which C accepts. C draws a bill (No. 3) at 3 months for £100 in his favour on D. D accepts and C endorses this bill over to B
Jan.   4 B endorses both bills (No. 2 and No. 3) over to A
April 6 A notifies B that C's acceptance for £400 (No. 2) was presented by A and dishonoured B immediately pays £400 to A

The other bills are paid on the due dates. Show how these transactions would appear in the ledger of B. Purchases and Sales Accounts need not be shown and Journal entries are not required.

(Institute of Bankers)

9 William Ashton is a boatbuilder. On 1st January he had a capital of £23,760, bills payable current No. 135, £640; No. 136, £728; No. 137, £320 and having received on account of ships in progress, Owl, £6,849 and Hawk, £3,500. A mortgage to P Piper for £8,000 existed on his works and plant, which were valued as follows: freehold works and buildings £9,127, fixed plant and machinery £7,826, dry dock £6,284, loose plant and rolling stock £2,788.

He owed to Brown & Co., £848, Jones & Co., £1,653, Robinson & Co., £984. He had cash at bankers £2,796 and in office £120. His bills receivable in hand were No. 186, £329; No. 187, £546; No. 188, £490.

He had three boats under construction, on which he had expended in work and materials: Owl £7,126; Hawk £4,291; Sparrow £835. The stock of stores and materials on hand, valued at cost price, was £4,724.

You are required to make the necessary opening entries.

(RSA adapted)

Chapter Twenty Seven

Consignment Accounts and Joint Ventures

Goods on Consignment

When goods are sent to an agent *on consignment*, it is understood that he is to sell them at the best price above cost he can get. Goods on consignment are not dispatched in fulfilment of an order. The agent expects to receive a commission on the value at which he disposes of the consignment.

The Pro-Forma Invoice

The cost price of the consignment appears on a *pro-forma*, or temporary, invoice addressed to the agent, or *consigneee*, on shipment of the goods. Two accounts are opened in the ledger to record this action:

1 Goods Consigned Account.

2 Consignment Account.

EX. 27/1   On 1st February, I consigned to my agent, Mr Mohamed Ali, Nairobi, Kenya, forty cases of goods value (at cost) £1,000, for which I sent him a pro-forma invoice:

GOODS CONSIGNED ACCOUNT

	£			£
		Feb. 1 Consignment Account J		1,000

CONSIGNMENT ACCOUNT

		£
Feb. 1 Goods Consigned J		1,000

Goods Consigned Account

This account simply records the cost price of the consignment. It is eventually transferred to the credit side of the Trading Account and added to the total annual turnover.

Consignment Account

This is in effect a combined Trading and Profit and Loss Account. Its purpose is to show the profit or loss made on a particular consignment. The debit side shows:

(a) Cost of the goods.

(b) All the 'outgoings', such as the cost of carriage to docks, insurance and freight.

(c) The agent's own expenses, plus his commission, when these are known.

EX. 27/2   On 15th February, the following charges were paid on shipment of the goods (example 27/1), and posted to the Consignment Account from the credit side of the Cash Book:

CONSIGNMENT ACCOUNT
(M ALI, NAIROBI)

			£
Feb.	1 Goods Consigned	J	1,000
	15 Cash:	CB	
	Carriage to docks and dock charges		5
	Insurance		7
	Freight		20

EX. 27/3   On 24th April, I received from my agent, M Ali, an *Account Sales*, which read as follows:

ACCOUNT SALES
FROM MOHAMED ALI, NAIROBI, KENYA

	£	£
Consignment as detailed in your Pro-forma dated 1st February, 19.3:		
Sold to Patel and Shah, Nairobi		1,400
Less Sundry Charges:		
Landing and dock charges	10	
Import duty	47	
Commission at 10%	130	
Del Credere at 1%*	13	143	200
		1,200
Bankers draft in settlement enclosed		

EX. 27/4   The above details are entered in the Consignment Account (debit) and in the personal account of M Ali (credit) respectively:

CONSIGNMENT ACCOUNT
(M ALI, NAIROBI)

19.3			£	£	19.3			£
Feb.	1 Goods Consigned	J		1,000	April 24 M Ali, Nairobi		J	1,400
	15 Cash:	CB						
	Carriage to docks and dock charges			5				
	Insurance			7				
	Freight			20				
April 24 M Ali		J						
	Import duty		47					
	Landing and dock charges		10					
	Commission at 10%		130					
	Del Credere at 1%		13					
				200				
	Profit and Loss A/c	T		168				
				1,400				1,400

M ALI, NAIROBI

19.3			£	19.3			£	£
April 24 Consignment Account		J	1,400	April 24 Consignment Account		J		
				Import duty			47	
				Landing and dock charges			10	
				Commission at 10%			130	
				Del Credere at 1%			13	
								200
				Cash		CB		1,200
			1,400					1,400

Del Credere: Agents are not usually liable for the payment of the goods they sell. If, however, they guarantee payment, or pay for them themselves, then they are entitled to an extra commission called del credere.

The Goods Consigned Account is now transferred to the Trading Account.

GOODS CONSIGNED

19·3			£	19·3			£
April 24	Trading Account	T	1,000	Feb. 1	Consignment Account	J	1,000

Unsold Stock on Consignment

EX. 27/5 Suppose that only three quarters of the consignment (thirty cases out of the forty cases shipped) had been sold by the end of my financial year, which fell on 30th June, 19·3. Then $\frac{1}{4}$ of the cost of the goods plus $\frac{1}{4}$ of the charges incurred by me and my agent (the consignee) are carried down to the debit side of the Consignment Account to show the total value of *unsold stock on consignment*. The agent's commission on the value of the part that was actually sold, is of course not included in computing the proportion of charges to be added to the value of unsold stock on consignment.

CONSIGNMENT ACCOUNT

19·3			£	£	19·3			£	£
Feb. 1	Goods Consigned	J		1,000	April 27	M Ali (Nairobi)	J		1,050
15	Cash:	CB				(Being sales of $\frac{3}{4}$ of			
	Carriage to docks and					the consignment)			
	dock charges			5	June 30	Value of unsold stock			250
	Insurance			7		*Add* Charges:			
	Freight			20		Carriage to dock			
April 24	M Ali:	J				etc.		5	
	Import Duty		47			Insurance		7	
	Landing and dock					Freight		20	
	charges		10			Duty		47	
	Commission at 10%					Landing charges		10	
	on £1,050		105			$\frac{1}{4}$ of		89 = 22	
	Del Credere at 1%					(nearest £)			
	(nearest £)		11			Balance	c/d		272
				173					
	Profit and Loss								
	Account	T	117						
				1,322					1,322
July 1	Unsold stock on								
	consignment	b/d		272					

Consignee's Ledger Accounts

EX. 27/6 M Ali's ledger accounts of his principal appears as follows:

JOHN FRY, LONDON

		£		£
April 24	Import Duty	47	Sundry Debtors	1,400
	Landing and dock charges	10		
	Commission	130		
	Del Credere	13		
	Cash	1,200		
		1,400		1,400

In the preceding examples the consignee, M Ali, was treated as a customer, not strictly as an agent. An agent does not normally handle the goods himself (they are dispatched direct to the customer) and even when he does, as in our example, he is not legally responsible for their payment (although he is under a moral obligation in that respect) unless there is a del credere arrangement.

If he is acting purely as an agent his gain out of the transaction is a commission, not a profit. His ledger, therefore, does not contain either a Purchases or a Sales Account. Yet, if he has stocks to dispose of on behalf of his principals, he must keep a record of them.

A Record of the Stocks on Consignment

If I were an agent with goods on consignment in hand for disposal on behalf of my principals, what sort of information would I wish to derive from each principal's stock record in my Stock Book?

Consider the following suggestions:

1 Quantity received.

2 Value of above.

3 Charges incurred on each consignment.

4 Quantity sold.

5 Value of above.

6 Commission due to me.

Consignee's Stock Account

Thus, assuming the above analysis were acceptable, Mohamed Ali's Stock Account against his principal, John Fry's name, would appear as follows:

EX. 27/7

STOCKS ON CONSIGNMENT

EX JOHN FRY, LONDON

Date of Pro-forma	Quantity IN	Cost Price £	Charges £	Date of Sale	Quantity OUT	Selling Price £	Commission and Del Credere £	Unsold Stock
19·3 Feb. 1	40 cases	1,000	57	19·3 April 24	30 cases	1,050	106	10 cases

Joint Ventures

A joint venture describes a particular business venture undertaken by two or more persons. It is a temporary partnership for the sole purpose of, and limited to that one undertaking. At its conclusion, the partnership is automatically dissolved.

EX. 27/8

I, John Fry, join with Allan Bray to purchase and then to sell, a quantity of surplus stock from a warehouse disposing of its assets at clearance prices. We agree to share profits (or losses) as to three-fifths Fry, two-fifths Bray. I purchase the goods paying £10,000 by cheque, having received £5,000 from Bray as his part of the outlay. Bray agrees to see to the advertising side of the sales drive, and he pays £400 for that service. On my part, I pay cheques for transport £50, and sundry other expenses, including warehousing, amounting to £300. I receive an Account Sales from Bray from which I see that he has sold two-thirds of the stock for £9,000 for which he has been paid by cheque. (All other items concerning his side of the venture, such as his outlay on advertising and his contributions of cash towards the purchase of the stock, appear on his Account Sales.) I sell the remaining one-third for £3,100 and I receive a cheque for that amount from my customer. The following are the steps I take to record these transactions:

EX. 27/9   A   1   Open a Joint Venture in Surplus Stocks Account (a memorandum account not involving any double-entries);

     2   Enter into this account every receipt (Cr.) and every payment (Dr.) including those of Bray (from his Account Sales).

The purpose of this account is to show at a glance the profit or loss made on the Venture.

B   1   Open a Joint Venture with Bray Account;

     2   Debit:

       (i)   All charges *I* have incurred—not those incurred by Bray.

       (ii)   Share of the profit due from Bray to me, transferred to Profit and Loss Account.

     3   Credit:

       (i)   All cash received from Bray.

       (ii)   Amount due to Bray (if any).

For the sake of clarity, my account as it appears in Bray's ledger is also shown below:

C   1   Debit:

       (i)   All cash paid by Bray either to me or for the purchase of Joint Venture goods.

       (ii)   All expenses incurred and paid for by Bray.

       (iii)   Share of profit due from me to Bray.

     2   Credit:

All cash received by Bray, eg., from sales of Joint Venture Goods.

In my ledger the balance in Bray's account represents the amount due to or from him.

JOINT VENTURE ACCOUNT

	£	£		£
Purchases		10,000	Cash (Bray)	9,000
Advertising (Bray)		400	Cash (Fry)	3,100
Cash:				
Transport		50		
Sundry Expenses		300		
Profit:				
Fry 3/5	810			
Bray 2/5	540			
		1,350		
		12,100		12,100

M BRAY

Purchases	10,000	Cash (½ cost of purchases)	5,000
Transport	50	Cash (Proceeds of sale effected by Fry)	3,100
Sundry Expenses	300	Cash (Balance due from Bray)	3,060
Share of Profit transferred to			
Profit and Loss Account	810		
	11,160		11,160

IN BRAY'S LEDGER
J FRY

Cash:		Proceeds of sale	9,000
Purchases	5,000		
Advertising	400		
Share of Profit to Profit and Loss			
Account	540		
Cash to Fry (Balance)	3,060		
	9,000		9,000

Exercise 27

1 On 1st January, 19·1, Benson of London sent 100 cases of goods to Sutton, his agent abroad, on consignment terms. The cost of the goods was £30 a case. Freight and other expenses paid by Benson amounted to £120.

The agent paid £240 for duty and landing charges. By 31st March he had sold eighty cases for £3,420. He deducted £171 for commission together with the duty he had paid, and sent a remittance for the balance to Benson.

Show the necessary entries in Benson's books to record these matters including the appropriate transfer to general profit and loss account.

(RSA II)

2 On 1st July, 19·2, Smithson of London sent 100 cases of goods to Jackson of Melbourne, Australia, on consignment terms. Smithson paid £80 per case for these goods, and it was agreed that he should bear all the expenses of the consignment. He paid freight and insurance amounting to £240.

On 31st December, 19·2, Smithson received an account sales from Jackson showing that sixty cases had been sold for £6,900. Jackson had paid duty and landing charges on the whole consignment amounting to £220. His selling expenses were £70 and he was entitled to a commission of 5% on the gross value of the goods sold.

Jackson enclosed with the account sales a remittance for the amount due from him to Smithson.

You are required to set out the ledger accounts, in Smithson's books, for the above transactions, and to show the transfer to Smithson's Profit and Loss Account at 31st December, 19·2.

(RSA II)

3 On 1st January, 1972, Ian Pearson of Bristol consigned goods to his agent, R Groom, in Australia by the s.s. *Borodino*, goods costing £21,000. In shipping the goods Pearson paid the following expenses:

	£
Freight	1,900
Marine Insurance	85
Haulage Charges	25

An Account Sales received by Pearson from Groom showed that Groom had disposed of nine-tenths of the goods for £28,000 and forwarded a remittance to Pearson, less his commission of 5%, on Gross Sales and his expenses in connection with the consignment, ie., Duty and Landing Charges £890. You are required to show the necessary consignment accounts in the books of Pearson, whose accounting year ended on 30th April.

4 On 20th December, 1974, S Bentall of London consigned to Zeno & Co., his agent in Saigon, forty cases of goods invoiced pro-forma at £120 per case. Bentall paid carriage charges of £42 and insurance £64.

The consignee paid landing charges of £158 on 19th January, and, on 26th February, rendered an account sales showing that thirty cases had realised £7,000 gross. The consignee's selling expenses amounted to £250, and in addition he was entitled to a commission of 4% on all sales and an additional del credere commission of 1% in respect of all credit sales which, in fact, accounted for £4,000 of the total. The account sales was accompanied by a remittance for the balance due to Bentall. Bentall's financial year ends on 28th February.

Show in the books of Bentall:

(a) the consignment account;

(b) Zeno & Co's account;

(c) Goods on Consignment account;

all ruled off at 28th February, 1974.

5 On 1st April, 19·1, The Export Co. consigned seventy-two cases of cutlery to A Dennis & Co., of Kingston, Jamaica, and forwarded a pro-forma invoice at the cost price of £427. On the same day the consignors paid freight charges £1·00 and insurance 50p per case.

On 1st August, 19·1, the following was received by the consignor together with the bill as stated:

Account Sales of part consignment of seventy-two cases received from The Export Co., per s.s. *Empire* by Dennis & Co., up to 30th June, 19·1.

	£	£
72 cases at £9 per case		648
Less		
Landing Charges, etc.	36	
Commission due to us	33	
		69
Sight draft herewith for		579

Dennis & Co.

Record these transactions in the books of The Export Co., showing the profit on the consignment.

(RSA)

6 On 1st January, 19·1, A N Exporter forwarded a consignment of 200 cases of tropical helmets to A Trader, his agent in West Africa, together with a pro-forma invoice for £360. On the following day, the consignor paid the freight charges amounting to £55 and insurance charges £9. On 15th March, 19·1, an Account Sales was received from the agent showing that 150 cases had been sold for £380, and that landing and storage charges on the consignment amounting to £28 had been paid by the agent. The agent's commission of 5% of the gross sales was deducted and the balance due was remitted by sight draft.

Record these transactions in the books of the consignor showing the profit or loss on the consignment.

(RSA)

7 On 1st January, 19·1, A Exporter & Co. forwarded a consignment of 100 card indexes to J Dyke, his agent in South Africa, and also sent a pro-forma invoice showing the price at £7·50 each. On 7th January, 19·1, the firm paid freight and insurance charges on the consignment amounting to £65.

On 30th June, 19·1, an account sales was received from the agent showing that fifty cabinets had been sold at £10 each and that various landing and storage charges had been paid by him on the whole of the consignment amounting to £85. The agent also deducted his commission of 5% of the gross sales, forwarded a draft for the net proceeds of the sale, and intimated that the balance would be sold shortly at the same price. Record these transactions in the books of the consignor, showing the profit or loss at the 30th June, 19·1.

(RSA)

8 On 1st October, 19·1, C D, an Exporter, consigned to G H & Co., 200 cases of goods costing the exporter £50 per case. The exporter paid insurance £150 and freight £600. G H & Co., were entitled to a commission of 5% on gross sales. The consignees paid customs duty £400 and landing and warehouse charges of £300 on behalf of C D. On 8th December, 19·1, C D received a cheque for £1,050 from the insurance company in full settlement of a claim for twenty cases of the consignment lost in transit. On 31st March, 19·2, G H & Co., accounted for the sale of 140 cases for £11,200 and remitted the net amount due to C D. You are required to show the accounts necessary to record in C D's ledger the foregoing transactions, and the transfer to profit and loss account at 31st March, 19·2.

9 Adams and Bell were art dealers who agreed to purchase certain pictures on joint account, the arrangement being that the party effecting the sale was to be allowed a commission of 5% on the amount realised, the remaining profit being divided equally.

On 25th June, 19·1, Adams bought three pictures for £1,600, and Bell purchased two others for £1,350. Expenses of £35 were incurred, of which Adams paid £25 and Bell £10.

On 17th July Adams sold one of the pictures for £600 and on 25th July forwarded another picture to Bell, the cost of carriage and insurance (paid by Adams) being £7. Bell sold this picture on 5th August for £720 and on the same day sent Adams a cheque for the amount realised, less 5%. The pictures purchased by Bell were sold by him on 10th and 29th July for £850 and £780 respectively.

At 30th September the remaining picture was still unsold, and it was arranged that Adams should take this over for £400. On 5th October the amount due from one party to the other was settled by cheque.

Prepare a general statement showing the result of the venture and write up the Joint Account as it would appear in the books of Adams.

(RSA)

10 Ragg and Stone decide to enter into a Joint Venture for the sale of second-hand cars and it is agreed that the profits or losses incurred are to be shared in the proportion 2:1 respectively. Ragg contributes 5 cars valued at £750 each and Stone puts up £2,000 which is paid into a Joint Venture Cash Account. These transactions take place on 1st January. The following expenses are paid by Stone out of Joint Venture Cash:

	£
Advertising	70
Hire of Show Room	10
Commissionaire's Wages	6
Hire of Carpet	3

Ragg provides flowers for the showroom and pays a florist £2 for them. He also provides a shorthand-typist-receptionist and charges the Joint Venture with £8.

Two cars are sold for £1,720. As Stone is rather short of cash, it is agreed that this amount be paid into the Joint Venture Cash Account so that Stone can withdraw £1,500 at once.

Two further cars are sold for £1,850 but this sum is kept by Ragg who wants to buy more cars. At the end of two weeks it is agreed to close the Joint Venture, the one unsold car being taken back by Ragg at the original transfer price.

You are required to show the Joint Venture Accounts in the books of Ragg and Stone, and also the Memorandum Joint Venture Account. Show also how the Joint Venture Accounts are completed and closed off.

11 Samson and Delilah entered into a joint venture to buy and sell scrap metal. Profits and losses were to be shared: Samson 3/5ths; Delilah 2/5ths.

On 5th October Samson bought metal for £600. He incurred various expenses amounting to £260. On 13th October, he bought a further £1,200 worth, which he sold the same day for £1,400. The buyer paid £800 cash, which Samson banked, and paid the balance with a cheque which Samson endorsed to Delilah who paid it into her own bank account. On 18th October part of the original stock bought by Samson was sold for £400, which Samson used to buy a motor lorry for the purposes of the venture. Delilah provided for the venture, from her own stocks, metal worth £1,000 on 20th October. Her yard was used as the base for the venture's operations and it was agreed that she should receive from the venture £200 for rent and services. Between 20th October and 31st December various sales totalling £1,800 were made, all the proceeds being collected by Delilah. At 31st December Delilah took over the remaining stocks at an agreed value of £200 and Samson took over the lorry at an agreed value of £360. The venture then closed, and on 15th January the sum required in full settlement between Samson and Delilah was duly paid.

You are required to produce:

(a) A memorandum account for the venture, showing the net profit.

(b) The joint venture accounts appearing in the books of:
   (i) Delilah.
   (ii) Samson.

Chapter Twenty Eight

Partnership Accounts

Why Partnership?

At a certain stage in the development of his business, the sole trader might consider the advisability of taking a partner into his business for all or some of the following reasons:

1 To provide extra capital for expanding the business.

2 To help improve management of a growing firm. The newcomer might have certain qualifications which would improve the capacity or the efficiency of the business.

3 The newcomer might be a family friend or a young relative who would share the burden of responsibilities and would carry on the business on the retirement of the older member.

The choice of partner is of the utmost importance; it should be made from people the trader knows intimately, because each partner may contract on behalf of the firm without the knowledge of the other partner; unless a partner's powers are limited by agreement *and those dealing with him are aware of such agreement.*

Definition

A partnership is an association of two to twenty persons in industry or commerce. There is no maximum limit for professional bodies such as solicitors, accountants, members of the Stock Exchange, provided the approval of the Department of Trade and Industry is obtained for this purpose.

Partner's Liability

Every one of the partners is individually liable for the total debts of the firm. Should the business go into liquidation, the partners would contribute a proportion of the debts corresponding to the ratio in which they shared profits and losses. Otherwise, each partner is liable to the full extent of his private property, such as his house.

The Limited Partnership Act 1907

A partnership may have members whose liability is limited to the capital they have invested in the firm. However, they may not take any part in the management of the business. In a limited partnership, one member at least is a limited partner and one member at least a general partner.

The Partnership Act of 1890

The Partnership Act of 1890 governs the legal aspects of partnerships. It lays down the maximum number of partners which has already been quoted above. If persons enter into partnership with one another without drawing up an article or deed of partnership, then every clause of the Act (Section 24) would have effect without qualification. The following are the accounting requirements of the Act in the absence of a deed between the partners:

1 Profits or losses must be shared equally (irrespective of the relative magnitude of each partner's contribution to capital).

2 Interest on capital is not allowed.

3 Interest on drawings is not chargeable by the firm.

4 Salaries to partners are not allowed.

5 A partner who has contributed a sum of money in excess of the capital he has invested (ie. a loan to the firm), is entitled to interest upon the extra amount.

These provisions of the Act might be qualified or altered if the partners wisely decide to draw up an agreement between them. In such a deed, or article of partnership, the following are the accounting matters which would usually be covered:

1 The capital to be contributed by each partner.

2 The ratio in which profits or losses are to be shared.

3 The rate of interest, if any, to be allowed on capital.

4 The rate of interest, if any, chargeable on partners' drawings.

5 Salaries, if any, payable to the partners.

The Ratio of the Share of Profits

In the absence of an agreement between the partners, the provisions of the Act would be enforced, that no matter what the proportion of capital contributed by each partner, they share profits or losses equally. But if there is an agreement which provides that profits are to be shared in proportion to the capital contributed by each partner, then if A and B contributed £5,000 and £3,000 respectively (Total £8,000), A would receive 5/8ths and B 3/8ths of the profits. This is a fair arrangement, provided that the partners share the responsibility equally between them.

Interest on Capital

A businessman asks himself: 'Is the return on the capital I have invested in my business approximately equal to the interest or profit I would have received if I had invested it in some other enterprise?' To ensure that he receives at least a basic return, the concept of interest on capital has been devised. This provides for an agreed interest, to be allowed to the partners, on the capital they have invested, *before* the trading profits are shared.

The Appropriation Account*

Thus, suppose:

1 The Net Trading Profit of the firm (the profit with which you are now familiar, as in a sole trader's business) is £4,000.

2 Interest on capital at 5% per annum is to be allowed.

Then the *Appropriation Account* appears as follows:

EX. 28/1

PROFIT AND LOSS ACCOUNT

		£			£
Sundry expenses		6,000	Gross profit	b/d	10,000
Net trading profit	c/d	4,000			
		10,000			10,000

APPROPRIATION ACCOUNT

	£			£
Interest on Capital:		Net Trading Profit	b/d	4,000
A: 5% on £5,000	250			
B: 5% on £3,000	150			
	400			
Share of Profit: (Balance)				
A: 3/5ths (of £3,600)	2,160			
B: 2/5ths (of £3,600)	1,440			
	4,000			4,000

Another reason for interest on capital is to even out to some extent an unequal contribution of capital from each partner, if profits are still shared equally. In such a case, in accordance with their deed of partnership only the partner contributing the greater capital (the senior partner) might be allowed interest on his capital. This reduces share of profits, to the disadvantage of the junior partner, who is not compensated by interest on *his* capital. Usually, however, interest on capital applies to both partners.

EX. 28/2

I GO INTO PARTNERSHIP WITH M RICH

I, John Fry, went into partnership with my friend, M Rich. Our respective contributions to capital were: J Fry £10,000; M Rich £5,000. Profits to be shared equally. Interest on capital to be allowed at 5% per year. Consider the effect of interest on capital in this instance on the distribution of profit, say £3,000, if (i) it is shared equally, without interest, and (ii) shared equally, but with interest:

(i)

APPROPRIATION ACCOUNT

	£			£
Share of Profit:		Net trading profit	b/d	3,000
J Fry	1,500			
M Rich	1,500			
	3,000			3,000

*This is a second section of the profit and loss account specifically to show how the trading profit has been used up, or appropriated.

(ii)

APPROPRIATION ACCOUNT

	£			£
Interest on Capital:		Net trading profit	b/d	3,000
J Fry	500			
M Rich	250			
Share of Profit:				
J Fry	1,125			
M Rich	1,125			
	3,000			3,000

Total received in (ii): J Fry $500 + 1,125 = £1,625$

M Rich $250 + 1,125 = £1,375$

£3,000

Interest on Drawings

It is to the advantage of the firm not to encourage the withdrawal of funds by partners for their personal use before the end of the financial year. Such withdrawals of cash might help to weaken the financial position of the firm. The provision of interest on drawings in the partnership agreement deters the partners from appropriating money for their personal use before the end of the year, when it is due to them; but if such drawings are made, the firm is compensated by the interest chargeable to the partners. For example:

EX. 28/3

1 The accounting year ends on 31st December.

2 I, John Fry, am entitled to £1,000 per year drawings, to be credited or paid to me on 31st December.

3 Interest at 5% per annum is chargeable on moneys drawn before the end of the year.

4 I draw £600 on 1st August (five months before it is due to me).

Then I, (ie. my Current Account[1]), is debited with £12·50:

$$\frac{5}{100} \times 600 \times \frac{5}{12} = £12 \cdot 50$$

(this figure will be shown as £12 when it recurs in the following examples).

and the Appropriation Account is credited with that amount.

Partners' Salaries

If my partner, M Rich, agreed to be responsible for an aspect of the business in which he is particularly qualified, he might be entitled to a salary, quite apart from his share of the business profits. Suppose he is a qualified accountant as well as a businessman, and he agrees to act as the Secretary of the firm. He has two functions, each carrying its own burden; each ought to have its own return:

1 He has invested his capital in the business; therefore he is entitled to a share of the profits.

2 As a qualified accountant, he has undertaken to be responsible for the proper maintenance of the firm's accounts, and so he is entitled to a salary for that additional service, say, £1,000 per year.

[1]See Chapter 13 on Proprietor's Current Account.

The Appropriation Account now appears as follows:

APPROPRIATION ACCOUNT

	£			£
Interest on Capital:		Net Trading Profit	b/d	4,000
J Fry	500	Interest on Drawings:		
M Rich	250	J Fry		12
Salary—M Rich	1,000			
Share of Profit:				
J Fry ½ share	1,131			
M Rich ½ share	1,131			
	4,012			4,012

Alternative Vertical form:

APPROPRIATION ACCOUNT

			£	£	£
Net Trading Profit	b/d			4,000	
Interest on Drawings				12	4,012
Interest on Capital	Fry		500		
	Rich		250	750	
Salaries	Rich			1,000	1,750
Share of Profit	Fry		1,131		
	Rich		1,131		2,262

Partners' Capital Accounts

In partnership accounting, each partner has his own, separate, capital account. The capital accounts are said to be *fixed*, that is, no entries are made in them apart from the original capital and any subsequent additions to or reductions of capital. It is possible, but not advisable, to have fluctuating capital accounts (as for sole traders, with which you are familiar) in which all the transactions of a partner with the firm might be shown. The Partnership's Capital Accounts are set out as follows:

CAPITAL ACCOUNTS

			J Fry	M Rich
	Jan. 1 Cash		£10,000	£5,000

Partners' Current Accounts

Each partner has a current account of his own in which his transactions with the firm are recorded. The transactions of Fry and Rich with the firm, so far recorded in the foregoing examples, appear in their respective current accounts as follows:

EX. 28/4

CURRENT ACCOUNTS

Cash:			J Fry £	M Rich £				J Fry £	M Rich £
Aug. 1 Drawings			600		Dec. 31 Interest on				
Dec. 31 Drawings			400		Capital			500	250
31 Interest on					Salaries				1,000
drawings			12		Share of Profit			1,131	1,131
Balance	c/d		619	2,381					
			1,631	2,381				1,631	2,381
					Jan. 1 Balance	b/d		619	2,381

A COMPREHENSIVE EXAMPLE

The above provisions (*with additional items*), drawn together in a deed of partnership, are briefly expressed below:

Contributions of Capital:

J Fry £10,000; M Rich £5,000.

Interest on capital allowed at 5% per annum.

Interest on drawings chargeable at 5% per annum.

Salary of £1,000 per annum to M Rich and J Fry respectively.

During the first year's trading, the following amounts were drawn by the partners for their private use:

J Fry: 1st August £600   M Rich: 30th September £800

31st December £600   31st December £200

Net trading profit for year ended 31st December, 19·1, £4,000.

EX. 28/5   The above are entered in a complete set of accounts in the firm's ledger as follows:

CAPITAL ACCOUNTS

	J Fry £	M Rich £	19·1			J Fry £	M Rich £
£			Jan. 1	Cash		10,000	5,000

CURRENT ACCOUNTS

		Int. on Drawings					
Aug. 1	Cash-Drawings	600		Dec. 31	Interest on		
1	Interest on				Capital T	500	250
	Drawings	12	12		Partners		
Sept. 30	Cash-Drawings		800		Salaries T	1,000	1,000
30	Interest on				Share of Profit T	636	636
	Drawings	10	10				
		600	200				
Dec. 31	Trans. to Interest on Drawings A/c	22					
Dec. 31	Balances c/d	924	876				
		2,136	1,886				2,136	1,886
				Jan. 1	Balance b/d	924	876

INTEREST ON CAPITAL

Dec. 31	Current Accounts: Fry	500	Dec. 31	Appropriation Account T	750
	Rich	250			
		750			750

INTEREST ON DRAWINGS

Dec. 31	Appropriation Account T	22	Dec. 31	Current Accounts T	22

PARTNERS SALARIES

Dec. 31	Current Accounts T	2,000	Dec. 31	Appropriation Account T	2,000

APPROPRIATION ACCOUNT
FOR YEAR ENDED 31ST DECEMBER, 19·1

Interest on Capital:	Fry	500		Net Trading Profit	b/d		4,000
	Rich	250	750	Interest on Drawings:	Fry	12	
Salaries	Fry	1,000			Rich	10	22
	Rich	1,000					
			2,000				
Share of Profit	Fry	636					
	Rich	636					
			4,022				4,022

EX. 28/6   The following extract from the Partners' Balance Sheet shows how the Capital and Current Accounts are set out:

BALANCE SHEET (EXTRACT)
AS AT 31ST DECEMBER, 19·1

	J Fry £	M Rich £	£
Capital Accounts	10,000	5,000	15,000
Current Accounts:			
Interest on Capital	500	250	
Salaries	1,000	1,000	
Share of Profit	636	636	
	2,136	1,886	
Less Drawings	1,200	1,000	
Interest on Drawings	12	10	
	1,212	1,010	
Balances	924	876	1,800

EX. 28/7   If one of the current accounts were in debit, it would be indicated by (Dr.) after the figure. The last line of the above example (example 28/6) would then appear as follows:

	£	£	£
Balances	924	876 (Dr.)	48

Exercise 28

1 Black and White are in partnership. From the following information write up Black's current account in Black and White's ledger:

		£
1 Oct. 1970	Black's credit balance	600
30 Sept. 1971	share of profit	1,400
	interest on capital	60
	salary	1,500
	drawings during year	3,000

Balance the account on 30th September, 1971.

(*RSA 1971*)

2 Jackson is a partner in a business and is entitled to one-third of the net profit of the firm. From the following particulars write up the Capital and Current accounts of Jackson for the year to 31st December, 1968, as they would appear in the Ledger of the partnership.

1968		£
Jan. 1	Balance on Jackson's Capital Account (credit)	3,000
1	Balance on Jackson's Current Account (credit)	450
May 1	Additional capital brought in by Jackson	600
Dec. 31	Jackson's Drawings for the year	1,600
31	Interest allowed on Jackson's capital	170
31	Jackson's salary	800
31	Net Profit for the year (after adjustment of partners' salaries and interest) divisible between the partners	6,300
31	Amount transferred from Jackson's Current Account to his Capital Account	1,400

(*RSA I 1969*)

3 Wheel and Barrow are in partnership under an agreement which provides that profits and losses shall be shared three-fifths and two-fifths respectively, and that before this division is made, Barrow shall be entitled to a salary of £1,200 per annum and partners shall be credited with 8% per annum interest on their capitals which are as follows:

Wheel £10,000

Barrow £4,000

The profit for the year ended 31st December, 1970, before making any of these adjustments amounted to £8,830.

Write up the Profit and Loss Appropriation Account for the year.

(*RSA I 1971*)

4 Badger and Coote carry on business in partnership, sharing profits in the proportion of three-fifths and two-fifths respectively.

On 1st April, 1969, the Capital Accounts of the partners showed the following credit balances: Badger, £10,000; Coote, £6,000; and the Current Accounts: Badger, £400 credit balance and Coote, £150 debit balance.

The Partnership Agreement provides that the partners shall be allowed interest on capital at 5% per annum and that Coote shall be entitled to a salary of £1,200 per annum. During the year ended 31st March, 1970, the partners' drawings were: Badger, £4,000 and Coote, £3,750.

The profit for the year, prior to making any of the foregoing adjustments, was £8,000. You are required to write up the Appropriation Section of the Profit and Loss Account for the year ended 31st March, 1970 and the Current Accounts of the partners.

(*RSA I 1970*)

5 Hayes and Harlington are in partnership. On 30th June, 1973, their Capital Accounts (unchanged since 1st July, 1972) are: Hayes, £15,000; Harlington, £10,000. Their deed of partnership provides that, after the net profit for any year has been ascertained, the balance available will be applied as follows:

(a) Harlington is to receive a salary of £1,200.

(b) Each partner is to be credited with interest on capital at 6% per annum.

(c) After providing for (a) and (b) the balance remaining available is to be divided equally between the partners.

You are required to draw up the partnership Appropriation Account for the year ended 30th June, 1973. The net profit as shown by the Trading and Profit and Loss Account was £6,250.

(*RSA I*)

6 The partnership agreement between L Hemp, T Wool and M Cotton contains the following provisions:

(a) The partners' fixed capitals shall be: Hemp, £12,000; Wool, £10,000; Cotton, £8,000.

(b) Wool and Cotton are to receive salaries of £800 and £600 respectively.

(c) Interest on capital is to be calculated at 6% per annum.

(d) Hemp, Wool and Cotton are to share profits and losses in the ratios 3:2:1.

(e) No interest is to be charged on drawings or current accounts.

On 1st January, 19·1, the balances on current accounts were:
Hemp Cr. £700; Wool Cr. £400; Cotton Dr. £100.
During the year the drawings were:
Hemp, £2,500; Wool, £1,800; Cotton, £1,200.
The Profit and Loss Account for the year showed a profit of £8,900 before charging interest on capital or on partners' salaries.
Show the Capital and Current Accounts of Hemp, Wool and Cotton as at 31st December, 19·1, after division of the profit.

(RSA I)

7 Root and Branch are in partnership, sharing profits and losses equally. On 1st January, 19·3, the following balances appeared in the partners' personal accounts:

Capital Accounts: Root, £4,000; Branch, £3,000.

Current Accounts–Credit balances: Root, £17; Branch, £20.

From the above and the details which follow, show the Balance Sheet of the partnership at 31st December, 19·3. Net profit for the year was £3,678 after providing for interest on capital Root, £200 and Branch, £150.

	£
Partners drawings for the year:	
Root	2,000
Branch	2,000
Sundry creditors	1,980
Sundry debtors	2,980
Provision for bad and doubtful debts	150
Stock	2,760
Amounts pre-paid	40
Furniture and Fixtures	470
Machinery and equipment at cost	2,600
Depreciation provided for machinery and equipment	1,250
Cash at bank	1,535
Petty cash	60

Set out the Balance Sheet in Vertical form to show clearly the amount of Fixed and Current Assets, the amount of Current Liability and working capital.

8 Peele and Mellis conduct business in partnership on the following terms:

(a) Interest is to be allowed on partners' capital accounts at 6% per annum.

(b) Peele is to be credited with a partnership salary of £750 per annum.

(c) The balance of profit in any year is to be shared equally by the partners.

After preparing their Trading and Profit and Loss Account for the year ended 31st March, 19·2, but before making any provision for Interest on Capital or for Peele's partnership salary, the following balances remained on the books:

	Dr. £	Cr. £
Capital Accounts: Peele (as on 1st April, 19·1)		1,000
Mellis (as on 1st April, 19·1)		2,000
Current Accounts: Peele		220
Mellis		100
Drawings Account: Peele	890	
Mellis	500	
Profit and Loss Account—Net Profit for year		4,500
Stock—31st March, 19·2	1,400	
Goodwill Account	1,000	
Plant and Machinery, at cost	3,000	
Depreciation		600
Fixtures and Fittings, at cost	1,800	
Depreciation		950
Trade Debtors and Creditors	3,500	850
Loan from H Oldcastle, and accrued interest		2,120
Rent accrued due at 31st March, 19·2		150
Insurance unexpired at 31st March, 19·2	95	
Cash at bank: Current Account	305	
	12,490	12,490

It is agreed by the partners to reduce the book value of Goodwill by writing off £250 at 31st March, 19·2 (to be charged to the Appropriation Section of the Profit and Loss Account).

You are asked to prepare the Appropriation Section of the firm's Profit and Loss Account and the partners' current accounts for the year ended 31st March, 19·2 together with the Balance Sheet as on that date.

(RSA I)

9 Baker and Grocer are in partnership sharing profits and losses equally. Interest on capital is allowed at 5% per annum. From the following Trial Balance (extracted after the Trading and Profit and Loss Accounts had been completed) prepare the partners' Profit and Loss Appropriation Account and Current Accounts for the year ended 30th September, 1970, and a Balance Sheet on that date, showing the working capital of the partnership. Show interest charges to the nearest £.

	£	£
Capital: Baker (1st October, 1969)		7,000
Grocer		5,000
Current Accounts: Baker (1st October, 1969)		275
Grocer	125	
Net trading profit for the year ended 30th September, 1970		3,600
Drawings during year ended 30th September, 1970:		
Baker (£700 drawn on 28.2.70)	1,400	
Grocer (£800 drawn on 30.4.70)	1,700	
Creditors		450
Rates		50
Machinery	10,000	
Shop Fittings	900	
Stock	1,700	
Debtors	30	
Bank Balance	400	
Cash in hand	60	
Insurance	60	
	16,375	16,375

During the year ended 30th September, 1970, the following depreciation had been written off:

Machinery £500.

Shop Fittings £100.

(RSA I 1970)

10 Sam and Bill are in partnership sharing profits equally and the following trial balance was extracted from their books at 31st December, 1970:

	£	£
Capital: Sam		19,124
Bill		17,347
Freehold premises at cost	22,500	
Motor vans at cost	6,000	
Provision for depreciation of motor vans at 31st December, 1969		3,400
Sales		112,442
Purchases	80,248	
Debtors and creditors	10,261	7,419
Bad debts	427	
Provision for doubtful debts at 31st December, 1969		381
Rent and Rates	1,050	
General expenses	1,192	
Salaries and Wages	9,819	
Motor expenses	1,002	
Lighting and Heating	284	
Drawings: Sam	4,808	
Bill	5,013	
Stock in trade, 31st December, 1969	14,242	
Bank	3,267	
	160,113	160,113

You are given the following additional information:

(i) Stock in trade at 31st December, 1970, £15,172.

(ii) Rates paid in advance 31st December, 1970, £80.

(iii) Depreciation is to be charged on the motor vans at the annual rate of 20% of cost.

(iv) Provision for doubtful debts is to be increased by £82.

(v) Lighting and Heating due at 31st December, 1970, £62.

(vi) During 1970 Sam took goods for his own use for which £124 has been paid but no entries have been made in the books to record this transaction.

You are asked to prepare a trading and profit and loss account for 1970 and a balance sheet at 31st December, 1970.

(RSA II 1971)

11 Rathlin and Lambay were partners sharing profits and losses in the ratio of 3:2. The following trial balance was extracted from their books as on 31st December, 19·3:

TRIAL BALANCE

	£	£
Capital account balances 1st January, 19·3:		
Rathlin		28,000
Lambay		14,000
Drawings:		
Rathlin	6,800	
Lambay	4,400	
Furniture and Fittings (cost £1,700)	1,360	
Stock in trade 31st December, 19·2	21,000	
Trade debtors and trade creditors	16,328	12,750
Purchases	152,000	
Sales		206,000
Freehold properties at cost	18,500	
Wages and Salaries	25,454	
Rates	300	
General expenses	9,832	
Balance at bank	2,408	
Discounts allowed	4,154	
Discounts received		1,630
Rents received		156
	262,536	262,536

You are given the following additional information:

(a) Stock in trade 31st December, 19·3, £23,500.

(b) Wages and salaries outstanding 31st December, 19·3, £304.

(c) Rates paid in advance at 31st December, 19·3, £60.

(d) Rent received £156 includes £12 for the month of January, 19·4.

(e) Depreciation on furniture and fittings is to be provided at the rate of 10% per annum on cost.

(f) The partners are to be credited with interest at the rate of 5% per annum on the balances on their capital accounts as at 1st January, 19·3. They are also to be charged with interest on their drawings: Rathlin is to bear £170 and Lambay £110.

You are required to prepare a trading and profit and loss account for the year 19·3 and a balance sheet as on 31st December, 19·3.

(RSA II)

12 Taylor and Wells are partners. Their agreement provides that interest shall be allowed on partners' capitals (calculated on balances at 1st January in each year) at 5% per annum and charged on drawings. Profits and losses are shared in the proportions Taylor two-thirds, and Wells one-third.

The following Trial Balance was extracted from the books as on 31st December, 19·1:

TRIAL BALANCE

	£	£
Capital accounts:		
Taylor		12,000
Wells		10,000
Drawings:		
Taylor	4,800	
Wells	3,000	
Stock in trade 1st January, 19·1	15,400	
Debtors	12,670	
Creditors		9,880
Purchases	97,800	
Sales		128,600
Wages and Salaries	10,580	
Rent and Rates	850	
Bad debts	1,470	
Returns Inwards	1,200	
Returns Outwards		800
Lease of Premises	1,400	
General expenses	7,150	
Provision for Bad Debts at 1st January, 19·1		600
Furniture and Fittings	5,200	
Balance at bank	90	
Discounts allowed	2,530	
Discounts received		2,260
	164,140	164,140

You are given the following information:

(a) A purchase invoice for £330 had been entered twice in the purchases journal in December 19·1, and posted twice to the supplier's account, but no payment had been made before the end of the year.

(b) Stock in trade at 31st December, 19·1, was valued at £18,600.

(c) Wages outstanding at 31st December, 19·1, amounted to £220.

(d) Rates paid in advance at 31st December, 19·1, amounted to £40.

(e) The provision for bad debts is to be increased to £740.

(f) The lease of the premises expires on 31st December, 19·4.

(g) Provide depreciation on Furniture and Fittings at 5% per annum.

(h) Interest on drawings to be charged for 19·1 amount to £130 for Taylor and £110 for Wells.

Prepare the Trading and Profit and Loss Account for 19·1 and the Balance Sheet at that date.

(*RSA II*)

13 Langston and Kent were in partnership sharing profits equally. The partnership was commenced on 1st January, 1971, and on that date each partner contributed £6,500 as his capital. The partners' drawings during 1971 were Langston, £2,140 and Kent, £1,975.

The following information was extracted from the books at 31st December, 1972:

TOTAL BANK ACCOUNT FOR 1972

	£		£
Opening balance	2,648	Cash paid to suppliers	35,391
Cash received from customers	55,871	Rent and Rates	1,750
		General expenses	10,431
		Drawings:	
		Langston	3,076
		Kent	3,144
		Closing balance	4,727
	58,519		58,519

	31st Dec., 1971	31st Dec., 1972
	£	£
Stock	5,171	5,348
Debtors	3,774	3,922
Creditors for Purchases	1,926	2,284

Motor Vans which cost £5,200 on 1st January, 1971, are still in use and it was decided when they were purchased that they should be subject to an annual depreciation charge of 25% on cost.

You are required to prepare Langston and Kent's trading and profit and loss account for 1972 and balance sheet as at 31st December, 1971.

(*RSA II 1973*)

Chapter Twenty Nine

Admission of Partner

Payment of Premium by New Partner

I, John Fry, and my partner, Martin Rich, think that with some extra capital our business could be expanded. We therefore invite our mutual friend, Sam Cook, to join our business. He brings in his Capital £5,000, plus £2,000 as a *Premium* for the privilege of coming into an established business. It is agreed that profits or losses are to be divided as to:

Fry one-half; the remainder: Rich three-fifths; Cook two-fifths.

EX. 29/1   On 1st January, 19·3, Cook's contributions are placed into the firm's bank and the postings are made to his Capital Account and to a Premium Account:

CASH BOOK

19·3			£
Jan.	1	S Cook:	
		Capital Account	5,000
		Premium Account	2,000

CAPITAL ACCOUNTS

				£ J Fry	£ M Rich	£ S Cook
19·3						
Jan.	1	Balances b/d		10,000	5,000	
	1	Cash				5,000

PREMIUM ACCOUNT

19·3			
Jan.	1	Cash—S Cook	2,000

What Happens to the Premium

Now, the premium may either be:

1 Withdrawn from the firm for the original partners' own use, divided between them in the ratio of their original agreement, that is, in equal shares.

2 Placed into their capital accounts in equal shares.

Method 1:

Premium Withdrawn

EX. 29/2   The reason for the following entries is merely to record the fact that S Cook paid a premium of £2,000 on coming into the business. It would have been possible (though not businesslike) for him to have made a *Direct Payment* to the partners, outside the firm, when no entries at all would have been made in the firm's books. The sequence of the entries below is evident:

(a) Pay premium into bank—Debit Cash Book.

(b) Credit Premium Account.

(c) Transfer Premium Account to Current Accounts of the two original partners in proportions in which they shared profits and losses.

(d) Withdraw premium: Credit Cash Book; debit Current Accounts.

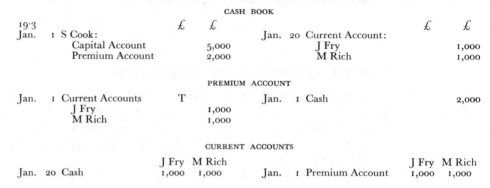

CASH BOOK

19·3			£	£	Jan.	20	Current Account:		£	£
Jan.	1	S Cook:					J Fry			1,000
		Capital Account	5,000				M Rich			1,000
		Premium Account	2,000							

PREMIUM ACCOUNT

Jan.	1	Current Accounts	T		Jan.	1	Cash		2,000
		J Fry		1,000					
		M Rich		1,000					

CURRENT ACCOUNTS

			J Fry	M Rich				J Fry	M Rich
Jan.	20	Cash	1,000	1,000	Jan.	1	Premium Account	1,000	1,000

Method 2:

Premium Added to Original Partners' Capital

The book entries required here are simply a transfer of Premium to Capital Accounts instead of to Current Accounts:

EX. 29/3

CAPITAL ACCOUNTS

			£	£	£
			J Fry	M Rich	S Cook
Jan.	1	Balances b/d	10,000	5,000	
	1	Cash			5,000
	1	Premium	1,000	1,000	

Effects of Adding the Premium to Capital

1 Increases the firm's total capital from £20,000 to £22,000. This widens the scope of the firm's activities to the benefit of all three partners.

2 Interest on Capital makes the retention of the premium in the business more advantageous to Fry and Rich.

3 The extra interest, however, reduces the total profit to be shared, and Sam Cook here is at a distinct disadvantage.

(Which method would Cook favour, method 1 or 2?)

Admission of a Partner who Cannot Contribute any Premium

Suppose that instead of S Cook, Rich and I take C Faith into partnership. Faith can contribute £5,000 Capital but no premium. We accept him because he has considerable business experience and many contacts in certain areas of the business world which we presume will ultimately benefit the firm.

Goodwill*

It is agreed therefore that a Goodwill Account for £5,000 should be opened and *capitalised* (added to Capital Account) in favour of Rich and I: (shared in the proportions in which profits and losses are shared).

EX. 29/4

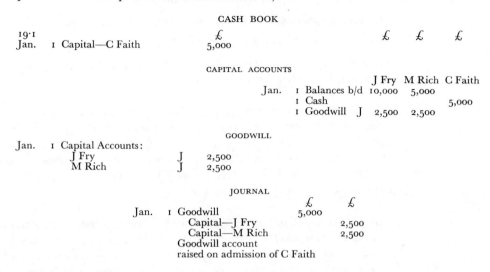

CASH BOOK

			£		£	£	£
19·1							
Jan.	1	Capital—C Faith	5,000				

CAPITAL ACCOUNTS

				J Fry	M Rich	C Faith
Jan.	1	Balances b/d		10,000	5,000	
	1	Cash				5,000
	1	Goodwill	J	2,500	2,500	

GOODWILL

Jan.	1	Capital Accounts:		
		J Fry	J	2,500
		M Rich	J	2,500

JOURNAL

			£	£
Jan.	1	Goodwill	5,000	
		Capital—J Fry		2,500
		Capital—M Rich		2,500
		Goodwill account		
		raised on admission of C Faith		

How does this Goodwill of £5,000, representing nothing but intangible assets, favour Rich and me? Here again it is interest on capital that makes the nominally increased capital desirable to us. Not only do we receive additional interest (as against the low figure Faith can expect as interest on *his* capital), but since interest reduces the total profit available for distribution, Faith's share of it is even less than it would have been if the extra interest on capital had not been deducted from it.

Exercise 29

1 Two partners, John and Peter, with capital respectively of £5,000 and £3,000, share profits and losses equally. They admit Amos as a third partner into their business. He brings in a capital of £4,000 and £2,000 as a premium for the privilege of entering a going concern. The £6,000 is paid into the firm's bank. It is understood that John and Peter retain the premium in equal shares for their own personal use. Record these matters in the firm's ledger.

2 Partners R and S, each with capital of £5,000 and £3,000 respectively, share profits and losses equally. They admit T into the business on the following conditions:

(i)   T is to bring into the business £2,000 as capital and £2,000 as premium.

(ii) The total amount is to be paid into the firm's banking account.

(iii) The premium is to be paid out to R and S in the proportions in which they share profits and losses.

Record the above matters in the firm's books.

---

*Goodwill describes the total value of such advantages as the firm's good name—its reputation, its creditworthiness—its customers, its average annual sales over a given number of years. These are sometimes called the firm's Intangible Assets, as against its Tangible Assets, such as machinery, stock, debtors, etc.

3 Partners Ex and Dart, each with capital of £6,000, share profits or losses equally. They admit Wey into their business on the following terms on 31st January, 19·1:

(i) Wey is to pay: Capital £6,000; Premium £2,000.

(ii) The premium is to remain in the business.

(iii) Profits and Losses to be shared equally between the partners.

(iv) Interest at 5% per annum to be allowed on capital.

Make the necessary entries in the firm's ledger and show the Appropriation Account as on 31st December, 19·1.

4 Hove and Rye are in partnership, sharing profits and losses equally. Each contributes a capital of £8,000. They then admit Hastings into the partnership. Hastings can contribute only £4,000 as his capital; he is unable to offer any more cash as premium. It is therefore agreed that a Goodwill Account shall be raised for £4,000 and that the capital accounts of Rye and Hove shall be credited with £2,000 each. Make the necessary entries in the firm's ledger.

5 Partners Bill and Tom, each with capital of £8,000, share profits and losses equally. They admit Jim into the partnership. Jim's contribution to capital is £4,000 but he is unable to offer any premium. It is therefore agreed to open a Goodwill Account for £4,000, capitalised equally in favour of Bill and Tom. If in future profits are to be shared in proportion to their capital, what ratio of the profits may each partner expect?

6 A and B are partners sharing profits in the same proportion as their capital, which is £6,000 and £3,000 respectively. They agree to admit their Manager, C, into partnership. Under the original agreement C was to pay £3,000 to A and B by way of premium for admission to the firm, and was to pay in a further £3,000 as his capital in the business.

C, however, is only able to raise £4,000; it is, therefore, agreed that a Goodwill Account of £8,000 is to be created, and £1,000 only paid to A and B by way of cash premium.

Prepare the necessary entries to record these transactions.

(RSA)

7 Partners Alp and Bell share profits and losses, Alp three-fifths and Bell two-fifths. On 1st January, 1976, the following credit balances appeared in their ledger:

	Alp £	Bell £
Capital Accounts	12,000	9,000
Current Accounts	300	200

They decided to admit Coyn into their firm on 1st January, 1976. Coyn's capital contribution of £7,000 and his payment of £2,000 as premium, a cheque for a total value of £9,000, was paid into the partnership bank. The premium was retained in the business.

Coyn's share of profit or loss was to be one-quarter and the remainder was to be shared between Alp and Bell equally. Interest on drawings was chargeable at 5%; Interest on capital at 5% (to nearest £).

On 31st December, 1976, after the Trading and Profit and Loss Account had been prepared, the following balances appeared in the firm's books:

	£	£
Capital Accounts (Cr.)		
Alp	12,000	
Bell	9,000	
Coyn	7,000	
		28,000
Current Accounts (Cr.)		
Alp	300	
Bell	200	
		500
Drawings		
Alp		5,000
Bell		4,000
Coyn		2,500
Goodwill		2,000
Freehold Premises		20,000
Furniture and Fixtures		1,600
Mortgage on Freehold Premises		7,000
Trade Debtors		7,000
Trade Creditors		4,000
Expenses due and unpaid		200
Provision for Bad Debts		200
Stock 31st December		5,400
Cash at bank		5,100
Expenses prepaid		300
Net Profit for year		11,000

Depreciation of 10% on Furniture and Fixtures has not been accounted for.

You are required to give:

(a) Capital and Current Accounts at 31st December, 1976.

(b) Appropriation Account.

(c) Balance Sheet as at 31st December, 1976.

Chapter Thirty

Purchase of a Business by Partnership

A SIMPLE EXAMPLE

Mark and Luke acquire John's business for £13,000. The following was John's balance sheet:

	£		£
Capital	10,000	Sundry Assets	12,000
Creditors	2,000		
	12,000		12,000

Mark and Luke each pay £6,500 and agree to share profits and losses equally. They open their books through the Journal Opening Entries:

JOURNAL

	£	£
Sundry Assets	12,000	
Goodwill	3,000	
Creditors		2,000
Vendor (Seller)—John		13,000
Assets and liabilities acquired on purchase of business	15,000	15,000

GOODWILL is the excess of credits over debits and it is a payment for the firms good reputation, list of customers and other advantages of a going concern.

THE PURCHASE PRICE of the business represents the respective capitals of Mark and Luke, £6,500 each. It was paid to John before the business was established. The Vendor's Account must therefore be transferred to Capital Accounts:

JOURNAL

	£	£
Vendor—John	13,000	
Capital		
Mark		6,500
Luke		6,500
Purchase price paid for John's business	13,000	13,000

LEDGER

VENDOR

		£			£
Capital—Mark	J	6,500	Balance	J	13,000
Luke	J	6,500			
		13,000			13,000

CAPITAL

		Mark	Luke
		£	£
Vendor	J	6,500	6,500

238

GOODWILL

		£
Balance	J	3,000

SUNDRY ASSETS

		£
Balance	J	12,000

A MORE REALISTIC EXAMPLE

My partners, M Rich, S Cook and I, John Fry, having been in business together for some years, think it would be a good idea to purchase another business and thus widen our activities by acquiring the assets of an established firm. Our balance sheet at the time stood as follows:

	£			£
Capital			Premises	15,000
Fry	10,000		Machinery	343
Rich	5,000		Furniture	100
Cook	5,000		Stock	457
		20,000	Debtors	6,000
Sundry creditors		1,900		
		21,900		21,900

Tangible and Intangible Assets and Goodwill

The assets we are acquiring consist generally of:

1 Tangible assets, such as Machinery, Furniture and Stock, as well as

2 its intangible assets, such as its annual turnover, customers, good reputation of many years' standing, which together represent the Goodwill of the business.

We decided to consider the purchase of S Booth's business. He presented to us his balance sheet:

EX. 30/1

BALANCE SHEET OF S BOOTH
AS AT 30TH NOVEMBER, 19·

	£		£
Capital	9,500	Machinery	4,500
Creditors	1,300	Furniture and Fittings	2,200
		Stock	1,700
		Debtors	2,000
		Cash at bank	400
	10,800		10,800

Revaluation of Assets

After examining the above, Rich, Cook and I told Booth that we thought the values of Machinery and Furniture and Fittings were over-estimated. He agreed to the following revaluations:

Machinery £4,000

Furniture and Fittings £2,000

The purchase price was agreed at £12,000, excluding the cash at bank which, it was agreed, he would retain. Rich, Cook and I paid Booth £4,000 each from our private resources. This represents additional contributions to our respective capital accounts.

It will be seen on inspection of Booth's balance sheet that, *at the revised values*[1], the assets, less the liabilities comes to no more than £8,400 although the purchase price had been agreed at £12,000. The difference of £3,600 represents the value of Goodwill. Other methods of assessing Goodwill are beyond the scope of this book.

On concluding the purchasing negotiations, the following entries are made in our journal:

EX. 30/2

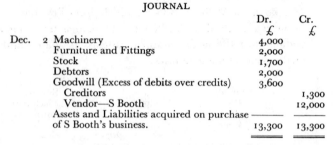

			Dr. £	Cr. £
Dec.	2	Machinery	4,000	
		Furniture and Fittings	2,000	
		Stock	1,700	
		Debtors	2,000	
		Goodwill (Excess of debits over credits)	3,600	
		Creditors		1,300
		Vendor—S Booth		12,000
		Assets and Liabilities acquired on purchase of S Booth's business.	13,300	13,300

The above items are posted to their respective ledger accounts, new accounts being opened where necessary, such as a Vendor's Account and a Goodwill Account.

EX. 30/3

VENDOR—S BOOTH

			£
Dec. 2 Balance	J		12,000

GOODWILL

Dec.	2 Balance	J	3,600

Purchase Price as Part of Capital

This is part of the capital of our business. It must therefore be transferred to capital account:

EX. 30/4

JOURNAL

		Dr. £	Cr. £
Vendor		12,000	
Capital			
J Fry			4,000
M Rich			4,000
S Cook			4,000
Purchase price of business			

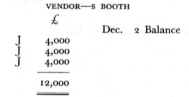

VENDOR—S BOOTH

			£				£
Dec.	2 Capital			Dec.	2 Balance	J	12,000
	J Fry	J	4,000				
	M Rich	J	4,000				
	S Cook	J	4,000				
			12,000				12,000

CAPITAL ACCOUNTS

			£ J Fry	£ M Rich	£ S Cook
Dec.	2 Balance b/d		10,000	5,000	5,000
	2 Vendor J		4,000	4,000	4,000

[1]We are only concerned with the cost of Booth's assets to us; we are not concerned with the values as they appeared in his books.

Goodwill Account

This might be transferred to the Appropriation Section of the Profit and Loss Account and thus closed. But the transferring is usually done in instalments, year by year, so that the available profits for distribution are not wiped out. For example one year after the purchase of the business, £600 might be transferred to Profit and Loss Account, reducing the balance of Goodwill Account to £3,000:

EX. 30/5

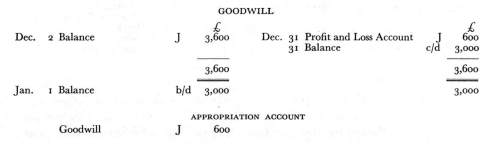

GOODWILL

			£				£
Dec.	2 Balance	J	3,600	Dec. 31 Profit and Loss Account	J	600
				31 Balance	c/d	3,000
			3,600			3,600
Jan.	1 Balance	b/d	3,000			3,000

APPROPRIATION ACCOUNT

Goodwill	J	600	

The Partnership Balance Sheet to Date

On 31st December, 19·7, our balance sheet included all the assets my partnership business originally possessed as well as those purchased from vendor S Booth. The capital of each partner as shown in the balance sheet, corresponds with the figures so far used; so do the figures for Machinery and Furniture. All other figures are necessarily assumed (depreciation on Machinery and Furniture is ignored):

EX. 30/6

BALANCE SHEET OF FRY, RICH AND COOK
AS AT 31ST DECEMBER, 19·7

CAPITAL ACCOUNTS	£	£	FIXED ASSETS	£	£
J Fry	14,000		Goodwill		3,600
M Rich	9,000		Freehold Premises		15,000
S Cook	9,000		Machinery	4,000	
		32,000	New machinery	343	
CURRENT LIABILITIES					4,343
Creditors		3,200	Furniture	100	
			New furniture	2,000	
					2,100
					25,043
			CURRENT ASSETS		
			Stock	2,157	
			Debtors	5,000	
			Cash at bank	3,000	
					10,157
		35,200			35,200

Exercise 30

1 Austin Coe purchases R Dunn's business on the basis of Dunn's balance sheet shown below:

BALANCE SHEET OF R DUNN
AS AT 1ST JANUARY, 19·1

	£		£
Capital	10,000	FIXED ASSETS	
CURRENT LIABILITIES		Freehold property	6,000
Sundry Creditors	3,000	Furniture	300
		CURRENT ASSETS	
		Stock	2,200
		Debtors	3,500
		Cash at bank	1,000
	13,000		13,000

Austin Coe agrees to take over all the assets and liabilities, with the exception of cash at bank, at the values shown in the balance sheet, for the sum of £10,000.

Record the above, in Coe's books and show his balance sheet as at 1st January, 19·1.

2 L May and D Rose enter into partnership to purchase the business of K Price as from 1st July, 19·1. They have agreed to share profits and losses equally and the purchase is to be on the basis of Price's last balance sheet, shown below:

BALANCE SHEET OF K PRICE
AS AT 1ST JULY, 19·1

	£		£	£
Capital—K Price	15,000	FIXED ASSETS		
CURRENT LIABILITIES		Freehold Property	11,500	
Sundry Creditors	3,900	Furniture and Fixtures	300	
				11,800
		CURRENT ASSETS		
		Sundry Debtors	3,100	
		Stock	3,550	
		Cash at bank	450	
				7,100
	18,900			18,900

May and Rose each contribute £9,000 in cash as capital, which was paid into the firm's banking account. The purchase price £16,500 was paid by cheque direct to Price (ie. before the firm's banking account had been opened). The partners took over all the assets and liabilities, except the cash at bank.

Record the above in the partners' books. Show the firm's balance sheet as at 1st July, 19·1.

3 A Morton and S Kenyon enter into partnership to purchase the business of B Burton as from 1st January, 19·1, based upon Burton's balance sheet, shown below:

BALANCE SHEET OF B BURTON
AS AT 1ST JANUARY, 19·1

	£		£	£
Capital	19,000	FIXED ASSETS		
CURRENT LIABILITIES		Freehold Property	8,000	
Sundry Creditors	4,400	Machinery	4,400	
		Fixtures and Fittings	700	
				13,100
		CURRENT ASSETS		
		Sundry Debtors	3,700	
		Stock	5,800	
		Cash at bank	800	
				10,300
	23,400			23,400

The agreed purchase price of £21,000 is paid in equal shares by Morton and Kenyon direct to Burton (ie., before the firm's banking account has been opened). A banking account is then opened and the two partners each pay £1,500 into it. All the assets (with the exception of cash) and the liabilities are taken over, but the partners decide to revalue the assets, and the following reductions are made:

The stock is reduced to £3,300; Fixtures and Fittings to £400; Machinery to £3,600. It is understood that as a result of these reductions, the value of Goodwill, included in the purchase price, will appreciate.

Record the above by journal entries and show the opening balance sheet of the partnership.

4 A, a sole trader owning an established business, took B into partnership on 1st January, 19·1, at which date the goodwill of the business was agreed to be worth £6,000. A's capital (exclusive of goodwill) was £10,000 and B brought in £3,000 as his capital. Interest on Capital Accounts was to be allowed at 5%, and A and B were to divide the remaining profit in the ratio of 2:1.

The profit for the year, before charging interest, was £2,600. Calculate the division of this sum between A and B on the alternative assumptions that:

(i) Goodwill was ignored on B's entering the business.

(ii) Goodwill was taken into account at its correct value.

(*RSA*)

5 George Wright and Henry Dobson enter into partnership upon equal terms, to acquire the business carried on by Amos Atkinson. The business was taken over as at 1st January, 19·1, on the basis of the last certified balance sheet which was as follows:

AMOS ATKINSON'S BALANCE SHEET
AS AT 31ST DECEMBER, 19·1

LIABILITIES	£	ASSETS	£
Capital Account		Freehold premises	14,200
Amos Atkinson	26,000	Plant and Machinery	8,100
Sundry Creditors	3,400	Furniture and Fittings	600
Reserve for bad debts	300	Stock in trade	4,100
		Sundry debtors	2,700
	29,700		29,700

The purchase price was agreed at £28,000 and was paid in equal shares by Wright and Dobson direct to Atkinson. A Bank Account was opened in the name of the firm, into which each partner paid the sum of £1,000. For the purpose of the partnership the assets were revalued, and the following reductions in value were made:

Plant and Machinery, £500; Stock, £450; Furniture and Fittings, £200.

A Goodwill Account is to be raised in the partnership books for the difference between the total purchase price paid and the amended valuation.

You are required to make the journal entries necessary to record the above transactions in the books of Messrs Wright and Dobson, and prepare the balance sheet as at the commencement of the new partnership.

(*RSA*)

Chapter Thirty One

Dissolution of Partnership

The expression *dissolution* applies not only when a partnership is being completely liquidated but also as part of the reconstitution of the firm when for example another partner is admitted or another business is purchased. In each case the partners are required to dissolve and to reconstitute their firm.

The present Chapter deals with the accounting processes involved when a partnership is broken up and the business is completely closed down. These processes may be expressed under three headings:

1 Selling up ('realising the value of') the assets.

2 Paying off the creditors.

3 Sharing the profits or losses between the partners on realisation of the assets.

Assuming the assets have been sold and the money for them received, the following is the order of priority in which the various classes of creditors are paid, each class being paid before the claims of the succeeding one is dealt with:

1 Sundry trade and expense creditors. If the available cash is insufficient, then the partners must contribute additional funds to meet the deficiency in proportion to their capital. Where any partner is unable to contribute more cash, then the others must pay his share.

2 The repayment of partner(s)' loan(s) to the firm.

3 The repayment of the partners' capital contributions.

4 The surplus, or loss, to be divided in proportion in which profits or losses are shared.

My Partners and I Decide to Part Company

After some years of partnership, my two partners and I decided that we could employ ourselves more profitably in other commercial or industrial activities. We therefore agreed to dissolve our partnership. On 31st December, 19·8, when profits were being shared as to J Fry ½ and of the remainder: M Rich 3/5 and S Cook 2/5, the firm's balance sheet stood as follows:

EX. 31/1

BALANCE SHEET OF FRY, RICH AND COOK
AS AT 31ST DECEMBER, 19·8

	£	£		£	£
CAPITAL ACCOUNTS			FIXED ASSETS		
J Fry	16,000		Freehold Premises	15,000	
M Rich	10,000		Machinery and Plant*	4,343	
S Cook	10,000		Furniture and Fixtures	2,100	
		36,000			21,443
CURRENT LIABILITIES			CURRENT ASSETS		
Creditors		3,500	Stock	3,200	
			Debtors	5,557	
			Cash at bank	9,300	
					18,057
		39,500			39,500

Closing the Books

In order to close the books, the following steps are taken:

1 A Realisation Account is opened and all the assets are transferred to it:
Credit asset account, thus closing it;
Debit realisation account.

2 As the assets are sold and the moneys for them are received:
Debit cash book;
Credit Realisation Account.

3 If any of the assets are taken by the partners for their own use:
Credit Realisation Account;
Debit relevant partner's Capital Account. (In example 31/3 Cook has taken furniture value £200 for his own use.)

4 Pay the creditors:
Credit cash book;
Debit Creditors' Accounts.

5 Pay the dissolution expenses:
Credit cash book;
Debit Realisation Account.

6 Proceeds on realisation of assets:
Debit cash book;
Credit Realisation Account.

7 Transfer partners' Current Accounts to their respective Capital Accounts and close the Current Accounts.

8 Balance the Capital Accounts.

9 Balance Realisation Account. That balance represents the profit or loss made on completion of the above transactions.

10 Balance the Cash Book.

---

*Plant describes the larger pieces of machinery. The expression is used here only to introduce it to the student. Otherwise it is difficult to understand eg. electric generating plant or the plant used in foundries, at so insignificant a figure as £4,000.

When the above entries have been made as shown in example 31/2 below, all the accounts will have been closed, except the Capital Accounts, the Cash Book and the Realisation Account.

EX. 31/2

FREEHOLD PREMISES

			£				£
Dec. 31	Balance	b/d	15,000	Dec. 31	Realisation		15,000

MACHINERY AND PLANT

Dec. 31	Balance	b/d	4,343	Dec. 31	Realisation		4,343

FURNITURE AND FITTINGS

Dec. 31	Balance	b/d	2,100	Dec. 31	Realisation		2,100

STOCK

Dec. 31	Balance	b/d	3,200	Dec. 31	Realisation		3,200

DEBTORS

Dec. 31	Balance	b/d	5,557	Dec. 31	Realisation		5,557

CREDITORS

Dec. 31	Cash		3,500	Dec. 31	Balance	b/d	3,500

EX. 31/3

REALISATION ACCOUNTS

		£			£
Dec. 31	Freehold Premises	15,000	Dec. 31	Cash:	
	Machinery and Plant	4,343		Proceeds on Realisation of	
	Furniture and Fixtures	2,100		Assets	34,200
	Stock	3,200		S Cook Capital Account:	
	Debtors	5,557		Furniture taken for own use	200
	Cash				
	Dissolution Expenses	500			
	Capital Accounts:				
	J Fry ½	1,850			
	M Rich 3/10	1,110			
	S Cook 1/5	740			
		3,700			
	Being profit on realisation	34,400			34,400

CASH BOOK

			£	£				£
Dec. 31	Balance	b/d		9,300	Dec. 31	Creditors		3,500
	Proceeds from assets:					Dissolution expenses		500
	Freehold premises	20,000				Balance	c/d	39,500
	Machinery and							
	Plant	3,900						
	Furniture, etc.	1,500						
	Stock	3,800						
	Debtors	5,000						
	Realisation Account			34,200				
				43,500				43,500
	Balance	b/d		39,500	Dec. 31	Capital Accounts:		
						J Fry		17,850
						M Rich		11,110
						S Cook		10,540
				39,500				39,500

CAPITAL ACCOUNTS

		£ J Fry	£ M Rich	£ S Cook			£ J Fry	£ M Rich	£ S Cook
Dec. 31	Realisation Account			200	Dec. 31	Balances Realisation	16,000	10,000	10,000
	Cash	17,850	11,110	10,540		Account	1,850	1,110	740
		17,850	11,110	10,740			17,850	11,110	10,740

The balance of the Realisation Account is transferred to Capital Accounts in the proportions in which profits or losses are shared.

In the Capital Accounts, the sum of the partners' balances should be precisely equal to the balance at bank, according to the cash book.

The debit side of the Cash Book shows that all the assets except Premises and Stock, have been sold at less than their book values. Also some debtors have not paid. The balance of the Cash Book is transferred to the Capital Accounts *to pay off each partner's claim, as shown by his credit balance.*

All the accounts in the partnership's books are now closed and the partnership is dissolved.

Partners' Capital Account in Deficiency (with a Debit Balance)

If on the sale of the assets a loss is sustained and its proportionate transfer to capital accounts puts one of the partners in deficiency, then the remaining partners must each pay into bank sufficient cash to clear the balance, as in the following example:

EX. 31/4 L and M in partnership, share profits three-fifths and two-fifths respectively. They decide to dissolve the partnership on 31st March, 19·1. At that date the firm's Balance Sheet appeared as follows:

BALANCE SHEET
AS AT 31ST MARCH, 19·1

	£	£		£
Capital Accounts			Sundry Assets	5,400
L	9,000		Stock	7,350
M	1,500		Cash at bank	1,350
		10,500		
Creditors		3,600		
		14,100		14,100

The assets realised £4,200 and the stock £4,350.
The expenses of dissolution came to £570.

On compiling the Realisation Account, a loss was seen to have been made and M was placed in debt to the firm. This obliged him to pay into the bank a sufficient cash amount to clear the sum due to L.

EX. 31/5

REALISATION ACCOUNT

	£		£	£
Total Assets	5,400	Mar. 31 Cash:		
Stock	7,350	Proceeds of sale of assets		8,550
Cash:		Balance transferred to capital		
Dissolution Expenses	570	Accounts, being loss on realisation:		
		L	3,180	
		M	1,590	
				4,770
	13,320			13,320

CASH BOOK

		£			£
Mar. 31	Balance	1,350	Mar. 31	Creditors	3,600
	Proceeds of sale of assets	8,550		Dissolution Expenses	570
	Capital—M; being cash paid			Capital—L	5,820
	to balance deficiency	90			
		9,990			9,990

CAPITAL ACCOUNTS

			£ L	£ M				£ L	£ M
Mar. 31	Realisation Account				Mar. 31	Balances	b/d	9,000	1,500
	Share of loss		3,180	1,590		Balance	c/d		90
	Balance	c/d	5,820						
			9,000	1,590				9,000	1,590
Mar. 31	Balance	b/d		90	Mar. 31	Balance	b/d	5,820	
	Cash		5,820			Cash			90
			5,820	90				5,820	90

If M had not paid £90 into bank, L would have had to do so, in order to clear the firm's overdraft, which is equal to the debit balance in M's Capital Account.

If all capital accounts were in deficiency, then partners would have to contribute sufficient cash (in proportion to share of profits) to meet creditors' claims in full, as already stated above.

The Rule in Garner v. Murray

Complications arise if in a partnership of three or more members, one partner's capital account has a debit balance, that is, a deficiency. The simplest solution is for that partner to pay into bank sufficient cash to balance his capital account. If, however, he cannot, then in accordance with the ruling of the court in the case known as Garner v. Murray (1904), the other partners must contribute the necessary cash to balance the deficiency in proportion to the balances in their capital accounts as shown in the last balance sheet before dissolution of the partnership—not in proportion in which they shared profits and losses. As the discrepancy between the two ratios might be considerable, the Deed of Partnership drawn up at the inception of the business provides that normal Profit and Loss Sharing Ratios shall be used, thus nullifying the rule in Garner v. Murray.

EX. 31/6   On 31st December, 19·1, the capital accounts of a partnership showed:

A, £8,000; B, £2,000; C, £1,000

They shared profits and losses as to: A, $\frac{1}{2}$; B, $\frac{1}{4}$; C, $\frac{1}{4}$. On dissolution of the partnership and the realisation of all the assets on 10th May, 19·2, but before finally closing the capital accounts by the distribution of the cash at bank, C's capital showed a deficiency of £800. The partners' balance sheet appeared:

BALANCE SHEET
AS AT 10TH MAY, 19·2

		£	£		£
Capital Accounts:				Cash at bank	8,200
	A	4,500			
	B	5,100			
		9,600			
Less C in deficiency		1,400	8,200		
			8,200		8,200

C cannot provide additional cash to close any part of his deficiency; A and B must therefore pay it off by transfer from their capital accounts in the proportions of their respective capital accounts shown in the last balance sheet before dissolution (31st December, 19·1):

$$\frac{A}{A+B} \times \text{Deficiency}; \quad \frac{B}{A+B} \times \text{Deficiency}.$$

That is, A, $\frac{8,000}{10,000} \times 1,400 = £1,120$;

B, $\frac{2,000}{10,000} \times 1,400 = £280$.

Then: £1,120 + £280 = £1,400 = C's deficiency

The necessary adjustments are now made in the capital accounts:

CAPITAL ACCOUNTS
(AFTER REALISATION)

		£ A	£ B	£ C			£ A	£ B	£ C
Balance				1,400	Balances		4,500	5,100	
Contra: C		1,120	280		Contra: A				1,120
Balances	c/d	3,380	4,820		B				280
		4,500	5,100	1,400			4,500	5,100	1,400
Cash		3,380	4,820		Balances	b/d	3,380	4,820	

Exercise 31

1 Barney and Good are in partnership, sharing profits and losses two-thirds and one-third respectively. On 31st January, 1976, their Balance Sheet appeared as follows:

BALANCE SHEET OF BARNEY AND GOOD
AS AT 31ST JANUARY, 1976

LIABILITIES	£	£	ASSETS	£
Capital Accounts			Machinery	3,000
Barney	7,600		Stock 31st January 1976	8,400
Good	3,800		Sundry debtors	4,200
		11,400	Cash at bank	1,400
Sundry Creditors		5,600		
		17,000		17,000

On that date it was decided to dissolve the partnership. The assets read as follows: Stock £9,000, Debtors £4,050; Barney took over the Machinery at an agreed price of £2,900. Dissolution expenses came to £182. Make the necessary entries to close the books of the partnership, and show the Ledger Accounts in their final form.

2 A and B, trading in partnership, decide as on 31st March, 19·1, to dissolve partnership and to liquidate their business.

Their Balance Sheet as on that date was as follows:

BALANCE SHEET
AS AT 31ST MARCH, 19·

	£		£
Capital Account: A	2,000	Cash	1,800
Capital Account: B	1,500	Sundry debtors	2,800
Sundry Creditors	2,750	Other assets	850
		Goodwill	800
	6,250		6,250

Profits and losses are shared equally.

The debtors realised £2,700, other assets £950, and the goodwill of the business was sold for £400. The expenses of liquidation amounted to £100.

Prepare the necessary accounts to show the result of the realisation as it would appear in the books of the firm, and the position of the two partners as regards the disposal of the balance of cash remaining after satisfying the firm's liabilities.

(RSA)

3 R and S were in partnership, sharing profits and losses in the proportions: R two-thirds and S one-third. The balance sheet of the firm as on 31st December, 19·1, was as follows:

BALANCE SHEET
AS AT 31ST DECEMBER, 19·1

	£	£		£	£
Capital Accounts			Freehold Property		4,700
R	14,000		Furniture		430
S	9,500		Stock in trade		12,840
		23,500	Debtors	13,540	
Creditors		11,720	*Less* provision for bad debts	310	
					13,230
			Balance at bank		4,020
		35,220			35,220

The partnership was dissolved on the date of the above balance sheet, R agreeing to take over the freehold property at a valuation of £5,000 in part-settlement of the amount due to him.

The furniture was sold for £374 and the stock for £11,930. £12,940 was collected from the debtors, and the remaining debtors were written off. The expenses of realisation amounted to £94. The creditors were paid in full.

Each partner was paid the amount due to him.

You are required to show the realisation account, the cash account, and the partners' capital accounts as they would appear after recording all these matters.

(RSA II)

4 Black and White, in partnership, share profits and losses, two-thirds and one-third respectively. The following balance sheet was brought out on 31st January, 1973:

BALANCE SHEET OF BLACK AND WHITE
AS AT 31ST JANUARY, 1973

	£		£
Capital Accounts		FIXED ASSETS	
Black	7,600	Furniture	3,000
White	3,800		
	11,400	CURRENT ASSETS	
Current Liabilities		Stock	8,400
CURRENT LIABILITIES		Debtors	4,200
Creditors	5,600	Cash	1,400
	17,000		17,000

On 31st January, 1973, the partners decided to dissolve their business and the assets were disposed of as follows: Stock realised £9,000; the debtors paid £4,050; Black took over the furniture at an agreed value of £2,900. £182 was paid to cover the expenses of realisation.

You are required to show the necessary closing accounts on dissolution of the partnership, ascertaining the profit or loss made on realisation and the amount payable to each partner.

5 Long and Short were in partnership sharing profits in the ratio of 3:2. The balance sheet of the firm on 31st December, 1970, was as follows:

Capital:	£		Fixed assets	£
Long	19,240		Fixed assets	26,200
Short	14,438		Current assets	16,906
	33,678			
Creditors	9,428			
	43,106			43,106

On 31st December, 1971, current assets amounted to £19,852 and creditors were £9,374. Each partner drew £1,500 in 1971. There had been no capital expenditure during the year.

On 1st January, 1972, Long and Short agreed to wind up their business and they ceased to trade on that day. During January, 1972, they sold the plant for £25,200 and current assets (other than cash) at their book value, and the creditors were paid off in full. On 31st January, 1972, the partners withdrew the amounts due to them.

You are required to give:

(a) A calculation of the profit for 1971.

(b) Realisation account, cash account and partners' capital accounts to record the realisation.

Ignore depreciation.

(RSA II 1972)

6 T and J were partners, sharing profits and losses, two-thirds to T and one-third to J.

BALANCE SHEET
AS AT 31ST MARCH, 1969

Capital Accounts	£	£		£	£
T	8,200		Plant and Machinery		3,680
J	5,000		Stock		7,790
		13,200	Debtors	7,100	
Sundry Creditors		3,950	*Less* Provision	500	
Bank overdraft		920			6,600
		18,070			18,070

The Profit and Loss Account for the year ended 31st March, 1970, showed a net loss of £1,440 after charging £390 for depreciation for plant.

During the year to 31st March, 1970, the drawings of the partners were as follows:

T £2,500

J £2,000

At 31st March, 1970, the firm's liabilities were:

Creditors £5,420
Bank Overdraft £1,236

No fixed assets were acquired during the year to 31st March, 1970, and no plant and machinery was sold or discarded.

The partnership was dissolved as from 1st April, 1970, when T took over the plant at an agreed figure of £2,500. The creditors were settled for £5,268 and the stock and debtors realised £12,552.

You are required:

(a) To set out the Balance Sheet of the partnership on 31st March, 1970.

(b) To show the entries in the Realisation Account, the Bank Account and the Partners' Capital Accounts after the dissolution was completed.

7 X, Y and Z were in partnership, sharing profits and losses in ratio 2:2:1.
At 31st October, 1975, when the partnership was dissolved, their balance sheet was as follows:

	£	£		£
Capital Accounts			Freehold Premises	10,000
Y	12,000		Stock	4,850
Z	8,000	20,000	Sundry Debtors	9,262
Current Accounts			Cash	1,882
Y	500		Current Account—X	2,000
Z	360	860		
Sundry Creditors		7,134		
		27,994		27,994

Premises realised £9,000, Stock £4,400. Except for a bad debt of £60, debtors realised their book value. Creditors were paid in full, discounts of £248 being received. Dissolution expenses came to £200. X was unable to contribute any part of his deficiency to the firm.

Show the Realisation Account and the Capital and Current Accounts of the partners after the entries required to close the partnership book have been effected.

Chapter Thirty Two

Limited Liability Companies and their Accounts

The Capital of a Sole Trader and his Vulnerability

Although a sole trader and his business are said to be separate entities (Chapter 2), the trader is fully liable for the payment of his creditors, even to the extent of his personal property—his house and its contents, for example, should his business become insolvent. The capital of a sole trader (or that of a partnership) is usually small. Substantial capital for expansion on a large scale is difficult to find. A number of possible ways of increasing the capital of a sole trader, *to a small extent*, have been illustrated in previous chapters on partnerships.

Limited Liability Companies

A company's capital is made up by the contributions of its members. In return for cash, they receive share certificates each one having a face value (called 'value at par') fixed by the company's promoters (those who launch, or *float*, the company).

A company's capital, then, is divided into shares, eg. of £1 each, at par. Those who purchase them, the subscribers, become:

(a) Shareholders and are called 'members' of the company.

(b) Part owners of the company. They have invested capital in the company; they are investors.

EX. 32/1   A company's liability is limited to the extent of the capital invested in it. If I bought 1,000 £1 shares in a company, my loss, should the company be declared insolvent, would not exceed £1,000. My private property would not be involved in any way. I should lose part or all of my investment of £1,000, but no more.

Private Companies

A private company:

(i) Has a minimum of two members and a maximum of 50, excluding its employers and employees.

(ii) May not invite the public to subscribe to its capital—the public at large may not be offered membership.

(iii) Has its right to transfer shares restricted.

(iv) Has shares that are not quoted on the Stock Exchange.

Public Companies

A public company:

(i) Has a minimum of seven members,

(ii) has no maximum limit of membership.

(iii) has shares bought and sold through brokers on the Stock Exchange. Buying and selling involves *transferring* shares from seller to buyer.

The Registration of a Company

When a company is formed, the following documents (among others required by the Companies Act) are 'filed with' (handed in to) the Registrar of Companies:

(a) MEMORANDUM OF ASSOCIATION

An application for registration made to the Registrar of Companies and signed by the applicants, the 'signatories'. It defines the Company's relationship with the world outside and includes:

(i) The name of the proposed company, with 'Limited' at the end of it.

(ii) The address of the Registered Office; whether it is to be in England or Scotland. When the company establishes itself at a definite address, the Registrar is informed.

(iii) The objects of the company; what its business is going to be. This is very broadly defined, to allow the company the maximum freedom to expand in the future if desired.

(iv) The declaration that the liability of its members is limited.

(v) The amount of share capital with which the company is to be registered.

(b) ARTICLES OF ASSOCIATION

Defines the relationship of the company's members with each other, and also describes the internal arrangements and organisation of the company. In the absence of Articles of Association, the company must be governed by Table A, an appendix to the Companies Act, consisting of a model set of Articles.

(c) CERTIFICATE OF INCORPORATION

When the above documents, properly stamped, are lodged with and accepted by the Registrar of Companies, a Certificate of Incorporation is issued, which must be prominently displayed in the company's registered office. The company is then said to have been formed and may, broadly speaking, commence business.

A Joint Stock* Company is a Legal Entity

Just as the sole trader is separate from his business, so a company is separate from its members. It has, so to speak, a life of its own; it is described as a 'separate entity'. Its members may come and go but the company itself may continue indefinitely. It may own property, it may sue and be sued and it may carry on business. A company is a

---

*Stock: describes a block of shares. When a number of people, each with a block of shares, join together in business, it may be described as a joint stock company; alternatively called a limited company.

'legal person' and its activities are restricted by the terms of its Memorandum of Association.

The Company's Directors Control its Activities

Although shareholders are, in the final analysis, in control of the company, it would be impractical for them all to take part in its day-to-day business. They therefore vote for and elect directors from amongst themselves who are made responsible for all aspects of the organisation and the running of the business. Voting power is proportional to shareholdings. At the Annual General Meeting (A.G.M.), to which all shareholders are invited, the directors report upon the company's progress and they support the financial aspects of their report with a set of Final Accounts for the year.

The Prospectus

Gives full details of the company's proposed activities and invites the public to apply for shares. An Application Form is attached to the prospectus.

Issue of Share Capital (or 'the Issue of Shares')

The total share capital of a company is described as the Authorised Share Capital. Alternative expressions to 'authorised' are 'registered' and 'nominal' share capital. The part of the authorised capital that is actually offered to, and purchased by the public is the Issued Capital. Thus, if the authorised capital consisted of 160,000 ordinary shares of £1 each, of these only 100,000 shares might be issued. The capital of the company would then be described as:

AUTHORISED CAPITAL:
160,000 Ordinary Shares of £1 each

ISSUED CAPITAL:
100,000 Ordinary Shares of £1 each

The Issued Capital is not always fully called up. In such cases, the shareholders are required to pay in stages. For example:

1 Payment for part of the share value is sent to the company, together with the Application Form for the shares—called the *Application money*.

2 Another part is paid when the company accepts the application, and shares are actually allotted to the applicant—called the *Allotment money*.

EX. 32/2 The following example illustrates these matters:

On 1st January, 19·8, A and B Hope Co., Ltd. is registered with a nominal capital of £160,000, divided into 160,000 ordinary shares of £1 each. 100,000 shares were issued to the public and fully subscribed (bought up). By 31st March, 19·8, £0·50 per share on Application and Allotment had been received by the company, and £0·25 per share had been paid at First Call by all but two shareholders, each holding 1,000 shares. These matters may be set out concisely as follows:

	£	£
Authorised, Nominal or Registered Capital		160,000
Issued Capital		100,000
Called up Capital		75,000
Uncalled Capital		25,000
Paid up Capital	75,000	
Less unpaid amount (*Calls in arrear*)	1,500	
		73,500
Calls in arrear		1,500

The ledger accounts recording the above appear as follows. (The numbers in the folio columns against the item indicate the sequence of entries):

1 THE APPLICATIONS AND ALLOTMENTS RECORDED:

CASH BOOK

19·8			£
Jan.	1	Application and Allotment A/c	1	75,000

APPLICATION & ALLOTMENT

| Jan. | 1 | Ordinary Share Capital A/c | J | 3 | 75,000 | | Jan. | 1 | Cash | CB | 2 | 75,000 |

ORDINARY SHARE CAPITAL

| | | | | | | Jan. | 1 | Application & Allotment | J | 4 | 75,000 |

2 THE FIRST AND FINAL CALL RECORDED:

At some convenient time before 31st March, a debit entry is made in the First and Final Call Account for the remaining 25,000 shares, and a corresponding credit entry is made in the Ordinary Share Capital Account. By 31st March, all but six shareholders, each holding 1,000 shares, had paid up:

CASH BOOK

19·8				£
Jan.	1	Application and Allotment	1	75,000
Mar.	31	First and Final Call	7	23,500

APPLICATION AND ALLOTMENT

| Jan. | 1 | Ordinary Share Capital | J | 3 | 75,000 | | Jan. | 1 | Cash | CB | 2 | 75,000 |

FIRST AND FINAL CALL

Feb.	28	Ordinary Share Capital	J	5	25,000		Mar.	31	Cash	CB	8	23,500
								Balance (Calls in arrears)	c/d		1,500
			9	25,000							25,000
April	1	Balance b/d (Calls in arrears)	12	1,500							

ORDINARY SHARE CAPITAL

						Jan.	1	Application and Allotment	J	4	75,000
						Feb.	28	First and Final Call	J	6	25,000

The above feature in the balance sheet as follows:

BALANCE SHEET
AS AT 31ST MARCH, 19·8

	£
AUTHORISED CAPITAL	
160,000 Ordinary Shares of £1 each	160,000
ISSUED CAPITAL	
100,000 Ordinary Shares of £1 each	100,000
Less Calls in arrear	25,000
	75,000

Calls in Advance

If a company is empowered by its articles to accept Calls in Advance, it may accept such payments and may pay interest as for a loan. The interest is payable without regard to the question of profit or loss. Calls in Advance first appear on the debit side of the cash book, then they are posted to the credit side of the Calls in Advance Account (or the accounts of the shareholders concerned). If such a balance is outstanding when a balance sheet is being prepared, it will appear under its own heading on the liabilities side.

The Capital of a Company; Ordinary Shares

In Example 32/1, I bought 1,000 ordinary shares of £1 each, for which I paid £1,000. This, together with the payments made by all the other shareholders, constitutes the Company's Ordinary Share capital. When at the end of the year the profit of the company is known (when it is 'declared'), I am, in common with all the other ordinary shareholders, entitled to a share of that profit, I am entitled to my 'dividend' of the profit. The market value of shares varies according to demand for them. Suppose that:

(i) Company A has issued £1 ordinary shares, the issue is said to be at par, as stated above.

(ii) If its price on the Stock Exchange rises to, say, £1·25, it is said to be 'at a premium' of £0·25 each.

(iii) If its price falls to, say, £0·90, it is said to be 'at a discount' of £0·10 per share.

The Issue of Shares at a Premium

Once they are issued, shares are bought and sold on the Stock Exchange. Like any other commodity, their prices rise or fall in response to demand for them. If demand for a particular share is high, its price rises above its face or nominal value—above its value at par. The excess of the market price over its value at par, is called the premium. Premiums are in the nature of capital profit; they appear under a 'Share Premium Account'. One must constantly bear in mind that *the Share Capital Account always shows the nominal value of the shares*—the value at par.

EX. 32/3

The market price of Company A's £1 Ordinary Shares has increased to £1·25 since they were issued. The Company, seeking additional capital, issued a further 20,000 shares, at a premium of 25p per share. The following are the necessary entries in the Company's books:

CASH BOOK

Proceeds of sale of 20,000
Ordinary Shares of £1 at £1·25
    Ordinary Shares Capital Account   20,000
    Ordinary Share Premium Account   5,000

ORDINARY SHARE CAPITAL
    Balance   100,000
    Cash (new issue)   20,000

ORDINARY SHARE PREMIUM
    Cash   5,000

The above appear in the balance sheet as follows:

BALANCE SHEET
AUTHORISED CAPITAL
    120,000 Ordinary Shares of £1 each   120,000

ISSUED CAPITAL
    120,000 Ordinary Shares of £1 each   120,000
CAPITAL RESERVE
    Premium on Shares   5,000

The Issue of Shares at a Discount

If the market price of the shares discussed above, are below par, then they are said to be at a discount. Suppose a new issue of 20,000 Ordinary Shares of £1 each is made at 90p, the appropriate entries in the books appear as follows:

CASH BOOK

Proceeds of Sale of 20,000 Ordinary Shares of £1 each at 90p	18,000	

ORDINARY SHARE CAPITAL

Balance (say)		100,000
Cash (new issue)		18,000
Discount on Ordinary Shares	J	2,000

DISCOUNT ON ORDINARY SHARES

Ordinary Shares Capital	J	2,000

BALANCE SHEET
(last item on Assets side)

FICTITIOUS ASSETS	
Discount on Ordinary Share	2,000

The Capital of a Company; Preference Shares

Preference shares are described according to the percentage rate of dividend they offer; for example 5% preference shares or 6% preference shares. Preference shareholders of 5% preference shares would expect to receive a dividend of 5% on their holding, *before* the dividend (if any) due to ordinary shareholders is computed. Thus, it is possible that after preference shareholders' claims have been met, the profit might be exhausted and none left for ordinary shareholders. Preference shareholders have the advantage over ordinary shareholders in that they have prior claim on profits. But if profits are high, the dividend to ordinary shareholders would probably be greater than the interest to preference shareholders. Most preference shares are 'cumulative'. If in any one year the company makes a loss, or if profits are low, no dividends may be forthcoming. The interest due to cumulative preference shareholders is then carried forward to the following year. Non-cumulative preference shareholders must forfeit their expectations in a non-profit year.

The procedure for recording Preference shares in the Company's books is the same as that for Ordinary shares. There is a separate set of corresponding accounts for each class of shares and Debentures. (See below for the meaning of Debentures.)

The Capital of a Company; Deferred Shares

Deferred shareholders are entitled to dividends only after all other classes have received payment of dividend. Where Deferred shares exist, Ordinary shares are given priority (after Preference shares) up to a limited amount of the total available for distribution, and thereafter the balance is shared between Ordinary and Deferred shares.

The Appropriation Account

As in partnership accounts, the purpose of the second section of a company's profit and loss account, the Appropriation Account, is to show the manner in which the trading profit has been used or appropriated. Items which are *debited* to appropriation include:

Dividends on preference shares, Dividends on ordinary shares, General Reserve, Preliminary Expenses written off, Goodwill written off, Corporation Tax.

The ledger account of each item is credited with the appropriate amount.

EX. 32/4 On 30th November, 19·6, A Bates Ltd. was floated with an authorised capital of £90,000, consisting of 20,000 5% preference shares of £1 each and 70,000 ordinary shares of £1 each. The company issued 20,000 5% preference shares and 50,000 ordinary shares. The profit at the end of the first year's trading, was £10,000.

Proposed dividend to 5% preference shareholders came to:

$$\frac{5}{100} \times 20,000 = £1,000$$

Proposed dividend to ordinary shareholders was computed as follows:

Profit minus dividend to preference shareholders = Dividend to ordinary shareholders.

That is: £10,000 − £1,000 = £9,000

Then, percentage of profit to ordinary shareholders is

$$\frac{9,000}{50,000} \times 100 = 18\%$$

These items appear in the company's appropriation account as follows:

APPROPRIATION ACCOUNT

	£			£
Preference share dividend	1,000	Net trading profit	b/d	10,000
Ordinary share dividend	9,000			

General Reserve

Whenever profits justify it, part of them is transferred to a General Reserve Account (debit Appropriation; credit General Reserve) in order to strengthen the financial position of the business. In Chapter 19 on Depreciation, the nature of profit as additional cash, was explained and how a provision for depreciation sets aside part of the profit, for replacement of fixed assets or any other purpose. The same principle applies to General Reserve. Part of the profits are set aside against unforeseen contingencies and thus the finances of the business are strengthened.

EX. 32/5

In the above example (example 32/4), it can be seen at a glance that the £9,000 proposed dividend on ordinary shares, a dividend of no less than 18%, is very high. If the company declared 10% to ordinary shareholders, it could transfer part of the remainder to General Reserve and let the balance of the Appropriation Account, called the *undistributed profit*, be carried forward to next year. When these suggestions are carried out, the Appropriation Account (example 32/4) continues as follows:

APPROPRIATION ACCOUNT
(YEAR 1)

		£			£
Preference share dividend		1,000	Net trading profit	b/d	10,000
Ordinary share dividend		5,000			
General Reserve		2,000			
Balance	c/d	2,000			
		10,000			10,000
			Balance (Undistributed or Retained profits)	b/d	2,000

The undistributed, or retained, profits are carried forward to the Appropriation Account of Year 2 as follows:

APPROPRIATION ACCOUNT
(YEAR 2)

(CREDIT SIDE ONLY)

		£
Net trading profit Year 2	b/d (say)	13,000
Balance Year 1	b/f	2,000

Preliminary or Formation Expenses

These are legal expenses and accountants' and other expenses incurred during the course of the company's formation. The account is written off against profits over the early years of the Company's life, until it is exhausted:

EX. 32/6   Suppose Preliminary Expenses, incurred in floating A Bates Ltd. (Example 32/4) came to £1,500, then the following are the relevant entries:

PRELIMINARY EXPENSES

19·6		£	19·7			£
Nov. 30	Cash	1,500	Dec. 31	Transferred to Profit and Loss Account (say)		500
				Balance	c/d	1,000
		1,500				1,500
19·8						
Jan. 1	Balance	b/d 1,000				

Goodwill

If the company were formed by the purchase of an existing business (Chapter 34), part of the purchase price would most probably be for the goodwill of the old business.* Such payment is for avoiding the troubles and anxieties in building up a new business; for taking over a going concern; for taking over an established list of clients; for using the good reputation of an old-established firm. All these and other such intangible assets are concerned not with actual cash but with the important influence they exercise on the early success of the new venture, and these together have a certain monetary value, described as Goodwill. Like Preliminary Expenses, Goodwill, too, is written off against profits year by year until it is exhausted and the account is closed.

EX. 32/7   On 30th November, 19·6, the Goodwill Account had a balance of £3,000. On 31st December, 19·7, £500 was transferred to Appropriation Account:

GOODWILL

19·6		£	19·7			£
Nov. 30	Balance	3,000				
			Dec. 31	Profit and Loss Account		500
			31	Balance	c/d	2,500
		3,000				3,000
19·8						
Jan. 1	Balance	b/d 2,500				

---

*The principles of accounting involved in the Purchase of a Business by a Company are exactly the same as those for the purchase of a business by a sole trader or partnership (Chapter 30). The main difference is that part or whole payment to the vendor might be in the Company's Shares. Optional exercises are offered at the end of this chapter.

All the examples so far given, together appear in the Appropriation Account as follows:

EX. 32/8

APPROPRIATION ACCOUNT
AS AT 31ST DECEMBER, 19·7

	£			£
Dividends		Net trading profit	b/d	13,000
6% Preference shares	1,000	Balance 31st December, 19·6	b/f	2,000
Ordinary shares	5,000			
General Reserve	2,000			
Preliminary Expenses	500			
Goodwill	500			
Balance	6,000			
	15,000			15,000
		Balance	b/d	6,000

Corporation Tax

This, too, appears in the Appropriation Account, but the treatment of taxation is beyond the scope of this work.

Debentures

Debentures are certificates issued by the company, as receipts for loans made to the company by investors. Debentures may be issued against the security of the company's assets. If the security comprises the whole of the company's assets, it is described as a *floating charge*. A floating charge does not prevent a company from using its assets in the ordinary way of business, or even of disposing of them, since a floating charge does not specify any particular asset. *Mortgage debentures*, on the other hand are issued against the security of certain specific items of the company's assets, and these (as all other charges of the company's property) must be registered with the Registrar of Companies and, of course they must not be disposed of. Each debenture is usually of a high value (eg. £100). Debentures are recorded in the account books in a manner similar to the recording of an issue of shares. They are described according to the interest payable to the holders, eg. 5%, 6% or 7% Debentures. Payment of interest to debenture holders has priority over every other creditors' claims. It must be paid whether or not a profit has been made. Therein lies their attraction to some investors. Debenture interest is charged as an expense in the first section of the Profit and Loss Account; it is not charged to Appropriation since payment of it is not dependent upon profit or loss. It is usually paid half-yearly. Debenture holders are not members of the company; they may be described as loan creditors of the company. Debentures are classified on the liabilities side of the balance sheet under Loan Capital.

Directors' Salaries

Directors' salaries, directors' commissions, and any other directors' emoluments are charged to the first section of the Profit and Loss Account, not to Appropriation, since they are not dependent upon the extent of profit made.

The above examples, together with various assumed Assets and Liabilities, appear in the company's balance sheet at the end of the financial year as follows:

EX. 32/9

BALANCE SHEET OF A BATES LTD
AS AT 31ST DECEMBER, 19·7

	£	£		Cost £	Accumulated Depreciation £	Net £
AUTHORISED CAPITAL			FIXED ASSETS			
20,000 5% Preference Shares of £1 each	20,000		Goodwill	3,000	500	2,500
70,000 Ordinary Shares of £1 each	70,000		Freehold Premises	30,000		30,000
			Machinery	10,000	2,000	8,000
	90,000		Furniture and Fittings	500	100	400
			Motor Vans	1,000	200	800
ISSUED CAPITAL						
20,000 5% Preference Shares of £1 each				44,500	2,800	41,700
fully paid	20,000					
50,000 Ordinary Shares of £1 each			INVESTMENTS			43,000
fully paid	50,000		CURRENT ASSETS			
		70,000	Stock	10,000		
CAPITAL RESERVES			Debtors	7,000		
Premium on Ordinary Shares		10,000	Cash at bank	4,300		
REVENUE RESERVES					21,300	
General Reserve Account	1,000		CURRENT LIABILITIES			
Profit and Loss Account	6,000		Proposed Dividends:			
		7,000	Preference Shares	1,000		
			Ordinary Shares	5,000		
BOOK VALUE OF CAPITAL		87,000			6,000	
LOAN CAPITAL			Creditors	3,500		
7% Debentures		10,000			9,500	
			WORKING CAPITAL			11,800
			PRELIMINARY EXPENSES			500
		97,000				97,000

BALANCE SHEET OF A BATES LTD
AS AT 31ST DECEMBER, 19·7

	Cost £	Accumulated Depreciation £	Net £
FIXED ASSETS			
Goodwill	3,000	500	2,500
Freehold Premises	30,000		30,000
Plant and Machinery	10,000	2,000	8,000
Furniture and Fittings	500	100	400
Motor Vans	1,000	200	800
	44,500	2,800	41,700
INVESTMENTS			43,000
CURRENT ASSETS			
Stock	10,000		
Debtors	7,000		
Cash at bank	4,300	21,300	
CURRENT LIABILITIES			
Proposed dividends			
Preference Shares	1,000		
Ordinary Shares	5,000		
Sundry Creditors	3,500	9,500	
WORKING CAPITAL		11,800	
LOAN CAPITAL			
7% Debentures		10,000	1,800
NET ASSETS			86,500
(INTANGIBLE ASSETS)*			
Preliminary Expenses			500
			87,000

*This apt heading is no longer used. It is placed here as a guide to the student. Another item that is placed under this heading is Discount on Shares Account.

REPRESENTED BY

	Authorised	Issued	
Share Capital			
20,000 5% Preference Shares of £1 each	20,000	20,000	
70, Ordinary Shares of £1 each	70,000	50,000	
	90,000		70,000

CAPITAL RESERVES			
Premium on Ordinary Shares			10,000
REVENUE RESERVES			
General Reserve Account		1,000	
Profit and Loss Account		6,000	7,000
MEMBER'S INTEREST			87,000

In the above example, the shares are fully called up. Where they are only partly called up, it is that value and not the full amount which appears in the Share Capital Account and therefore also in the Balance Sheet.

EX. 32/10   Suppose that of the 50,000 ordinary shares in example 32/9, 12,000 had not yet been called up. The relevant entry in the Balance Sheet then appears as follows:

BALANCE SHEET (EXTRACT)

LIABILITIES SIDE

	£	£
ISSUED CAPITAL		
50,000 Ordinary Shares of £1 each	50,000	
Less Uncalled Shares	12,000	
		38,000

Exercise 32

1   The following is the balance sheet of Ficus Ltd., a manufacturing company:

BALANCE SHEET

AS AT 31ST DECEMBER, 1970

	£		£
Share capital	24,000	Freehold buildings	15,000
Net Profit	7,000	Plant and Machinery	10,500
7% Debentures	10,000	Stock	8,500
Creditors	8,000	Debtors	9,000
		Bank balance	6,000
	49,000		49,000

You are required to calculate:

(a) Capital employed.

(b) Current assets.

(c) Current liabilities.

(d) Working capital.

(*RSA II 1971*)

2   The following information is given on AB Limited:

Authorised capital £300,000, consisting of 30,000 7% preference shares of £1 each and 270,000 ordinary shares of £1 each. All the preference shares are issued and fully paid; 150,000 ordinary shares are issued, £0·75 per share paid. The following additional information is given as at 30th June, 1976:

Fixed Assets (at cost) £135,000.
Provision for depreciation on fixed assets £30,375.
Revenue Reserves £45,000.
Current Assets £94,125.
Current Liabilities £11,250.

You are required to give a classified balance sheet as at 30th June, 1976, showing the working capital of the company.

3 AB Ltd., was formed and commenced trading on 1st January, 19·1. The authorised capital was £20,000 divided into 20,000 ordinary shares of £1 each, all of which were issued at £1·50 each and fully paid. The following balances remained on the books after the revenue accounts had been closed at 31st December, 19·1:

The Share Capital Account, £20,000; preliminary expenses, £500; sundry creditors, £4,820; freehold premises, £9,800 (cost £10,000 *less* depreciation £200); cash in hand £120; Profit and Loss Account (Cr.), £2,000; Share Premium Account, £10,000; goodwill at cost, £10,000; machinery, £6,800 (cost £8,500, *less* depreciation £1,700); general reserve, £1,000; sundry debtors, £7,975; stocks as valued by officials of the company, £2,270; provision for dividend, £1,000; provision for bad debts, £50; and balance with bank, £1,405.
Draft the Balance Sheet as at 31st December, 19·1, for presentation to the members of the company.

(RSA)

4 CD Ltd., manufacturers, had an Authorised Capital of £150,000 of which £100,000 was in Ordinary Shares of £1 each and the balance in 5% Preference Shares of £1 each. From the following list of balances at 30th June, 19·1, prepare the Balance Sheet of the company at that date for presentation to the members:

Formation expenses, £2,050; Ordinary Share Capital Account, £100,000; cash in hand, £255; sundry creditors, £14,326; General Reserve Account, £30,000; leasehold premises at cost, £42,000, *less* depreciation £8,000; stocks on hand as valued by officials of the company, £15,826; Profit and Loss Account—undistributed profits, £23,739; machinery at cost, £126,056, *less* depreciation £16,056; equipment and tools at cost, £10,763, *less* depreciation £5,382; Preference Share Call Account (Dr.) £150; Preference Share Capital Account, £50,000; office furniture at cost, £2,978, *less* depreciation £952; sundry debtors, £37,377; balance at bank, £11,000.

(RSA)

5 (a) Make a list of as many items as you can that would appear in a company's Appropriation Account.

(b) What does 'Limited liability' mean to a shareholder in a company?

(c) What considerations would govern your decision to invest in:

(i) Ordinary shares.

(ii) Preference shares.

(iii) Mortgage debentures.

6 B Smith Co. Ltd., has an authorised capital of £100,000 divided into 200,000 shares of £0·50 each. On 31st December, 1976, the following balances were extracted from the company's books:

	£
Share Capital (fully paid)	60,000
Profit and Loss Account (Cr.)	20,960
General Reserve	10,000
Machinery and Plant (at cost)	68,000
Furniture and Fixtures (at cost)	6,000
Provision for depreciation	
Machinery and Plant	19,400
Furniture and Fixtures	1,600
Stocks	14,800
Sundry debtors	9,560
Sundry creditors	4,680
Cash at bank	18,280

The end of the financial year being 31st December, 1976, it was decided to transfer £4,000 to General Reserve and to propose a dividend of 20% on the ordinary shares. You are required to prepare the Appropriation Account for the year ended 31st December, 1976, and a Balance Sheet as at that date. Prepare the Balance Sheet in a manner which will show the figures for:

(a) total of fixed assets;

(b) total of current assets;

(c) total of current liabilities;

(d) total of revenue reserves;

(e) the working capital;

(f) the net book value of the assets;

(g) the capital employed.

7 From the following information you are required to make up the liabilities side only of LM Limited's balance sheet as at 31st December, 1975:

Authorised capital £150,000, consisting of 30,000 7% preference shares of £1 each and 120,000 ordinary shares of £1 each. All the preference shares and 90,000 ordinary shares were issued and fully paid. The net trading profit for the year came to £19,575 and the balance of the Appropriation Account brought forward from 1974 was £2,025. It is proposed to pay the year's dividends on the preference shares; to credit dividends on ordinary shares account with 10% on ordinary shares.

8 The balance sheets of Blue Sea Ltd., at 31st December, 1971, and 31st December 1972, are as follows:

	1971 £	1971 £	1972 £	1972 £
Fixed assets				
Plant at cost	40,000		60,000	
Less depreciation	18,300		24,500	
		21,700		35,500
Transport at cost	5,000		6,000	
Less depreciation	2,400		3,900	
		2,600		2,100
Current assets				
Stock	7,138		10,242	
Debtors	5,209		7,116	
Bank	4,163		4,295	
		16,510		21,653
		40,810		59,253
Share capital		20,000		30,000
Retained profit		11,332		13,119
Debentures				5,000
Current liabilities		9,478		11,134
		40,810		59,253

You are required to redraft these two balance sheets to show the working capital and the capital employed at the 31st December, 1971, and at the 31st December, 1972. No dividends were paid for 1972 and none are proposed.

(RSA II 1973)

9 Parsons Ltd., has an authorised capital of £300,000 divided into 1,000,000 ordinary shares of £0·25 each and 50,000 8% preference shares of £1 each. After ascertaining the net profit for the year ended 31st March, 1969, the following balances remained in the ledger:

	Dr. £	Cr. £
50,000 8% Preference shares of £1 each		50,000
600,000 Ordinary shares of £0.25 each		150,000
Profit and Loss Account		26,800
General Reserve		16,780
Trade Debtors	10,300	
Trade Creditors		6,520
Stock in trade	12,900	
Freehold Property at cost	126,900	
Plant and Machinery at cost	140,000	
Provision for depreciation on Plant and Machinery		60,000
Furniture and Fittings at cost	8,000	
Provision for depreciation on Furniture and Fittings		4,000
Cash at bank	16,000	

After extracting the above balances, it was decided to pay a full year's dividend on the preference shares and the directors decided to recommend a dividend of 6% on the ordinary shares and to transfer £9,000 to General Reserve. You are required to prepare:

(a) The Appropriation Account for the year ended 31st March, 1969.

(b) The Balance Sheet as at that date. (Ignore Taxation.)

10 The following balances were shown in the books of Day and Dobson Ltd., after closing the Profit and Loss Account for the year ending 1971:

	£
Ordinary share capital, fully paid	100,000
5% Preference share capital, fully paid	100,000
Freehold land and buildings at cost	320,000
Plant and Machinery at cost	21,200
Plant and Machinery provision for depreciation	7,220
Formation expenses	470
Creditors and accrued expenses	36,110
General Reserve	12,500
Balance at bank	14,360
Provision for Bad Debts	1,270
Profit and Loss Account—Undistributed profit at 30th June, 1970	92,680
6% Debentures—secured on land	40,000
Debtors and payments in advance	40,190
Net profit for year ending 30th June, 1971	53,110
Interim dividend paid on Ordinary shares	1,500
Interim dividend paid on Preference shares	2,500
Stocks as valued by the directors at 30th June, 1971	40,270
Interest on Debentures paid	2,400
Share Capital—Authorised 250,000 shares of £1 each	

It was resolved that:

(i) The sum of £5,000 be transferred to General Reserve.

(ii) The final dividend on the preference shares be paid.

(iii) A final dividend of £0·05 per share on the ordinary shares be paid.

Set out these balances in the form of a trial balance, prepare the Appropriation Account to show the proposed distribution, and draw up the balance sheet as at 30th June, 1971, for presentation at the annual general meeting of the members of the company.

11 Oxbridge Limited has an authorised share capital of £500,000 of which £250,000 is in preference shares of £1 each and the balance in ordinary shares of £0·25 each. The following balances were left in the books of the company after the Profit and Loss Account for the year ending 31st March, 19·1, had been prepared:

Ordinary Share Capital £250,000; 6% Preference Share Capital £250,000; Freehold Properties at cost £350,000; General Reserve £250,000; Stock on hand as valued by officials of the company £215,928; Creditors and accrued charges £125,976; Share Premium £25,000; Leasehold Properties at cost £125,000; Provision for Depreciation of leases £25,000; Fixtures and Fittings at cost £245,000; Provision for Depreciation of Fixtures and Fittings £45,000; Debtors and payments in advance £20,576; Balance at bank and Cash in hand £250,312; and Profit and Loss Account—undistributed profit £235,840.

It was resolved that:

(i)   A transfer of £50,000 to General Reserve be made.

(ii) Provision for a dividend for the year on the preference shares be made.

(iii) Provision for a dividend of £0·10 per share on the ordinary shares be made.

Prepare the Appropriation Account to give effect to these resolutions and the Balance Sheet at 31st March, 19·1, for presentation to the members of the company.

(RSA II)

12 The following Trial Balance was extracted from the books of Box Ltd., at 31st December, 1970:

TRIAL BALANCE

	£	£
Share capital; authorised and issued 40,000 shares of £1 each		40,000
Stock in trade, 1st January 1970	13,428	
8% Debentures		20,000
Share premium		10,000
Freehold property (at cost)	50,000	
Furniture and Fittings (at cost)	3,000	
Bad debts	601	
Wages and Salaries	9,820	
Purchases	90,620	
Sales		121,498
Provision for bad debts, 1st January, 1970		250
Provision for depreciation of Furniture and Fittings, 1st January, 1970		750
Insurance	693	
Office expenses	1,142	
Balance at bank	14,294	
Debenture interest paid to 1st July, 1970	800	
Rates	210	
Profit and Loss Account balance at 1st January, 1970		2,900
Trade debtors	16,923	
Trade creditors		12,989
Rent received		390
Directors' salaries	6,000	
General expenses	1,246	
	208,777	208,777

You are given the following information:

(a) Stock in trade 31st December, 1970, £16,426.

(b) The provision for bad debts is to be increased to £300.

(c) £796 has been included in the wages and salaries account which represents the wages cost of extending the company's freehold property.

(d) Rent receivable due at 31st December, 1970, £130.

(e) Insurance paid in advance at 31st December, 1970, amounted to £86.

(f) Depreciation of furniture and fittings is to be provided for at the rate of 5% per annum on cost.

(g) £7,000 is to be transferred to General Reserve and provision is to be made for a dividend of 10% on the issued capital.

You are required to prepare a Trading and Profit and Loss Account for the year 1970 and a Balance Sheet as at 31st December, 1970.
Ignore taxation.

(*RSA II 1971*)

13 Martin Ltd., manufactures desks of one type only. The following Trial Balance was extracted from the company's books on 31st December, 1970:

TRIAL BALANCE

	£	£
Share capital authorised and issued 70,000 shares of £1 each		70,000
Freehold premises at cost	40,000	
Plant and machinery at cost	10,000	
Provision for depreciation of plant and machinery to 1st January, 1970		5,000
Stock of raw materials 1st January, 1970	6,950	
Stock of finished desks in warehouse (300 desks) 1st January, 1970	6,000	
Balance at bank	4,960	
Bad debts	691	
Provision for doubtful debts 1st January, 1970		290
Debtors and Creditors	11,492	10,611
Directors' remuneration	8,000	
Manufacturing wages	8,249	
Sales (5,400 desks)		135,000
Raw material purchased	122,440	
Salaries	4,228	
Rates	420	
General expenses	1,701	
Profit and Loss Account balance at 1st January, 1970		4,230
	225,131	225,131

You are given the following information:

(a) Stock of raw materials 31st December, 1970, £9,839.

(b) During 1970, 6,440 desks were completed and transferred from the factory to the warehouse. The desks transferred and the stocks of completed desks are to be valued at cost.

(c) There were no stocks of partly finished desks at 1st January, 1970, or at 31st December, 1970.

(d) Rates paid in advance 31st December, 1970, £60.

(e) The provision for doubtful debts is to be increased to £325.

(f) Provision for depreciation of plant and machinery is to be made at 10% per annum on cost.

(g) The directors have recommended a dividend of 10% on the issued capital.

(h) General expenses outstanding 31st December, 1970, £89.

You are required to prepare Manufacturing, Trading and Profit and Loss Accounts for the year 1970 and a Balance Sheet as on 31st December, 1970. Ignore taxation.

(RSA II 1971)

14 The summarised accounts of Estimates Ltd., for 1971 were as follows:

TRADING AND PROFIT AND LOSS ACCOUNT FOR 1971

	£		£
Materials consumed and wages	19,243	Sales	26,835
Depreciation	2,225		
	21,468		
Gross profit	5,367		
	26,835		26,835
Expenses	3,578	Gross profit	5,367
Net profit	1,789		
	5,367		5,367

BALANCE SHEET
AS AT 31ST DECEMBER, 1971

	£		£	£
Share capital	17,500	Fixed assets:		
Profit and Loss Account	4,120	Buildings at cost		8,000
		Plant (purchased		
	21,620	1st January, 1969) cost	17,800	
Current liabilities	2,138	*Less* depreciation	6,675	
				11,125
				19,125
		Current assets:		
		Stocks	2,181	
		Debtors	1,464	
		Cash	988	
				4,633
	23,758			23,758

The directors of Estimates Ltd. decide that the time is ripe to expand the business. They anticipate that the 1971 turnover can be doubled in 1972 and they make the following consequential estimates:

(i)   A new building costing £4,000 will be required.

(ii) Additional plant with an eight-year life and costing £9,000 will be required.

(iii) The cost of materials consumed and wages will be doubled.

(iv) The cost of expenses will be increased by £1,789.

(v)   At the end of 1972 stocks will have increased to £3,246, debtors to £2,219 and current liabilities to £3,462.

Required, on the assumption that the above estimates are fulfilled.

(a) a total cash amount for 1972,

(b) a summarised trading and profit and loss account for 1972 and a balance sheet as at 31st December, 1972.

Notes:

(i) Stocks consist of raw materials only: no manufactured or partly manufactured goods are on hand at the beginning or at the end of the year;

(ii) no dividends have been paid and none are proposed;

(iii) assume that the company's bankers have agreed to grant any necessary overdraft.

(RSA II 1972)

15 Swinford is the proprietor of a small manufacturing business, but he also makes an occasional deal in house property. The accounts of his business for 1971 and 1972 are as follows:

	1971 £	1972 £
Sales (manufactured goods)	26,240	31,970
Sales (of houses)	11,810	16,360
	38,050	48,330
Cost of manufactured goods sold	18,160	23,550
Cost of houses sold	10,600	12,320
	28,760	35,870
Gross profit	9,290	12,460
	38,050	48,330
Administration Expenses (for Manufacturing business)	6,900	7,300
Expenses of house sales	320	630
Net profit	2,070	4,530
	9,290	12,460

Swinford takes the view that because of his increase in turnover and net profit he should expand his manufacturing business. He proposes to double his production capacity by installing new plant at a cost of £14,500. He approaches Stroker for a loan of £15,000 at 8% for this development.

You are asked to prepare a report for Stroker giving your views of the proposal and to support them with whatever financial statements you are able to prepare on the basis of the information provided in this question.

(RSA II 1973)

16 The following is the balance sheet of M Rose at 31st December 1976:

BALANCE SHEET OF M ROSE
AS AT 31ST DECEMBER, 1976

	£		£
Capital Account	16,000	Fixed Assets	12,000
Sundry Creditors	1,000	Current Assets	4,500
		Cash at bank	500
	17,000		17,000

On 31st December, 1976, the business was acquired by RS Limited with a nominal capital of 25,000 Ordinary shares of £1 each. The Company took over all the assets except Cash at bank and undertook to pay off the creditors.

The purchase price was £19,000, consisting of 17,000 Ordinary shares and the balance in cash. On 1st February, 1977, the balance of the shares was issued to the public and by 28th February, all moneys due had been received and the purchase price had been paid.

You are required to show the necessary entries in the company's books and a balance sheet as at 28th February, 1977.

17 The Balance Sheet of two partners, Pride and Dixon, at 31st December, 19.1, was as follows:

BALANCE SHEET OF PRIDE AND DIXON

AS AT 31 T DECEMBER, 19·1

Capital Account			Goodwill		375
Pride	7,125		Land and Buildings		4,650
Dixon	10,854		Machinery and Plant		4,080
		17,979	Fixtures and Fittings		625
Bills payable		450	Stock		7,335
Sundry Creditors		1,875	Bills Receivable		600
Bank Overdraft		696	Debtors	3,510	
			Less Provision for Bad Debts	175	
					3,335
		21,000			21,000

On 31st December, 19.1, the business was acquired by Pride and Co. Ltd., with a nominal capital of 22,500 Ordinary Shares of £1 each and 22,500 5% Preference Shares at £1 each.

The Company took over all the assets except the Bills Receivable and undertook to pay off the Sundry Creditors, but not the Bank Overdraft nor the Bills Payable. The purchase price was £22,500 consisting of 15,000 £1 Ordinary Shares and 6,000 £1 Preference Shares and the balance in cash. The Land and Buildings were valued at £5,700, and the Machinery and Plant at £3,750.

On the 28th February, 19.2, the balance of the Ordinary Shares was issued to the public and by 31st March all moneys due had been received; the purchase consideration was also discharged on 31st March.

You are required to give:

(i)   The Journal entries in the books of Pride and Co. Ltd.

(ii) The Balance Sheet as at 31st March, 19.2.

Chapter Thirty Three

Flow of Funds*

It is only since the late 1960s that the study of the flow of funds and how it is best controlled has come into increasing prominence. A Flow of Funds Statement shows concisely the ever-changing nature of working capital (the excess of current assets over current liabilities) during the process of day-to-day business, and the fluidity (or cash position) of the business. There is a flow of creditors to stock (purchases); stock to debtors (sales); debtors to cash (payments in); cash to creditors (payments out), and so on. Thus, cash is not only taken into account in its most liquid form, ie. money, but also in the form of credit. My creditors are a form of cash because as long as I do not pay them, I use the money due to them for other purposes. At the same time, some of them represent the stocks of goods in my warehouse. It is assumed that I will pay them. Similarly, my debtors are a form of cash from which I am deprived, as long as they do not pay me. It is assumed that they will pay me. It is relevant to remind ourselves that when creditors (liabilities) are reduced on being paid off, cash (assets) are also reduced by the same amount; and the working capital remains unchanged. All these changes in current assets and current liabilities are reflected in the fluctuations of working capital, which increases when profits are made and decreases when losses are sustained. Profits are the excess of revenue over expenditure—ultimately cash.

The two most important Flow of Fund Statements are concerned with flow of cash and working capital respectively. The object is to see that there is always sufficient liquidity of assets for the requirements of the business. A businessman must know not only the extent of his profits, but he must also make sure of the adequacy of his cash resources and the working capital of his business to meet future contingencies. Favourable figures for both these resources are essential for the firm's survival. Many firms nowadays, therefore, produce periodical statements which show the state of their finances—their cash flow and working capital positions at any point in time— present position or future estimates. Future estimates or assessments are described as projections or budgets, which enable managers to plan ahead, perhaps for an increase in capital in the form of additional cash from external sources (eg. a new issue of shares, or a bank overdraft).

Changes occur in the value of fixed assets which, when increased, imply an outflow of cash and when decreased imply an increase in cash. Share or loan capital may be increased by a new issue of shares (or by the contribution of extra cash in a sole-trading firm, from the proprietor's private resources); and decreased by the redemption of debentures or the payment of dividends and taxes. A less obvious source of cash is depreciation. A motor van purchased this year for £2,000, reduces funds by that amount. Next year, however, when 20% depreciation (a reserve) is written off, profits are decreased by £400 but sources of cash are increased by the

---

*Alternative expressions for Flow of Funds are: Cash Flow; Sources and Applications of Funds; Movement of Funds.

same amount. That £400, and the reserve for depreciation in every subsequent year, until the whole cost of the motor van is written off, may be used in any way that is necessary or expedient for the welfare of the business, not necessarily for the replacement of the motor van. Therefore, when computing flow of cash, the reserve for depreciation is classified as a source of funds—it is added back to profits. After all, depreciation is retained profits—profits put aside for some future use, and it is there to be added to other sources of funds when required.

The following classification of sources of funds and their use or application during an accounting period are shown below:

SOURCES	APPLICATIONS
Increase of Share or Loan Capital	Redemption of Loan Capital
	Payment of dividends and taxes
Profits (before taxation)	Losses, eg. Proprietor's drawings
Depreciation charged against current profits	
Increases in creditors (purchases of stocks)	Decreases in creditors (reduction in outstanding balances)
Decreases in assets (payment by debtors)	Increases in assets (sales of goods).

Explanations have already been given on depreciation and the increase of capital as sources and how they are applied. Creditors, too, when they are increased, are sources of new assets (eg. Stock). Yet, such increases cause a decrease in cash as well. If payment is made by a bank overdraft, that implies a release of additional cash into the business, for a short period. The decrease in assets (excepting depreciation), shows that they have been converted into cash, as when stocks have been sold for cash or when debtors have paid. By whatever value the assets fall, a corresponding value is added to cash, ultimately.

Cash Flow Statement

A Cash Flow Statement is intended to explain how funds have moved during a given financial year. The information is obtained from figures given in the opening and closing balance sheets of the year or period concerned. The following example should clarify the explanations given above:

EX. 33/1   The following are the balance sheets of R Crowe, a trader, for the years ended 31st December, 1975 and 1976. Crowe is unable to understand why his cash position has shown a considerable improvement in 1976, especially as his net profit for 1976 has not increased and his drawings are greater in 1976 than in 1975. You are required to prepare for Crowe a Cash Flow Statement for the year ended 31st December, 1976, showing how the improvement in his cash position has occurred.

BALANCE SHEETS AS AT 31ST DECEMBER

	1975 £	1976 £		£	1975 £	£	1976 £
Capital Account	10,400	11,000	FIXED ASSETS				
Add Net Profit	3,600	3,560	Premises at cost		7,200		7,200
			Machinery at cost	5,000		5,000	
	14,000	14,560	*Less* Depreciation	2,000		3,000	
Less Drawings	3,000	3,300			3,000		2,000
	11,000	11,260			10,200		9,200

273

CURRENT LIABILITIES			CURRENT ASSETS		
Trade creditors	2,900	1,880	Stocks	1,050	1,120
Bank overdraft	550		Trade debtors	3,200	2,000
		3,450	Cash at bank		820
				4,250	3,940
	14,450	13,140		14,450	13,140

SOLUTION:

	£
Bank overdraft as at 1st January, 1976	550
Cash at bank as at 31st December, 1976	820
Total paid into bank in 1976	1,370

CASH FLOW STATEMENT
FOR YEAR ENDED 31ST DECEMBER, 1976

	£	£	£
Sources of Cash			
Net Profit	3,560		
Add back Depreciation	1,000		
		4,560	
Reduction in debtors		1,200	
			5,760
Applications of Cash			
Drawings	3,300		
Reduction in creditors	1,020		
Increase in Stock	70	4,390	
Increase in Cash during 1976			1,370

WORKING CAPITAL

	1975 £	1976 £
Current Assets	4,250	3,940
Current Liabilities	3,450	1,880
Working Capital	800	2,060

Working Capital 1976	2,060
Working Capital 1975	800
Increase in Working Capital	1,260

The following is a rather more comprehensive example:

EX. 33/2 From the following balance sheets and appropriation account of Marigold Ltd. you are required to show how the profits for year 1971 have been used up.

BALANCE SHEETS AS AT 31ST MARCH

	1970 £	1971 £		1970 £	1971 £
Issued Capital	225,000	225,000	Freehold Property	110,250	108,045
Profit and Loss Account	30,000	36,750	Machinery and Plant	114,750	148,500
General Reserve	37,500	37,500	Work in Progress	45,000	41,250
Redeemable Debentures	37,500	33,750	Stock of materials	26,250	33,750
Creditors	45,000	67,500	Debtors	56,250	71,250
Bank Overdraft		2,295	Cash at bank	22,500	
	375,000	402,795		375,000	402,795

APPROPRIATION ACCOUNT

Dividend paid			27,000	Balance 31st March, 1970	b/d	30,000
Balance 31st March, 1971	c/d		36,750	Net Profit 31st March, 1971		33,750
			63,750			63,750

	1970	1971
	£	£
Machinery and Plant—Cost at 31st March	127,500	177,750

The above statement shows the flow of funds into the business and how they have been controlled and used up. The statement also discloses the manner in which changes have occurred in the working capital during the course of the year, as the following Flow of Funds Statement clearly explains:

FLOW OF FUNDS STATEMENT
FOR YEAR ENDED 31ST MARCH, 1971

	£	£
SOURCES OF FUNDS		
Net Profit for year ended 31st March, 1971		33,750
Depreciation		
Freehold Property		2,205
Machinery and Plant		
31st March, 1970	114,750	
Cost of new machinery	50,250	
	165,000	
Less value at 31st March, 1971	148,500	
		16,500
Creditors—increase		22,500
Work in Progress—decrease		3,750
Cash at bank = £22,500 + £2,295 overdraft repaid		24,795
		103,500
APPLICATIONS OF FUNDS		
Dividend paid		27,000
Debentures redeemed		3,750
Machinery and Plant purchased during year		50,250
Stock of Materials—increase		7,500
Debtors—increase		15,000
		103,500

The following is an analysis of the Working Capital at 31st March, 1971:

	1970	1971
	£	£
CURRENT ASSETS		
Work in Progress	45,000	41,250
Stock of materials	26,250	33,750
Debtors	56,250	71,250
Cash at bank	22,500	
	150,000	146,250
CURRENT LIABILITIES		
Creditors	45,000	67,500
Bank Overdraft		2,295
	45,000	69,795
Working Capital	105,000	76,455
Decrease in the Working Capital 31st March, 1971		28,545

Computed as follows		
New Machinery	50,250	
Depreciation Freehold Property	2,205	52,455
Reductions		
Dividend paid	27,000	
Debentures redeemed	3,750	
New Machinery purchased	50,250	81,000

Decrease in the Working Capital 31st March, 1971   28,545

Exercise 33

1   The following are the balance sheets of M Cramer for the years ended 31st December, 1975 and 1976. Cramer's cash position, you will observe, has greatly improved in 1976, although his net profit for 1976 has not increased and furthermore his drawings are greater in 1976 than in 1975.

Required:

Prepare Cramer's Flow of Funds Statement for the year ended 31st December, 1976 to show why his cash position has improved.

BALANCE SHEETS
AS AT 31ST DECEMBER

	1975 £	1976 £		1975 £	1976 £
Capital Account	2,600	2,750	FIXED ASSETS (at cost)	2,550	2,300
Add Net Profit	900	890			
			CURRENT ASSETS		
	3,500	3,640	Sundry Current Assets	1,063	780
Less Drawings	750	825	Cash at Bank		205
	2,750	2,815			
CURRENT LIABILITIES					
Trade creditors	725	470			
Bank overdraft	138 863				
	3,613	3,285		3,613	3,285

Note: No new fixed assets were bought during 1976.

2   The balance sheet of a limited company as on 31st December, 19·1 was as follows:

	£		£
Issued Capital	100,000	Fixed Assets	72,300
Reserves	20,000	Stock	72,500
Debentures	50,000	Debtors and Prepayments	22,400
Current Liabilities	5,500	Bank	8,300
	175,500		175,500

(a)   What was the amount of the company's working capital at that date?

(b)   During the year ended 31st December, 19·1, the company earned a net profit of £19,700 after charging £4,800 for depreciation of the fixed assets, new fixed assets were bought at a cost of £18,600, and old ones sold for £1,300.

Calculate the amount of working capital at the end of the year.

(c)   The following appropriations are proposed out of the profit for 19·1: The transfer of £5,000 to general reserve and the declaration of dividends amounting to £7,500. What effect will each of these have on the working capital, and why?

(*RSA*)

3 The balance sheets of Narrow Waters Ltd. at 31st December, 1970, and 31st December, 1971, are as follows:

	1970 £	£	1971 £	£
FIXED ASSETS				
Plant at cost	42,000		59,500	
Less Depreciation	14,850		20,240	
		27,150		39,260
Transport at cost	5,100		6,800	
Less Depreciation	1,700		2,650	
		3,400		4,150
		30,550		43,410
CURRENT ASSETS				
Stock	9,179		11,421	
Debtors	7,241		8,219	
Bank	6,118			
	22,538		19,640	
Less				
Current liabilities	8,864		10,712	
Dividend	3,000		3,000	
Bank Overdraft	—		3,184	
	11,864		16,896	
Working capital		10,674		2,744
		41,224		46,154
REPRESENTED BY				
Share capital		30,000		30,000
Profit and loss		11,224		16,154
		41,224		46,154

Required:

(a) a flow of funds statement for 1971; and

(b) a brief comment on the financial policy followed by the directors of Narrow Waters Ltd. in 1971.

(Institute of Bankers 1972)

Chapter Thirty Four

Mechanised Accounting

It is essential that the accounts of a growing business should be able to provide accurate information on demand, immediately, if possible. Manual (handwritten) systems cannot meet this requirement rapidly. This brief introduction to mechanised accounting sets out to show that mechanised accounting is a desirable alternative.

Manual Methods

The conventional manual sales ledger system with the three separate entries (Sales-book-ledger-statement) is slow and error-prone, even when operated by highly-qualified bookkeepers. As the volume of work increases with the growth of the business, the recording of transactions tends to lag behind the actual invoicing of the goods and the receipt of cash. Maintaining up-to-date accounts and producing up-to-the-minute information at short notice becomes difficult. Above all, the dispatch of the monthly statements is held up, which results in giving debtors extended credit, slows cash flow, and may also result in incurring losses in interest charges.

The 'three-in-one' systems reproduce the ledger account, the statement, and the sales sheet (which becomes part of the sales book when filed) simultaneously. They save time and reduce the areas in which errors might occur, but they cannot eliminate calculation errors or errors due to fatigue. Mechanised accounting eliminates those human disabilities, although the manual accounting procedures in use may remain unaltered. The information on the 'media' (original documents—invoice copies, paying-in slips, credit and debit note copies, cheque book stubs) is fed into the machine, which processes it.

Mechanised Accounting Methods

Mechanised accounting is speedy and it keeps ledger accounts up-to-date at all times. Thus, credit control (the calling-in of debts when they fall due for payment, hence a smooth cash flow) is more easily maintained. Accounting machines are constructed to add as well as subtract, and they may or may not supply 'particulars', or the details, shown on the media. The more complex electronic and computer methods, such as punched card accounting machines and electronic computers, have certain basic components which were first used in scientific research and calculations. Apart from the input and output units, the electronic computer stores information ie. it has a 'memory' unit. In the medium-sized and bigger businesses electronic computers are used for day-to-day accounting, pay roll and stock control, as well as more complex calculations.

At the present stage of our studies, it is sufficient to understand how a 'three-in-one' system, using a horizontal ledger, operates. For purposes of explanation and examples, the method applicable to Sales will be used, which may equally be applied to Purchases. A sales ledger card (or 'account card' as it is sometimes called, a term which includes purchases ledger cards) and a corresponding statement (sent to customers, usually at the end of each month) show the current balance of the customer's account at any moment.

The following example recapitulates what has already been said in previous chapters regarding the 'horizontal' ledger:

			£
Feb.	1	Amount due from M Kim (a customer)	200
	7	Sold to M Kim goods value	150
	15	Received cheque from M Kim	200
	25	M Kim returned goods; a credit note was sent to him	10
	28	Sold to M Kim goods value	90

These transactions appear on M Kim's account card as follows:

Ref. 81 Account Card of M Kim

				Debit £	Credit £	New Balance £
1976 Feb.	1	Balance	(or a symbol)			200
	7	Sales	(or a reference number)	150		350
	15	Cash	,, ,, ,, ,,		200	150
	25	Returns	,, ,, ,, ,,		10	140
	28	Sales	,, ,, ,, ,,	90		230

The last figure in the 'New Balance' column always shows the amount due. Each account card has a reference number; M Kim's number is 81.

The following are the steps taken to record credit sales:

1 Take a batch of invoices and give each a date and a number.

2 Arrange the invoices in the numerical order corresponding to that of the customers' ledger cards.

3 Produce the total value of the batch on an adding machine. This is called a 'pre-list'.

4 Select the relevant account cards from the file and 'marry' them to their respective invoices.

5 Insert a Sales Day Book Sheet, called a Sales Sheet or, more technically, an Action Sheet, which is chemically sensitised to make a carbon unnecessary.

6 Insert the ledger card into the machine for posting the sale.

7 Strike keys representing customer's outstanding balance and the proof-code. Striking in this instance does not mean printing—no printing takes place, but a mechanism is stimulated to produce a second proof-code. The new proof-code is a number representing a mathematical relationship between the previous proof-code number and the customer's outstanding balance. The proof-code is automatically computed by the machine. When a new transaction is to be recorded, the operator first causes the machine to pick up the account balance and the last proof-code number. The machine will then decide whether or not the correct balance has been picked up.

8 If not correct, the machine rejects the new entry (the keys do not function); try again with the correct figures!
   If correct, the machine accepts the new entry (with copies on Statement and Sales Sheet). Type the reference number, the amount in the debit column, and the amount of sales tax (such as VAT) if applicable.

9 The machine computes and updates the outstanding balance on the ledger card and then prints the new proof-code. Also, by the time the batch of invoices have

been entered in their respective ledger accounts, the machine has accumulated each invoice total and at the pressure of a key, it produces a grand total for the batch, below the entries in the debit column of the Sales Sheet.

10 Check that total with the one on the pre-list. If incorrect, find the error, which must be in the batch just posted, and adjust.

11 Carry out the same procedure for cash received and all other credit entries.

The Control Card

A 'master' ledger card, called the Control Card, is a mechanised version of a Control Account (Chapter 22).

1 Remove previous documents from machine. Clear the machine.

2 Insert the Control Card. Strike the figures of the outstanding balance and those of the last proof-code showing on the card.

3 If the correct outstanding balance has been struck, the machine will accept the new entries: (a) Batch number; (b) Batch totals (debit and credit). The machine will now up-date the outstanding balance; it will also create and print a new proof-code.

The sum of the balances on all the customers' account cards will be equal to the New Balance on the Control Card.

The Sales Sheet Shows:

(a) date of posting; (b) batch reference number; (c) details in words or code numbers; (d) value of each invoice; (e) total of each batch; (f) amount of each credit entry; (g) a figure for comparison with the up-dated Control Card New Balance.

Revisionary and More Difficult Exercises

1 You are keeping the books of W Wright a wholesaler. Wellmaker is a supplier of goods. On 1st May, 1975, Wellmaker is owed £200. The day books show the following transactions took place during the month of May 1975.

Date		Book	Page	Amount
1975				£
May	5	Purchases	7	300
	7	Returns	3	10
	9	Cash		
		Bank column	9	285
		Discount		15
	16	Purchase	19	170
	22	Purchase	30	150
	27	Returns	4	15

(a) Write up Wellmaker's account in W Wright's ledger.

(b) What is the purpose of the folio column?

(c) In which of W Wright's ledgers should this account appear?

(d) Is the final balance on the account a debit or credit balance?

(*RSA 1975*)

2 The following figures are taken from a metal merchant's books as at 31st December, 1974:

	Tonnes	£
Stock of copper in warehouse 1st January, 1974	500	350,000
Purchases for the year	10,825	7,361,000
Sales for the year	9,525	6,857,000

There were no weight gains or losses during the year.
The market price of copper on 31st December, 1974 was £650 per ton.

You are required:

(a) To calculate the tonnage and value of the stock at 31st December, 1974;

(b) To prepare the Trading Account for the year ended 31st December, 1974.

(*RSA 1975*)

3 (a) What would be the effect on gross profit of an increase in the rate of turnover of stock? Assume that buying and selling prices remain constant.

(b) A trader's turnover for 1971 is £64,740. What additional information would you require in order to calculate his rate of turnover of stock?

(c) The average value of stock, at cost price, held by S Lark during the year 1971 was £3,550. His rate of turnover of stock was 12. He made an average percentage of gross profit on sales of 20%.

Calculate: (i) the cost of goods sold,

(ii) the gross profit,

(iii) the turnover,

for the year 1971.

(d) In the early part of 1972 Lark started an advertising campaign estimated to cost £2,350. He expects to sell more goods as a result of this and estimates that his selling and administrative expenses will increase by £300.

Assuming that Lark will maintain his average stock at the same value and sell at the same margin of gross profit, calculate what will have to be his rate of turnover of stock to achieve *at least* the same net profit as in 1971. (Give your answer to the nearest whole number.)

(University of London GCE O level)

4 The following personal account appeared in S Engineer's ledger on 1st January, 1975. L Beech—a credit balance of £160. During January 1975 the following transactions took place relating to this account:

Jan. 9 Bought goods from L Beech for £60 less 20% trade discount.
11 Paid L Beech by cheque the amount standing to the credit of his account on 1st January less 2½% cash discount.
18 Returned damaged goods purchased from L Beech on January 9 at the catalogue price of £10.

(a) Make the necessary entries in the personal account of L Beech and balance the account at 31st January, 1974.

(b) Name the book of original entry in which each of these transactions would appear.

(RSA 1975)

5 N Ramrod keeps cash and bank records. At the close of business on 29th May, 1975 he reached the bottom of a page and carried forward the following:

	Discount £	Cash £	Bank £	
Total B/F	27·40	114·10	214·30	Debit side
Total B/F	40·10	74·50	210·00	Credit side

The following sums were received on 30th May, 1975:
Cheque from J Cuthbertson for £120 in settlement of an account for £125.
Cash from N Green £40.
Cheque from Brian Way for £75 in settlement of an account for £76·50.
The following payments were made on 30th May, 1975:
Cheque to Morris Brown for £140·40.
Cheque to local council in payment of rates for the half year £150·40.
N Ramrod cashed a cheque for private drawings £50, and took £50 from the office cash for the same purpose.
Write up N Ramrod's cash and bank records and balance them at close of business on 30th May, 1975.
Note: The business will be closed on 31st May, 1975.

(RSA 1975)

6 On 31st October, 1975 the Cash Book of N Orange showed a balance at bank of £570. An examination of his records located the following errors:

(1) Orange paid to R Jones £175 by cheque on 15th October. This cheque was entered in the Cash Book as £195.

(2) Bank charges not recorded in the Cash Book amounted to £25.

(3) A cheque dated 19th October, value £150, payable to T Jack was not paid by the Bank until the 5th November.

(4) Orange on 23rd October received from W Green a cheque, value £125. This cheque was dishonoured on the 29th October. No entry for the dishonour has been made in the Cash Book.

(5) On the 31st October a cheque, value £200, received from F Brown was banked; however the bank statement was not credited until 1st November.

You are required to:

(1) Make the necessary entries in the Cash Book in order to show the revised Cash Book balance at the 31st October, 1975.

(2) Prepare a statement reconciling the corrected Cash Book balance with the Bank Statement at 31st October, 1975.

(3) State the balance at Bank at 31st October, 1975 as shown by the Bank Statements.

(RSA 1975)

7 On 31st December, 19·1, C Dee's Bank Statement showed a balance in his favour of £650. On comparing the Statement with his Cash Book he found that the following entries in the Cash Book had not yet been entered on the Statement:

Cheques paid in 30th December, £125.
Cheques drawn up to 31st December, £275.

and the following entries on the Statement had not yet been entered in his Cash Book:

Bank charges for the half year to 31st December, £26.
Payment direct to the Bank by one of his debtors, £116.

Draw up a Bank Reconciliation Statement so as to show the bank balance according to his Cash Book on 31st December, 19·1.

8 On 31st March, 19·1, the balance in the bank account as shown in the Cash Book of S Crowe was £573. On checking the Cash Book with the Bank Statement, he discovered the following differences:

(a) Cheques credited in the Cash Book but not yet presented for payment, £312.

(b) The bank statement does not include cheques paid into the bank on 31st March, and debited in the Cash Book on that day, £124.

(c) The bank had charged his account with £15 bank charges, and had credited his account with £30, representing a dividend received by the bank on behalf of Crowe. Neither of these items had been entered in the Cash Book.

You are required:

(a) to adjust the Cash Book balance, and

(b) to reconcile the adjusted balance showing the amount which should appear on the Bank Statement at 31st March, 19·1.

(RSA 1970)

9 From the following information prepare a Bank Reconciliation Statement to show the balance in the Cash Book on 31st December, 1971.

	£
Bank statement (credit balance)	6,295·55
Cheques issued but unpresented at 31st December, 1971	196·71
Bank charges not entered in Cash Book	35·50
Cheques paid in but not credited in bank statement at 31st December, 1971	965·95
Bank dividends received by 31st December, 1971 but not entered in Cash Book	14·52
Cheques returned by the Bank marked 'refer to drawer' not adjusted in Cash Book	56·90

(JMB 1972)

10 The following is the cash book of C Croydon for the month of September 19·1:

19·1			£		19·1				£	
Sept.	2	To C Par	26	b	Sept.	3	By Milford Co.		168	b
	6	L Prescot & Son	198	b		14	D Blaydon		375	b
	10	S Athan	657	b		27	L Ditton		201	
	23	I Ryde	401	b		30	N Milton		66	
	30	S Seaford Ltd.	296			30	Wages		250	b
						30	Bank Charges		8	b
						30	N York		160	
						30	Balance	c/d	350	
			1,578						1,578	

The above cash book was checked with the bank statement and all items marked 'b' were shown therein.

All cheques drawn before September, 19·1, had been presented for payment except one for £43.

Prepare the bank reconciliation statement at 30th September, 19·1.

(RSA II)

11 Rowney, a trader, pays all his business takings into his bank. The balance shown by his bank's statement at 1st January, 19·2 agreed with the balance shown by his cash book as at that date, and the following statement shows in the form of a summary all the figures appearing on the bank's statement for 19·2:

	£
Balance in hand 31st December, 19·1	368
Amounts paid in by Rowney and credited by the bank in 19·2	12,429
Cheques drawn by Rowney and paid by the bank in 19·2	12,241
Bank charges for 19·2	20
There were no other entries on the bank statement during 19·2	

On 31st December, 19·2, Rowney had drawn two cheques for £34 and £38 respectively, which are not included in the total shown above, having been paid by the bank in 19·3.

You are asked to prepare:

(a) a summary of the bank statement for 19·2;

(b) a summary of the bank account in the books of Rowney for 19·2 and

(c) a bank reconcilation statement at 31st December, 19·2.

(RSA II)

12 The ledger card of B Parkes in the books of R Foster for February 1975 was as follows:

B Parkes

1975			Dr.	Cr.	Balance
			£	£	£
Feb.	3	Goods		460	460
	6	Returns	40		420
	20	Cheque	200		220
		Discount	10		210

(a) State the meaning of each entry in the debit and credit columns, naming the book of original entry from which the item is posted.

(b) What does the balance of £210 represent?

(*RSA I 1975*)

13 It is essential that both accounting staff and the public understand the modern terminology used in the presentation of accounts.

You are therefore required to choose four of the terms listed below and briefly describe their meanings.

(a) Cost of goods sold; (b) Net worth; (c) Working capital; (d) First in, first out (F.I.F.O.); (e) Capital expenditure; (f) Revenue expenditure.

(*RSA 1975*)

14 What effect would the following transactions have on (a) the assets and (b) the liabilities (including capital) of a wholesaler?

(i) Purchased on credit, goods for re-sale £420.

(ii) Paid creditors accounts amounting to £260 by cheque £247, the remainder being allowed as cash discount.

(iii) Received £342 from debtors in settlement of accounts amounting to £360 less cash discount allowed.

(iv) Paid one year's interest at 8% per annum on a loan of £1,000.

(v) Purchased new fittings on credit £240.

(vi) Received invoice from Builders Ltd. for repairs to premises £70.

Your answer is to be presented in the following form:

Effect on liabilities (incl. capital)	*Effect on assets*
(i)	
(ii)	
and so on.	

You are required to show, under the appropriate heading, the item affected and the amount of increase or decrease. Indicate an increase by the sign + (plus) and a decrease by the sign − (minus) and the amount. If there is no effect write the words 'no effect'.

(*University of London GCE O level*)

15 (a) How would you distinguish between capital expenditure and revenue expenditure?

(b) State, with reasons, in which of the two categories you would place each of the following items:

(i) cost of repairs to plant, £792;

(ii) cost of an addition to an existing machine which will improve its performance, £600;

(iii) cost of repairing and replacing woodwork, which had been destroyed by woodworm, in a building which had been in the same ownership since it was built, £2,000.

Would it make any difference to your answer if you were told that the building had been purchased recently, and its state was known when the contract to buy it was signed?

(Institute of Bankers 1971)

16 N Lirn closed his Books of Account on 31st October, 1975 and prepared a trial balance at that date. He subsequently located the following discrepancies.

(a) N Lirn received a letter from R Fir stating that Fir would not allow Lirn to take the £20 cash discount which Lirn had deducted from his last payment.

(b) N Lirn had erroneously charged £200 to furniture and fittings instead of wages.

(c) Depreciation not deducted from plant and machinery, 10 per cent on net book value. (Plant cost £8,000, depreciation to 31st October, 1974 £3,000.)

(d) Credit note £100 for short delivery of oil from Lubricants Ltd. Not wishing to reopen his books of prime entry he decided to pass all of the adjustments through his General Journal.

You are required to:

Make the necessary adjusting journal entries with suitable narration explaining each entry.

(RSA 1975)

17 A set of accounts was prepared for the year ended 31st December, 1974 and the following errors were subsequently discovered:

(a) Stock at 31st December, 1974 was found to be under-valued by £50.

(b) The purchase of a second-hand typewriter £25 had been included under the heading of repairs and renewal. Depreciation of Office Equipment had been provided at 10% and should be adjusted after the correction of the error.

(c) During the year the owner had taken goods from stock for his private use £60 (cost) but no entry had been made in the books to record this transaction.

Prepare journal entries to correct these errors or omissions and state the effect that the correction of each error or omission would have on the gross profit, net profit and balance sheet, naming the items affected on the balance sheet.

(RSA 1975)

18 You are presented with a Trading and Profit and Loss Account for the year ended 31st December, 19·1, and a Balance Sheet at that date. The accounts show a gross profit of £10,650 and a net profit of £5,120.

A careful check of the accounts on which the statements have been based revealed the following:

(i) General rates include payment of £150 for the half-year ending 31st March, 19·2.

(ii) Bank charges of £6 for the quarter ended 31st December, 19·1 were not notified by the bank until after the accounts had been closed.

(iii) The proprietor had withdrawn goods costing £100 for his own use during the year and had not recorded this fact.

(iv) Depreciation amounting to £20 had not been provided on shop equipment.

(v) Goods sold on credit for £30 had been returned by the buyer, P Dunn and included in Stock. The return had not been entered in the books.

(vi) A display stand, valued in the books at £25, had been destroyed by fire, and a claim against XY Insurance Co. Ltd., in respect of this had been agreed at £20. Entries had not been made to record either the loss of the stand or the insurance claim.

(vii) An invoice for £15 in respect of the press advertisement of a Christmas sale was received after the end of the year and had not been taken into account.

You are required:

(a) To prepare journal entries in respect of the above items to correct the accounts; and

(b) to calculate the adjusted figures of gross and net profit.

(JMB)

19 The following matters arose in the course of trading of a Limited Company.

(a) An invoice for the purchase of goods amounting to £1,407 was entered in the purchase journal as £1,047.

(b) On the last day of the year, goods were received on sale-or-return terms together with a pro-forma invoice for £660. No entries were made in the books of account but it was found that the goods had all been included in the stock at the end of the year at £660.

(c) Goods amounting to £200 had been sold to A Merchant, who paid this sum, less 2½% cash discount. It was subsequently discovered that an error had been made, the goods were returned, and a credit note for £200 was issued.

Show how the records would be adjusted.

(RSA II)

20 (a) Smith, a trader, received from his solicitor a cheque for £74 which represented the proceeds of collecting a debt due to him from Jones, a customer, less the solicitor's charges £6. Show the entry in Smith's journal to record this matter.

(b) Jackson, a trader, sells a van for £470 in cash. Out of the proceeds he pays £210 to Murphy, a creditor, and lodges the balance in his bank. Show the entries in Jackson's journal to record these matters.

(c) A cheque for £50, which had been received by a trader from his customer Paterson in settlement of an account due, was dishonoured and returned by the bank. The trader receives information that Paterson is bankrupt and unlikely to be able to pay any part of the amount due. Show the entries in the trader's journal to record these matters.

Note: In all cases cash is to be journalised.

(RSA II)

21 (a) How would each of the following errors affect the agreement of the totals of a trial balance?

(i) A receipt from a debtor correctly entered in the cash book as £248 was posted to the debtor's account as £284.

(ii) Goods purchased from F Derby were correctly entered in the purchases book as £462 but were posted to Derby's account as £402.

(iii) Sales on credit made to S Barrow £179 were incorrectly entered in the sales book as £197 and posted as that amount.

(iv) A page of the sales book correctly totalled as £8,846 was transferred to the next page as £8,946.

(v) A discount of £12 allowed to L Barlow, a debtor, was correctly recorded in the cash book but omitted from Barlow's account.

Your answer is to be presented in the following form:

Excess of debit over credit	*Excess of credit over debit*
(i)	
(ii)	

and so on.

State the amount of the excess *in each case.* If there is no effect write the words 'no effect' in each column.

(b) On 31st November, 1971 L Howard drew up the following trial balance:

	Dr. £	Cr. £
Capital		3,400
Drawings	2,764	
Stock (1st July, 1971)	3,417	
Purchases	27,994	
Sales		33,704
Trade debtors	2,858	
Trade creditors		5,066
Business expenses	4,947	
Fixtures and fittings	457	
Suspense account		267
	42,437	42,437

The suspense account was included as the trial balance did not balance. During the month of December 1971 the following errors were discovered. These errors accounted for the 'difference'.

(i) Goods invoiced to L Rust at £139 and correctly entered in the sales book had been posted to Rust's account as £193.

(ii) A purchase of goods from F Williams £121 had been entered on the wrong side of his account.

(iii) Business expenses paid by cheque and correctly entered in the cash book as £130 had been posted to the Business Expenses Account as £120.

(iv) A purchase of fittings £158 had been entered in the purchases account as £185.

(v) Goods £46 had been invoiced to Howard (the proprietor) and entered in the sales account but no other entry had been made.

Re-write the trial balance as it should have been if the errors had not been made. Write up the suspense account as it would appear *after* the errors have been corrected and balance it as at 31st December, 1971.

(*University of London GCE O level 1972*)

22 Scott was in business on his own account and during the year to 31st December, 19·1.

(a) He used goods, valued at £69, for private purposes.

(b) He purchased a motor van for £1,340, including £48 for tax and insurance paid in advance. He received an allowance of £350 on an old van taken in part exchange and paid the balance in cash. The old van stood in Scott's books at £380.

(c) A cheque for £100 received from Smith, a customer, settlement of the latter's account for that sum, was dishonoured and returned by the bank. Scott is of the opinion that nothing can be recovered from Smith.

(d) On 1st July, 19·1, he lent £100, privately and free of interest, to a senior employee. He later decided that the debt should be shown in the books as a business asset. The arrangements for repayment were that £20 should be deducted each month from the employee's salary, commencing in August, 19.1. These matters were all carried out but no entries were made in the books.

Give the journal entries in Scott's books to record these matters. (*RSA II*)

23 The trial balance of Crane Ltd., was extracted on 31st December, 19·1, and failed to agree. The trading and profit and loss account and balance sheet were prepared using the figures shown in the trial balance and the difference on the trial balance was shown in the balance sheet in a suspense account. The net profit shown was £8,290. The following errors were discovered later:

(i) A debit balance of £72 on the account of Hopkins, a customer, had been omitted from the trial balance.

(ii) Goods valued at £150 (selling price) were returned by a customer on 31st December, 19·1. No entry for the return of these goods had been made in the books and they had not been included in closing stock. The cost of the goods was £100.

(iii) The sales journal was under-cast by £220.

(iv) The wages cost of extending the company's freehold property amounted to £800. This amount has been included in the wages account.

(v) The purchase journal was over-cast by £300.

(vi) The total of discounts allowed for the month of April, 19·1, amounting to £142 had been credited to discounts received account.

(vii) Returns inwards amounting to £48 had been posted to the personal accounts only.

You are required:

(a) To show which side of the trial balance was in excess by reason of *each* error and by how much the trial balance was out of balance as a result.

(b) To show your calculation of the correct net profit.

Note: You are to assume that no control accounts are maintained for the purchases and sales ledgers.

(RSA II)

24 From the following trial balance and the notes appended below, prepare the Profit and Loss Account for the year ended 31st December, 1974 and a Balance Sheet as at that date.

TRIAL BALANCE OF A M DEALER
DECEMBER 31ST, 1974

	£	£
Capital		66,365
Cash at Bank—Deposit A/c	50,000	
Cash at Bank—Current A/c	14,622	
Cash in Hand	374	
Debtors	30,003	
Creditors		34,681
Drawings	10,000	
Investments	5,000	
Office Furniture and Fittings	10,100	
Office Machines	4,000	
Motor Car	1,600	
Commission Received		53,740
Consultation Fees		1,250
Interest		2,476
Rent and Rates	5,240	
Salaries and National Insurance	21,478	
Travel and Entertaining	2,472	
Advertising	728	
Insurance	224	
Trade Subscriptions	1,280	
Telephone and Cables	1,284	
Sundry Expenses	107	
	158,512	158,512

Notes:

(a) No Trading Account is required.

(b) Depreciate Office Furniture and Fittings and Office Machines by 10 per cent. Depreciate Motor Car by 20 per cent.

(c) Insurance paid in advance £34.

(d) Rates paid in advance £80.

(e) Advertising expenses accrued £72.

(RSA 1975)

25 (a) On 1st November, 19.1, Property, Ltd., purchased freehold premises, part of which were let at a rent of £40 a month, and paid (including the deposit) a total of £15,058, made up as follows:

	£	£
Purchase price		15,000
Add Water rate, proportion for five months to 31st March, 19·2	14	
Rent due from tenant for September and October, 19·1	80	
		94
		15,094
Less General rates, proportion for the month of October, 19·1		36
		15,058

No personal accounts were opened.
Show the entries in the Journal of Property Ltd.
Cash is to be journalised.

(b) On 31st December, 19·1, Poulton, a trader, paid £174 to a firm of builders. £54 was for repairs to Poulton's private house and £120 represented repairs to Poulton's business premises. It was agreed that the landlord of the business premises should bear £40 of the cost of repairs and that this amount should be deducted from the quarter's rent of £100 due on 31st December. On that date Poulton paid the amount due to the landlord. Show the entries in Poulton's journal.

Notes: No personal account is to be opened for the landlord. Cash is to be journalised.

(*RSA II*)

26 (a) On 1st January, 1971 W Summer's Rates Account showed that rates amounting to £120 were outstanding. During the year 1971 he made the following payments by cheque:

		£
Jan. 14	Rates for half year 1st October, 1970 to 31st March, 1971	240
June 20	Rates for half year 1st April, 1971 to 30th September, 1971	256
Dec. 15	Rates for half year 1st October, 1971 to 31st March, 1972	256

Write up Summer's Rates Account for the year 1971 and balance the account assuming that Summer prepares his final accounts at 31st December, 1971.

(b) State what information you derive from each of the entries in the following accounts which appeared in Summer's ledger. Your answer should indicate the nature of any transactions which have taken place.

Dr.				F Goode				Cr.
1971			£	1971				£
Dec. 10	Bank		220	Dec. 1	Balance	b/d		220
21	Purchases returns		34	17	Purchases			334
31	Balance	c/d	300					
			554					554
				1972				
				Jan. 1	Balance	b/d		300

Dr.				Fixtures and Fittings				Cr.
1971			£	1971				£
Jan. 1	Balance	b/d	580	Dec. 31	Depreciation			31
July 14	F Tate & Co.		240	31	Balance	c/d		789
			820					820
1972								
Jan. 1	Balance	b/d	789					

(c) L Parker sells goods on commission for Endor Ltd. On 1st July 1971, £165 was due to him from Endor Ltd. Parker is entitled to a commission of 10% on sales made by him.

From the following information draw up the account of Endor Ltd. in Parker's books for the quarter ended 30th September, 1971 and for the quarter ended 31st December, 1971.

	Value of goods sold £	Commission received £
Quarter ended 30th September, 1971	4,800	525
Quarter ended 31st December, 1971	3,950	415

(University of London GCE O level 1972)

27 F Stokes prepared his final accounts on 30th June, 1970. On 1st July, 1970 the following balances appeared (among others) in his ledger:

	Debit £	Credit £
Rates Account		60
Insurance Account	15	
Loan Account (F Williams)		1,000
Interest on Loan Account		25

(a) What information can you derive from each of these balances?

(b) Open the accounts named above and enter the balances.

(c) During the six months ended 31st December, 1970 the following transactions took place affecting these accounts:

1970
July 10 Paid half year's rates to 30th September, 1970 £120.
Sept. 30 Paid six months interest at 10% per annum on loan from F Williams together with a capital repayment of £200.
Oct.   1 Paid annual insurance premium £36 to 30th September, 1971.
Dec. 29 Paid rates for half year to 31st March, 1971 £120.

Make the entries which arise from these transactions in the accounts which you have opened.

(d) Stokes balanced his accounts and prepared his final accounts at 31st December, 1970. Balance the accounts which you have already opened incorporating any necessary adjustments, showing transfers to final accounts where appropriate and bringing down balances where necessary.

Note: Only the accounts named at the beginning of the question are required.

(University of London GCE O level 1971)

28 The following Balance Sheet was prepared by L B Jay on 1st November, 1975.

L B JAY
BALANCE SHEET AS AT 1ST NOVEMBER, 1975

	£		£	£
Capital	18,000	FIXED ASSETS		
		Land and Buildings (net)	10,500	
		Motor Vehicles (net)	3,000	13,500
CURRENT LIABILITIES		CURRENT ASSETS		
Creditors	2,550	Stock	4,000	
		Debtors	2,000	
		Cash at bank	1,000	
		Cash in hand	50	7,050
	20,550			20,550

L B Jay later found that the Balance Sheet was not correct due to errors and omissions subsequently located and now listed hereunder.

(i)   Stock had been over-valued by £300.

(ii) A motor vehicle had been completely destroyed in a road crash on 1st November, 1975, value (net) £800. (Note: ignore insurance.)

(iii) Included in creditors was a Bad Debt Provision of £450.

(iv) Depreciation on land and buildings of 10% on the net balances had been omitted.

You are required to:

(a)   Produce an amended Balance Sheet for Mr Jay as at 1st November, 1975, showing clearly how you calculated Mr Jay's revised capital.

(b)   Calculate Mr Jay's working capital from the revised Balance Sheet.

(RSA 1975)

29 K S King has a small business and does not keep proper accounts. At the end of the year 1972 he submits the following statement. This contains errors of several different sorts, purporting to show his profit. You are required to draw up a proper Trading and Profit and Loss Account.

STATEMENT OF TRADING

	£	£		£	£
Stock 1st January, 1972	1,215		Sales	21,300	
Less Stock 31st December, 1971	1,140	75	*Less* Purchases	10,300	11,000
Carriage on goods bought		125	Goods returned to suppliers		210
Carriage on goods sold		215	Discount allowed		465
Light and Heat		95			
Rent and Rates		525			
Office expenses		150			
Office salaries		1,600			
Wages		6,140			
Depreciation		210			
Sales return		650			
Drawings		950			
New office furniture		220			
Profit		720			
		11,675			11,675

Note: There is an outstanding electricity bill for the quarter ended 31st December, 1972 of £17. (Add this to Light and Heat Account.)

(RSA)

30 Angus Brown is a retail trader. From the following information prepare a Trading and Profit and Loss Account for the year ended 31st December, 1974 and a Balance Sheet on that date.

TRIAL BALANCE
31ST DECEMBER, 1974

	£	£
Capital 1st January, 1974		6,400
Land and Buildings	5,000	
Motor Vehicles (cost £1,200)	600	
Drawings	1,400	
Stock	910	
Bank overdraft		96
Sales		14,260
Purchases	11,100	
Motor Expenses	310	
Sundry Expenses	106	
Wages	1,560	
Debtors	820	
Creditors		1,210
Rates and Insurance	160	
	21,966	21,966

The following items should be taken into consideration:

(a) Stock at 31st December, 1974 £1,820.

(b) A provision for doubtful debts of 5% on the debtors at 31st December, 1974 is to be created.

(c) Depreciation is to be provided on motor vehicles at 20% on cost.

(d) Rates prepaid at 31st December, 1974 £12.

(e) Motor expenses bill for December £26 is owing at 31st December, 1974.

(f) Sundry expenses includes £15 for a private telephone bill of Angus Brown.

(g) A cheque for £250 was paid to a creditor on 31st December, 1974 but had not been entered in the books at the time of extracting the Trial Balance.

(RSA 1975)

31 From the following information set out B Dickson's Balance Sheet as at 31st May, 1975. Your Balance Sheet should clearly show the totals of the following:

Fixed assets, current assets, current liabilities.

	£	£
Capital 1st June, 1974		10,000
Motor Vans at cost	4,000	
Provision for depreciation		1,500
Fixtures and fittings at cost	1,500	
Provision for depreciation		1,250
Stock	4,000	
Debtors	950	
Balance in bank	1,200	
Cash in hand	70	
Trade creditors		450
Sundry unpaid expenses		140
Rates in advance	150	
Drawings (cash)	1,400	
Stock taken by B Dickson	700	
Net profit for year		630
	13,970	13,970

(RSA 1975)

32 From the following information relating to the purchase, depreciation and sale of machinery you are required

(a) to prepare:

    (i) the machinery asset account,

    (ii) the machinery aggregate depreciation account, and

    (iii) the machinery sales and disposals account,

for the year ended 31st December, 1970, and

(b) to show how the machinery would appear in the fixed assets section of the Balance Sheet as at that date.

1970		£
Jan. 1	Balance brought forward:	
	Machinery asset account	5,000
	Machinery aggregate depreciation account	2,000
	Purchased new machinery	6,000
Mar. 31	Machinery purchased on 1st January, 1968 at a cost of £2,500 was sold for	1,400
April 1	Purchased new machinery	3,800
June 30	An item of machinery purchased for £2,000 on 1st April, 1970 was sold for	2,100
Sept. 30	An item of machinery purchased on 1st April, 1970 for £1,000 was damaged beyond repair and sold as scrap	150
Dec. 31	Purchased new machinery	2,500

Depreciation is provided at the rate of 20% per annum on the written down value and is calculated on each completed calendar month for which the machinery is held.

(JMB 1971)

33 The bus service to Low Bottom Hamlet has been withdrawn, and Jones the grocer has started a minibus service to the local town charging 10p per return journey.

(a) From the following figures prepare an account showing the profit and loss on the undertaking for the first month of operation, 1st August to 31st August, 19·1.

	£
Tax and insurance per annum	288
Cost of minibus, to be written off over a period of five years	1,500
Fares collected	90
Petrol and Oil	30

10% of fares to be set aside for repairs and maintenance.

(b) Comment on the profitability of the undertaking.

(RSA 1972)

34 You are given the following information about the car running expenses for 19·1 of Smith, a trader:

19·1		£
Jan. 1	Insurance paid in advance	21
July 1	Insurance paid for the year to 30th June, 19·2	38
Dec. 31	Total payments during the year for spare parts, repairs and running expenses	329
Dec. 31	Spare parts purchased during the year not used	13
Dec. 31	Liability for repairs	22

The depreciation charge for 19·1 is calculated at £100.

One-quarter of the total costs for 19·1 are to be treated as Smith's private expenditure and three-quarters as a business expense.

Show the car running expenses account in Smith's books for 19·1 after the books had been closed off for the year.

(RSA II)

35 On 1st April, 1972 Smallpiece Manufacturing Company purchased machinery at a cost of £50,000. It was decided to write off 10% of the cost of the machinery each year including a full 10% in the year of purchase.

On 1st January, 1974 the Company purchased additional machinery for £12,000, including installation.

On 1st September, 1974 the Company sold a machine for £7,500 which had been installed on 1st April, 1972 at a cost of £10,000.

The Company closes its books on 31st March, in each year.

Show the Machinery Account for the period from 1st April, 1972 to 31st March, 1975.

(RSA 1975)

36 (a) The following balances were extracted from the accounts of F Fraser at 31st December, 1970.

Prepare Fraser's Trading and Profit and Loss Accounts for the year ended 31st December, 1970.

	Dr.	Cr.
	£	£
Purchases	16,720	
Sales		21,885
Sales returns	135	
Stock (at cost) 1st January, 1970	2,880	
Delivery of goods sold	242	
Rent and rates	1,425	
Bad debts	103	
Light and heat	142	
Insurance	45	
Discount received		204
Discount allowed	296	
Wages of shop assistant	728	
Bank charges and interest	41	

The following matters are to be bought into account:

(i) On 31st December, 1970 stock was valued, at cost, £2,740.

(ii) Rates £230 for the half year to 31st March, 1971 were paid and are included in the balance of rent and rates account.

(iii) Fraser's annual rent was £960. Rent for December 1970 had not been paid.

(iv) A provision for bad debts of £40 is to be created.

(b) (i) What is the amount of Fraser's turnover for the year 1970?

(ii) Calculate his rate of turnover of stock for the year.

(iii) During the year Fraser had purchased a delivery van for £960. To what extent (if any) do you think this would affect Fraser's profit for the year?

(University of London GCE O level 1971)

37 A coal merchant on 31st December, 19·1, had the following stocks of coal and coke in his yard:

Grade I coal 60 tons
Grade II coal 50 tons
Coke 15 tons

The prices at 31st December, 19·1, were as follows:

	Cost Price per ton £	Selling Price per ton £
Grade I coal	12·00	15·00
Grade II coal	10·00	11·00
Coke	8·00	7·00

(a) Prepare a statement showing the calculation of the stock valuation at 31st December, 19·1.

(b) Assuming his stock of coal and coke on 1st January, 19·1, was £600 write up the Stock Account for the year ended 31st December, 19·1.

38 Ashford Ltd., commenced business on 1st January, 1968, and its accounts were made up annually to 31st December. The following figures were extracted from the company's books:

	Sales £	Purchases £	Increase (+) or decrease (−) in stock during year £
1968	30,000	31,000	+9,000
1969	41,000	29,000	−3,000
1970	58,000	47,000	+4,000
1971	90,000	82,000	+9,000
1972	114,000	103,000	+11,000

	Selling Expenses £	Rent £	General Expenses £
1968	900	2,500	3,500
1969	1,100	2,500	4,000
1970	1,600	2,500	4,400
1971	2,900	5,000	6,500
1972	4,000	5,000	7,900

You are required to give:

(a) A statement showing the book value of the stock on 31st December each year from 1968 to 1972 inclusive.

(b) Trading and profit and loss accounts in column form for each of the five years to 31st December, 1972.

(c) A brief discussion of the implications of these figures and the inferences you would draw from them.

(RSA II 1973)

39 (a) When a business is divided into departments indirect costs and overhead expenses are usually proportionately allocated to each department. Suggest *four* ways in which this division may be carried out.

(b) What method of allocation would you use for *each* of the following expenses?

(i) National Insurance contributions.

(ii) Heating and Lighting.

(iii) Printing and Stationery.

(iv) Advertising.

(RSA II)

40 From the following information relating to the firm of Radio Services you are required to prepare Trading and Profit and Loss Accounts to show the gross and net profits of the Servicing Department and the Commercial Sales Department. The accounts should be prepared in column form. A Balance Sheet is *not* required.

A BROWN TRADING AS

RADIO SERVICES

TRIAL BALANCE AT 31ST DECEMBER, 19·1

	Dr. £	Cr. £
Capital		5,000
Stock (at 1st January, 19·1):		
TV and radio sets	1,500	
Servicing supplies	300	
Purchases:		
TV sets for re-sale	2,650	
Radios for re-sale	1,340	
Spare parts for servicing dept.	600	
Test meter for use in servicing dept.	350	
Sales of Radio and TV sets		5,620
Income from servicing		3,970
Debtors	880	
Creditors		150
Rent, Rates and Insurance	650	
Furniture and Fittings	1,300	
Servicing equipment (at 1st January, 19·1)	850	
Office expenses	380	
Bank balance	750	
Provision for bad debts		30
Carriage on goods sold	20	
Wages:		
Service engineer	1,200	
Sales staff	650	
Advertising	100	
Drawings	1,250	
	14,770	14,770

Notes:

(a) Servicing equipment is to be depreciated at 10% on written down value, a full year's charge being made in the year of acquisition.

(b) Furniture and Fittings are to be depreciated at 5% on written down value.

(c) Expenses, except where otherwise indicated, are to be allocated 3/5ths to the servicing department and 2/5ths to the commercial sales department.

(d) Stock at 31st December was:
TV and Radio sets for re-sale £1,200
Servicing supplies   £250

(*JMB 1971*)

41 Lynchester Traders sell goods of two main types (A and B) and the business is organised on a departmental basis. The firm's Trial Balance at 31st December, 19·1, was as follows:

	Dr. £	Cr. £
Stock at 1st January, 19·1 Dept.:		
A	4,210	
B	3,150	
Sales:		
A		34,250
B		24,900
Returns inwards:		
A	620	
B	240	
Purchases:		
A	17,290	
B	15,130	
Capital		25,000
Property	10,000	
Office salaries	4,160	
Selling expenses	4,260	
Warehouse expenses	3,490	
Carriage outwards	650	
Rates and Insurance	3,620	
Miscellaneous expenses	2,890	
Sundry debtors and creditors	10,100	4,510
Fixtures and Fittings	5,900	
Bank	2,950	
	88,660	88,660

The following matters are to be taken into account:

(a) Depreciate fixtures and fittings by 10% on written down value.

(b) Value of stock at 31st December, 19·1

Department A £3,820
B £4,240

(c) £150, included in sundry debtors, in respect of a credit sale by Department A is to be written off as a bad debt

(d) All expenses (including depreciation) should be apportioned on the basis of 3/5ths to Department A and 2/5ths to Department B.

You are required to prepare departmental Trading and Profit and Loss Accounts for the year ended 31st December, 19·1, and a Balance Sheet at that date.

(*JMB 1973*)

TOP LOCK BOAT HIRE
TRIAL BALANCE 31ST DECEMBER 1974

	£	£
Capital		16,000
Drawings—cash	1,435	
Cruisers	10,000	
Rowing boats	500	
Boat house and landing stage	7,000	
Stock of gas containers, 1st January, 1974	10	
Purchases		
Petrol and Oil	700	
Groceries	3,000	
Gas	90	
Sales		
Petrol and Oil		1,000
Groceries		4,000
Gas containers		110
Hiring fees received		
Cruisers		4,000
Rowing boats		950
Deposits on rowing boats not reclaimed		5
Repair and maintenance		
Cruisers	450	
Rowing boats	90	
Canal dues, insurance		
Cruisers	250	
Rowing boats	50	
Rates	100	
Repairs to property	350	
Lighting and heating	40	
Cash in hand and bank	2,000	
	26,065	26,065

Notes:

Rates include £20 paid in advance for 3 months to March 1975.

As far as possible all stocks are cleared at the end of each season.

A deposit of £1 is charged on all rowing boats hired out. Five people did not return the boat and forfeited the £1. Four boats had been recovered, but one completely lost is to be written off. The book value of this boat was £18 on 1st January, 1974. Cruisers are to be depreciated by 10%.

Groceries taken by proprietor for private use totalled £400. No entries have been made in books for this item.

(a) Prepare a revenue account to show the profit or loss on the undertaking for the year ended 31st December, 1974, and a Balance Sheet on that date.
The revenue account should show as far as possible, the profit or loss on each of the activities: groceries, petrol and oil, gas cylinders, cruisers, rowing boats.

(b) 'Although the profit or loss has been shown on each activity, this is not a true departmental business as no one part could exist without all the others.'

Comment very briefly on this statement.

(University of London GCE O level 1975)

43 (a) A duplicating agency which does not keep personal accounts for its suppliers, had a stock of stationery at 1st January, 1969, valued at £154, and at 31st December, 1969, £207. At 1st January, 1969, the agency owed £53 to its stationery suppliers and at 31st December, 1969, the amount owing was £27. During the year £1,168 had been paid to suppliers of stationery.

Write up the Stationery Account for the year, showing the amount to be transferred to Profit and Loss Account.

(b) You are employed as a bought ledger clerk by P Smith, a retail clothier. Invoices are checked on receipt and not entered in the ledger until passed.

At 1st August, 1972, there was no balance on the bought ledger account of G J Suppliers Ltd., settlement having been made on 31st July, 1972. An invoice dated 16th July for £160 had not been passed as correct until 3rd August.

The invoices received from G H Suppliers Ltd. in August were as follows: 5th August, £170; 8th August, £80; 19th August, £104; 26th August, £78; but of these the invoice for £104 had not been approved by the end of the month. During August goods valued at £36 had been returned and a credit note dated 28th August for this amount was received. On 30th August a cheque was paid of £390 after allowing for cash discount of 2½%.

You are required to write up the account of G J Suppliers Ltd. in the bought ledger of P Smith for the month of August.

(RSA I 1973)

44 Each of the following transactions of a sole trader affects either the Balance Sheet only, or the Trading and Profit and Loss Account only, or in some cases both.

(i) The trader settles an account for £100, due to a creditor, by sending the creditor a cheque for £97·50, the balance being allowed as discount.

(ii) The trader withdraws £60 from his business account at the bank for his personal expenses.

(iii) A debtor's account for £25, being irrecoverable, is written off as a bad debt.

(iv) A second-hand motor van, costing £425 and standing in the books at that figure, is sold on credit for exactly that sum.

(v) A debtor, who owes £50, settles his debts in full.

(vi) At the close of the trading year an entry is passed for bank charges, £9·37½.

(vii) The trader moves into new premises, which he rents. In consequence, his old premises, which he owned freehold and which stand in the books at £6,500, are sold for £7,000.

(viii) Machinery, the cost of which was £2,000, had been depreciated by £600. It is to be written down by a further £200 at the close of this trading year.

You are required to write down the words Balance Sheet or Profit and Loss Account, as may be appropriate, against each of the items (i) to (viii). If in your judgement the correct answer should be both, write down the word 'both'.

(RSA)

45 On the evening of 31st December, 1970, a fire destroyed a large part of the stock in trade of Hart, a trader.

The following information is available from the books:

	£
Debtors for sales, 31st December, 1969	9,485
Creditors for purchases, 31st December, 1969	7,162
Debtors for sales, 31st December, 1970	10,241
Creditors for purchases, 31st December, 1970	8,645
Payments to suppliers in 1970	92,461
Receipts from customers in 1970	121,848
Stock in trade, 31st December, 1969	13,249
Stock in trade, 1st January, 1971 (on the morning after the fire)	3,261

Hart sells all his goods at a price which gives him a fixed gross profit rate of 25% on sales.

You are required to give a calculation of the value of Hart's stock that was destroyed on 31st December, 1970.

(Institute of Bankers 1971)

46 G E Jones, a café proprietor had not kept any books and asks you to prepare a statement of his profit or loss for the year ended 30th June, 1972. He gives you the following information:

	July 1st, 1971 £	June 30th, 1972 £
Cash in hand and at Bank	350	400
Stock	200	210
Furniture	400	350
Crockery, cutlery, glass, etc.	250	280
Rates unpaid		30

	£
Cash withdrawn by Jones during the year	1,300
Meals taken by his family	500
Car expenses paid from business account	400

Mr Jones admits that one half of the car expenses are for private purposes.

Prepare the statement of profit and loss for the year ended 30th June, 1972, and a Balance Sheet on that date.

(RSA I 1972)

47 William Granford is considering setting up business on his own account. He is employed at present by a large company at an annual salary of £5,000 a year and he can expect to remain in this employment at the same salary for many years.

Granford owns securities worth £40,000 comprising investments in local authority mortgages at 10 per cent. He could withdraw the full amount immediately without suffering any penalty.

He is considering the following alternatives:

(i) He could invest £20,000 in a business which he would manage on a full time basis: the annual costs and revenues are expected to be:

	£
Sales	130,000
Cost of goods sold	95,000
General expenses (including depreciation)	29,000

(ii) He could invest £40,000 in a business which would not require his attention; the annual costs and revenues are expected to be:

	£
Sales	260,000
Costs of goods sold	188,000
General expenses (including depreciation and manager's salary)	67,000

Required:

(a) The preparation of statements comparing the results of the different possibilities open to Granford and the advice you would give him as to the course of action he should follow on the assumption that price levels will be stable.

(b) How would your advice be affected on the basis of the following changed expectations:

(i)   Granford's salary to be increased to £6,000 per annum;

(ii) the rate of interest on investments to go up to 14 per cent;

Note: The costs and revenues from the business which Granford is considering remain unchanged.

Ignore taxation.

(RSA 1975)

8 On 1st January, 1966, Bashford Ltd. purchased three type A machines for £1,600 each. Depreciation at the rate of 10% per annum of cost is credited each year to a 'Provision for depreciation account' and debited to profit and loss account. The company's accounting year ends on 31st December.

The directors decided, as the result of changes in demand for the company's product, to sell one type A machine on 30th June, 1967. The price realised was £800. On 1st July, 1967, one type B machine, costing £2,000, was purchased to develop a new product. On 1st January, 1968, both remaining type A machines were sold for a total price of £1,000 and two more type B machines were purchased for £2,000 each.

You are required:

(i)   to set out the machinery account and the provision for depreciation account for the three years 1966, 1967 and 1968; and

(ii) to show the entry for machinery in the balance sheet dated 31st December, 1968.

(Institute of Bankers 1970)

9 Wholesalers Ltd. keeps three sales ledgers, one for each of its areas. Transactions for the month of May 1975 are shown below:

		Birmingham £	Leeds £	London £
1975				
May	1 Balance: Dr.	700	400	500
	Cr.	12		
	31 Sales	18,000	16,500	21,000
	Returns	70	43	110
	Payments received	17,900	16,400	20,000
	Discounts allowed	210	170	200
	Balance Cr.			10

On 31st May, 1975 the following changes were made:

(i)   An account with a debit balance of £150 was moved from Leeds to London.

(ii) An account with a debit balance of £25 was transferred from the London sales ledger to the purchase ledger.

(iii) An account in the purchase ledger showing a credit balance of £30 was offset against the same person's account in the Birmingham sales ledger.

From the information given set out the sales ledger control account for each area ledger.

(University of London GCE O level 1975)

50

J R BROWN

TRADING ACCOUNT

FOR THE YEAR ENDED 31ST DECEMBER, 1975

	£		£
Stock 1st January, 1975	2,000	Sales	25,000
Purchases	14,000		
	16,000		
Stock 31st December, 1975	2,500		
	13,500		
Gross Profit	11,500		
	25,000		25,000

PROFIT AND LOSS ACCOUNT

FOR THE YEAR ENDED 31ST DECEMBER, 1975

Administration expenses	2,000	Gross profit	11,500
Selling expenses	3,500		
Net profit	6,000		
	11,500		11,500

On 1st January, 1976, J R Brown expresses his dissatisfaction with the account shown above, and considers mounting an advertising campaign which he anticipates will increase his profit.

He makes the following estimates:

(i) The campaign will cost £1,500 and last for twelve months.

(ii) Sales will increase by 50%.

(iii) Administration expenses will not change.

(iv) Selling expenses, other than advertising will increase to £4,000.

(v) Stock will be kept at the level of £2,500

(vi) There will be no changes in price per unit of either purchases or sales.

(a) Prepare estimated Trading Profit and Loss Accounts for the next twelve months. The capital employed in the business is £20,000.

(b) Calculate the following for the year ended 31st December, 1975, and the estimated figure for the year ended 31st December, 1976:
Percentage of net profit to capital employed, net profit to turnover, gross profit to turnover, total expenses to turnover.

(c) Comment briefly on J R Brown's policy.

(University of London GCE O level 1976)

51 (a) What do you understand by the term 'Credit Limit'?

(b) J Twister is a customer of Luckman & Co. Ltd., with a credit limit on his account of £200. Luckman & Co. Ltd. allow their customers 4% for payment within one month.

1st May, 1975 J Twister owed £170, for goods purchased on 24th April, 1975.

Luckman & Co. Ltd. received the following orders from Twister during the month of May 1975:

			£
1975			
May 3	for goods to the value of		150
10	,, ,, ,, ,, ,, ,,		200
27	,, ,, ,, ,, ,, ,,		150

The following transactions also took place:

May	15	Goods returned to value of	20
	15	Cash received	144
	20	,, ,,	144
	26	,, ,,	192

Set out J Twister's account in Luckman's ledger. The account should be set out showing the running balance, and entries dated to show clearly when each order should be delivered.

(c) Write a short explanation of the transactions which have taken place.

(University of London GCE O level 1975)

The following figures relating to the year 19·1 were extracted from the books of a trader:

	£
Debit balances on Sales Ledger Control Account 1st January, 19·1	5,721
Sales per sales journal	61,272
Discounts allowed per cash book	1,497
Cash and cheques received from customers on account of credit sales	58,921

During 19·1 debit balances on the sales ledger amounting to £391 were set off against credit balances of that amount in the Bought Ledger. A customer's cheque amounting to £103, dishonoured by the bank, was re-presented and paid; this cheque has been included twice in the total of receipts shown above. The relevant entries for these matters in the customers' personal accounts have been made.
The balance of £192 on one sales ledger account has been written off as bad. The bookkeeper was unable to reconcile the balance on the sales ledger control account with the list of balances he extracted from the sales ledger and on rechecking he discovered the following errors:

(a) The sales journal had been under cast by £300.

(b) A debit balance of £149 on the personal account of a customer had been omitted from the list of balances.

(c) A sales invoice for £221 entered in the sales journal had not been posted to the customer's personal account.

(d) Discounts allowed, amounting to £22, had been credited to the personal account of the customer but had not been entered elsewhere.

(e) A sales invoice for £74 had been entered twice in the sales journal and posted twice to the personal account of the customer.

You should assume that all these matters have been corrected and are now required to prepare a sales ledger control account for 19·1.

(RSA II)

Enterprise Ltd., show the following totals of transactions with Debtors and Creditors in the year to 30th September, 1976, detailed postings for which have been made to the personal accounts in each separate ledger.

You are required to write up the Sales Ledger Control Account and Purchases Ledger Control Account for the year as they would appear in the General Ledger.

Note: Only these two accounts are required.

Balances at 1st October, 1975:

	£
On Sales Ledger (*Less* Credit Balances £493)	101,000
On Purchases Ledger	71,250
On Bills Payable Register	45,000
On Bills Receivable Register	115,325

Transactions during the year to 30th September, 1976:

Purchases per Day Book	412,500
Sales per Day Book	479,000
Returns Outwards	2,710
Returns Inwards	4,200
Bills accepted by the Company for goods purchased	214,080
Bills accepted by Debtors for goods sold to them	375,000
Bills Receivable Dishonoured	750
Bad Debts written off	590
Debit Balances in Sales Ledger transferred to Purchases Ledger	250

Extract from Cash Receipts and Payments:

RECEIPTS	£	PAYMENTS	£
Debtors on account of Credit Sales	100,000	Creditors	130,645
Discounts allowed £2,000		Discounts received £3,765	
Cash Sales	5,235	Cash Purchases	2,800
Bills discounted less Discount £1,200	325,225	Bills paid at maturity	212,500
Bills collected at maturity	124,560		
Bad debts written off in September 1975 recovered in January 1976 not included in the amount of £100,000 mentioned above	1,115		

54 T Brown, a retailer, had not kept proper books of account for the year ended 31st December, 19·1. He was, however, able to provide the following information:

SUMMARY OF THE BANK CASH BOOK FOR 19·1

	£		£
Trading receipts banked	23,790	Balance at 1st January, 19·1	700
		Trade creditors	20,100
		Rent and Rates	320
		Lighting and Heating	200
		General expenses	630
		Drawings	900
		Balance at 31st December, 19·1	940
	23,790		23,790

	1st Jan., 1971	31st Dec., 1971
Balances at:	£	£
Stock	3,000	4,200
Trade debtors	1,500	1,700
General expenses accrued due, not yet paid	120	90
Rates paid in advance	30	40
Motor vehicles	2,900	2,400
Trade creditors	1,200	1,350

From the above information you are required to prepare a Trading and Profit and Loss Account for the year ended 31st December, 1971, and a Balance Sheet at that date.

(*JMB*)

55 The following information is extracted from the books of Denston at 31st December, 1969.

TOTAL BANK ACCOUNT FOR 1969

	£		£
Opening balance	821	Cash paid to suppliers	18,624
Cash received from credit customers	24,264	Salaries	2,249
Closing balance	1,030	Rent and Rates	824
		Lighting and Heating	168
		General expenses	1,781
		Drawings	2,469
	26,115		26,115

	31st Dec., 1968	31st Dec., 1969
	£	£
Stock in trade	2,141	2,648
Debtors	3,219	3,388
Creditors for:		
Purchases	1,842	1,891
Lighting and Heating	31	42
Rent and Rates paid in advance	100	120
Fixed assets	2,200	see note

You are required to give:

Denston's trading and profit and loss account for 1969 and his balance sheet at 31st December, 1969.

Note: Depreciation at the rate of 10% per annum on the opening balance is to be charged on fixed assets.

(Institute of Bankers 1970)

56 Karisma is in business on his own account. He kept a full set of books. His trading year ended on 30th June. On 30th June, 1976, his premises were badly damaged by a fire and although most of his business records were saved his Bank Cash Book and Sales Ledger were destroyed together with all his Bank Paying-in Books.

The following balances were extracted from the Private Ledger at 30th June, 1976:

	£	£
Capital at 1st July, 1975		8,656
Fittings and Equipment at 1st July, 1975	3,142	
Stock at 1st July, 1975	4,418	
Sales for year to 30th June, 1976 per Sales Book		18,230
Purchases for year to 30th June, 1976	11,368	
Rents and Rates paid	592	
Sales Ledger Control A/c (Debtors) at 1st July, 1975	1,544	
Bought Ledger Control A/c (Creditors) at 1st July, 1975		1,618
General Expenses unpaid at 1st July, 1975		248
Postage, Packing and Stationery paid	298	
Drawings for year	4,030	
Salaries and Commission paid	1,444	
General Expenses paid	586	
Commission owing at 30th June, 1976		280
Light and Heat paid	136	
Light and Heat owing at 30th June, 1976		34

From the file containing the Bank Reconciliation Statements it was ascertained that the Balance at Bank on 1st July, 1975 was £1,418. Karisma keeps a card index of all his customers and obtains from them details of sums owing by them. This amounted to £1,982 at 30th June, 1976, so far as could be ascertained. Suppliers were owed £1,432 for goods at this date, and there was £164 owing for general expenses. No discounts were allowed or received and there were no bad debts.

Stock at cost on 30th June, 1976 was valued at £3,794.

You are required to reconstruct the Cash Book, and then to prepare a Trading and Profit and Loss Account for the year ended 30th June, 1976, and a Balance Sheet at that date.

57 The following is a summary of the cash book of Benworth Social Club for the year to 31st December, 19·2:

CASH BOOK

	£	£		£
Balance at bank, 1st January 19·2		360	Restaurant and bar supplies	6,000
Members' subscriptions:			Wages	2,120
for 19·2	2,660		Printing, Stationery and Postages	140
for 19·3	100		General Expenses	1,830
		2,760	Balance at bank, 31st December, 19·2	1,030
Restaurant and bar takings		8,000		
		11,120		11,120

Additional information is obtained as follows:

	31st Dec., 19·1 £	31st Dec., 19·2 £
Freehold Premises	5,000	5,000
Furniture	3,620	3,620
Stock of Restaurant and bar supplies	618	548
Creditors for Restaurant and bar supplies	450	490

You are required to prepare:

(a) A Trading Account for the Restaurant and Bar for 19·2.

(b) An Income and Expenditure Account for the year 19·2.

(c) A Balance Sheet on 31st December, 19·2.

Note: Ignore depreciation.

(*RSA II*)

58 A summary of the cash book of the Explorers Club for the year 1971 is given below:

CASH BOOK

	£	£		£
Balance at bank and cash in hand, 1st January, 1971		249	Furniture and Equipment	2,000
Subscriptions:			Rent and Rates	940
for 1970	22		Insurance	52
for 1971	5,291		Wages	3,043
for 1972	102		Printing and Stationery	520
		5,415	General expenses	1,232
Bar and dining room sales		16,292	Magazines	75
Hire of rooms		201	Payments for supplies for bar and dining room	10,481
Sale of old magazines		25	Balance at bank and cash in hand, 31st December, 1971	3,839
		22,182		22,182

You are given the following additional information:

(a)

	31st Dec., 1970 £	31st Dec., 1971 £
Bar and dining room stocks	1,420	1,629
Creditors for supplies of refreshments	891	942
Rent due	40	50
Wages outstanding	82	
Rates paid in advance	120	

(b) In 1970 subscriptions amounting to £85 were received for 1971.

(c) The club does not take credit in the accounts for any subscriptions due but not received at the end of the year.

(d) A provision of £600 is to be made for depreciation of Furniture and Equipment. (Furniture and Equipment appeared at £10,000 in the Balance Sheet at 31st December, 1970.)

(e) On 31st December, 1971, the treasurer received £20 representing subscriptions for 1971 and he paid £2 for stationery. No entries have been made in the cash book given above to record these matters.

You are required to prepare a Bar and Dining-room Trading Account and an Income and Expenditure Account for the year 1971, and a Balance Sheet as at 31st December, 1971.

(RSA II 1972)

59 The secretary of the Marathon Sports Club has prepared the following statement:

BALANCE SHEET
FOR THE YEAR ENDED 30TH APRIL, 1976

	£		£
Paid for Bar Supplies	11,604	Cash at Bank 1st May	2,660
Payments for		Subscription for year ended	
Wages	3,548	30th April, 1975	656
Secretary's Expenses	1,576	30th April, 1976	6,700
Extension of Premises	2,280	30th April, 1977	196
New Billiard table, etc.	1,520	Bar Sales	16,428
Light and heat	424	Receipts from	
Stationery and postage	868	Entertainments	340
Telephone	252	Telephone	116
General Expenses	3,364	Raffles	504
Balance at Bank per Bank statement	1,484		
Loss for Year	680		
	27,600		27,600

Some members were not satisfied with the above statement and asked a professional accountant to audit the books and to prepare proper accounts.

He obtained the following information in addition to the figures set out above.

(1) The Club owned the premises which had cost £9,600 when purchased some years ago.

(2) At 1st May, 1975 creditors for bar supplies were owed £232; the telephone account for £116 owing at 30th April, 1975 had not been paid; the Club owned Billiard Tables and other equipment valued at £5,680 and there were Bar stocks £1,256 (cost).

(3) During the month of April 1975, £76 had been received from members in respect of subscriptions for the year commencing 1st May, 1975.

(4) Cheques drawn and entered in the Cash Book in the last week of April 1976 none of which was presented until after 1st May, 1976 amounted to £256. £936 had been paid into bank on 30th April, 1976 and entered in the Club Cash Book but this was not credited in the books of the bank until the following day.

(5) At 30th April, 1976 the Bar stocks amounted to £1,048: creditors were owed £276 for bar supplies and £780 was still owing to the builder in respect of the extension to the premises. £68 was owed for electric light.

You are required to prepare:

(a) a Bar Trading Account for year ended 30th April, 1976;

(b) an Income and Expenditure Account (including profit or loss on the Bar) for year ended 30th April, 1976;

(c) a Balance Sheet as at 30th April, 1976.

Notes:

(i) No credit is to be taken in the annual accounts for subscriptions due but not received.

(ii) Ignore depreciation of fixed assets.

(iii) The item of wages is to be charged to Income and Expenditure Account.

60 The Deep Tunnel Mineral Mine is worked by G Miner in business on his own. The trial balance set out below was extracted from his books on 31st December, 1975.

	£	£
Capital		26,000
Drawings	3,000	
Machinery and plant	7,000	
Buildings	3,000	
Land	9,000	
Motor lorries	4,000	
Stock of mineral for sale, 1st January, 1975	600	
Debtors	1,750	
Cash in hand and at bank	1,000	
Insurance	1,000	
Sundry mining expenses	150	
Sales		20,000
Miners' wages	7,000	
Fuel and power for mine	1,500	
Office salaries	1,500	
Office expenses	1,000	
Lorry drivers' wages	3,000	
Lorry expenses	1,500	
	46,000	46,000

The following information is to be taken into consideration:

(a) Stocks awaiting sale were valued at £1,000,

(b) Depreciate machinery and plant by 10%,

(c) Depreciate motor lorries by 20%,

(d) Miners' wages unpaid £150,

(e) Drivers' wages unpaid £100,

(f) Fuel account unpaid £20 (lorry expenses),

(g) The extraction of mineral during the year has reduced the value of the land by £500,

(h) Insurance paid in advance £150,

(i) Insurance to be divided 4/5 to mine and 1/5 office.

Prepare Production, Trading, and Profit and Loss Accounts for the year ended 31st December, 1975, and a Balance Sheet on that date.

(University of London GCE O level 1976)

61 From the following details extracted from S Turner's books prepare:

(i) a Manufacturing Account;

(ii) a Trading Account;

(iii) a Profit and Loss Account;

for the year ended 31st December, 1972.

	£	£
Stocks (1st January, 1972)		
raw materials	1,841	
finished goods	5,697	
		7,538
Purchases of raw materials		13,843
Sales of finished goods		59,756
Manufacturing expenses		914
Factory power, light and heat		893
Office power, light and heat		96
Rates (4/5 factory, 1/5 offices)		555
Insurance (4/5 factory, 1/5 offices)		70
Carriage on raw materials		97
Carriage on sales		289
Wages		
Factory		14,748
Office		1,980
Salesmen		2,435
Salaries		
Factory		4,800
Administration		2,200
Commission to salesmen		4,714
Advertising		2,500
Depreciation		
Machinery		3,150
Furniture and fittings		86
Stocks (31st December, 1972)		
Raw materials		1,698
Finished goods		5,186

From your accounts state:

(a) the cost of raw materials used;

(b) the cost of goods sold;

(c) the total of selling expenses.

(University of London GCE O level 1973)

62 You are required to prepare a Manufacturing Account, Trading Account and a Profit and Loss Account for the year 1971 for Painter Ltd. from the figures given below. Indicate in the accounts the significance of the various sub-totals and balances carried down.

	£
Stocks on 1st January, 1971	
Raw materials at cost	6,000
Work in progress at factory cost	3,290
Finished goods at factory cost	7,280
Purchases of raw materials	42,940
Purchases of finished goods for resale—all sold in 1971	1,240
Manufacturing wages	60,984
Factory expenses	17,891
Office and administration expenses	8,922
Depreciation of plant and machinery	7,000
Factory power	4,982
Travellers' salaries and commissions	6,921
Delivery expenses	4,228
Advertising	2,989
Rates and insurance	800
Light and heat	400
Sales	172,498
Stocks at 31st December, 1971	
Raw materials at cost	8,921
Work in progress at factory cost	4,557
Finished goods at factory cost	9,480

Note: Three-quarters of (i) rates and insurance and (ii) light and heat are to be allocated to factory and one-quarter to office.

(*RSA II 1972*)

63 From the following information prepare Manufacturing, Trading and Profit and Loss Accounts for the year ended 31st December, 1970. A balance sheet is not required:

MANUFOAM LTD.

	£
Stock at 1st January, 1970:	
Raw Materials	54,000
Work in progress	20,000
Finished goods	85,500
Purchases of raw materials	356,000
Manufacturing expenses:	
Direct	106,000
Overheads	42,500
Sales	680,000
Profit and Loss Account Credit balance at 1st January, 1970	60,000
Factory premises (Cost)	450,000
Administration expenses	25,200
Warehouse expenses	5,000
General reserve	40,000
Debtors	52,500
Creditors	32,600
Bank overdraft	45,100
Plant and Machinery at cost	395,000
Aggregate depreciation:	
Factory Premises	102,000
Plant and Machinery	132,000
Share Capital (authorised)	750,000
Share Capital (issued)	500,000

(a) Stock at 31st December, 1970:
Raw materials £79,600
Work in progress £15,500
Finished goods £96,200

(b) Depreciation to be provided:
Factory premises—5% on cost
Plant and Machinery—10% on cost

(*JMB 1971*)

64 Engineering Products Ltd., manufacture a standard accessory for supply to the motor industry. The following figures were extracted from the books of the company on 31st December, 1972:

	£
Purchases of raw material	20,000
Manufacturing wages	10,000
Salaries of administrative staff	4,750
Factory expenses	13,850
Depreciation of machinery	5,000
Stocks at 1st January, 1972:	
Raw materials	2,800
Finished goods (320 units)	6,400

(a) 1/5th of the salaries of administrative staff related to factory supervisors and balances to sales staff.

(b) All the goods in stock at 1st January, 1972, were sold at their valuation plus 60% for overheads.

2,000 units were produced during the year and of these 1,900 were sold at factory cost plus 75% for overheads. (The overheads are to cover administrative costs, selling expenses and profit.)

(c) Stocks at 31st December, 1972, were:
Raw materials £4,600
Finished goods 100 units

(d) Selling Expenses were £10,400 and General Expenses were £8,500 (both excluding salaries in (a) above).

You are required to prepare Manufacturing, Trading and Profit and Loss Accounts for the year ended 31st December, 1972.

(JMB 1973)

65 The summarised Manufacturing and Profit and Loss Account of Pentlow Ltd., for 1969 was as follows:

	£
Raw materials used	10,000
Wages	8,000
Prime cost	18,000
Factory accommodation	5,000
Depreciation	3,000
Manufacturing cost	26,000
Administration expenses	9,000
	35,000
Net profit	5,000
Sales (40,000 units at £1 each)	40,000

The sales department estimates that turnover could be doubled in 1970 if the selling price were reduced by 10%.

The management are considering alternative production plans:

(a) To work a second shift for which the wages cost would be time-and-a-half the day rate. Administration costs would increase by £2,000 per annum, but factory accommodation cost and the depreciation charge would be unchanged.

(b) To rent extra space, which would increase the cost for factory accommodation to £10,000 per annum, and to double plant capacity, which would increase the depreciation charge to £6,000 per annum. Administration costs would be increased by £4,000 per annum. Wages rates would be the same as for 1969.

In both alternatives the cost of raw materials and labour time for production per unit of finished goods would remain unchanged.

You are required to give:

(a) Summarised Manufacturing and Profit and Loss Accounts for 1970:

    (i) Based on the estimates given above to meet the cost of the doubled sales demand; and

    (ii) As they would appear if only a 50% increase in production was needed to meet the sales demand for the product.

    Assume for part (ii) that administration expenses would increase by half the amount given above: any other assumptions must be consistent with the data given.

(b) Brief comments on the results disclosed by your calculations.

The summary accounts should be presented in the form given in the questions and separate statements for alternatives (a) and (b) are required.

(Institute of Bankers 1970)

66 From the following information relating to Tape Supplies Limited prepare and close the following accounts: Total Debtors, Total Creditors, Bills Receivable, Bills Payable and Bank:

BALANCES AT 1ST JUNE, 1972

	Dr. £	Cr. £
Total Debtors Account	10,960	
Total Creditors Account		14,840
Bills Receivable Account	6,290	
Bills Payable Account		6,320
Bank Account	1,400	

1972
June 2 A Smith Limited accepted Bill of Exchange for £6,250
    3 Bill of Exchange for £650 drawn by F Townley fell due and was discharged
    3 Discounted a Bill of £5,150 (bank charges were £26)
    6 Bill for £1,290 due to be met by Robinson was dishonoured
    8 Accepted a Bill drawn by L Jackson, a creditor, for £2,650 in respect of this amount owed to him
    9 Endorsed Bill Receivable for £500 and transferred it to M Motors Ltd., in payment of part of debt due to them
   16 Informed by bank that a Bill for £255 discounted on 8th April has been dishonoured
   21 M Robinson accepted a new Bill for £1,320 (ie. the amount due on 6th June plus interest of £30)
   29 Accepted a Bill for £2,400 drawn by R Haigh

(JMB 1972)

67 (a) Describe the use of Control Accounts in a system of self-balancing ledgers.

   (b) From the following information prepare a Sales Ledger Control Account on 31st March, 1971:

1971		£
Mar. 1	Total of the debit balances on debtors' accounts	21,000
Mar. 31	Sales for the month	58,840
	Cash received from debtors	46,810
	Discount allowed	2,400
	Bills of Exchange accepted	3,800
	Bills of Exchange dishonoured	412
	Goods returned by customers	3,000

(JMB 1972)

68 Smith Bros. consigned 150 cases of goods valued at £16 each to their agent, Giovanni Morrelli, of Milan, on 15th February, 1971. Smith Bros. paid freight charges of £140 and insurance premiums of £50. The cases were received by Morrelli on 27th February and up to 31st March he sold 120 cases at £28 per case.

Morrelli is entitled to a commission of 5% on gross proceeds and on 2nd April he submits an Account Sales to Smith Bros. which shows landing charges of £290 and selling expenses of £68.

On 12th April Smith Bros. drew a bill of exchange on Morrelli for the net amount due and the bill was accepted.

No further transactions took place before 30th April on which date Smith Bros. closed their accounts.

You are required to record the above transactions in the ledger of the consignor and to balance the accounts at 30th April.

(JMB 1972)

69 The following is the balance sheet of Oldster and Youngster who are in partnership as retail traders, sharing profits and losses in the ratio of 2:1:

BALANCE SHEET
AS AT 31ST DECEMBER, 1970

	£	£		£
Capital:			Furniture and Fittings	2,900
Oldster	8,300		Stock	7,200
Youngster	2,400		Debtors	1,200
		10,700	Cash in hand and at bank	500
Creditors		1,100		
		11,800		11,800

During January, 1971, they:

Wrote down the Furniture and Fittings by £200;

Received payment of £250 from the debtors;

Paid the creditors £150;

Made cash sales of one-sixth of the stock for £1,700.

You are required to:

(a) Re-draft the Balance Sheet as at 31st January, 1971, and state, as at that date, the amount of:

  (i) The capital owned by the partnership.

  (ii) The total capital employed in the business.

  (iii) The working capital.

(RSA I 1971)

70 Laxton and Bexley were in partnership sharing profits equally. The following information was extracted from their books at 31st December, 1971:

TOTAL BANK ACCOUNT FOR 1971

	£		£
Opening balance	768	Cash paid to suppliers	24,171
Cash received from credit customers	39,847	Salaries	6,319
		Insurances	129
		Rent and Rates	980
		General expenses	1,197
		Lighting and Heating	218
		Drawings:	
		Laxton	1,762
		Bexley	1,696
		Closing balance	4,143
	40,615		40,615

	31st Dec., 1970	31st Dec., 1971
	£	£
Stock	2,529	2,876
Debtors	3,171	3,349
Creditors for:		
Purchases	1,622	2,048
Rates	44	56
Insurance paid in advance	28	24

Delivery vans which cost £3,500 on 1st January, 1970, are still in use and are to be written down by an annual depreciation charge of 20% on cost.

Laxton and Bexley entered into partnership on 1st January, 1970, and each partner contributed £3,250 as his capital. The net profit for 1970 was £3,808 and the partners drawings during 1970 were: Laxton, £1,382 and Bexley, £1,296.

Required:

Laxton and Bexley's trading and profit and loss account for 1971 and balance sheet as at 31st December, 1971.

(*RSA II 1972*)

71 The following information has been taken from the incomplete records of Marsh and Jackson who are in partnership:

RECEIPTS DURING YEAR	£
Cash sales	3,280
Debtors for credit sales	31,640

PAYMENTS DURING YEAR	
Creditors for credit purchases	25,750
Salaries and Wages	3,250
Rates	120
Rent	300
Delivery expenses	620
Miscellaneous administrative expenses	2,563
Heating and Lighting	1,290
Drawings:	
Marsh	2,100
Jackson	1,950

BALANCES	1st Jan., 1970	31st Dec., 1970
	£	£
Trade debtors	4,270	5,180
Trade creditors	8,360	7,210
Bank	120(Dr.)	
Stock	5,840	7,390
Fixtures and Fittings	2,070	
Motor vehicles	400	
Capital		
Marsh	2,000	
Jackson	2,000	
Current account		
Marsh	240(Cr.)	
Jackson	100(Cr.)	

The following should be noted:

(a) Depreciation is to be provided by the reducing balance method at 10% on fixtures and fittings and 20% on the motor vehicle.

(b) Rates amounting to £80 were due but unpaid for the half-year ending 31st March, 1971.

(c) £100 had been paid in advance in respect of rent for the half-year ending 30th June, 1971.

You are required to prepare Trading, Profit and Loss and Appropriation Accounts for the year ended 31st December, 1970, and a Balance Sheet at that date.

(JMB 1971)

72 Boxted and Preston were in partnership sharing profits equally. The following information was extracted from their books at 31st December, 1970:

TOTAL BANK ACCOUNT FOR 1970

	£		£
Opening balance	942	Cash paid to suppliers	26,214
Cash received from credit customers	41,629	Rent and Rates	1,020
		Lighting and Heating	241
		Salaries	6,864
		Insurances	148
		General expenses	1,281
		Drawings:	
		Boxted	1,874
		Preston	1,728
		Closing balance	3,201
	42,571		42,571

	31st Dec., 1969	31st Dec., 1970
	£	£
Stock	2,714	3,029
Debtors	3,328	3,594
Creditors for:		
Purchases	1,712	2,326
Rates	55	64
Insurances paid in advance	31	38

Motor vans which cost £3,000 on 1st January, 1969, are still in use and are to be written down by an annual depreciation of 25% on cost.

Boxted and Preston entered into partnership on 1st January, 1969, and each partner contributed £3,500 as his capital. The net profit for 1969 was £3,244 and the partners' drawings during 1969 were: Boxted, £1,412 and Preston, £1,334.

You are required to give:

Boxted and Preston's trading and profit and loss account for 1970 and balance sheet as at 31st December, 1970.

(Institute of Bankers 1971)

73 Sawyer and Finn are partners sharing profits and losses in the ratio 2/3 and 1/3 respectively. The following is their Balance Sheet as at 31st December, 1972:

	£	£		£	£
Capital:			Premises	10,000	
Sawyer	6,000		Fixtures and Fittings	1,500	
Finn	3,000		Motor Van	500	
		9,000			12,000
Creditors	2,500		Stock	1,700	
			Debtors	1,500	
Bank Overdraft	4,000		Cash in hand	300	
		6,500			3,500
		15,500			15,500

On 1st January, 1973, Thom was admitted to the partnership and paid into the Bank £5,000 as capital. It was agreed that future profits and losses should be shared in the ratio: Sawyer $\frac{1}{4}$; Finn $\frac{1}{4}$; and Thom $\frac{1}{2}$.

It was also agreed that, prior to the admission of Thom, the following adjustments be made in the accounts of Sawyer and Finn:

(i) Premises to be revalued at £14,000.

(ii) £200 to be written off the stock figure.

(iii) Goodwill of £3,000 be created.

(iv) Bad debts of £100 to be written off.

(v) A provision for bad debts equal to 5% of the debtors be made.

You are required to prepare:

(a) Journal entries (including Bank) to record:
  (i) The adjustments in the books of Sawyer and Finn.
  (ii) The receipt of Thom's capital.

(b) The Balance Sheet of the new partnership at 1st January, 1973.

(JMB 1973)

74 X and Y are partners in a business sharing profits and losses in the proportions of 4 and 3. Their Balance Sheet at 31st December, 1965, was:

Capital Accounts	£	Fixed Assets	£
X	16,000	Plant and Machinery	9,200
Y	13,000	Furniture and Fittings	560
Current Liabilities		Motor Vans	1,540
Creditors	7,500	Current Assets	
Bills payable	2,400	Stock	7,580
		Debtors	16,200
		Cash	3,820
	38,900		38,900

They agree to take into partnership, Z, who is in a similar line of business. His Balance Sheet at 31st December, 1965, contained the following details:

Plant and Machinery £4,300; Furniture and Fittings £240; Motor Vans £720; Debtors £5,600; Stock £2,460 and Creditors £3,170.

It is agreed that Z should introduce sufficient cash to make up his capital to £12,000, after reducing the value of his stock by 10% and making a provision for bad debts of 5% of the debtors.

X and Y's goodwill is to be valued at £2,800 and their plant and machinery and motor vans are revalued at £9,500 and £1,940 respectively at which amounts the new firm is to take them over. It is agreed also that profits in the new firm shall be shared equally and that X shall draw out a sum of money which will leave his capital the same as Y's.

Show the necessary journal entries, including those relating to cash, in the books of X and Y and the Balance Sheet of X, Y and Z.

75

LIGHT AND DARK
BALANCE SHEET
AS AT 31ST DECEMBER, 1974

Capital	£	£	FIXED ASSETS	£	£
Light	14,000		Premises	20,000	
Dark	14,000		Fixtures	5,000	
		28,000			25,000
CURRENT ACCOUNTS			CURRENT ASSETS		
Light	150		Stock	4,000	
Dark	200		Debtors	1,300	
		350	Cash at bank	450	
Creditors		2,500	Cash in hand	100	
					5,850
		30,850			30,850

On 1st January, 1975 the partners agreed to admit Twilight as a partner under the following conditions:

(a) A goodwill account was created at £12,000, £6,000 to be credited to Light and £6,000 to Dark. The goodwill account to be written off over the first three years of the new partnership.

(b) Twilight to introduce £10,000 as new capital, part of which was used on 1st January to purchase new fixtures and fittings £4,000, and additional stock £3,000.

(c) Profits and losses to be divided in proportion to capital accounts.

(d) Interest on capital to be allowed at 7% per annum.

(e) Twilight to receive £2,000 per annum as a salary.

During the year ended 31st December, 1975 the partners' drawings were as follows:
Light £2,100, Dark £1,600, Twilight £2,200

The net trading profit (before writing off goodwill or allowing for Twilight's salary) amounted to £10,000 for that year.

Prepare:

(i) The balance sheet of the new partnership on 1st January, 1975.

(ii) A profit and loss appropriation account for the year ended 31st December, 1975.

(iii) The partners' current accounts for the same year.

(University of London GCE O level 1976)

76 (a) Black and White agreed to form a partnership to purchase a business run by Green for £40,000.

GREEN'S BALANCE SHEET ON 31ST MAY, 1975

	£		£
Capital	27,000	Premises	20,000
Creditors	670	Stock	7,000
		Debtors	200
		Cash in bank	400
		Cash in hand	70
	27,670		27,670

In addition to the above, the half-year rates of £150 for the period 1st April, to 30th September, 1975 had not been paid.

Black and White agreed to take over all assets except cash in hand and bank at book value and to meet all liabilities including rates.

1975
June 2 Black and White opened a bank account and paid in £25,000 each.
A cheque for £40,000 was drawn for the purchase of the business.
A new delivery van was purchased and paid for by cheque for £4,000.
New furniture and fittings were purchased and paid for by cheque £3,000.
Rates were paid by cheque £150.

Set out the Balance Sheet of Black and White after the above transactions had taken place on June 2nd, 1975.

(b) (i) Assuming that Black and White could safely invest their money to earn 7% per annum and that Black could earn £2,000 and White £2,500 per annum, what is the lowest acceptable amount of net profit in any year?

(ii) The partners estimate that their business expenses will total £2,500 per annum. The average mark up on the goods they sell is 25% of selling price. Stock will be kept at £7,000.

Set out an estimated Trading and Profit and Loss Account for the next twelve months showing the sales required to give the minimum net profit.

(iii) What is the lowest acceptable rate of turnover?

(iv) Calculate the working capital on June 2nd, 1975.

(University of London GCE O level 1975)

77 Excel Traders Ltd. has an authorised capital of £100,000 divided into 100,000 ordinary shares of £1 each.

The following balances were extracted from the books at 31st December, 1970:

	£
Issued capital (fully paid)	60,000
Reserve (1st January, 1970)	10,000
Profit and Loss Account (credit balance 1st January, 1970)	1,460
Profit for year to 31st December, 1970	14,670
Fixtures and fittings at cost	4,800
Machinery at cost	37,000
Provisions for depreciation	
Fixtures and fittings	1,600
Machinery	14,500
Freehold premises at cost	48,000
Stock	8,850
Sundry debtors	9,250
Provision for bad debts	370
Sundry creditors	3,440
Bank overdraft	1,860

The directors decided to transfer £3,000 to reserve and to recommend a dividend of 15% on the issued ordinary shares.

Prepare the Appropriation Account of the company for the year ended 31st December 1970 and a Balance Sheet as at that date.

Notes:

The assets and liabilities are to be grouped under appropriate headings.

Omission of appropriate sub-headings and inclusion of items under a wrong heading will be penalised.

(University of London GCE O level 1971)

78 On 1st February, 19·1, Alpha and Beta, who were trading in partnership, sharing profits and losses in the proportions of two-thirds and one-third respectively decided to wind up their business.

On the cessation of trading, the Balance Sheet was as follows:

BALANCE SHEET
1ST FEBRUARY, 19·1

	£		£
Alpha Capital Account	3,500	Freehold Factory	4,218
Beta Capital Account	1,500	Machinery	1,707
Alpha Current Account	276	Debtors	625
Creditors	1,592	Stock	458
Bank overdraft	402	Beta Current Account	262
	7,270		7,270

The assets were sold for the following prices: Freehold Factory £7,000; Machinery £1,000; Stock £300. £600 was collected from the Debtors and the dissolution expenses came to £150. Creditors were paid in full.

Prepare the necessary accounts to show result of realisation and the manner in which the partners' capital accounts were closed.

(RSA)

79 The following balances were extracted from the books of Co-operative Suppliers Limited at 31st December, 1971:

	Dr. £	Cr. £
Preference Share Capital £1 each fully paid		20,000
Ordinary Share Capital		90,000
Freehold Land (at cost)	40,000	
Buildings (cost £100,000)	75,000	
Motor Vehicles and Equipment (cost £24,000)	15,000	
Sundry debtors	54,920	
Sundry creditors		25,170
Sales		361,324
Purchases	279,218	
Goods returned	1,304	1,042
Warehouse Wages	8,760	
Salaries	21,800	
Office expenses	7,100	
Motor Vehicle expenses	6,300	
Warehouse expenses	5,600	
Carriage Inwards	1,452	
Carriage Outwards	974	
Stock at 1st January, 1971	17,120	
Profit and Loss Account balance at 1st January, 1971		12,000
Cash at bank	5,488	
6% Debentures		20,000
Interest on Debentures (half-year to 30th June, 1971)	600	
Preference Share dividends (half-year)	700	
Bad debts	2,800	
Provision for bad debts		3,400
General Reserve		11,200
	544,136	544,136

The Authorised Capital of the company is £140,000 divided into 20,000 7% Preference Shares of £1 each and 120,000 Ordinary Shares of £1 each of which £0·75 has been paid.

You are required to prepare Trading, Profit and Loss and Appropriation of Profit Accounts for the year ended 31st December, 1971, and a Balance Sheet as at that date, after taking account of the following:

(a) Stock at 31st December, 1971, was valued at £21,300.

(b) The adjustment of the provision of bad debts to 5% of debtors.

(c) Depreciation of motor vehicles and equipment at the rate of 20% per annum of written down value.

(d) Depreciation of buildings at the rate of 5% per annum of cost.

(e) Provision for a final dividend of £9,000 on the ordinary shares.

(f) The transfer of £12,000 to General Reserve.

Ignore taxation.

(JMB 1972)

80 The following trial balance was extracted from the books of Pelargonium Ltd. at 31st December, 1974.

	£	£
Share capital authorised and issued 160,000 shares of £1 each		160,000
Freehold premises at cost	101,000	
Plant and machinery at cost	40,000	
Stock in trade at 1st January, 1974	51,352	
Balance at bank	4,289	
Provision for depreciation of plant and machinery to 1st January, 1974		20,000
Bad debts	820	
Provision for doubtful debts at 1st January, 1974		390
Directors' remuneration	14,000	
Debtors and creditors	17,492	13,298
Profit and loss account balance at 1st January, 1974		12,448
Purchases	142,998	
Sales		194,542
General expenses	6,242	
Wages	19,285	
Rents and rates	3,200	
	400,678	400,678

You are given the following additional information:

(a) The provision for doubtful debts is to be increased to £500.

(b) Stock in trade at 31st December, 1974 was £56,788.

(c) Wages outstanding at 31st December, 1974 amounted to £482.

(d) Provision for depreciation of plant and machinery is to be made at the rate of 10% per annum on cost.

(e) Rent and rates amounting to £350 were paid in advance at 31st December, 1974.

(f) The directors propose to pay a dividend of 5% on the issued capital and to transfer £6,000 to General Reserve.

You are required to prepare a trading and profit and loss account for the year 1974 and a balance sheet at 31st December, 1974.
Ignore taxation.

(RSA II May 1975)

81 'The valuation of assets does not influence the measurement of profit. Profit is calculated by simply charging expenditure against income.'
Discuss this statement.

(RSA II May 1975)

82 Growit Ltd. sells house plants and vegetables. The firm's accounts for 1973 and 1974 are as follows:

	1973 £	1974 £
Sales (house plants)	52,600	61,740
Sales (vegetables)	25,200	33,860
	77,800	95,600
Cost of house plants sold	34,240	46,280
Cost of vegetables sold	22,600	24,980
	56,840	71,260
Gross Profit	20,960	24,340
	77,800	95,600
Sundry expenses incurred		
in connection with house plants	8,240	8,980
in connection with vegetables	1,220	1,840
Net profit	11,500	13,520
	20,960	24,340

After seeing the accounts, the directors of Growit Ltd. became optimistic and propose to expand the business by spending £30,000 on the purchase of new facilities to increase the output and sales of house plants.

You have been asked to give your opinion of the proposed expansion and are required to prepare a report, and any financial statements you consider appropriate, for the directors of Growit Ltd.

(RSA II May 1975)

83 The summarised balance sheets of Glenstead Ltd. at the end of 1973 and 1974 are as follows:

	31st December 1973 £	31st December 1974 £
Buildings at cost	80,000	100,000
Plant at cost less depreciation	51,600	65,400
Transport at cost less depreciation	7,100	8,400
Stock	17,150	24,370
Debtors	12,280	14,610
Bank balance	10,740	1,220
	178,870	214,000
Share capital	125,000	125,000
Retained profit	33,785	36,840
Debenture repayable 1985	—	20,000
Creditors for purchases and expenses	12,085	23,660
Dividend payable	8,000	8,500
	178,870	214,000

Note: The dividend is usually paid in early April in the year following the accounting date.

Required:

(a) State the amount of the current assets, the current liabilities, the working capital and the working capital ratio at 31st December, 1973 and at 31st December, 1974. Present your answer in the following form:

	1973	1974
Current assets		
Current liabilities		
Working capital		
Working capital ratio		

(b) Comment briefly on the changes that have taken place during 1974 in Glenstead's working capital.

(RSA II June 1975)

84 The summarised accounts of Forwardlook Ltd. for 1974 were as follows:

TRADING AND PROFIT AND LOSS ACCOUNT FOR 1974

	£		£
Materials consumed and wages	38,486	Sales	53,670
Depreciation	4,450		
	42,936		
Gross Profit	10,734		
	53,670		53,670
Expenses	7,156	Gross Profit	10,734
Net Profit	3,578		
	10,734		10,734

BALANCE SHEET 31ST DECEMBER, 1974

	£		£	£
Share capital	35,000	FIXED ASSETS		
Profit and Loss Account	8,240	Building at costs		16,000
		Plant (purchased		
	43,240	1st January, 1972) cost	35,600	
		Less depreciation	13,350	22,250
CURRENT LIABILITIES				38,250
Supplier of materials	4,276			
		CURRENT ASSETS		
		Stock	4,362	
		Debtors	2,928	
		Cash	1,976	9,266
	47,516			47,516

The directors of Forwardlook Ltd. decide to expand the business and they anticipate that the 1974 turnover will be doubled in 1975. They make the following consequential estimates:

(i) a new building costing £8,000 will be required, and will be paid for in January 1975;

(ii) additional plant with an eight year life and costing £18,000 will be required, and will be paid for in January 1975;

(iii) the cost of materials consumed and wages will be doubled;

(iv) the cost of expenses will be increased by £3,578;

(v) at the end of 1975 stocks will have increased to £6,492, debtors to £4,438 and current liabilities for supplier of materials to £6,924.

Required, on the assumption that the above estimates are fulfilled:

(a) a total cash account for 1975;

(b) a summarised trading and profit and loss account for 1975 and a balance sheet as at 31st December, 1975.

Notes:

(i) Stocks consist of raw materials only; no manufactured or partly manufactured goods are on hand at the beginning or at the end of the year;

(ii) no dividends have been paid and none are proposed;

(iii) assume that the company's bankers have agreed to grant any necessary overdraft.

(RSA June 1975)

85 The Balance Sheet of Gort Ltd., at 31st December, 1971, was as follows:

BALANCE SHEET

	£	£		£	£
Share capital		50,000	FIXED ASSETS		
Profit and Loss Account		11,621	Buildings at cost		30,000
		———	Plant at cost	25,000	
		61,621	*Less* depreciation	9,250	
				———	15,750
CURRENT LIABILITIES					———
Creditors for					45,750
purchases	4,419				
expenses	246		CURRENT ASSETS		
Dividend for 1971	2,500		Stocks	11,223	
	———	7,165	Debtors	8,542	
			Bank	3,271	
				———	23,036
		68,786			68,786

The Authorised Capital of Gort Ltd. is £50,000 divided into 50,000 shares of £1 each. During 1972:

(a) goods costing £57,126 were purchased;

(b) salaries paid were £18,726;

(c) general administration expenses paid were £2,498;

(d) sales to customers amounted to £84,482;

(e) the dividend for 1971 was paid;

(f) the charge for depreciation of plant for 1972 was £3,500.

As at 31st December, 1972,

(g) creditors for purchases were £5,964 and for general administration expenses £265;

(h) debtors for sales were £9,628;

(i) stock in trade was valued at £12,126;

(j) a dividend of £2,700 was proposed for 1972.

Gort passed all its receipts and payments through its bank account.

You are required to give:

(a) A summary of Gort's bank account for 1972.

(b) A Trading and Profit and Loss Account for 1972 and a Balance Sheet on 31st December, 1972.

Ignore taxation.

(*RSA II 1973*)

86 L Stone, a wholesaler decides to convert his business into a private company as from 1st January, 1975. The following is his balance sheet at that date:

	£		£
Capital Account	15,000	Leasehold Property	7,500
Creditors	5,400	Machinery	6,600
Bank Overdraft	2,100	Delivery vans	1,500
Loan from R Adams	7,500	Sundry debtors	7,500
		Stock	6,900
	30,000		30,000

The company was incorporated as L Stone Ltd., with an authorised capital of £37,500 divided into 37,500 ordinary shares of £1 each. The purchase price of the business was agreed at £22,500 and the company was to take over the assets and liabilities at the values shown in the above balance sheet, except for the freehold property which was to be revalued at £11,250. The purchase price was to be satisfied by the issue to L Stone of 22,500 Ordinary Shares of £1 credited as fully paid. To pay the bank overdraft and to provide additional working capital it was arranged to issue the 15,000 remaining Ordinary Shares to two other persons at a premium of 25p per share. All these arrangements were completed by 1st January, 1975.

(a) Show how the above transactions would be recorded in the journal and cash book of the company.

(b) Draft the company's opening balance sheet.

Answers to Exercises

CB=Cash Book; SB=Sales Book; PB=Purchases Book; J=Journal; PCB=Petty Cash Book; TB=Trial Balance; P&L=Profit and Loss; BS=Balance Sheet; GP=Gross Profit; NP=Net Profit; BRS=Bank Reconciliation Statement.

Chapter 1

1 Left side. **2** Credit. **3** From the account's point of view. **4** 'Buying on Credit', see text. **5** (a) I owe my creditors value; (b) My debtors owe me value. **6** Office Furniture Dr., A Price Cr.; Office Machinery Dr., B Thomas Cr.; Office Furniture Dr., Slikfiles Cr.; Office Machinery Dr., Speedadders Cr. **7** Machinery Dr., Machine Tools Ltd. Cr.; Motor Van Dr., Excel Cars Co. Cr.; Fixtures and Fittings Dr., Contelves Ltd. Cr.

Chapter 2

1 CB (debit) balance £10,000; TB totals £20,930. **2** CB (debit) balance £4,663; TB totals £5,558. **3** CB (debit) balance £14,380; TB totals £15,110. **4** CB (debit) balance £7,815; TB totals £8,055.

Chapter 3

1–9 See text. **10** CB £80; TB totals £140. **11** CB £202; TB totals £641. **12** CB £7,960; TB totals £8,457. **13** CB: 31st Oct. £4,771; 30th Nov. £4,992;TB: 31st Oct. £5,682; 30th Nov. £6,370. **14** See text. **15** D Cox's account: Debit: Balance £107, Sales £186, £52. Credit: Cash £107, £119, Balance c/d £119. **16** R White's account: Debit: Balance £160, Sales £30, Carriage £5, Sales £105; Credit: Cash £100, £95, Balance c/d £105. **17** S Monk's account: Credit: Balance £90, Purchases £60. Debit: Cash £150.

Chapter 4

1 TB totals £26,000; GP £6,000; NP £4,000; BS totals £14,000. **2** (a) GP £3,882; NP £2,338; BS totals £16,682; (b) GP £7,500; NP £3,920; BS totals £21,710. Only *total* debtors and *total* creditors should be shown in the balance sheet. **3** CB £8,840; TB £10,200; GP £245; NP £100; BS totals £9,550. **4** CB £6,449; TB £9,548; GP £452; NP £178; BS £8,271.

Chapter 5

1 TB £650. **2** Cash £56; TB £666. **3** Cash £702; Capital £1,136;TB £2,246; GP £250; NP £136; BS £1,613. **4** Cash £3,080; GP £785; NP £175; BS £5,340. **5** GP £1,180; NP £530; BS £10,830. **6** M Bell's account: Debit: Balance £100, Sales £70. Credit: Cash £100, Returns £10, Balance c/d £60. **7** J Peel's account: Credit: Balance £500, Purchases £450. Debit: Returns £40, Cash £460, Carriage £10, Balance c/d £440. **8** J Jones's account: Credit: Balance £170, Purchases £150. Debit: Returns £20, Cash £170, Balance c/d £130.

Chapter 6

1–2 See text. **3** SB total £128; PB total £85; TB £213. **4** SB total £1,690; PB total £970; TB £10,690; GP £790; NP £390; BS £9,310. **5** (a) PB, Purchases, Metal Supplies Co.; (b) SB, S Daniel & Sons, Sales; (c) CB, Salaries, CB; (d) Returns Outwards Book. Metal Supplies Co., Returns Outwards Account. **6** Balances at 31st December: Morton £52 (Cr.), Coles £211 (Dr.), Purchases £8,918 (Dr.), Sales £16,199 (Cr.), Returns Inwards £138 (Dr.), Returns Outwards £121 (Cr.). **7** Increases: (a) £20; (b) £60; No change (c) and (d).

Chapter 7

1 GP £700. **2** 31st August GP £890, 30th September GP £673. **3** Cash 30th June £3,827, 31st July £3,975. TB: 30th June £6,382, 31st July £6,271. 30th June GP £563, NP £338, BS £5,322. 31st July GP £5,305. **4** Stock 30th September £620. **5** (a) 6 times; (b) 45%; (c) 33⅓%. **6** Stock at close £1,300. **7** (a) See text; (b) BS £10,700; (c) Liabilities: Creditors £400; Assets: Cash at bank £3,640. **8** Loss of Stock £7,220. **9** Loss of stock £8,200. **10** £5,600. **11** (a) Increase £20; (b) Decrease £60; (c) No effect; (d) Increase £649; (e) No effect. **12** Purchases £14,750. **13** GP £4,900. **14** £1,050. **15** (i) GP

£30,000, NP £10,000; (ii) Cost of goods £50,000; (iii) Turnover £80,000; (iv) 60%; (v) 37½%; (vi) 12½%. **16** (i) £5,000; (ii) £5,800. **17** GP £14,070; Stock turn approx 5¼ times.

Chapter 8

1 Total £291. **2** Total £1,700+£455=£2,155. **3** £81, £60, £90, £60, total £291. **4** TB totals £486·50. **5** (a) Russell = Credit balance £294·80; (b) Current Liabilities; (c) £206. **6** See text. **7** TB totals £582.

Chapter 9

1 TB £4,267; GP £245; Net Loss £79; BS totals £3,921. **2** TB totals £8,908; Gross Loss £189·25; Net Loss £704·60; BS totals £7,752·65. **3** R Shipper's Credit balance £570. **4** T Rose: Debit balance £292. **5** A Bird: No balance. **6** G Root: Debit balance £171. **7** L Kent: Debit balance £168. **8** L Trent: Credit balance £50. **9** A Thorn: Credit balance £292. **10** Debit balances: Driver £70; Porter £140; Guard £80. **11** Sales Ledger: Debit balances: Lawson £297; James £224. Purchases Ledger: Credit balance: Jack £210. **12** Crombie: Debit balance £176; Sales total £28,844. **13** TB correct credit entries: Capital, Sales, Returns Outwards, Discounts Received, Sundry Creditors, Bank Overdraft. Totals £55,230; GP £16,885; NP £9,055; BS totals £17,305.

Chapter 10

1 Balances b/d: Cash £128; Bank £299; Discounts Allowed: £5; Discounts Received £4. **2** Bank balance b/d £634·08; Discounts Allowed £2·50; Discounts Received £5. **3** Balances b/d: Cash £10; Bank £310; Discounts Allowed £95; Discounts Received £70. **4** Bank balance b/d £593; Discounts Allowed £3; Discounts Received £5.

Chapter 11

1 BRS; Cash Book balance *less* lodgements not credited £160; *Add* Unpresented cheques £350; Adjusted Cash Book: Balance (Drs) £450 + Debtor £180; *Credit*: Bank charges £20. Adjusted balance £610. **2** Bank Statement balance £420; *Add* Bank charges £2 + standing order £5·25 Returned cheque £41·10; *Less* unpresented cheques £25·40+£37·95. **3** Adjusted cash book: Balance (Dr.) £740·80 + Interest £73·50. *Credit*: Insurance £25·70; Adjusted balance £788·60. BRS: Bank statement balance £819 *less* unpresented cheques £32·70 + £168·44 = £201·14. *Add* lodgements not credited £170·74. **4** Bank Cash Book: *Add* to amounts brought forward: *Debit*: £94·70 + £2; £1,170·73 + £78. *Credit*: £78·67; £1,317·10 + £5 + £2·50. Credit balance (Overdraft) brought down £75·87. **5** Cash Book: *Debit*: £1,017·12 + £5·75 + £16·06; *Credit*: £10·50 + £4·22. Adjusted Balances £1,024·21. BRS: Cash Book balance £1,017·12. *Add* unpresented cheques £115·10 + £237·50 + £38 = £390·60. *Less* lodgements not shown £185·15. Balance per Bank statement = £1,222·57. **6** BRS: Bank Statement Balance £257·95: *Less* unpresented cheques £18·35 + £20·95. *Add* lodgements not shown £73·50. Cash Book balance £310·50. **7** Cash Book: *Debit balance* £30 + giro credit £70. *Credit* Insurance standing order £10. Balance c/d £90. BRS Bank Statement balance £290 *Less* unpresented cheques £40 + £160 = £200. CB balance £90. **8** BRS Bank Statement balance £473; *Add* Bank charges £3 + lodgements not shown £85 = £561; *Less* unpresented cheques £78 + £146 + £116 = £340 + omissions from CB £299 = £639. Cash book balance (Overdraft) = £78. (a) Before balancing on 31st December enter (i) *Debit* £299; (ii) *Credit* £3. **9** (a) Cash book: *Debit*: Balance £1,568 + dividends £36. *Credit*: Bank charges £7·50 + Economic Research £25. Balance c/d £1,571·50. (b) BRS Bank Statement balances £1,472 *Add* lodgements not shown £125 + £49 + £3·50 = £177·50 *Less* unpresented cheques £28 + £50; Balance per CB 31st March £1,571·50.

Chapter 12

1 *Debit* £16·40 + £33·60; *Credit* Stationery £10·30, Expenses £10·50, Postage £3, Cleaners £7; Ledger Account £7·45; Total £38·25; balance c/d £11·75. Cash to make up imprest £38·25. **2** *Debit* £2 + £18; *Credit* total £18 + balance £2 = £20. **3** (a) (i) PB; (ii) PB; (iii) Returns Inwards Book; (iv) Petty cash; (v) CB; (vi) SB; (b) (i) Supplies Invoice; (ii) Supplies invoice; (iii) Credit note; (iv) BRS bill; (v) Pay-in slip; (vi) Copy of Sales invoice. **4** *Debit* £25. *Credit* total £15·75. Balance c/d £9·25; Cash to make up imprest £25·75. **5** *Debit* £20: *Credit* total £12·50. Balance c/d £7·50; Cash to make up imprest £12·50.

Chapter 13

1 *Assets*: Premises, Machinery, Furniture, Stock, Debtors, Bank. *Liabilities*: Capital + Profit − Drawings, Creditors. BS totals £31,890. **2** GP £5,973; NP £1,510; BS totals £15,844; *Assets*: Fixed £14,309, Current £1,535; Capital + Profit £15,000, Current liabilities £844.

3 (a) Fixed Assets: Premises, Machinery, Furniture, Motor Vans; Current Assets: Stock, Debtors, Bank, Liabilities: Capital + Profit − Drawings £31,000; Current Liabilities: Creditors £890. Totals £31,890; (b) Drawings decreases Cash on Assets side and decreases capital on Liabilities side. **4** Fixed Assets: Premises, Vehicles; Current Assets: Stock, Debtors, Expenses paid in advance, cash; Liabilities: Capital + Profit − Drawings; Current Liabilities: Creditors, Expenses accrued, Bank Overdraft. **5** Effect on Capital: (i) None; (ii) Decrease by £20 through reduced profit; (iii) Increase by the profit £25; (iv) None. **6** (i) Both; (ii) BS; (iii) Both; (iv) BS; (v) BS; (vi) P&L; (vii) Both. **7** See text.

Chapter 14

1 See text. **2** Right-hand side: Fixed Assets: Premises, Motor Vans; Total £3,300; Current Assets: Stock, Debtors, Insurance pre-paid; Total £5,865, *Less* Current Liabilities: Creditors, Wages due, Bank Overdraft; Total £5,055; Working Capital £810. Left-hand side: Capital *less* Net loss, *less* drawings = £4,110. It is the value of stock which produces a working capital. Stock must therefore quickly be sold to meet creditors' claims. **3** (i) None; (ii) Increase by £25; (iii) None (long-term liability); (iv) None; (v) None; (vi) Decrease by £10. **4** Fixed Assets £11,048; Current Assets £7,960; Current Liabilities £4,546; Working Capital £3,414; Long-term Liability £3,000; Capital (excess of assets over liabilities) £11,462. Jones is solvent and very well able to meet his obligations. **5** 2nd March: Cash £240, Creditors £1,765, Debtors £695, Machinery £1,550, Stock £1,710, Loan Account £500, Capital: Credit: Balance b/d £2,355, Additional profit £45. Debit: Stock re-valued £320, Loss on Machinery £150, Balance c/d £1,930. BS totals £4,195. **6** TB totals £1,920 (Credit side: Capital £900, Sales £840, Proctor £180). GP £500; NP £433; Working capital £883; BS totals £1,333. **7** Adjusted capital = £13,582·75. **8** (a) GP £500; GP as percentage of turnover = 33⅓%. BS totals £1,440; (b) No difference, because value of stock is assessed at lowest cost. (See text.) **9** See text. **10** Fixed Assets: £6,980; Current Assets: £7,260; Capital: £4,040; Loan Account: £8,000; Current Liabilities: £2,200; BS totals £14,240. **11** (a) 18%; (b) 10%; (c) 20%; (d) 5 years; (e) £29,000; (f) £30,500; (g) £12,500; (h) £7,500; (i) £40,000; (j) 25%; (k) £42,000; (l) £23,000; (m) £10,000; (n) £2,500; (o) £1,400.

Chapter 15

1 (a) Revenue; (b) Capital; (c) Capital; (d) Revenue; (e) Capital. **2** (a) Capital; (b) Capital; (c) Capital; (d) Revenue. **3** See text. **4** (a) See text; (b) Revenue; (c) Increase of profit by £200. **5** (a) Expense; Asset; Asset; Expense; Asset; Expense; Asset; (b) Capital; (c) See text. **6** (a) Capital; (b) Revenue; (c) Revenue; (d) Capital. **7** Balance b/d (Dr.) £5,420. **8** (a) A. Capital £199; B. Liabilities £5,520; C. Assets £3,675; D. Assets £8,481; E. Liabilities £8,580; (b) Fixed Assets; Long-term Liabilities; Current Liabilities; Current Assets. The excess of Current Assets over Current Liabilities = Working Capital; (c) False; False; By the reduction of cash. **9** (a) See text; (b) Revenue; Capital; Revenue. Yes, Capital, because damaged woodwork would have had to be *replaced* before the building could be occupied.

Chapter 16

1 (a) Machinery Dr. Makeshift Cr.; Office Furniture Dr. Penner & Co. Cr.; Smith Dr. Smithson Cr.; Jay Dr. Jones Cr.; Able Dr. Cain Cr.; (b) Sales Dr. Office Furniture Cr.; Office Machinery Dr. Purchases Cr.; (c) Drawings Dr. Purchases Cr.; Drawings Dr. Wages Cr.; (d) Autovans Ltd. Dr. Motor Vans Cr.; Drawings Dr. Office Expenses Cr. **2** (a) Fixtures and Fittings Dr. Purchases Cr.; (b) Watson Dr. Weston Cr.; (c) Johnson Dr. Johnston Cr.; (d) Stock Account Dr. Trading Account Cr. **3** Totals: Sales £173; Purchases £275; Returns Inwards Book £4; CB: Discount Allowed £4; Bank Dr.: £192, £76; Bank Cr.: £40, £33, £50; Journal: 3rd March Office Furniture Dr. Office Supplies Ltd. Cr. 7th March Bird & Sons Dr. Purchases Cr.; 6th March Returns Inwards (or Packing Case Account) Dr. A Gunn Cr. **4** (a) Motor Vans Dr. Car Cr. £500; Carr Dr. Motor Vans Cr. £100; P&L Account Dr. Motor Vans Cr. £40; (b) Wright Dr. Wrightson Cr. £5; (c) Machinery Dr. £250; Wages £150 and Purchases £100 Cr. **5** Green Dr. Discounts Received Cr.; Brown Dr. Returns Outwards Cr.; (a) Purchases Dr. Pink & Co. Cr.; (b) Drawings Dr. Sales Cr.; (a) Gray Dr. Sales Cr.; (b) Office Furniture Dr. C Gray Cr. **6** (a) Interest Dr. Tardy Cr.; (b) Motor Vans Dr. Dove & Co. Cr. £725; Dove & Co. Dr. Motor Vans Cr. £100; (c) Discounts Received Dr. Jones Cr.; (d) Machinery Dr. Purchases Cr.; (e) Derby & Co. Dr. Sales Cr. **7** (a) Discounts Received Dr. Waterways Ltd. Cr.; (b) Repairs to Premises Account. Dr. Builders Ltd. Cr.. **8** (a) Premises Dr. Purchases Cr.; (b) Hunter Dr. Hunt Cr.; (c) P&L Account Dr. Office Machinery Cr. £20. **9** (a) P&L Account Dr. Machinery Cr.; (b) Premises Dr. Wages Cr.; (c) Legal Expenses Dr. Turney Cr.; (d) Drawings Dr. Purchases Cr. **10** (i) Credit CB, Debit Customer; or more precisely, Journalise first; (ii) J; (iii) PCB; (iv) PB; (v) J. But if credit note is for Return Inwards, then RIB; (vii) J or Returns Outwards Book (as v); (vi) SB. **11** Balance b/d

(Dr.) £208.　**12** (a) Debit; Debit; Credit; Debit; Debit; (b) See text.　**13** (i) Machinery Dr. Purchases Cr.; (ii) Sales Dr. Suspense Account Cr. £100; Suspense Account Dr. Drawings Cr. £100; (iii) Browne Dr. Brownson Cr.; (iv) Capital Dr. Reynolds Loan Account Cr.; (b) Profit increase by £400 and reduced by £100. Net increase of profit £300.　**14** (a) Cr. £6; Cr. £24; Dr. £100; Cr. £2; Dr. £3. (b) Debit of TB greater than credit by £71. (c) Suspense Account: Debit: £100, £3. Credit £6, £24, £2. Balance £71.　**15** (i) Suspense Dr. Sales Cr.; (iii) Discounts Allowed Dr. Suspense Cr.; (iii) Kay Dr. Jay Cr.; (iv) Sales Dr. Office Furniture Cr. Suspense Account: Debit £90; Credit £60. Balance (TB error) £30.　**16** (a) Suspense Dr. Purchase Cr.; (b) Machinery Dr. Suspense Cr.; (c) Suspense Dr. A Swindel Cr.; (d) Suspense Dr. R Tee Cr. Suspense Account: Dr. Purchases £120 A Swindel £70 R Tee £5; Cr. Machinery £135. TB error £60.　**17** (i) Suspense Dr. General expenses Cr.; (ii) Office Furniture Dr. Office Expenses Cr.; (iii) Discounts Dr. Suspense Cr.; (iv) Suspense Dr. Returns Outwards Cr.; (v) Suspense Dr. Sales Cr. Suspense Account: Dr. General Expenses £100 Returns Outwards £148 Sales £90; Cr. Discounts £40, TB error £298.　**18** Journal Opening Entries: Credit Loan Account and H Tims; Debit remaining items. Difference is Capital £4,778. TB: Debit Premises £4,000, Fixtures £416, Stock £396, Bank £350, Cash £112, Roberts £47, Pope £85, Discounts £2 ,Purchases £543·20. Wages £40, Cleaning £2, Expenses £1, Postage £2. Credit: Tims £36, Keeping £243·20, Fix £242, Loan Account Walters £500, Sales £175, Returns Outwards £22, Capital £4,778. Totals £5,996·20. Gross Loss £442·20, Net Loss £489·20, BS totals £5,310.

Chapter 17

1 Rent Account: Dr. March, June, September at £117 December Balance c/d £117, total £468. Cr. December P&L Account £468, total £468 1st January Balance b/d £117.　**2** Rent: Dr. Balance £750 Balance c/d £250, total £1,000; Cr. P&L Account £1,000, total £1,000, 1st January Balance b/d £250. Rates: Dr. Balance £500; Cr. Balance c/d £125, P&L Account £375. Wages: Credit balance b/d £500. Interest: Credit balance b/d £100. Insurance: Dr. Balance b/d £30.　**3** Dr. Cash £64, £54, £42, £47. Balance c/d £82 total £289. Cr. Balance b/d £64. P&L Account £225, total £289. Balance b/d £82.　**4** (a) Rent Account Dr. Cash: 4 entries of £200. 31st December Balance c/d £200, total £1,000. Cr. Balance b/d £200, P&L Account £800, total £1,000. Balance b/d £200; (b) £200 would appear in the BS under Current Liabilities, as Rent due.　**5** Dr. January £240 March £72, total £312, Balance b/d (amount prepaid) £168 September Cash £8. Cr. P&L Account £120 + £24 = £144, Balance c/d £168, total £312.　**6** Rent Receivable Account: Cr. March, June, September at £78 December Balance c/d £78, total £312. Dr. P&L Account £132, total £312, Balance b/d £78.　**7** Rent Payable: Dr. March, June, September at £425, December Balance c/d £425, total £1,700. Cr. December P&L Account £1,700, total £1,700. Balance b/d £425. Rent Receivable: Cr. August–November £75, total £150. Dr. P&L Account £150.　**8** Rent Receivable: Dr. 1st January Balance b/d—Hill £80, 31st December P&L Account: Hill £12 × £80 = £960, Dale £12 × £120 = £1,440, Balance c/d £80, total £2,560. Cr. January, Balance b/d—Dale £120, 31st December Cash—Hill 1st January 1972—31st January 1973 = £1,120; Cash—Dale 10 months to 30th November 1972 £1,200, Balance Dale c/d £120.　**9** Rent and rates: Dr. Balance £40, July 19·1—April 19·2 Rent = £4 × £100, Rates = £2 × £85. June 19·2 Balance c/d £100, total £710, Balance b/d £42·50. Cr. Balance b/d £100, Balance c/d £42·50, 30th June 19·2 P&L Account £567·50, total £710. 1st July 19·2, Balance b/d £100.　**10** GP (including Carriage Inwards added to Purchases) £17,438; NP £4,661. BS totals £27,228.　**11** Cr.: Balance £16, Insurance £14 c/d Balance: Drawings Account £94 + P&L Account £94, total £218, Balance b/d £13. Dr.: Balance £12, Cash £193. Balance c/d £13, total £218. Balance b/d £14.

Chapter 18

1 Scott Account: Dr. Balance £340; Cr. Bad Debts £340. Prince: Dr.: Balance £500; Cr. Cash £175, Bad Debts £325. Bad Debts Account: Dr. Scott £340, Prince £325. Cr. P&L Account £665. Bad Debts Recovered Account Cr. Cash—Scott £340; Dr. P&L Account £340. (Bad Debts Recovered may be incorporated with Bad Debts Account—Not essential to have two accounts): Journal entries to precede Ledger entries.　**2** Provision for Bad and Doubtful Debts Account: Cr. Balance £350, P&L Account £50; Dr. Balance c/d £400. Bad Debts Dr. Customer £130, Cr. P&L Account £130.　**3** Cr. December 19·1 P&L Account £500, December 19·2 P&L Account £150; Dr. December 19·2 Balance c/d £650, Cr. December 19·2 Balance b/d £650. Corresponding entries in P&L Accounts 19·1, 19·2. BS 19·1 Assets side: Debtors *Less* Provision £9,500; BS 19·2 Debtors, *Less* Provision £12,350.　**4** Entries as in No. 3. (a) 19·1 Cr. P&L Account £400; (b) Cr. P&L Account £100; (c) Dr. P&L Account £150. BS: 19·1 Debtors £8,000 *Less* Provision £400; 19·2 Debtors £10,000 *Less* Provision £500; 19·3 Debtors £7,000 *Less* Provision £350.　**5** Provision for Bad Debts Account in the following sequence: Cr. £300, Dr. £400, Balance c/d £500, total £900; Cr. total £900, therefore P&L

Account £600. BS Debtors £10,000 *Less* Provision £500. **6** Provision for Bad Debts Account: Dr. Bad Debts £185, Balance c/d £200, total £385; Cr. Balance b/d £175, Bad Debts Recovered £30, total £385, therefore P&L Account £180. BS: Debtors £4,000 *Less* Provision £200. **7** Provision for Bad Debts Account = 1974 Dr. Bad Debts £137, Balance c/d £200, total £337; Cr. Balance £240, total £337 therefore P&L Account £97. 1975 Dr. Bad Debts £129, Balance c/d £250, total £379; Cr. Balance b/d £200, Bad Debts Recovered £26, total £153, therefore P&L £153. BS 1974 Debtors £4,000 *Less* Provision £200; 1975 Debtors £5,000 *Less* Provision £250. **8** Provision for Bad Debts Account: Dr. Bad Debts June/November £281, Balance c/d £217 (5% Provision). Cr. January Balance b/d £161, November Dividend Abel £12. December Bad Debts Recovered £20. Total £498 therefore P&L Account £305. **9** Provision for Bad Debts = Dr. Bad Debts May/November £268, Balance c/d (5% Provision on £5,360) £268; Cr. Balance b/d £225, Bad Debts Recovered £36, total £536, P&L £275. **10** Provision for Bad Debts: Credit side only: December 19·1 P&L Account £77, December 19·2 P&L Account £47, total £124. January 19·3 Balance b/d £72. **11** Bad Debts Account: Dr. £27, £87, £6, £8, £12; Cr. Bad Debts Recovered £75, P&L Account £65, total £140. Provision for Bad Debts: Cr. Balance b/d £111; Dr. P&L £24, Balance c/d £87, total £111. P&L Account: Dr. Bad Debts £65, Legal Charges £8·40; Cr. Interest £3, Provision for Bad Debt £24. **12** Calculations of correct NP: Plus: Rates £36, Drawings (from wages) £1,040; Minus: Electricity £22, Debtors £120, Provision for Bad Debts £64; Difference = +£870. Add to wrong NP of £2,000 = £2,870. BS: Capital Net £5,830, Current Liabilities £1,222; Fixed Assets £3,600, Current Assets £3,452; Totals £7,052. **13** GP (including Carriage Inwards £120, Wages £2,837) £1,665; NP £35; BS: Capital Net £12,909, Current Liabilities £8,675; Fixed Assets £1,900, Current Assets £19,684; Totals £21,584. **14** GP £16,632, NP £6,605. BS Capital Net £25,983 Current Liabilities £5,673; Fixed Assets £12,200, Current Assets £19,456. Totals £25,983. Working Capital £13,783.

Chapter 19

1 (a) See text; (b) Journal Dr. Machinery £187·50, Fixtures £37·50; Cr. Depreciation £225. **2** (a) Machinery Account Dr. £2,000 Cr. Depreciation: 19·1 £200, 19·2 £180, 19·3 £162; Balance c/d in 19·3 to debit side £1,458; (b) Machinery Account Cr. Depreciation for 3 years at £200 = £600 Balance c/d to debit side £1,400. On straight line Method Depreciation over 3 years greater by £58. **3** Depreciation Account: Cr. December 1970 P&L Account Van £1,150; January 1971 Balance b/d £150, December 1971 P&L Account Van £1,112 + Van £2,150 = £262; January 1972 Balance b/d £412 December 1972 P&L Account £247; January 1973 Balance b/d £659. **4** Machinery Account: Dr. January 1968 Cash £1,500 Cr. December 1968 Depreciation £130, Balance c/d £1,370. December 1969 Depreciation £130 Balance c/d £1,240. **5** Machinery Account: 1967 Dr. Cash £3,000, Cr. P&L £300 Balance c/d £2,700. 1968 Dr. Balance b/d £2,700 Cash £600; Cr. P&L: Machine 1 £300 Machine 2 £40, total £340, Balance c/d £2,960. 1969 Dr. Balance b/d £2,960 Cr. P&L £360 Balance c/d £2,600. Balance Sheet 1969 Machinery £2,960 *Less* Depreciation £360 = £2,600. **6** Packing Machine Account: 1970 Dr. Cash (1) £720, Cash (2) £1,920, total £2,640. 1970 Cr. 31st October Depreciation (1) £135, Cash (1) £500, 31st December P&L Account (1) £85, Depreciation (2) £96, Balance c/d £1,824. **7** Journal: Cash Dr. Machinery Cr. £300; Machinery Dr. P&L Cr. £50; Machinery Dr. M & P Ltd. Cr. £7,000; Machinery Dr. Wages Cr. £300; M & P Ltd. Dr. Cash Cr. £3,000. **8** Motor Vehicles Account 19·1 Dr. January Balance (1) £200, February Cash (2) £800, Cash (Car) £600; Cr. Depreciation £320, Balance c/d £1,280; 19·2 Dr. Balance b/d £1,280. 19·3 Dr. P&L Account £66. Cr. Cash (Car) £450, Depreciation (Car) £96, Depreciation (Vans) £160 Balance c/d £640. **9** (a) Motor Vehicles Account: Dr. Balance (a) £600, (b) £500 = £1,100, Cash £80, BCM Ltd. £900; Cr. 31st March Depreciation (a) £30 Cash, (a) £520, Loss transferred to P&L (a) £50, 31st December Depreciation (b) £50 + £4 = £54, Depreciation (c) £23, Balance c/d £1,403; (**b**) Savage is a motor vehicles dealer; balance of £1,403 represents stock of vehicles at close of year. Therefore Current Assets. **10** Journal: 19·1 P&L Account Dr. Depreciation Cr. £300; 19·2 P&L Account Dr. Depreciation Cr. £390; 19·3 P&L Account Dr. Depreciation Cr. £506; 19·4 1st January Balance b/d Machinery Account = £5,594. **11** (a) Motor Lorries Account: Dr. 19·1/19·3 Cash (a), (b), (c), (d), (e) £9,600 + £2,700 = £12,300. Cr. January 19·3. Motor Lorries Disposals Account (a) £2,400, December Balance c/d £9,900. Depreciation Account: Cr.: December 19·1 P&L (a–d) £1,920; 19·2 P&L (a–d) £1,920 Balance b/d £3,360. Dr. 1st January 19·3 Motor Lorries Disposals (a) £480, Balance c/d £3,360. Motor Lorries Disposals Account Cr. 19·3 January Cash (a) £1,500 Depreciation (a) £480, December P&L (a) £420. Dr. Transfer to Motor Lorries Account £2,400; (b) Machinery Account: Dr. 19·1 Cash (a–d) £8,000, 19·2 Cash (e–f) £4,800. Cr. 19·2/19·3 Machinery Disposals (a–b) at £2,000 each. Balance c/d £10,800. Depreciation Account: Cr. December 19·1 P&L (a–d) £800, 19·2 P&L (b–d) £600, P&L (e–f) £480, 19·3 P&L (c–f) £880; Dr. January 19·2 Machinery Disposals £200, 19·3 Machinery Disposals £400 December Balance c/d £2,160. Machinery Disposals Account: Cr. 19·2 January Cash (a) £1,722, Depreciation (a) £200,

December P&L (a) £78. 19·3 January Cash (b) £1,625, Depreciation (b) £400; Dr. December 19·2 Machinery (a) £2,000, December 19·3 P&L (b) £25, Machinery (b) £2,000. BS 19·3, Machinery £10,800 *Less* Depreciation £2,160 = £8,640. **12** NP £1,943; Capital £2,133, Current Liabilities £3,251; Fixed Assets £2,630, Current Assets £2,754. Totals £5,384. Working Capital deficiency £497. **13** GP (including Carriage Inwards £246) £9,920: NP £1,955; Capital £11,655, Current Liabilities £2,350; Fixed Assets £7,500, Current Assets £6,505. Totals £14,005. (b) Working Capital £4,155; (c) GP would decrease by £155, NP would therefore decrease by same amount. **14** TB credit side: Creditors, Sales, Bank Overdraft, Returns Outwards, Commission Received, Discounts Received. Totals £25,968. GP £6,666; NP £1,297; Capital £6,100, Current Liabilities £1,545, Current Assets £5,765, Fixed Assets £1,880. Totals £7,645. **15** NP £5,746; Capital Net £18,596; Current Liabilities £3,083, Current Assets £19,438, Fixed Assets £2,241. Totals £21,679. **16** GP £22,841, NP £9,520 (including Provisions for Bad Debts £59). Capital £26,363. Current Liabilities £7,220. Current Assets £19,343 (including total Provision for Bad Debts £339), Fixed Assets £14,240. Totals £33,583.

Chapter 20

1 GP: A £5,175; B £3,500. **2** GP: Copper £2,375, Tin £225, Lead £300, Zinc £800. **3** (a) Suggested analysis columns: Details, Net Values, Invoice Totals, Television, Refrigerators Radios, Sundries; (b) Total Sales is posted to a nominal ledger. **4** Wills: Dr. Balance £165; Law Dr. Balance £93; Bottomley Dr. Balance £48; Benn Dr. Balance £476; Lister Dr. Balance £221. Carriage Dr. £15 (when paid). Discounts Allowed Dr. £10. Sales Account: Cr. Total £1,053; Sweets £438, Tobacco £132, Cigarettes £468, Carriage (included because it is charged to the Customer) £15. **5** GP: Total £10,935; Purchases £9,925; Service & Repairs £1,010. NP: £8,700. BS: Capital £15,200, Current Liabilities £2,593; Current Assets £16,588, Fixed Assets £1,205. Totals £17,793.

Chapter 22

1 (a) and (b) See text. **2** Assets: Fixed £11,520; Current £6,480; *Less* Current Liabilities £1,202 = Working Capital £5,278; Capital + Profit − Drawings = £16,798. **3** Totals £20,313; Debit balance b/d £9,446. **4** Totals £14,422; Debit balance b/d £7,654; Credit balance b/d £131. **5** Sales: Totals £33,759; Debit balance b/d £12,158; Credit balance b/d £121. Purchases: Totals £29,114; Credit balance b/d £13,218; Debit balance b/d £102. **6** Sales: Totals £71,034; Debit balance b/d £5,322; Credit balance b/d £124. 'Increase in Provision for doubtful debts' is irrelevant. Purchases: Totals: £48,602; Credit balance b/d £5,528. **7** Sales: Totals £678,841; Debit balance b/d £83,932.

Chapter 23

1 1st January Capital £12,000 − 31st December Capital £7,000 = Net increase £5,000 − New Capital £2,000 = NP £3,000. **2** GP £2,600; NP £1,970; BS: Capital Net £5,040; Assets: Fixed £4,200, Current £840, total £5,040. **3** Statement of Affairs: Assets: Van, Stock, Debtors, Bank, Cash = £2,000. *Less* Liabilities: Creditors = Capital £1,050. Totals £2,000. Statement of Profit Capital: 1st January £1,000; 30th June £1,050; Net increase £50; *Add* drawings £530, *Less* additions to capital £400, NP = £180. **4** Statement of Affairs 1st January, Assets total £5,580 *Less* Creditors £960 = Capital £4,620. Statement of Affairs 31st December, Assets total £6,720 *Less* Creditors £1,000 = Capital £5,720. Statement of Profit 31st December: Net Increase of Capital £1,100 + Drawings £1,200 − New Capital £400 = NP £1,900. **5** Statement of Affairs 31st December, Assets total £5,640; *Less* Liabilities: Loan Account, creditors = Capital £3,400. Statement of Profit Capital 31st December − Capital 1st January = Net increase £400 + Drawings £832 − Interest £50 = NP £1,182. **6** P&L Account: Debit: Purchases, *Less* closing stock = £1,500 plus Motor expenses, Insurance, Rent, depreciation. Credit: Receipts + debtors £150. NP £1,930. Totals £4,150. BS: £3,000 + Profit − Drawings = £3,530. Assets: Van £800, Equipment £1,170, stock £250, debtors £150, Bank £1,160. Total £3,530. Cash Book: Debit: Capital, Takings. Credit: total of items listed £5,840. Balance 30th June £1,160. **7** Statement of Affairs 1st January: Liabilities: Loan Account £3,000 Creditors £2,918, remaining items are assets. Total £29,684. Capital £23,766. Statement of Affairs 31st December. Liabilities: Loan Account £3,000, Creditors £2,184, Bank Overdraft £628: Remaining items assets. Total £30,244. Capital £26,832 − Drawings £2,400 = £24,432. Statement of Profit: Capital 31st December £24,432 − Capital 1st January £23,766 = Net increase of Capital £666 + Drawings £2,400 = NP for year £3,066. **8** Journal: Debit: Premises, Vans, Stock, Debtors, Insurance Bank. Total £19,195. Credit: Remaining 4 items. Difference is Capital £9,265. Books required: Ledger, CB, J, PB, SB, Returns Inwards Book, Returns Outwards Book, PCB. **9** Statement of Affairs 31st December. Totals £4,950. Capital £3,075. Statement of Profit: Capital 31st December £3,075 + Drawings £500 − Car £200 = £3,375. Deduct Capital 1st January £5,500. Net Loss = £2,125. **10** Total Debtors

Account: Dr. Balance £6,000. Cr. Cash £55,530, Balance c/d £5,750, total £61,280. Difference = Sales £55,280. Total Creditors Account: Cr. Balance £2,100. Dr. Cash £46,320, Balance c/d £2,740, total £49,060. Difference = Purchases £46,960. GP £5,550. **11** Total Debtors Account and Total Creditors Account: Set out as in **10**: Sales £4,212; Purchases £4,049. GP (including Cash Sales £1,863) £2,004. NP (including Provision for Bad Debts £150 and Depreciation £58), £426. BS totals £4,018. [Deduct Drawings of goods £38 from Debtors and from Capital (Total Drawings £574)]. Cash 31st December £352 (including starting Dr. balance £33). **12** Calculations: CB: Balance 31st December £2,768. Sales £71,122. Purchases £60,236. Total expenses Account: Dr. Cash £2,923; Cr. Balance £86, Balance (amount prepaid) c/d £40, total £2,923. Expenses for year to P&L Account £2,797. GP £9,686 (including £2,000); NP £973. BS totals £9,942. **13** BS 31st December, 1971 totals £22,328. Assets: Fixed £1,378; Current £20,850. Liabilities: Capital £12,290 + £2,710 + £800 = £15,800 *Less* Drawings £3,330. Creditors £7,332. Difference of the two sides £2,526 = Net Profit. Trading and P&L Account: Order of entries: (Leave spaces for missing items, then calculate.) Stock 1st January (Dr.), Stock 31st December (Cr.), Expenses, NP (from BS), totals of P&L Account £13,566, GP £13,566, Sales £13,566 × 5 = £67,830; totals Trading Account £77,050; £77,050 − £13,566 = £63,484; £63,484 − £8,920 = Purchases (including Drawings £40) £54,564. **14** Bank balance 31st December, 1969 £150; Calculated credit purchases £80; TB credit side: Capital £980, Sales £10,460, Creditors £550, totals £11,990. GP £3,080; NP £720; BS totals £1,610. **15** Bank Account Balance 31st December, 1971 £590. GP £3,878. NP £3,315, BS totals £1,225. **16** Purchases £3,736 + £239 = £3,975 − Stock 31st March, 1970 £300 = Cost of Sales £3,675. GP = 33⅓% on cost = £1,225. Sales £4,020 + £250 + £5 + Drawings (balance) £625 = £4,090. Paper bags £18 + £2 − £5 = £15, NP £642. BS Assets: Fixed £450; Current: Stocks £300 + £5, Prepayments £10, Bank £503, Cash £5. Liabilities Capital £1,017, Creditors £239, Gas £10, Bags £2, Others £5; Totals £1,273.

Chapter 24

1 Loss £5. **2** Surplus £323 (Profit on refreshments £35). **3** Surplus £42. Accumulated Fund 31st December, 19·2 = £123. **4** Loss £180. Subs. £810 = [(£750 + £10) = £760 + £20 + £40 − £10] = £810. BS totals £110. **5** Surplus £22. BS totals £409. **6** Surplus £57. BS totals £860 [Subs. in advance £3 (Liability); Subs. due £10 (Assets)]. **7** Receipts and Payments balance 31st December, 1968. £230; Inc and Exp Account Loss £80. (Rates £60 − £10 − £10 = £40; Subs £350 − £5 + £15 = £360; Tournament £70 − £40 = £30.) **8** Surplus £231, Depreciation £750 + £160 − £800 = £110; Profit on refreshments £255 − (£140 + £15 − £9) = £109. **9** Inc and Exp Account Surplus £64: Subs £600, Dance profit £60; Profit on refreshments £160 − (£120 + £30 − £20) = £30. BS totals £596. **10** Inc and Exp Account: Loss £14. Subs Account to be shown: Cr. Bad Debts £15, Cash (£20 + £140 + £25) = £185, Amount due for 1970 c/d £18. Dr. Subs due £35, Payment in advance £25 c/d, Balance to Inc and Exp Account £158. **11** Subs Account (a): Cr. Balance £43, Cash £837, Balance c/d £76. Dr. Balance £69, Balance c/d £29, Balance to Inc and Exp Account £858. Subs Account (b) 19·1: Cr. Cash £325, Subs due c/d £25; Dr. Subs in advance £40 + Balance to Inc and Exp Account £310. 19·2: Cr. Prepayment b/d from 19·1,£40, Cash £340, Subs due c/d £15; Dr. Subs due b/d from 19·1 £25, Subs in advance c/d £20. Inc and Exp Account £350. **12** Surplus £580; BS totals £8,105. **13** Calculations: Total Creditors (or Creditors Control Account) Purchases £9,521. Subs Account: Cr. Subs in advance b/d £25, Cash (£31 + £6,671 + £89) = £6,791. Balance c/d £56; Dr. Subs in arrear b/d £42, Balance c/d £89, Balance to Inc and Exp Account £6,741. Newspapers and Periodicals: Dr. Cash £74, Balance c/d £28; Cr. Balance b/d £26, Cash £8, Inc and Exp Account £68. Journal: 1st January Assets £10,007 − Liabilities £478 = Capital £9,529. Bar Trading Account: GP £1,455. Inc and Exp Account Surplus £784 (Wages £5,405 − £492 = £4,913); BS; Premises £5,000 + £492 + £620 = £6,112, Furniture £2,700; Current Assets £2,146. Capital £10,313, Current Liabilities £645. Totals £10,958.

Chapter 25

1 (b) GP £1,538. **2** Materials used £13,700 + Wages = Prime Cost of Production £25,700; Factory Overheads £1,000 Factory (or Direct) Cost of Production £26,700. GP £11,700. NP £8,700. **3** Materials used £19,597 + Wages = Prime Cost of Production £46,027; Factory overheads £12,913; Cost of Production £57,767; GP £16,070. Administration £3,725 + Selling and Distribution £4,170; NP £8,175. **4** Materials used £40,019 + Wages = Prime cost of Production £101,003; Factory overheads £30,773, Factory cost of Production £131,776; GP £42,949. Administration £9,222. Selling Expenses £14,138. NP £19,589. **5** (a) Cost of Materials used £20,678; Cost of Production £38,338; Percentage of Profit on Capital 22%; Turnover £48,716. (b) (i) Direct materials; (ii) Factory indirect expenses; (iii) Selling and Distribution; (iv) Direct labour; (v) Administration expenses; (vi) Factory indirect expenses; (vii) Direct expenses; (viii) Financial expenses. **6** Trading and P&L Account: GP Tavana

£32,000 (25%), Quick £43,000 (25%). (a) NP T £3,500, Q £8,700. BS. Premises: T £40,000, Q £41,000; Plant, *Less* aggregate depreciation: T £24,000, Q £22,200; Working Capital: T £26,500; Q £31,500. Capital Employed: T £90,500; Q £94,700; (b) Q is more successful than T. Sells more than T at same GP percentage. Q's resulting greater GP more than covers increased selling expenses. Q's lower administration expenses on a higher turnover, are lower than T's. All this on same amount of capital. Q better businessman than T.

Chapter 26

1 (i) Dr. Crow, Cr. Sales; Credit Crow, Debit B/R; Dr. Cash, Cr. B/R; (ii) (a) Cole's Account: Dr. 1st March Sales £800, Cr. 1st March B/R £800. B/R Account: Dr. 1st March Cole £800. Cr. 3rd April Cash £800; (b) Roe's Account = Dr. 10th March Sales £300; Cr. 10 March B/R £300. B/R Account: Dr. Roe £300; Cr. 15th March Cash (Bill discounted) £300. Discount on Bills Account: Dr. 15th March Cash £7; (c) Tyne's Account: Dr. 18th March Sales £700, 20th May B/R (dishonoured bill) £700, 21st May Interest £10; Cr. 18th March B/R £700, 21st May B/R £710. B/R Account: 18th March Tyne £700, 21st May Tyne £710; Cr. 20th May Tyne (bill discounted) £700. Interest Account Cr. 21st May Tyne £10. **2** Bates's Account: Dr. Sales £800, 4th September Cash (bill dishonoured) £800; Cr. 1st July B/R £800. B/R Account: Dr. Bates £800; Cr. 1st July Cash (bill discounted) £800. Discount on Bills Account: Dr. 4th September Cash £15. **3** A's Account: Dr. 30th June Balance £1,000, Interest £25, 1st October B/R (Retired) £1,025. Cr. 30th June B/R £1,025, 1st October Cash £650, B/R £375. B/R Account: Dr. 30th June A £1,025, 1st October A £375. Cr. 1st October A Bill retired £1,025. Discount on Bills Account: Dr. 1st October Cash £4·85. **4** X's Account: Dr. Balance £1,555, B/R (Bill withdrawn) £650, Interest £5·41, Interest £8·66. Cr. Cash £305, B/R (3 months) £600, B/R (5 months) £650, B/R £325, B/R £333·66. Cash—Interest £5·41. B/R Account: Dr. X £600, £650, £325, £333·66; Cr. Cash £600, X £650, Balance c/d £658·66. **5** Hull, Exeter Cr. respectively B/R £250, £400. Bristol, Cardiff Dr. respectively B/P £300, £100. B/R Account: Dr. Exeter, Hull; Cr. Cash—Bill discounted £400, Hull £250. B/P: Cr. Bristol, Cardiff; Dr. Cash £300 ,Balance c/d £100. Discount on Bills Account Dr. Cash—Exeter £2. Cash Book: Dr. £400, £250; Cr. £300, £2, Balance c/d £348. **6** A's Account: Cr. B/R Nos 1, 2, 3 at £400, Cash £100, B/R No. 4 £303·75. Dr. Sales £1,200. B/R No. 3 Retired £400, Interest £3·75. B/R Account: Dr. A's Account Bill Nos 1, 2, 3 at £400, No. 4 £303·75. Cr. Cash—Bill discounted £400, Cash £400, A's Account No. 3 retired £400, Cash—Bill discounted £303·75. Discount on Bills Account: Dr.2, £3·75. Interest Account: Cr. £3·75. **7** A's Account: Dr. £300, C (Bill discounted) £300; Cr. B/R £300, Bank £150, Bad Debts £150. C's Account: Cr. Balance £500, Bill dishonoured. A £300; Dr. B/R £300, Bank £190, Discount £10, Bank £300. B/R Account: Dr. A £300; Cr. C £300. Bad Debts Account: Dr. £150. Discounts Received Cr. £10. **8** A's Account: Cr. Purchases £800, B/dishonoured (2) £400; B/P (1) £300 (2) £400, (3) £100, Bank £400. C's Account: Dr. Sales £500, B/dishonoured (2) £400; Cr. B/R (2) £400, B/R D (3) £100, Balance c/d £400, B/P Account: Cr. A (1) £300; Dr. Bank £300. B/R Dr. C (2) £400, C (3) (D) £100; Cr. A (2) £400, (3) £100. **9** Journal: Debit total £47,282; Credit total £23,522; Therefore Capital = £23,760.

Chapter 27

1 Consignment Account: NP £561; Unsold Stock c/d to debit side £600 + £72 = £672 Sutton's Account: Dr. Consignment Account—Sale Proceeds £3,420; Cr. Duty £240, Commission £171, Cash—being balance £3,000. **2** Consignment Account NP £1,685; Unsold stock c/d £3,200 + £460 = £3,660. Jackson's Account: Dr. Consignment Account—Sale Proceeds £6,900; Cr. Duty, etc., selling expenses, Commission. Cash—being balance £6,265. **3** Consignment Account NP £5,090; Unsold stock c/d £2,100 + £290 = £2,390. Groom's Account: Dr. Consignment Account—Proceeds of Sale £28,000; Cr. Duty, etc. £890, commission £1,400, Sight draft (being balance) £25,710. **4** Consignment Account: (Commission includes 1% del credere £320), NP £1,368. Zeno's Account: Dr. Consignment Account Sale Proceeds £7,000; Cr. Charges £406, Commission and del credere £320; Sight draft £6,274. **5** Consignment Account: NP £44: Dennis & Co's Account: Sight draft £579. **6** Consignment Account: NP £22; Unsold Stock c/d £90 + £23 = £113. Cash received from A Trader £333. **7** NP £25: Unsold stock c/d £375 + £75 = £450. Sight draft £390. **8** NP £2,530. Consignment Account: Cr. Cash and Insurance claim £1,050. Sale Proceeds £11,200, Unsold Stock c/d £2,000 + £290 = £2,290. Cash from GH & Co. £9,940. **9** Joint Venture with Bell Account: Cr. Cash £600, Cash £720, Unsold Picture £400, Cash from Bell £47·25. Dr. Cash £1,600, Expenses £25, Carriage £7, Commission £30, P&L Account—½ share of profit £105·25. Joint Venture Account Cr. Proceeds of Sales: £600, £720, £850, £780. Picture to Adams £400. Dr. Purchases £2,950, Expenses £35, Carriage £7, Commissions £30, £36, £81·50. Share of Profit: £105·25 each partner. **10** In Ragg's books: Memorandum Joint Venture Account: Share of Profit Ragg £314, Stone £157: Joint Venture with Stone

Account. Dr. £3,750, £8, £2 Share of Profit £314. Cash to Stone £1,720. Cr. Sales £1,720, £1,850. Stone £750, Cash from Stone £1,474. In Stone's books: Joint Venture with Ragg Account: Cr. Cash from Ragg £1,720. Dr. Advertising £70, Showroom hire £10, Commission-aire £6, Carpet £3, Share of Profit £157, Cash to Ragg £1,474. Joint Venture Cash Account: Dr. Cash self £2,000, Ragg £1,720; Cr. Advertising £70, Showroom £10, Commissionaire £6, Carpet £3, Refund to self £1,500, Ragg £1,474, Self £657.   **11** Joint Venture Memorandum Account: Dr. Purchases £600, £1,200, £1,000; Sundry expenses £60, £200; Purchases of lorry £400; Rent £200. Cr. Sales: £1,400, £400, £1,800, Sale to Delilah £200, Sale of lorry to Samson £360. Profit: Samson £300, Delilah £200. In Delilah's Books: Joint Venture with Samson Account: Dr. Purchases £1,000. Rent £200, P&L Account share of profit £200, Cash to Samson £1,200. Cr. Cash from Samson £600, Cash from Sales £1,800, Purchases £200.

Chapter 28

1 Balance (Cr.) £560.   **2** Capital Account: Cr.: Balance £3,000, Cash £600, Current Account T £1,400. Current Account: Cr.: Balance £450, Interest on Capital £170, Salary £800, Share of Profit ⅓ £2,100; Dr. Cash (Drawings) £1,600, Capital T £1,400, Balance c/d £520.   **3** P&L. Appropriation Account: Share of Profit Wheel £3,906, Barrow £2,604.   **4** P&L. Appropriation Account: Share of Profit Badger £3,600, Coote £2,400.   **5** P&L Appropriation Account: Total Profit £3,550 equally divided at £1,775 each.   **6** Current Accounts: Cr.: Share of Profit Hemp £2,850, Wool £1,900, Cotton £950. Balances c/d to credit side Hemp £1,770, Wool £1,900, Cotton £730.   **7** Liabilities: Capital: Root £4,000, Branch £3,000; Current Accounts Root £56, Branch £9. Assets: Fixed £1,820 Current £7,225—Current Liabilities £1,980 = Working Capital £5,245.   **8** P&L Appropriation Account: Share of Profit Peele £1,660, Mellis £1,660. BS: Capital Peele £1,000, Mellis £2,000; Current Account Peele £1,800, Mellis £1,380; Long-term Liabilities: Loan Account £2,120; Current Liabilities £1,000. Assets: Fixed (including Goodwill £1,000 *less* amount written off £250=£750) £4,000, Current £5,300; Totals £9,300.   **9** Net Trading Profit £3,000 (ie. £3,600 *less* depreciation £600 which should have appeared in the main section of P&L Account); Working Capital £1,750; BS totals £12,050.   **10** GP £33,248 (including deduction of Drawings £124 from Purchases); Net Trading Profit £18,210; Share of Profit: Sam, Bill at £9,105. BS Capital £36,471, Current Accounts Sam £4,173, Bill £4,092, Current Liabilities £7,481. Assets: Fixed £23,900, Current £28,317; Totals £52,217.   **11** GP £56,500, Net Trading Profit £18,120, Share of Profit Rathlin £9,780, Lambass £6,520, BS Capital £42,000, Current Accounts: Rathlin £4,210, Lambass £2,710. Current Liabilities £13,066. Assets: Fixed £19,690, Current £42,296, Working Capital £29,230. Totals £48,920.   **12** GP £33,930 (including deduction £330 from Purchases), Net Trading Profit £12,680, Share of Profit Taylor £7,880, Wells £3,940. BS Capital £22,000. Current Accounts: Taylor £3,550, Wells £1,330, Current Liabilities £9,770 (including deduction £330 from Creditors), Assets: Fixed £5,990 Current £30,660; Totals £36,650.   **13** Calculations: Total Creditors Account: Purchases=£35,749; Total Debtors Account: Sales=£56,019; BS 1971: NP=Excess of Assets over Liabilities=£4,682. Final Accounts 1972: GP £20,447, Net Trading Profit £6,966, Share of Profit L £3,483, K £3,483; BS Capital £8,885+Profit in 1971, £13,567.

Chapter 29

1 and 2 See Ex 29/2 for identical entries.   **3** See Ex 29/3 for identical entries.   **4** See Ex 29/4 for identical entries.   **5** See Ex 29/4; Bill 5/12, Tom 5/12, Jim 1/6.   **6** Capital Accounts (Cr.): Balances A £6,000, B £3,000; C's Premium: A £666, B £334; Cash: C £3,000; Goodwill: A £5,334, B £2,666.   **7** Capital Accounts (Cr.): Balances: A £12,000, B £9,000; Cash: C £7,000; Premium: A £1,200, B £800. Appropriation Account: Net Trading Profit £10,840, Interest on Drawings A £62, B £50, C £31; Interest on Capital: A £660, B £490, C £350; Share of Profit A £3,556, B £3,556, C £2,371. Current Accounts: Balances b/d (Cr.) B £196, C £190; (Dr.) A £546, BS: Capital £30,000, Current Accounts £160 (Dr.), Mortgage £7,000, Creditors £4,000+£200. Assets: Fixed £23,440, Current £17,600; Totals £41,040.

Chapter 30

1 Goodwill £1,000. BS totals £13,000.   **2** Goodwill £1,950. BS totals £38,400.   **3** Goodwill £6,400. BS totals £28,400.   **4** Appropriation Account (i) Share of Profit A £1,300, B £650: Appropriation Account (ii) Share of Profit A £1,100, B £550.   **5** Goodwill £3,150, BS totals £33,400.

Chapter 31

1 Realisation Account: Share of Profit: Barney £112, Good £56. Bank balance transferred to Capital Accounts: Barney £4,812, Good £3,856.   **2** Realisation Account: Share of Loss: A £250, B £250. Bank balance transferred to Capital Accounts: A £1,750, B £1,250.   **3**

Realisation Accounts: Share of Loss: R £700, S £350. Bank balance transferred to Capital Accounts: R £8,300, S £9,150. **4** Realisation Account: Share of Profit: Black £112, White £56. Bank balance transferred to Capital Account: Black £4,812, White £3,856. **5** BS 31st December 1971 totals £46,052, NP (excess of Assets over Liabilities) £6,000 (Long £3,600, Short £2,400). Realisation Account: Share of Loss: Long £600, Short £400. Bank balance transferred to Capital Account: Long £20,740, Short £14,938. **6** BS 31st March, 1969 totals £13,916; Debtors and Stock £10,626 (excess of Liabilities over Assets). Realisation Account: Share of Profit: T £1,526, J £762. Bank balance transferred to Capital Accounts: T £2,766, J £3,282. **7** Realisation Account: Loss £1,462 (Dr.); Cr. Cash from Y £584, Z £292. Transfer balance £586 to Current Account X. Current Account Dr.: X: Balance £2,000, Realisation £586; Y: Transfer to Capital £500; Z Transfer to Capital £360. Cr.: X: Transfer to Capitals of Y £1,552 and Z £1,034; Y: Balance £500; Z: Balance £360. Capital Accounts Dr.: Y: from X's Current Account £1,552, Cash £10,948; Z: from X's Current Account £1,034, Cash £7,326. Cr.: Y: Balance £12,000, Transfer from Y's Current Account £500; Z: Balance £8,000. Transfer from Z's Current Account £360.

Chapter 32

1 (a) Capital employed £41,000; (b) Current assets £23,500; (c) Current liabilities £8,000; (d) Working capital £15,500. **2** Working capital £82,875; BS totals £187,500. **3** Working capital £5,900; BS totals £33,000. **4** Working capital £50,132; BS totals £203,589. **5** See text. **6** (a) £53,000; (b) £42,640; (c) £16,680; (d) £18,960; (e) £25,960; (f) £78,960; (g) £78,960. **7** Issued capital £120,000; Revenue Reserves £10,500; Current liabilities £11,100; Appropriation: Dr. Dividends: Preference Shares £2,100, Ordinary Shares £9,000; Balance c/d £10,500: Credit Net Trading Profit £19,575, Balance B/F from 1974 £2,025. **8** See example of 'Vertical' BS in text. **9** Appropriations: Balance c/d £4,800; BS: Issued Capital £200,000, Revenue Reserves £30,580, Current liabilities: Preference dividends £4,000, Ordinary dividends £9,000, Creditors £6,520 = £19,520. Fixed Assets Net £210,900, Current Assets £39,200. BS totals £250,100. **10** TB totals £442,890. Appropriation Dr. Dividends: Preference £5,000, Ordinary £6,500, Reserve £5,000. Balance c/d £126,890; Credit Balance 1970 b/d £92,680, Balance 1971 £53,110 *less* Debenture interest £2,400 = £50,710. BS Issued Capital £200,000, Revenue Reserves £144,390, Loan capital £40,000, Current liabilities (including dividends) £43,610. Assets: Fixed £333,980, Current £93,350. Preliminary expenses £470. Totals £428,000. **11** Appropriation: Balance c/d £70,840. BS Issued Capital £500,000, Capital Reserve £25,000, Revenue Reserve £370,840, Current liabilities £240,976. Assets: Fixed Net £650,000, Current £486,816, Working Capital £245,840 **12** GP £33,876, Net Trading Profit £13,766, Appropriation balance c/d £5,666. BS Capital £40,000, Capital Reserve £10,000, Revenue Reserve £12,666, Loan Capital £20,000, Current Liabilities £17,789. Assets: Fixed £52,896, Current £47,559; Totals £100,455. **13** Cost of Production £128,800 (including depreciation machinery), GP £21,000, Net Trading Profit £5,896, Appropriation Balance c/d £3,126. BS Capital £70,000. P&L Account £3,126. Assets: Fixed £44,000, Current £46,826, Current Liabilities £17,700. Working Capital £29,126. **14** To ascertain Cash received from debtors and paid to creditors, make up Total Debtors and Total Creditors accounts: Cash received £52,915, Cash paid £37,162. Cash Book balance (Cr.) £1,626, GP £12,899; NP £7,532. BS Capital £17,500, P&L Account £11,652, Current Liabilities £5,088. Assets: Fixed £28,775, Current £5,465; Totals £34,240. **15** Trading/Manufacturing Account 1971, 1972 in adjacent columns. Dr. Cost of Production £18,160 and £23,550. Cr. Sales £26,240 and £31,970. GP £8,080 and £8,420. Administration expenses £6,900 and £7,300, NP £1,180 and £1,120. Houses Account 1971 and 1972. Dr.: Cost £10,600 and £12,320, Cr.: Sales £11,810 and £16,360. GP £1,210 and £4,040. Expenses of house sales £320 and £630, NP £890 and £3,410. Manufacturing percentage of GP over turnover $1971 = \dfrac{8,080}{26,240} \times 100 = 31\%$ approx.; $1972 = \dfrac{8,420}{31,970} \times 100 = 26\%$ approx.

Computation to ascertain increase or decrease in capital

1972: Capital: Goods: Cost £23,550 + NP £1,120 = £24,670
              Houses: Cost £13,320 + NP £3,410 = £15,730

                                            £40,400

1973: Capital: Goods: Cost £18,160 + NP £1,180 = £19,340
              Houses: Cost £10,600 + NP £890 = £11,490

                                            £30,830

         Increase in Capital   £ 9,570

Required loan for manufactures. Therefore report mainly concerned with manufacturing side of Swinford's activities. Percentage of GP on Sales 1971 = 31%, 1972 = 26%. In 1972, 33⅓% increase in capital over 1971—from £30,830 to £40,400. Take into account loan of £15,000 at 8% interest = £1,200 per annum. Assuming that Swinford succeeded in doubling production and sales, then he would be able to pay the interest, and with the assistance of his side-line, the purchase and sale of houses (assuming figures remained constant), he would be able to repay the loan from Stroker. But if the full facts and figures were presented to Stroker, it is doubtful if he would advance the required £15,000 loan. **16** (i) Goodwill £3,500; (ii) Journal: (a) Dr. Vendor £19,000, Cr. Share Capital £17,000, Cash £2,000; (b) Dr. Application & Allotment Account £6,000, Cr. Share Capital £6,000. BS: Share Capital £25,000, Creditors £1,000; Assets: Goodwill £3,500, Fixed £12,000, Current £4,500, Cash at Bank £8,000 *less* to Vendor £2,000 = £6,000. Totals £26,000.   **17** (i) Goodwill £3,630; (ii) Journal (a) Dr. Vendor £22,500, Cr. Preference Share Capital £6,000, Ordinary Share Capital £15,000, Cash £1,500. (b) Dr. Application & Allotment Account £7,500 Cr. Ordinary Share Capital £7,500.

Chapter 33

1 Total paid into bank £343. Sources: Profit £890 + Depreciation £250 + Reduction in current assets £283 = £1,423. Applications: Drawings £825 + Reduction in creditors = £1,080 Increase in cash. Working Capital: 1975: £200; 1976: £515. Increase in Working Capital £315.   **2** (a) Working Capital 31st December 19·1 = £97,700. (b) Working Capital 1st January, 19·1 = £97,700 Add: Profit £19,700 + Depreciation £4,800 + Sale of fixed assets £1,300 = £123,500 − Purchase of fixed assets £18,600 = Working Capital at 31st December, 19·1 £104,900. (c) Working Capital available £104,900 − proposed dividend £7,500 + Available cash £97,400.   **3** (a) To arrive at Net Reduction in Working Capital: Increase in current liabilities £1,848 + Bank balance becoming bank overdraft £9,302 = £11,150; *Less*: Increase in stock £2,242 + Increase in debtors £978 = £3,220 = Net reduction £7,930. Sources: £7,930 + Profit £7,930 − Dividend £3,000 = £12,860. Applications: Investment in plant £17,500 − Depreciation £5,390 = £12,110; Investment in transport £1,700 − Depreciation £950 = £750; £12,110 + £750 = £12,860. Presume that the £3,000 dividend 1970 is paid, and additional £3,000 payable for 1971. (b) There seems to be the intention to invest substantially in more fixed assets, financed mainly by a reduction in Working Capital. Sales appear to be increasing, since debtors and stock have increased. Somehow more Working Capital must be made available, unless the bank overdraft can be used, until retained profits are available to finance that policy.

Printed and bound in Great Britain by Butler & Tanner Ltd, Frome and London